OXFORD ENGLISH MONOGRAPHS

General Editors

Women, Writing, and Fetishism 1890–1950

Female Cross-Gendering

CLARE L. TAYLOR

CLARENDON PRESS · OXFORD

OXFORD
UNIVERSITY PRESS

Great Clarendon Street, Oxford OX2 6DP

Oxford University Press is a department of the University of Oxford.
It furthers the University's objective of excellence in research, scholarship,
and education by publishing worldwide in

Oxford New York

Auckland Bangkok Buenos Aires Cape Town Chennai
Dar es Salaam Delhi Hong Kong Istanbul Karachi Kolkata
Kuala Lumpur Madrid Melbourne Mexico City Mumbai Nairobi
São Paulo Shanghai Taipei Tokyo Toronto

Oxford is a registered trade mark of Oxford University Press
in the UK and in certain other countries

Published in the United States
by Oxford University Press Inc., New York

British Library Cataloguing in Publication Data

Data available

Library of Congress Cataloging in Publication Data
Taylor, Clare L.
Women, writing, and fetishism, 1890–1950: female cross-gendering/Clare L. Taylor.
p. cm—(Oxford English monographs)
Includes bibliographical references and index.
1. American literature—Women authors—History and criticism. 2. English literature—Women
authors—History and criticism. 3. American literature—20th century—History and criticism.
4. English literature—20th century—History and criticism. 5. Modernism (Literature)—United
States. 6. Modernism (Literature)—Great Britain. 7. Women and literature—Great Britain.
8. Women and literature—United States. 9. Gender identity in literature. 10. Fetishism in
literature. 11. Sex role in literature. 12. Woman in literature. I. Title. II. Series.
PS151 .T39 2003   810.9'9287'0904—dc21   2002192571

ISBN 0-19-924410-3

1 3 5 7 9 10 8 6 4 2

Typeset by Hope Services (Abingdon) Ltd.
Printed in Great Britain
on acid-free paper by
Biddles Ltd,
Guildford and King's Lynn

Preface

The aim of this book is to reformulate the concept of fetishism as both a sexual practice for women and a textual practice for modernist women writers, with a focus on what I term 'female cross-gendering'. In the discourses of sexology and psychoanalysis female fetishism is not viewed as a viable explanation for female sexual 'inversion' or cross-gendering. But this study identifies a mode of representation that both inscribes female fetishism and reformulates Freudian fetishism to suggest that it enhances the sexual body/self. This work contributes to an ongoing debate within feminism about the nature of female fetishism, but also offers an extended literary analysis within a historical and theoretical frame.

The works of Sarah Grand, Radclyffe Hall, H.D., Djuna Barnes, and Anaïs Nin are read as entering into a dialogue with the discourses of sexology and psychoanalysis, and as an intimate modernist clique generating a specific model of female cross-gendering as a performance of fetishism. Fetishism itself, operating through disavowal and splitting, and anxiety about dismemberment, is read as a literary discourse. These components of fetishism speak volubly about the nature of women's writing and women's position within modernism. The introduction maps out the theoretical debate, and the first two chapters on Grand and Hall contextualize the development of female cross-gendering and fetishism within the progression from sexology to psychoanalysis, arguing ultimately for the perverse nature of the texts. Female fetishism is significantly expanded to include the object of desire as 'fetishized' in the analysis of H.D. In Chapters 4 and 5 on Barnes and Nin, female fetishism is seen as 'exhausting' its limits within the parameters of female modernism.

The idea for this project began with a reading of Jeanette Winterson's *The Passion*, and her interest in gendered embodiment, during the rise of performance theory. I became interested, however, in the operations of fetishism because of its seeming potential as a means of sexual and creative expression for women, rather than in the performative aspects of drag and transvestism. There has been important work in the recuperation of fetishism for women, the nature of cross-dressing in literary texts, and in the reformulation of 'female masculinity', but no extended analysis that brought all of these together. It seemed that there was a rich vein to be opened up concerning the cleavage of women, writing, and fetishism.

I would like to thank everyone who has supported me throughout the writing of this book, but particularly Dr Ros Ballaster, who supervised this work as a D.Phil. thesis, and my D.Phil. examiners Jeri Johnson and Dr Laura Marcus, who gave me the encouragement to publish. Finally I am grateful to the Oxford University Press readers for providing the impetus to take the ideas of fetishism further.

C.L.T.

Acknowledgements

Copyright permission is gratefully acknowledged for the following:

Tribute to Freud by Hilda Doolittle
Reprinted by permission of David R. Godine, Publisher, Inc.
Copyright © 1956 by Hilda Doolittle.

The Heavenly Twins by Sarah Grand. Copyright © by Sarah Grand.
Reprinted by permission of The University of Michigan Press.

Various excerpts by Djuna Barnes, from *Nightwood*, Copyright ©
1937 by Djuna Barnes. Used by permission of New Directions
Publishing Corporation.

Contents

INTRODUCTION   1

1. 'COVETED PLEASURES': INVERTS AND
   PERVERTS AT THE *FIN DE SIÈCLE*   24

2. 'A NEW PERVERSENESS': FEMALE CROSS-
   GENDERING AND THEORIES OF
   FETISHISM, 1915–1930   57

3. 'I AM HER': THE CROSS-GENDERED
   WOMAN AS FETISH OBJECT IN H.D.'S
   HER   105

4. 'SHE IS MYSELF': DJUNA BARNES'S
   NIGHTWOOD AND THE EXHAUSTION OF
   FEMALE FETISHISM   149

5. 'BECOMING DJUNA': ANAÏS NIN'S DIARIES
   AND FICTION   191

   AFTERWORD   229

BIBLIOGRAPHY   233

INDEX   249

Introduction

In 1929 Radclyffe Hall, who had recently unsuccessfully defended *The Well of Loneliness* on trial for obscenity, expressed anger at the public spectacle of Valerie Arkell-Smith cross-gendering as Colonel Barker (Barker at the time was facing her own trial after falsifying a marriage register). Hall called Barker a 'mad pervert of the most undesirable type', seeking to differentiate her congenital 'invert' Stephen Gordon, who was also partial to a man's dress shirt, from this 'masquerader' whose only motive, it seemed, was for financial gain. Barker could have restrained herself (instead of being perverse), Hall must have thought, while the invert was inherently incapable of denying her true nature. But motive (for sexual pleasure) is precisely what is at stake in this study of women, writing, cross-gendering, and fetishism 1890–1950, which examines the collision of the categories of invert and pervert in both an historical and theoretical frame through a re-evaluation of (female) perversion and fetishism. Part of this project is to re-read *The Well of Loneliness*, the classic text of sexual inversion—which rigorously polices its own means of production and reception with an introduction by prolific sexologist Havelock Ellis—as a subversive, perverse, modernist text.

In order to achieve this, Radclyffe Hall is placed in an intimate and symbiotic grouping which displays a specific sexual and textual 'perversity' through a narrative with fetishistic components. This group includes, primarily, Sarah Grand's *The Heavenly Twins*, H.D.'s *HER*, Djuna Barnes's *Nightwood*, and Anaïs Nin's *Ladders to Fire*. These texts all contribute to the debate about female fetishism, 'exceeding' the sexological and psychoanalytic inscriptions which inform them, and allowing for a vision of female fetishistic cross-gendering as a sexual performance which enhances the desirability of the body/self for both the subject and the object of her desire. The writers discussed here form an intimate clique (although they differ in their employment of fetishism): phrases and clusters of images recur from text to text; Nin in *Collages* writes

Djuna Barnes into her fiction as literary icon; Bryher poses H.D. as the object of her literary quest; Radclyffe Hall fictionalizes the lesbian coterie of Left Bank Paris, one of whose members was Barnes; she in turn wittily and cruelly parodied this circle in her *Ladies Almanack*. Moreover all the writers discussed here entered into a dialogue with the discourses of sexology and psychoanalysis. Sarah Grand made public statements concerning the political ramifications of male sexual behaviour, which was a primary concern of sexologists. Radclyffe Hall championed the theory of sexual inversion as promoted by Richard von Krafft-Ebing and Havelock Ellis, and *The Well of Loneliness* has been read as an endorsement of sexology. Anaïs Nin was in Freudian analysis during the 1930s—René Allendy and Otto Rank tried to 'cure' her of her diary-writing compulsion which they saw as preventing her from writing fiction—and then intermittently a Jungian for the rest of her life. Nin's fictional work in the wake of analysis has customarily been read as an incorporation of what Valerie Harms has called the 'analytic voice'.[1] H.D. was in analysis with Freud in order to cure her of her writer's block, and her fiction both before and after analysis exhibits, as Dianne Chisholm explains, 'a clinical interest in her own writing-subject . . . a serious commitment to an intertextual experimentation that in some way(s) incorporates Freud's text'.[2] Djuna Barnes, ostensibly dismissive of the therapeutic and intellectual possibilities of psychoanalysis, nevertheless has been seen to rewrite parodically the sexological and psychoanalytic inscriptions of the cross-gendered woman (in this case invert and lesbian).

CATEGORIES

The term 'cross-gendering' carries specific reference to a form of female masculinity, transvestism, and cross-dressing, but it is also used as a more general term, where appropriate, to cover a range of practices and identities. The choice of the term is symbolic, used to signify that even the more pejorative and delimiting inscriptions of

---

[1] Valerie Harms, 'Anaïs and Her Analysts, Rank and Allendy: The Creative and Destructive Aspects', in Suzanne Nalbantian (ed.), *Anaïs Nin: Literary Perspectives* (Basingstoke: Macmillan, 1997), 112–19: 117.

[2] Dianne Chisholm, *H.D.'s Freudian Poetics: Psychoanalysis in Translation* (Ithaca, NY: Cornell University Press, 1992), 22.

female cross-gendering in the clinical texts (inversion for instance) have the potential for a range of sexual possibilities not accounted for in that original inscription. It retains the meanings of inversion, still a current discourse in the 1920s, while also suggesting the fetishistic aspects (cross-dressing and transvestism). Although 'transgendered' is now used as an umbrella term to include a broad range of sexual identities and behaviours, including transvestism and cross-dressing, the term is too bound up with sex change and post-1950 sexual identities for use here. 'Transvestism', traced back to Magnus Hirschfeld's *Die Transvestiten* (1910), to mean the 'impulse to assume the external garb of a sex which is not apparently that of the subject as indicated by the sexual organs',[3] is too scientifically specific in its designation of male perversion (Edward Carpenter employed the term 'cross-dressing' as a translation of Hirschfeld's term).[4] A fusion of clinical terminology and cultural usage (although the distinction does not always apply) seemed the most appropriate coinage given that this study analyses the interrelation between clinical and literary texts.[5] As Chapter 1 outlines, a classificatory system cataloguing sexual identities flourished at the turn of the century; at stake in this taxonomic obsession was the status of women who desired other women.[6] While cross-gendering is intimately bound up with lesbianism in this work, I prefer to keep the categories separate and to protect the autonomy of both.

---

[3] Quoted in Havelock Ellis, *Studies in the Psychology of Sex*, vii. *Eonism and Other Supplementary Studies* (Philadelphia: F. A. Davis, 1928), 13.

[4] Edward Carpenter, 'On the Connection Between Homosexuality and Divination and the Importance of the Intermediate Sexes Generally in Early Civilizations', *American Journal of Religious Psychology and Education*, 4 (1911), 219–43. For an overview of the terms of categorization see Dave King, 'Gender Blending: Medical Perspectives and Technology', in Richard Ekins and Dave King (eds.), *Blending Genders: Social Aspects of Cross-Dressing and Sex–Changing* (London and New York: Routledge, 1996), 79–98.

[5] There are a plethora of terms most of which are both in clinical and cultural usage; 'cross-gender' itself is a term used occasionally in clinical practice as shorthand for both transvestite and transsexual behaviours. See Richard F. Docter, *Transvestites and Transsexuals: Toward a Theory of Cross-Gender Behaviour* (New York: Plenum Press, 1988). In the cultural arena, the term has been used by Alan Michael Parker and Mark Willhardt in their anthology of poems 'written in the voice of the opposite sex', *The Routledge Anthology of Cross-Gendered Verse* (London: Routledge, 1996).

[6] Although at the turn of the nineteenth century and in the early years of the twentieth, female cross-gendering 'was not bound up with any particular sexuality, and the differences among female masculinities were many and often quite subtle'. Laura Doan, *Fashioning Sapphism: The Origins of a Modern English Lesbian Culture* (New York: Columbia University Press, 2001), 181.

FETISHISM

Any discussion of fetishism must begin with Freud—in *Three Essays on the Theory of Sexuality* (1905) he was the first to establish a broad and flexible model for the concept, and he assigned to it, as Lacan and Granoff have stated, 'a particular position in the study of neurosis and perversion': fetishism is the only perversion that cannot be compared with a neurosis.[7] Defined early on as a deviation with respect to the sexual object, the fetish 'substitutes' for the sexual object itself and is characteristically an item of clothing, an inanimate object which bears an assignable relation to the person whom it replaces, or another part of the body (hair, foot, or hand). Later, in 'Fetishism' (1927), Freud analyses the role of castration in fetishism and suggests that the fetish represents the maternal phallus that the boy expects to see on his mother; the lack of it produces castration anxiety, alleviated only by a fetish which produces a split in the ego, allowing him to believe in the fantasy of his mother's penis, even if on some level he knows it not to be true (disavowal or *verleugnung*). Within this framework girls *cannot* be fetishists because the castration complex functions differently in women, who see a male body with a penis, and not the mother's that is said to be 'like' her own. Freud reworked his theory of fetishism at regular intervals throughout his life—indeed one of his last unfinished fragments is concerned with the subject. Freud also widens the concept of fetishism by comparing the operations of disavowal in the act of narcissism and mourning. In 'Mourning and Melancholia' (1917 [1915]), he observes that normal mourners who follow a normal grieving pattern will introject the lost object as both there and not there, simultaneously avowing and disavowing its loss, but will eventually accept the loss; other mourners will cling to the mode of disavowal and retain the object as both alive and dead in a split off part of their unconscious. This cleavage of mourning and fetishism is developed in the work of Judith Butler and Angela Moorjani. Carole-Anne Tyler reworks the connection of narcissism to fetishism to state that narcissism is 'critiqued and preserved by

⁷ Jacques Lacan and Wladimir Granoff, 'Fetishism: The Symbolic, the Imaginary and the Real', in Sandor Lorand and Michael Balint (eds.), *Perversions: Psychodynamics and Therapy* (1956; London: The Ortolan Press, 1965), 265–76: 265.

subjects through fetishistic disavowal of the other's difference, including that other which is the "self" '.[8]

Subsequent psychoanalysts, trading on the assumption established by Freud that women believe in their own genital castration, refused to ascribe fetishism to women. Despite Freud's assertions that women are clothes fetishists, transvestism was conceived as a male perversion. In the few extant cases of female fetishistic transvestism post-Freud, analysts emphasize the rarity of such a phenomenon, and that any material presented is not necessarily evidence of a sexual trend, but probably an indication of the masculinity complex, as Hyman S. Barahal concludes in his 1950s' study of a lesbian transvestite. Barahal traces her transvestism (which could be an undiagnosed symptom of transsexualism) to the competitive feelings she has towards men, who took her mother from her. Barahal leaves unanalysed the damage done to her ego because of her mother's expressed desire for a baby boy and her later feelings that femininity was something terrible, although he encourages his patient to experiment with accoutrements of femininity. Indeed the analysis, perhaps despite itself, enables the young woman to gain access to and to love her female body; what analysis seems to be consciously doing is what transvestism has already been unconsciously achieving.[9] Anna Freud recognizes that sex differences are often 'transgressed' in infantile transvestism, especially by girls, but that the clothes chosen are more often 'status symbols' rather than 'sex symbols'.[10] When transvestism becomes more than a bid for elevation of status, it is perceived to be the effect of penis envy, and a normal phase of development.

RECLAIMING FETISHISM FOR WOMEN

There has been a small but influential group of feminist theorists who have, however, sought to disprove the assumption that women are not prone to paraphilias, and there are a few case histories that

[8] Carole-Anne Tyler, 'Passing: Narcissism, Identity, and Difference', *differences: A Journal of Feminist Cultural Studies*, 6.2 and 3 (Summer/Fall 1994), 212–48: 219.

[9] Hyman S. Barahal, 'Female Transvestism and Homosexuality', *Psychiatric Quarterly*, 27 (1953), 390–438.

[10] Anna Freud, *Normality and Pathology in Childhood: Assessments of Development* (London: The Hogarth Press and the Institute of Psycho–Analysis, 1966), 203.

support this with regards to fetishistic cross-dressing. Frank Caprio relates, if anecdotally and sensationally, that one of his patients (a 'mannish lesbian') 'found it erotic to buy and wear men's shorts'; she behaved like a typical male transvestite, making efforts to conceal her male undergarments.[11] In the 1960s Robert Stoller treated a female transvestite who erotically fixated on men's jeans ('The excitement begins immediately—as I begin to pull them over my feet and up, towards my thighs'), and a woman who had intercourse with a male partner while dressed in male clothing.[12] One of the most detailed accounts of female transvestism as reported by Gutheil in the early 1920s is analysed in context in Chapter 2; George Zavitzianos's theories of female fetishistic homeovestism (the fetishizing of same sex clothing) are examined in Chapter 5. Feminist critic Carole-Anne Tyler stated that woman 'can fetishize her wound, the signs of her lack, and disavow her castration just as man does'.[13] Louise Kaplan, in an important study, argues that it is not that female perversions do not exist, but that they have been ignored or misread; she ascribes this to the fact that perversions have only previously been seen as pathologies of sexuality rather than of gender role identity.[14] In her analysis of *Madame Bovary*, the paradigmatic perverse text for Kaplan, she reads Emma Bovary as a fetishistic subject; she analyses the 'fluidity and uncertainty of her sexual identity' (specifically her voracious smoking, and the training of her waist in 'mannish-styled tight-fitting vest') as symptoms of *horigkeit* (a perversion which trades the abasement of one partner in a sexual scenario for the domination of another). The problem with Kaplan's reading, however, is that it does not pay sufficient attention to the presentation of Emma's perversion as sexual, as

---

[11] Frank S. Caprio, *Variations in Sexual Behaviour: A Psychodynamic Study of Deviations in Various Expressions of Sexual Behaviour* (1957; London: John Calder, 1966), 275. Caprio suggests, however, that this behaviour is merely a form of 'psychic identification with the opposite sex' (274).

[12] Robert J. Stoller, *Observing the Erotic Imagination* (New Haven: Yale University Press, 1985), 142–3. The mother had denied her daughter her first pair of jeans, and the woman subsequently stole a pair; the thrill of deceit and triumphalism contributed to her first orgasm in the presence of a female friend. Stoller does not comment on this fetishism, which seems intimately connected to the mother's prohibitions.

[13] Carole-Anne Tyler, 'The Feminine Look', in Martin Kreiswirth and Mark A. Cheetham (eds.), *Theory Between the Disciplines: Authority/Vision/Politics* (Ann Arbor: University of Michigan Press, 1990), 191–212: 206.

[14] Louise J. Kaplan, *Female Perversions: The Temptations of Madame Bovary* (1991; London: Penguin, 1993), 14.

pertaining to the enhancement of a specific female sexuality. According to Kaplan's perverse model, by submitting to Emma's masculine powers, Charles Bovary can express his 'forbidden femininity' and still be reassured of his masculinity; at the same time he can adore with impunity the femininities forbidden him. Meanwhile Emma's enthralment to Rodolphe is a 'hiding place for her masculine ambitions' rather than a site for sexual pleasure.[15] It is Kaplan's contention, following Karl Abraham and Joan Riviere, that in female perversions a 'display of stereotypical femininity acts as the disguise for what a woman experiences as a forbidden masculine striving.'[16] Following this logic, masculine wishes masquerade in the caricature of submissive femininity, while 'feminine wishes must disguise themselves in the caricature of masculine virility'.[17] In a discussion of homeovestism (the fetishizing of same sex clothes), the fetish (an item of feminine clothing) is used by women who are unsure of their femininity, not to confer on them an enhanced image of a sexual self, but to 'mask' masculine ambition. Kaplan advertises this model's universal applicability, but she cannot explain the presence of masculine accoutrements (the vest) and masculine behaviours (smoking, parting her hair on the side like a man) in the perverse practice of Emma Bovary. Kaplan's reading is a clinical analysis of female perversity which isolates the practice in terms of the acting out of a particular psychodrama. This symptomatic reading does not allow for the complexity of the fictive discourse, nor for the deviation from a clinical model.

Feminist theorists have been wary, though, of reappropriating fetishism as a female 'perverse' practice because of the implications of female genital lack. Elizabeth Grosz concurs with the logic that it 'makes no sense' for women to be fetishists. Since, according to the classic account, the fetish stands as testimony to, and in place of, the maternal phallus, female fetishism is a clinical impossibility because there is no reason for the girl to disavow her mother's castration; she has already understood and come to terms with her

---

[15] Ibid. 235.
[16] Ibid. 173. See Joan Riviere, 'Womanliness as Masquerade', *The International Journal of Psycho-Analysis*, 10 (1929), 303–13; and Karl Abraham, 'Manifestations of the Female Castration Complex' (1920), in *Selected Papers of Karl Abraham*, trans. Douglas Bryan and Alix Strachey (London: The Hogarth Press and the Institute of Psycho-Analysis, 1927), 338–69.
[17] Kaplan, *Female Perversions*, 236.

lack.[18] Lorraine Gamman and Merja Makinen in a first full-length work on the subject, however, attempt to bypass the Freudian model and posit a theory of female fetishism grounded in the pre-Oedipal relationship with the mother. This formulation 'challenges the phallocentric dominance of the castration complex within psychoanalytic theory', and argues for a new formulation of the female erotic.[19] They theoretically challenge the idea of the phallus as the only signifier of desire (although they are loathe to suggest an 'alternative' signifier to the phallus), and prefer to read female fetishism via Kleinian object-relations theory because it states that fetishism 'is as much about disavowal of *individuation* [separation from the mother] as it is about sexual difference', that it has a 'strong oral component', and that a narcissistic wound to the body image of either sex can lead to the creation of a pubertal fetish.[20] But the problem with these theories is that they return women to a space before the castration complex, and it is this that precipitates separation from the mother and the entry of the subject into the realm of language and desire; Gamman and Makinen's theory propels female fetishists back to a 'regressive and psychotic space'. To try to reject, bypass, or supplant the castration complex is, as Teresa de Lauretis argues, to 'find ourselves without symbolic means to signify desire'.[21] Sarah Kofman, whose reading of Freud

[18] Elizabeth Grosz, 'Lesbian Fetishism?', in Emily Apter and William Pietz (eds.), *Fetishism as Cultural Discourse* (Ithaca, NY, and London: Cornell University Press, 1993), 101–15: 101, 109.

[19] Lorraine Gamman and Merja Makinen, *Female Fetishism: A New Look* (London: Lawrence and Wishart, 1994), 105.

[20] Ibid. 111 (authors' emphasis and gloss). Analysts opposing the centrality of the phallus in the theory of castration, such as Nin's analyst Otto Rank, argue for the '*primal phantasies* of castration' to be the separation from the mother. Object-relations analysts such as M. Wulff generally agree that fetishism is a pre-Oedipal phenomenon with its source in a crisis of primary identification with the mother. The use of transitional objects by children, while usual, could be retained perversely as fetishes in order to restore retrogressively the mother's body. The fetish represents a substitute for the mother's breast and the mother's body. 'Fetishism and Object Choice in Early Childhood', *Psychoanalytic Quarterly*, 15 (1946), 465–8. Robert Dickes concludes that much of the research into both childhood and adult fetishism suggests that 'the fetish represents more than the female phallus'. 'Fetishistic Behaviour: A Contribution to Its Complex Development and Significance', *Journal of the American Psychoanalytic Association*, 11 (1963), 303–30: 320. For Dickes the fetish does not develop solely in the phallic stage, but can be traced back to transitional objects and comes to signify both parents as partial objects.

[21] Teresa de Lauretis, 'Perverse Desire: The Lure of the Mannish Lesbian', *Australian Feminist Studies*, 13 (Autumn 1991), 15–26: 17.

has been very influential for this study, opens up fetishism for women by suggesting that an oscillation between genders produces undecidability and a non-gendered fetishism. Yet it is this paradigm of undecidability that is most pertinent to women.[22] Fetishism in men works to sustain the ego and maximize pleasure, and this theory excludes women from a range of sexual pleasures. This study runs the risk of the dangers of recuperating fetishism, but inverts and subverts the Freudian model of male fetishism (which invests woman with a penis) to suggest, crucially, that for some women writers cross-gendering is a performance of fetishism which *enhances* the (female) body/self as a *sexual* body/self for the subject, and a desirable body/self for the object of her desire. The word 'enhance' is used to convey meanings of sexual confidence, personal esteem, and, as in male transvestism, genital pleasure. The cleavage of body/self signifies the coterminous nature of both components in the discourse of sexology and psychoanalysis, in which the perception of the self is generated through a stable conception of the body. This points to a serious challenge by women writers to sexological and psychoanalytic theory, and indeed one which writes them out of the parameters of the classic Freudian account.

Having identified the strain in women's writing which fixates on the body of the cross-gendered woman, the work of Teresa de Lauretis becomes very important to this study. In *The Practice of Love* de Lauretis re-examines the Freudian concept of perversion, as separate from the pathological, and its resignification in what she calls 'perverse desire', a 'type of desire fetishistic in a general sense and specifically homosexual or lesbian'. De Lauretis reads Freudian perversion as the 'very mode of being of sexuality', not a deformation of nature, nor 'a deviation from a biologically determined law that assigns one and only one type of object to the sexual drive, but . . . rather an inherent way of being of the drive itself, which continuously seeks out the objects best fitted to its aim of pleasure and satisfaction'.[23] She reworks the castration complex and the concept of the phallus for lesbian subjectivity, proposing a model of perverse desire 'based on the one perversion that Freud insisted was not open to

[22] Sarah Kofman, 'Ça cloche', in Philippe Lacoue-Labarthe and Jean-Luc Nancy (eds.), *Les Fins de l'homme: à partir du travail de Jacques Derrida* (Paris: Galilee, 1981).
[23] Teresa de Lauretis, 'Habit Changes', *differences: A Journal of Feminist Cultural Studies*, 6.2 and 3 (Summer/Autumn 1994), 296–313: 298–9.

women—fetishism'.[24] She works from Madelon Sprengnether's reading of castration as separation from the mother's body as 'the place where division occurs', rather than the locus of mythic unity: the mother's body is not just in the Symbolic, but is itself the Symbolic.[25] Using classic studies on female homosexuality, *The Well of Loneliness*, and contemporary fiction and film of Cherríe Moraga, Adrienne Rich, and Sheila McLaughlin, de Lauretis marks out a mode of desire that takes not the phallus as its signifier but something which resembles a fetish, and detects the operations of disavowal, which is at once the denial of, and belief in, castration. Importantly she does not lose the findings of object-relations theory, which are posed in the light of a rethinking of the terms of the castration complex with regards to the female body, asserting that what threatens the female subject is lack or loss of being, or a loss in being: 'thus the fantasmatic "lost object" of perverse desire is neither the mother's body nor the paternal phallus [as in male fetishism]; it is the subject's own lost body, which can be recovered in fantasy, in sexual practice, only *in and with* another woman.'[26] This is perverse desire (a form of lesbian desire) that has no relation to the masculinity complex, nor does it relate to an infantile attachment to the mother, but is based on 'the post-Oedipal disavowal of that loss'.

Emily Apter argues for the possibility of conceptualizing female subjectivity and fetishism both 'in terms of an aesthetics of ornamentation without immediate recourse to a compensatory emphasis on phallic cover-up'.[27] Apter seeks to 'unmask' the phallic theory of masquerade and displace it with 'epistemological categories for thinking female loss as something other than just penis envy or a masqueraded castration anxiety'.[28] Recognizing (as Freud had done) that the operations of disavowal are similar in fetishism and narcissism, de Lauretis notes that Apter perceives an 'intimate relation' between them: disavowal protects the subject not against phallic loss but against personal debasement and the loss of a part of the (female)

[24] De Lauretis, 'Perverse Desire', 17.

[25] Teresa de Lauretis, *The Practice of Love: Lesbian Sexuality and Perverse Desire* (Bloomington, Ind.: Indiana University Press, 1994), 163–6. See Madelon Sprengnether, *The Spectral Mother: Freud, Feminism, and Psychoanalysis* (Ithaca, NY: Cornell University Press, 1990), 233–46.

[26] De Lauretis, 'Habit Changes', 300 (de Lauretis's emphasis; my gloss).

[27] Emily Apter, *Feminizing the Fetish: Psychoanalysis and Narrative Obsession in Turn-of-the-Century France* (Ithaca, NY: Cornell University Press, 1991), 97–8.

[28] Ibid. 122.

self that was once valued. The connection between narcissism and
fetishism is upheld by de Lauretis and is dealt with primarily in
Chapters 3 and 4. Apter locates female fetishism in an erotic economy of loss, which enables a malleable and flexible theory of
fetishism to emerge. It is, however, perhaps too flexible: de Lauretis
is concerned that in 'severing the fetish from the castration complex'
(with its emphasis on genital/penile loss) and basing it in a 'generic
"female loss",' Apter 'loses sight of disavowal as a defense against
the specifically sexual loss or threat signified by castration'.[29]
   De Lauretis's theory itself has been contested: Elizabeth Grosz is
concerned about the status of psychoanalytic discourse and de
Lauretis's 'reliance on it as the sole explanatory framework in her
account of the structuring of lesbian desire'.[30] Most recently Judith
Halberstam, in a ground-breaking study, offers an alternative reading
of 'female masculinity', and suggests that it 'is a specific gender with
its own cultural history rather than simply a derivative of male masculinity'. Given this premiss, 'psychoanalytic approaches that assume
that female masculinity mimics male masculinity are not especially
helpful'.[31] Halberstam believes that de Lauretis is too wedded to
Freud's 'negative theory of sexuality—sexuality as perversion', which
leads her to overlook 'the masculine woman's account of her desire
and her gender in favour of a model of false consciousness in which
the masculine woman really wants to be feminine, but because she
cannot be, she must hate herself and women in general'.[32]
Halberstam reroutes her own reading of female cross-gendering,
including that of Stephen Gordon, back through sexology, significantly widening the concept of sexual inversion to include transsexuality and transgendering. In a sense though this is a retrogressive step,
and one that fails to analyse the intersection of avowed sexology and
disavowed psychoanalysis in *The Well*. Halberstam's study is
extremely important as a cultural history of female masculinity, but
it is not one that has much bearing on this project, which is concerned
with how modernist fictions by women challenge the inverted and
fetishistic logic of sexological/psychoanalytical literature which itself

[29] De Lauretis, *The Practice of Love*, 274–5.
[30] Elizabeth Grosz, *Space, Time, and Perversion: Essays on the Politics of Bodies*
(New York and London: Routledge, 1995), 168.
[31] Judith Halberstam, *Female Masculinity* (Durham, NC, and London: Duke
University Press, 1998), 77.
[32] Ibid. 103.

masculinizes the desiring woman. My purpose it not to reveal 'the essential femininity of the female body', which Halberstam justly opposes, but rather the *sexual* female body. While Halberstam is right to question wholesale subjection to the discourse of psychoanalysis which she diagnoses in de Lauretis, we must be aware that psychoanalysis is a language that entered the cultural and private domain and, arguably, had an influence in the early part of the twentieth century, on the formation of the self through developmental concepts and terminology (this influence is most felt in H.D. and Nin).

Despite recent readings against de Lauretis, and while I have my own reservations concerning the extent of her project, she provides the most significant interpretative framework for my own analysis—her reading of *The Well of Loneliness* carves out a space of possibility for female fetishism which allows this study to be written. But this study also significantly extends points de Lauretis left undeveloped or ignored: the object of lesbian desire; historicizing the idea of female fetishism within modernism; widening out applications of fetishism to women's writing; theorizing the interaction of literature and the discourses of science; expanding the range of fetishes to include the hand as both sexual instrument and writing tool. This last point extends to considering women's writing in this mode as employing the 'discourse of fetishism'. In the same way that some critics talk of (sexual) inversion as a textual practice, so I talk of fetishism.[33]

THE LITERARINESS OF FETISHISM

In her survey of the power of the image of the phallic mother in psychoanalysis and literary modernism, Marcia Ian argues that both discourses 'idealize the body as language, and language as material, by conflating language with the body'. She outlines the modernist overvaluation of the symbol in D. H. Lawrence's *The Plumed Serpent*, describing it as a 'fetishistic text that memorializes not only the horror of castration, but also that of hysterectomy, in other

---

[33] See Gregory W. Bredbeck 'Narcissus in the Wilde: Textual Cathexis and the Historical Origins of Queer Camp', in Moe Meyer (ed.), *The Politics and Poetics of Camp* (New York and London: Routledge, 1994), 51–74.

words, of the loss of generativity and referentiality itself'. Language becomes a 'cultural ritual capable of making ideas concrete', embodied, and material, of constituting that which has been experienced as absent or lost.[34] Ian's conflation of the literary symbol with the fetish acts as a precedent from which to begin speaking about texts in terms of 'perverse' practices. Angela Moorjani has perhaps gone furthest along this route, and, in her reading of literary texts, has 'extended the concept of fetish-words to fetish signs', relating to the 'mother-father phantasm'.[35] Moorjani's conception of female fetishism in its 'phallic' mode, which relies on the woman devaluing femaleness, envying the penis, wishing she could be a man, and 'acting out phallic rivalry', will not be supported in this study. But Moorjani also maps out and privileges what she calls the 'matric' mode, however, which derives from Louise Kaplan's designation of the 'female castration complex' as pertaining to the mutilation of the female genitalia. Matric castration anxiety finds expression in envy of the mother's fecundity, rivalry with women, homeovestism (which veils her desire to be a man), and devaluation of maleness. Female fetishism in this mode is a fetishization of what the father lacks. Moorjani explores this in the work of H.D., but I am more concerned here with how fetishism is instituted according to a maternal fantasy. Moorjani's work, while important for the expansion of fetishism into other discursive fields, does not attend to how the text functions with relation to fetishism, and her matric fetishism is perhaps too neat an inversion of the phallic: 'it would appear that both men and women, in a continuous to and fro between recognition and denial of loss, fetishize those part-objects which the parent of the opposite sex lacks.'[36]

Sarduy Severo argues that transvestism is 'probably the best metaphor for what writing is';[37] and the specific components of fetishism crucially speak of the literariness of the discourse: Freud himself stated in 'Fetishism' that the fetish has to be deciphered like

[34] Marcia Ian, *Remembering the Phallic Mother: Psychoanalysis, Modernism and the Fetish* (Ithaca, NY and London: Cornell University Press, 1993), 98, 116.
[35] Angela Moorjani, 'Fetishism, Gender Masquerade, and the Mother-Father Fantasy', in Joseph H. Smith and Afaf M. Mahfouz (eds.), *Psychoanalysis, Feminism and the Future of Gender*, vol. xiv of *Psychiatry and the Humanities* (Baltimore and London: Johns Hopkins University Press, 1994), 22–41: 23.
[36] Angela Moorjani, *The Aesthetics of Loss and Lessness* (London: Macmillan, 1992), 130.
[37] Sarduy Severo, 'Writing/Transvestism', *Review*, 9 (Fall 1973), 31–3: 33.

a message, a fragment of text.[38] As Lacan has extrapolated 'such an approach places the problem explicitly in the realm of the search for meaning in language'.[39] Indeed the fetish functions according to synecdoche (a part substituting for a whole), and as a signifier of 'undecidability'. Disavowal is perhaps the component of fetishism most easily translated into the 'literary'; Freud defined it as the negation of an idea through repression, but the affirmation of it on another level of consciousness. In literary terms disavowal denotes the 'unsaid' of a text, that which haunts the text itself; this is perhaps most evident in those modernist women's texts which police themselves most rigorously, which allow lesbian desire only to enter the text as encoded or barely expressed; as Terry Castle suggests: 'One might think of lesbianism as the "repressed idea" at the heart of patriarchal culture.'[40] This might explain the pervasive trope of silence/unarticulation in modernist women's writing. The fetishist's statement of disavowal—'I know that I am not, but I choose to believe that I am'; or 'I know that you are not, but I choose to believe that you are'—is the mode of fictional fantasy for the women writers under discussion in this study. As Lacan and Granoff state, fetishism positions the subject somewhere between the imaginary and the symbolic, an idea which comes to the fore in Nin's writing and the concept of *l'écriture feminine*. Disavowal generally resembles the oscillatory ambivalence that Marianne DeKoven calls the 'simultaneity of irresolvable contradictions' characteristic of modernist texts.[41] More specifically it is a facet of the encoding of lesbian cross-gendering, and in *The Well* for instance represents the oscillation between two conflicting models of female cross-gendering. Fetishistic disavowal, so necessary for sexual pleasure, is also translatable into the literary, an idea which is perhaps most suggestively stated in Roland Barthes's *The Pleasure of the Text*.

[38] Fetishism has been dealt with more widely as a cultural and filmic discourse. See Emily Apter and William Pietz (eds.), *Fetishism as Cultural Discourse* (Ithaca, NY: Cornell Unversity Press, 1993); and Gaylyn Studlar who argues with reference to the visual arts that the 'structure of fetishistic disavowal as a formulation of "I know but nevertheless" is critical to any theory of cinematic pleasure'. *In the Realm of Pleasure: Von Sternberg, Dietrich, and the Masochistic Aesthetic* (New York: Columbia University Press, 1988), 38.

[39] Lacan and Granoff, 'Fetishism', 267.

[40] Terry Castle, *The Apparitional Lesbian: Female Homosexuality and Modern Culture* (New York: Columbia University Press, 1993), 61–2.

[41] Marianne DeKoven, 'Gendered Doubleness and the "Origins" of Modernist Form', *Tulsa Studies in Women's Literature*, 8.1 (Spring 1989), 19–42: 21.

Barthes translates the fetishist mantra into '*I know these are only words but all the same . . .*', suggesting that the reader is seduced into accepting a text's 'reality', and foregrounding other splits that occur within the reader during textual seduction.[42] For Barthes, reading is a perverse activity, critics are voyeurs, and the text itself is a 'fetish object'.[43] For some perverts/readers, the sentence is itself a body which displays itself seductively, split into 'erotic sites', and the reader is free to enter the text where s/he chooses, to follow at her/his desire the slippages of the text where the 'garment gapes'. Pleasure involves the production of a cleavage between two 'surfaces' of a text: the effect is to bring something perverse into connection with raw language.

This splitting of the subject and the text is relevant for modernist texts by women that anxiously play with ideas of physical and textual dismemberment. The idea of stable bodies and selves and the effects of any threat to that body/self are translated into an idea of unity which is especially pertinent to modernist texts which are formally fragmented, and to women writers establishing a gendered self in writing. The discourse of fetishism can flourish in female modernist texts because fiction-writing was, or is represented as, a problematic task for the women writers discussed here: in *The Well*, Hall correlates the paucity of Stephen Gordon's emotional life and her inability to write good prose. Anaïs Nin underwent psychoanalysis in order to convert her diary writing into fiction. H.D. consulted Freud in the 1930s because of writer's block, and Barnes did not write another novel after *Nightwood*. All of the major texts discussed here with the exception of Sarah Grand's *The Heavenly Twins*, are *romans à clef*, a mode dominant in the late 1920s and 1930s particularly in expatriate Paris, around which all of the writers circulated. Nin ransacked her voluminous diary for material to be converted into fiction; H.D. obsessively rewrote a specific period of her life (1911–19); Radclyffe Hall continued her stylization of fantasized self-presentation in *The Well*, while Djuna Barnes told T. S. Eliot that *Nightwood* was to be regarded as semi-autobiography. (She later disavowed this assertion.) Semi-autobiography, split between the narcissism of autobiography, and the imaginative fantasy of fiction puts emphasis on another split which severs the 'narrating "I" ' from the 'narrated "I" ', accentuating the

[42] Roland Barthes, *The Pleasure of the Text*, trans. Richard Miller (1975; Oxford: Basil Blackwell, 1990), 47, Barthes's emphasis and ellipsis.
[43] Ibid. 27.

nature of the genre as the locus of fetishistic desire.[44] The status of fiction within autobiography is precisely, as Laura Marcus imagines, the 'what might have been, what could have been, what might yet be'.[45] As Marcus has theorized, autobiography has 'played a central role in feminist thought, in articulating conceptions of subjectivity'.[46] In semi-autobiographies/semi-fictions influenced by psychoanalysis or sexology, the stakes are raised over the production of subjectivity. In the modernist texts discussed here a number of familiar tropes emerge: the mirroring of psychoanalytic scenarios of the birth of the subject, narcissism associated with this stage of development, and the fragmentation of the self. For Bruce Mazlish, autobiography is analogous to the interpretive process of psychoanalysis:[47] in the constitution of the 'ideal self' a split is produced rendering the text susceptible to fetishism, particularly when there are anxieties concerning publishing (Nin feared a dispersal of the self, or not being able to contain her multiple selves).

WAYS OF READING

Given the literariness of fetishism it is curious that there have not been many extended literary analyses, which combine a historical and theoretical approach, as opposed to a socio-historical survey or a psychoanalytic treatise. Naomi Schor pioneered the appropriation of psychoanalytic concepts 'to ends for which they were not originally intended', in a short article on George Sand, reading her work in terms of sexual/textual fetishism.[48] Schor importantly argues for the possibility of female fetishism, noting that if one takes the splitting of the ego as one of the defining features of fetishism (to which the fetish bears testimony), then it becomes possible to envisage female fetishism. She provides a useful model of how to read literary texts as representative of a particular sexual/textual practice; in

[44] I have borrowed these terms from Sidonie Smith, *A Poetics of Women's Autobiography: Marginality and the Fictions of Self-Representation* (Bloomington, Ind.: Indiana University Press, 1987), 47.

[45] Laura Marcus, *Auto/biographical Discourses: Theory, Criticism, Practice* (Manchester: Manchester University Press, 1994), 280.

[46] Ibid. 279.

[47] Bruce Mazlish, 'Autobiography and Psychoanalysis: Between Truth and Self-Deception', *Encounter*, 35 (Oct. 1970), 28–37: 36.

[48] Naomi Schor, 'Female Fetishism: The Case of George Sand', *Poetics Today*, 6.1–2 (1985), 301–10: 301.

her analysis of Sand's *Léila*, she employs a flexible model of fetishism to argue that the text itself oscillates perversely, rejecting boundaries between characters and subverting the 'fiction of individuation that is the bedrock of conventional realism'.[49] Schor reads the exchange of female identities ('female travesty' or women dressing up as other women), and the blurring of difference 'within difference' as the most subversive form of 'bisextuality'. While Schor's seductive reading is undercut by her suggestion that the 'appropriation of fetishism' might be 'only the latest and most subtle form of "penis-envy"', the usefulness of her analysis remains.[50] While losing some of the specificities of the operations of fetishism as mapped out above (she confuses denial with disavowal for instance), Schor does advertise the potential of the 'mobility of the fetish', especially its applicability to textual strategies.[51]

Susan Gubar's work with Sandra M. Gilbert constitutes one of the most complete analytic catalogues of 'transvestite' fiction by women.[52] Gubar argues that cross-dressing in the modernist period was both a 'sexual statement' and social and political evidence of the 'rhetoric of costuming to redefine the female self'.[53] Female writers and artists exploited this rhetoric to 'transcend' categories of sex and gender, and the limits of 'humanness', ultimately to posit a radically 'redefined' female subject. In a movement too often thought of as male, female modernists 'in-vested' and 'di-vested' conventional forms of legitimacy to make a 'travesty' of sexual signs. But their theorization of the transgressive female subject is problematic: her entry into high modernism is clearly more complex than the 'transcendence' of categories of gender and sex Gubar suggests. Gertrude Stein within this model is the exemplary female cross-dresser who transfigures 'inversion' into 'con-version', converting the image of the invert into an icon of divinity. But the invocation of transcendence elides the complex and radical position

---

[49] Ibid. 307.

[50] Ibid. 308–9. In a later essay Schor suggests that it is extremely rare for women to fetishize sexually. She argues instead for the 'undecidability' of irony 'peeled off' from fetishism as a viable means of perverse expression for women. 'Fetishism and Its Ironies', *Nineteenth-Century French Studies*, 17 (Fall 1988), 89–97: 94–5.

[51] Schor, 'Female Fetishism', 304.

[52] See Sandra M. Gilbert and Susan Gubar, *No-Man's Land: The Place of the Woman Writer in the Twentieth Century*, i. *The War of Words* (New Haven and London: Yale University Press, 1988), and vol. ii, *Sexchanges* (1989).

[53] Susan Gubar, 'Blessings in Disguise: Cross-Dressing as Re-Dressing for Female Modernists', *The Massachusetts Review*, 22.3 (Autumn 1981), 477–508: 478.

that the cross-gendered woman occupies in modernism. Marjorie Garber, who sees cross-dressing as a mode of articulation that challenges the way in which 'cultural binarism is read', has contested Gilbert and Gubar on these grounds, seeing them as subsuming the figure of the cross-dresser within one of the two traditional genders, collapsing the 'space of possibility' created by transvestism and drag.[54]

The respective analyses of Garber, and Gilbert and Gubar, coincide on one point, however: that the transvestite puts into question categories of gender. Judith Butler's work in this field has of course been ground-breaking; gender impersonation, she theorizes, 'destabilizes the very distinctions between the natural and the artificial, depth and surface, inner and outer through which discourse about genders almost always operates'.[55] The 'performance of drag plays upon the distinction between the anatomy of the performer' and the gender that is being performed; in '*imitating gender, drag implicitly reveals the imitative structure of gender itself*' and its radical contingency, as well as its reliance on a repetitive discourse that resubstantiates its claims. The parody is not of an original but '*of* the very notion of an original'.[56] Butler's analysis offers a vision of radical possibilities which emanate from the location of strategies of subversive repetition. What is primarily and necessarily an unconscious process (the substantiation or 'materialization' of a gendered and sexed identity), is revisioned by Butler as a conscious 'task' to displace gender norms.[57] While it is precisely the tension between the conscious and the unconscious with which I am concerned, and while Butler certainly created a space for such discussions to take place, I will not be arguing for the radical and self-fulfilling possibilities these gender performances allow, but rather for ways in which scientific discourses are both incorporated and manipulated, consciously and unconsciously, overtly and covertly, textually and subtextually.

This study differs from those formerly undertaken because it is a literary analysis of fetishism, which combines a historical and theoretical approach. Aside from mapping the intersection of fiction and

---

[54] Marjorie Garber, *Vested Interests: Cross-Dressing and Cultural Anxiety* (1992; London: Penguin, 1993), 14, 9–10.

[55] Judith Butler, *Gender Trouble: Feminism and the Subversion of Identity* (London: Routledge, 1990), p. x.

[56] Ibid. 137–8.   [57] Ibid. 148.

autobiography, the readings in this study trace out a particular narrative trajectory that is interpreted against both sexological inscriptions of the female invert and psychoanalytic symbolizations of the masculine lesbian. The interpretative framework is multiple: to read the texts in terms of their symptomatic assimilation of clinical inscription on the one hand, and their discrete and covert symbolization of fetishism on the other. Reading the fiction against itself, exploiting the tropes of articulation and silence, and encodings of lesbian desire, generates a theory in which women writers are seen as exceeding the scientific theories of fetishism. The precise nature of female cross-gendering is read for its fetishistic possibilities, as a self-fulfilling fantasy on behalf of the female subject. In the literary analysis of each text certain themes and motifs are traced such as the symbolization of the hand as sexual instrument, writerly tool, and fetish object, in order to argue for the fetishistic nature of the texts themselves.

Psychoanalytic and sexological texts are of course already highly textually mediated. The case history has a narrative which undergoes successive mutations and permutations: it is disseminated in the public arena and then is re-narrativized. As Jay Prosser argues, for example, the case histories of sexual inversion are 'the narratives of inverts' lives and identification in their autobiographical recounting or translated into biography by the sexologist'.[58] Gender itself is perhaps the most contested 'text' or sign-system of all. Here it is read as radically unstable, requiring fetishism to stabilize it; this has its most terminal statement perhaps in Barnes's *Nightwood*, in which the cross-gendered woman is 'misread into conformity' by her lover. The focus on cross-dressing foregrounds this instability, as Laura Doan states: 'what clothing confirms for the cross-dresser and observer alike is not gender but gender's status as a fiction.'[59] The instability of gender's effects can lead to misreading, and female cross-gendering itself is highly contested; interpretations of the mirror scene in *The Well of Loneliness* in turn *reflect* the complex position of the cross-gendered woman and the desires she initiates and attracts; in Halberstam, Prosser, and de Lauretis she is recuperated for a defining theory of respectively female masculinity, transgendering, and (lesbian)

[58] Jay Prosser, 'Transsexuals and the Transsexologists: Inversion and the Emergence of Transsexual Subjectivity', in Lucy Bland and Laura Doan (eds.), *Sexology in Culture: Labelling Bodies and Desires* (Oxford and Cambridge: Polity Press, 1998), 116–23: 123.
[59] Doan, *Fashioning Sapphism*, 94.

perverse desire. Of course there are ways in which my own readings and writing are bound up with fetishism: any interpretation of fetishism runs the risk of being categorical, where the fetish is gender/sex.[60] Running risks is part of the pleasure of fetishism, and, in a Barthesian sense, a facet of the pleasure of reading. Elizabeth Grosz suggests that in wanting both to 'castrate' and preserve psychoanalysis, de Lauretis is herself succumbing to the disavowal of fetishism, and there is a danger that my own writing could become fixated by its object—female fetishism—and operate fetishistically, disavowing other readings/theories. Engaging with alternative readings of the texts carefully guards against this danger.

The first chapter of this study begins with a reading of Sarah Grand's *fin de siècle* New Woman novel *The Heavenly Twins*. Grand, who had made public statements on sexual and social purity in the 1890s, may seem a curious place to begin this study, but her representation of female cross-gendering employs many of the motifs that I have identified in the other texts: she both avows and forecloses the possibilities of sexual fetishism for women. Moreover, the novel's seeming 'uncontamination' by the discourses of sexology and psychoanalysis makes its representation of female cross-gendering 'ideal'. This chapter also contextualizes the reading of *The Heavenly Twins* with a brief overview of female cross-gendering in nineteenth-century literature, and an analysis of the inscription and manifestation of female cross-gendering as 'sexual inversion' in sexology, with an attempt to recover the fetishist and transvestite from these case histories. Chapter 2 follows with a brief reading of Christopher St John's *Hungerheart* to foreground the invisibility of female cross-gendering prior to the First World War, before embarking on a brief study of how the war legitimized certain modes of female masculinity. A reading of Bryher's early *romans à clef*, and her adherence to the model of sexual inversion, demonstrating both the existence of dualistic strategies of writing and the close relationship between literary texts of the period and the discourses of sexology and psychoanalysis, prefaces a close reading of motifs of perversion in Radclyffe Hall's *The Unlit Lamp*, and an extended analysis of both inversion and perversion in *The Well of*

[60] As Mary E. Galvin comments: 'The heterosexist society imbues its fetish (gender, sex) with inordinate power, the power of the universal, the ahistorical, the transcultural, the power of original immutable truth'. *Queer Poetics: Five Modernist Women Writers* (Westport, Conn., and London: Praeger, 1999), 2.

Loneliness. This extends de Lauretis's reading and deviates from it both in the comparison of Gutheil's case history of female fetishistic transvestism, and in the analysis of Hall's textual fetishism. This chapter analyses conflicting modes of female cross-gendering but privileges the fetishistic.

The figure missing from this chapter, who nevertheless haunts it, is Virginia Woolf who appeared as a witness for the defence during *The Well*'s obscenity trial. The identification of a particular narrative trajectory has necessary led to the exclusion of other 'cross-gendered' texts of the period, most notably Woolf's *Orlando*, published the same year as *The Well*. If a narrative of cross-gendering emerges from *Orlando*, Woolf's love letter to Vita Sackville-West, it is one that can more easily be co-opted by performance theory. Woolf was privy to the narrative of Sackville-West's mythic self-presentation which was the confirmation of the classic characteristics of the 'sexual invert'. Sackville-West's autobiographical narrative, begun in 1920, recalls her self-conscious cross-gendered exploits, and was supposed to offer the kind of personal testimony a 'professional scientist could acquire only after years of study'.[61] But what Sackville-West privileges in her own account is anathema to Woolf: while Sackville-West advanced the theory that 'cases of dual personality do exist, in which the feminine and masculine elements preponderate', Woolf theoretically adhered to the concept of a balance of masculine and feminine characteristics to create a figure of androgyny.[62] Woolf rewrites her lover's sexual subversiveness as the triumph of personality across three centuries; in each era she remains a consistent persona despite undergoing a 'sex change'. Woolf attaches no deep motivational psychology to this event: 'Let biologists and psychologists determine. It is enough for us to state a simple fact; Orlando was a man till the age of thirty; when he became a woman and has remained so ever since.'[63] Woolf does not enter into an overt dialogue with sexology and psychoanalysis, as do Grand, Hall, Nin, H.D., Barnes (and Bryher); rather Woolf constructs gendered identity as a form of dress which clothes a stable androgynous self: 'It was a change in Orlando herself that dictated

[61] Nigel Nicolson, *Portrait of a Marriage* (1973; London: Weidenfeld and Nicolson, 1990), 102.
[62] Ibid. 102.
[63] Virginia Woolf, *Orlando: A Biography* (London: The Hogarth Press, 1928), 127-8.

her choice of a woman's dress and of a woman's sex.'[64] Sandra
Gilbert comments that since only 'outwardly' does Orlando undergo
a 'sex change' he remains, in all other aspects, precisely as he always
had been: Woolf's 'transsexual . . . is no more than a transvestite'.[65]
While this identification of Orlando might suggest 'perversity', and
while I agree with Laura Marcus that Woolf's text 'disrupts' gender
categories, I have omitted Woolf's novel from this study because it
does not speak of the specificities of female fetishistic cross-
gendering, but rather addresses male-to-female con-version as
opposed to female per-version.[66] Gertrude Stein is also excluded.
Like Woolf, Stein tested the boundaries of biography in *The
Autobiography of Alice B. Toklas* (1933), and like Sackville-West,
Stein underwent a public gender-transformation, rewritten as a textual persona: she saw herself as 'a roman and Julius Caesar and a
bridge and a column and a pillar'.[67] In 'Lifting Belly' she presents
one lover's request 'Please be the man' with the other lover's eager
reply 'I am the man'.[68] Susan Gubar has argued for Stein's deliberately subversive analysis of lesbian role-play, but Stein in the words of
Gubar is like Woolf, more concerned with 'transcendence', desiring
to surpass 'not only the limits of gender, but also the confines of
humanness'.[69] Unlike *Orlando* and the work of Gertrude Stein the
texts in this study all 'convert' female sexual inversion into 'perverse'
fetishism.

   Chapter 3, meanwhile, analyses the shift away from the model of
inversion, to psychoanalytic cross-gendering, in H.D.'s *HER*. H.D.
was heavily invested in psychoanalytic theory, but readings of *HER*
and *Tribute to Freud* focusing on female cross-gendering demon-
strate that she was endlessly reformulating Freudian theory, particularly as it might relate to a maternal fantasy which could be
characterized as fetishistic. *HER* brings to the fore the motifs traced
in Chapters 1 and 2: fetishism is sexual and textual, registered here
as a linguistic crisis. In *HER*, as in Djuna Barnes's *Nightwood*,
which forms the basis of Chapter 4, cross-gendering is located in the

---

[64] Woolf, *Orlando*, 171.
[65] Sandra M. Gilbert, 'Costumes of the Mind: Transvestism as Metaphor in Modern
Literature', in Elizabeth Abel (ed.), *Writing and Sexual Difference* (1980; Brighton:
Harvester, 1982), 193–219: 206–7.
[66] Marcus, *Auto/biographical Discourses*, 126
[67] Gertrude Stein, 'A Sontina Followed By Another', in *The Yale Gertrude Stein*, ed.
Richard Kostelanetz (New Haven: Yale University Press, 1980), 296.
[68] Ibid. 51.   [69] Gubar, 'Blessings in Disguise', 493.

object of desire rather than the subject of the novel. Chapters 3 and 4 expand on the work of Emily Apter to verify the similarities between narcissism and fetishism in order to read 'sister-love' (the fusion of twin selves). In both novels the motif of being twinned with the cross-gendered woman forms the basis of fetishism. Barnes, however, in her radical linguistic, narrational, and representational experiments spells out the limits of female fetishism through motifs of 'impossibility' and exhaustion. Barnes's writing is 'haunted' by the (im)possibility of imagining a way out of the impasse of sexual dichotomies: the 'impossibility' of the representation of the cross-gendered woman, and the desires that circulate around her, are the expression and symptom of this. *Nightwood* itself is fetishistic: it disavows sexology and psychoanalysis while posing its own discourse according to their terms, and it is split from within by its inability to manage successfully the figuration of the cross-gendered Robin Vote. Finally, Chapter 5 examines Barnes's legacy in Anaïs Nin, another analysand, and her confrontation with Freudian concepts of the female subject. Nin is a particularly appropriate subject of this study: in the effort to 'convert' her diary writing into fiction she 'perverted' the Freudian text and proposed her own (problematic) model of female sexuality. One of the ways Nin tries to address the problems encountered by Barnes is to make the female subject diffuse and multiple, anticipating post-modern subject dispersal. Nin maps out other female fetishisms for women (homeovestism), but on the whole her work is the final statement on this particular narrative of female fetishism, a final disavowal.

'Coveted Pleasures'
Inverts and Perverts at the *Fin de Siècle*

CROSS-DRESSING AND EARLY MODERNISM IN
SARAH GRAND'S *THE HEAVENLY TWINS*

In 1890 Frances McFall attempted to publish 'The Tenor and the
Boy', a fantastical story of a young woman, Angelica, who cross-
dresses as 'the Boy' in order to conduct a relationship with a young
man, the Tenor. In 1892 it appeared as an 'interlude' in the privately
published novel *The Heavenly Twins*, for which McFall had restyled
herself as 'Sarah Grand', a manoeuvre described by Sandra M.
Gilbert and Susan Gubar as signalling 'a rebirth into linguistic
primacy'.[1] Eventually 'The Tenor and the Boy' was published as a
separate piece by Heinemann in 1899, and Grand also wrote a script
based on the story with Robert Buchanan for an unrealized play. In
1934 Grand agreed with the critic Bjornsen Bjornsen that 'The
Tenor and the Boy' might have been excised entirely from *The
Heavenly Twins* because it 'is not necessary to the story'.[2] She
always insisted that the novel's primary purpose was to draw attention to the dangers of venereal disease; within that remit, she had little reason to speak about 'The Tenor and the Boy'. Among the 'New
Woman' writers Grand was perhaps the one who put most empha-

---

[1] Sandra M. Gilbert and Susan Gubar, 'Ceremonies of the Alphabet: Female
Grandmatologies and the Female Autograph', in Domna C. Stanton (ed.), *The Female
Autograph: Theory and Practice of Autobiography from the Tenth to the Twentieth
Century* (1984; Chicago and London: University of Chicago Press, 1987), 21–48: 27.
Grand claimed not to have heard of the 'other' Sarah Grand, the mistress, and later wife,
of Talleyrand, and a woman of 'disreputable' character. See Gillian Kersley, *Darling
Madame: Sarah Grand and Devoted Friend* (London: Virago, 1983), 65–6. Gerd
Bjørhovde remarks on the choice of a female pen name when it was 'customary for
women writers to adopt male pseudonyms'. *Rebellious Structures: Women Writers and
the Crisis of the Novel 1880–1990* (Oslo: Norwegian University Press, 1987), 87. Gillian
Kersley provides a psychological explanation: after leaving her husband McFall constructed a personality 'that could stand alone' (51).
[2] Kersley, *Darling Madame*, 262.

sis on social purity, and her reputation suffered as a result. But it might be that her active concern with sexual purity—her knowledge was gleaned from her husband's treatment of men with VD in lock hospitals—perhaps enabled her to have a unique insight into female sexuality and cross-gendering which informed the 'interlude' of her novel.

Late in her life Grand felt that *The Heavenly Twins*, which was one of the most popular novels of the 1890s when commercially published by Heinemann in 1893, had spoilt her literary career because it 'diverted her activities into other channels and it took her a long time to get back again'.[3] What this publishing history suggests is that 'The Tenor and the Boy' occupied a peculiar position in Grand's oeuvre (it also preoccupied her to the end of her life), and its status was never fully resolved. It was both valued as a discrete literary project worthy of adaptation, and devalued as something that was always somewhat 'out of place'. Transplanted into the body of *The Heavenly Twins* text it dismembers it both generically and thematically, but without it *The Heavenly Twins*, entitled as such, would lack its *raison d'être* and its subversive core as represented in the twins Angelica and Diavolo: the twins' cross-dressing is the impetus for the subsequent action, as their mother foresees: 'I said, when those children changed clothes, it was unnatural, and would bring bad luck.'[4]

Prior to *The Heavenly Twins* Grand had begun her literary career with 'The Baby's Tragedy', a short story not published until the 1890s, and 'Two Dear Little Feet', a morality tale about constricting footwear, which was published in 1873. This was her first pronouncement on her obsession with clothes—as Gillian Kersley has documented, Grand's initial connection with the

---

[3] Ibid. 237.

[4] Sarah Grand, *The Heavenly Twins* (1893; Ann Arbor: University of Michigan Press, 1992), 106. Further references to this edition will be cited in the text. Although I do not endorse a contemporary review from the *Spectator* that the novel was 'thrown together in a haphazard fashion', I cannot fully agree with the modern view that the novel is unified. Although there is a thematic link with the other sections, as Carol A. Senf states in her introduction to this edition, the influence of the twins as played out in 'The Tenor and the Boy' is textually destabilizing. Significantly many *fin de siècle* reviewers were seduced by them, such as the *Punch* critic: 'I should have liked the Twins, and only the Twins, and nothing but the Twins' (Senf, pp. xxi, xi, xxii). A heated debate concerning the relevance of the twins was carried out in the *Pall Mall Gazette* in May 1893. See Robert Rowlette, 'Mark Twain, Sarah Grand, and *The Heavenly Twins*', *Mark Twain Journal*, 16.2 (Summer 1972), 17–18: 18.

suffrage movement grew out of her interest in the Rational Dress Society.[5] From 1879 to 1881 Grand wrote 'The Tenor and the Boy' at the same time as composing her novel *Ideala* (privately published in 1888). In 1891 she produced *A Domestic Experiment*, a story of female friendship, and the following year, *Singularly Deluded*, a 'cross-genre' piece (half-detective novel and half-adventure story) about a woman, cast, as Teresa Mangum notes, as a figure of 'literary transvestism' in the male role of detective and adventurer who pursues a man she thinks is her husband.[6] By 1893 *The Heavenly Twins* was a commercial bestseller, and entered the culture through parodies and cartoons, also eliciting letters from the medical establishment praising her on her well-informed knowledge of physiology and pathology. But for all its success it was also seen as a dangerous and perverting book: 'not healthy reading for the growing youth or maiden'.[7] Moreover the novel did not impress her reviewers, and after *The Beth Book* (1897), the third novel in the trilogy which comprised *Ideala* and *The Heavenly Twins*, Sarah Grand took notice of the critics, who thought her 'heavy handed', caring 'nothing about novel-writing as an art, except in so far that it can be used as a vehicle for her doctrines'.[8] She thenceforth confined her feminist politics to articles and lectures, while trying to improve the style of her fiction.

Grand's reputation floundered in the twentieth century. But in the 1990s, with the republication of *The Heavenly Twins* in 1992, critics and historians re-examined Grand's style and aesthetics. John Kucich's work is probably the most useful for this study, for while he does not ignore the archaisms of her writing, he believes that Grand's failure to resolve some of the more intractable problems of feminism, for instance 'the tension between women's sexual expression and their autonomy', is rather an exploration of the 'dynamism of her characters' impossible choices', because '[s]elf-contradiction

[5] Kersley, *Darling Madame*, 24. As Kersley notes, amongst Grand's strongest memories from childhood, was her repugnance for her brother's cast-off jacket: 'the torture of a soiled frock was soon surpassed by having to wear a boy's jacket for warmth in the autumn' (24). Kersley goes on to suggest that Grand's adoption of a new persona was consolidated through her clothing.
    [6] Teresa Mangum, *Married, Middlebrow, and Militant: Sarah Grand and the New Woman Novel* (Ann Arbor: University of Michigan Press, 1998), 52.
    [7] *Englishwoman's Review*, 24 (1893), 198.
    [8] Kersley, *Darling Madame*, 93; *The Athenaeum* (27 Nov. 1897). Quoted ibid. 93.

is the psychological state most interesting to her'.[9] Indeed, as Kucich points out, Angelica frames her cross-dressing within these terms, and Grand's interest in such psychological complexity had 'aesthetic consequences that cry out to be put in relation to modernist formal innovations'. Despite Grand's affirmation of realist traditions, Kucich talks of Grand's 'covert interest in antirealist aesthetics' which 'lies in the disjunctive form of the novels themselves'.[10]

With *The Heavenly Twins* Grand utilized the conventional form of the three-decker novel to carry an overtly sensational story which addressed pertinent contemporary issues such as the dangerous effects of male sexual behaviour on three women: Evadne Frayling, Angelica Hamilton-Wells, and Edith Beale. Evadne, who has been self-educated in pathology, anatomy, botany, and philosophy, marries a man to whom she is sexually attracted, but with whom she refuses to have sex after she discovers his promiscuity, and battles with her father who threatens to incarcerate her in a lunatic asylum. Taking an instant dislike to Edith's husband, her views are confirmed when Edith gives birth to a sickly child and then dies a terrible death from syphilis contracted from her husband. Within the bounds of a celibate marriage to Mr Kilroy, Angelica pursues her own desires, including cross-dressing as the 'Boy' and visiting her friend the Tenor. When the Tenor dies after a boating accident that is partly Angelica's fault, she resumes a life more suited to a wife. Evadne succumbs to a form of hysteria, diagnosed by her second husband Dr Galbraith, and tries to kill herself when she learns that she is pregnant. She is restored to mental health by Galbraith in what is a precarious conclusion to the novel.

The first two-thirds of the novel are largely written in the realist mode, but Grand systematically undermines this form from within. The focus for this subversion is Angelica: not only her cross-gendering but also the presentation of her consciousness, which in its fluidity and formlessness suggests what Bjørhovde has identified as the 'beginnings of modernism'.[11] This takes the form of flights of fancy, and dreams:

---

[9] John Kucich, 'Curious Dualities: *The Heavenly Twins* (1893) and Sarah Grand's Belated Modernist Aesthetics', in Barbara Leah Harman and Susan Meyer (eds.), *The New Nineteenth Century: Feminist Readings of Underread Victorian Fiction* (New York and London: Garland Publishing, 1996), 195–204: 196.

[10] Kucich, 'Curious Dualities', 197.

[11] Bjørhovde, *Rebellious Structures*, 110–15.

in her dream she saw a semblance, the semblance of a man, a changing semblance, the features of which she could not discern, although she tried with frenzied effort, because she knew that when she saw him fully face to face he would be hers. They were not in this world, nor in the next. They were not even in the universe. They were simply each the centre of a great light which formed a sphere about them, and separated them from one another; and heaven and hell, and earth and sky, and night and day, and life and death were all added to the glory of those spheres of light. And she knew *how*; but there is no word of human speech to express it. (293)

The eruption of fantasy into the main narrative finds its full expression, however, in 'The Tenor and the Boy'. Highly fantastical in mode, it takes place at night, anticipating the more radical gender deconstruction in Djuna Barnes's crepuscular *Nightwood*. The Tenor, committed to a vision of Angelica as the true embodiment of her name, can see no trace of her in her cross-dressed as the Boy (whom he also secretly desires); Angelica meanwhile uses her disguise to discourse on the nature of sexual identity and modern relationships.

The uncertain position of 'The Tenor and the Boy' in the text itself is magnified in the position that Angelica, as a cross-gendered woman, occupies in it. Never quite absorbed into the narrative as a whole, and exceeding the narrative constraints upon it, the representation of Angelica is proto-modernist. Emerging prior to Havelock Ellis's inscription of the female invert in *Studies in the Psychology of Sex* (1897), and too early for the effects of Richard von Krafft-Ebing's *Psychopathia Sexualis* (1886) to have been widely disseminated, 'The Tenor and the Boy' occupies a liminal position with regards to fictional representations of female cross-gendering, and inscribes its own fascinating model. While Grand was intimately concerned with female sexuality at a time when investigation into what was perceived as women's increasing masculinization was being conducted, and may have had access to *Psychopathia Sexualis*, 'The Tenor and the Boy' remains virtually uncontaminated by the discourse of sexology. Indeed female cross-gendering in 'The Tenor and the Boy' is the focus for a range of desires and pleasures which are not written into the sexological accounts. Grand's novel provides evidence that female writers were conceptualizing female sexual identity 'differently' before the cultural absorption of sexology and psychoanalysis was fully under way. Indeed, the text wittily plays with the range of meanings available at the time with

Angelica musing on the interrelation between (religious) conversion
and perversion: ' "I suppose you wouldn't like us to be converted?"
Angelica asked. "We call it *perverted*, dear child," said Mrs. Beale
. . . "I don't suppose they care a button what we call it," Angelica
decided off-hand, out of her own inner consciousness. "But you
would like us to be either "con" or "per," would you?" she asked the
bishop' (153). The opposing choices of 'con' and 'per' force any
inscription of 'in-version' out of the frame of 'The Tenor and the
Boy'.[12] Angelica later terms her cross-dressing as 'conversion': 'I
should hardly have thought it possible to convert a substantial
young woman into such a slender, delicate-looking boy as I make'
(452). The key word here is 'make', which suggests that Angelica's
con-version is a self-fulfilling fantasy rather than an innate biological inversion.

'COVETED PLEASURES': HOMOSEXUAL AND HETEROSEXUAL
DESIRE IN 'THE TENOR AND THE BOY'

Angelica's cross-gendering in childhood prefigures her more devastating experiment with the Tenor, but also testifies to her desire to
be liberated from the constraints of her sex. In the larger body of the
text, inversion is manifestly present in the polarization of gender
underscored from the outset in the naming of the twins as Angelica
and Diavolo. Angelica pursues the same right to education as her
brother, posing as him in the schoolroom; as a result of a liberal education she learns to value physical and mental health above all other
things. Indeed, her practical education prepares her to fight her twin
brother Diavolo for equality 'by hook, which she explains as being
the proper development of her muscles and physique generally, and
by crook, which she defines as circumventing the slave drivers of her
sex' (73). Angelica, in a fantasy of inversion, believes that she and
her twin 'were mixed somehow wrong, and I got his mind and he got
mine', that '*I* am Diavolo and *he* is me' (Grand's emphasis, 124).
Angelica certainly bears what were typically interpreted as the signs
of masculinity: she is wilful and assertive, and Diavolo, conversely,
refuses to accede to full masculinity by remaining a sensitive and

---

[12] Kenneth Burke plays with these prefixes in 'Version, Con-, Per-, and In-: Thoughts
on Djuna Barnes's Novel *Nightwood*', *Language as Symbolic Action: Essays on Life,
Literature and Method* (Berkeley: University of California Press, 1968), 240–53.

vulnerable boy. But while cross-gendered behaviour is presented as a corollary of that 'inversion', Grand does not impose a complete inversion of character. On the verge of womanhood, Angelica is persuaded by her mother to graduate to long dresses. The idea horrifies Diavolo, who is not prepared to enter into adulthood, but Angelica promises that when she does wear formal dresses 'it shall only be a disguise' (275). Angelica's behaviour suggests that she covertly supports and colludes in her brother's desire to remain in the undifferentiated realm of childhood. In adulthood she conducts a celibate relationship with her asexual and effeminate husband, whom she refers to as 'dear old Daddy'. Rejecting the idea of a conventional marriage after witnessing Edith's illness and death, and Evadne's frustration, she and Mr Kilroy enter into a pre-nuptial agreement in which she is granted freedom within marriage. According to this arrangement, she pursues her own desires, most notably that of cross-dressing, and enjoying the company of the Tenor while disguised as 'the Boy'. Grand insists that Angelica's main purpose in cross-dressing is to enjoy the benefit of 'free intercourse with [a] masculine mind', and Angelica, herself, later justifies her behaviour to the Tenor in the language of feminist insurrection:

There was no latitude allowed for my individuality. I was a girl, and therefore I was not supposed to have any bent . . . I had the ability to be something more that a young lady, fiddling away her time on useless trifles, but I was not allowed to apply it systematically, and ability is like steam—a great power when properly applied, a great danger otherwise . . . This is the explosion . . . I had the feeling, never actually formulated in words, but quite easy to interpret now, that if I broke down conventional obstacles—broke the hampering laws of society, I should have a chance—(450)

But this extract also figures Angelica's predicament in sexual terms: her cross-dressing is the explosion, rendered here as an orgasmic convulsion after the first break in the sentence. But it is a desire that can barely be spoken, cannot be 'formulated in words', but can be 'interpreted' after the event. Interpretation is the key to reading Grand's representation of female cross-gendering as a 'desiring' act. This should be compared with Angelica's dream in which she knows on some unconscious level, 'but there is no word of human speech to express it' (293).

With that in mind, Angelica's cross-dressing precipitates and invokes a series of complex erotic responses on behalf of the Tenor and Angelica herself. Prior to her cross-dressing experiment,

Angelica has denied herself any recognition of desire or passion. Her closest relationship is with her brother, and although she sought out her husband and asked him to marry her, this very assertion points to the sexual neutrality of Mr Kilroy, who admires Angelica's modernity, and grants her the freedom she craves under the letter of the law. Desire is not actively excised from the text, however: in one of the text's modernist digressions quoted above, Angelica dreams of a 'semblance of a man'. Up to this moment, as she admits, she has never 'felt a throb of passion. She had given the best love of her life to her brother, and had made no personal application of anything she had heard, or seen, or read of lovers, so that the possibility of ever having one of her own had never cost her a serious thought' (293). Significantly Angelica's dream is broken by Edith's screams as, close to death, she summons her family in order to denounce her husband and those 'who represent the arrangement of society which has made it possible for me and my child to be sacrificed in this way' (300). Angelica breaks Menteith's nose and then proposes celibate marriage to Mr Kilroy. It is only later while cross-dressed that Angelica feels the return of desire, and the very first effects of the cross-dressing are sexual as she is approached by a prostitute. The narrative then enters a world in which desire, according to Angelica's fantasies, is the modus operandi.

The Tenor desires Angelica both as she appears to him in church as an image of piety, *and* as the Angelica who cross-dresses as the Boy. For Angelica the act is presented as erotically fulfilling, and as a practice that fleetingly secures a sense of psychic and sexual health. Indeed the desires incited by her cross-dressing impact upon her own pleasure, and restructure it. As children, the twins had revelled in the subversive nature of their cross-gendering. At Evadne's wedding, they cross-dress as each other, and Diavolo enjoys a homo-erotic frisson:

Angelica obtained the coveted pleasure of acting as page to Evadne, and Diavolo escaped the trouble of having to hold up her train, and managed besides to have some fun with a small but amorous boy who was to have been Angelica's pair, and who, knowing nothing of the fraud which had been perpetrated, insisted on kissing the fair Diavolo, to that gentleman's lasting delight. (61)

While the emphasis is firmly on Diavolo's playful desires, Angelica's cross-dressing has already been described as a 'pleasure'.

The success and power of her 'adult' cross-dressing also facilitates a reading of the Tenor's response as homoerotic:

As he walked through the Close, still a little behind the Boy, he could not help noticing, by no means for the first time, but more particularly than usual, what a graceful creature the latter was. His slender figure showed to advantage in the light flannels. They made him look broader and more manly while leaving room for the free play of limb and muscle. He had knotted a crimson silk scarf round his neck, sailor fashion, and twisted a voluminous cummerbund of the same round his waist, carelessly, so that one heavily fringed end of it came loose, and now hung down to his knee, swaying with his body as he moved. (436)

On the one hand this scene of homosexual cruising points to the collapse of the images that the Tenor has of Angelica: the graceful woman, and the (unacknowledged) manly Boy. On the other, this sensual portrait, which acknowledges what the Tenor perceives to be the male body as erotic spectacle, is invested with a scopophilic energy and intensity which is immediately diffused by Angelica's accidental unmasking. In either case, it remains a testimony to the complex desires which female cross-gendering provokes. It is crucial that it is at this point that the Tenor recognizes that the Boy is at his most manly. Previously, he had been struck by the Boy's effeminacy: his voice is womanish and he calls him 'Maude', and likens him to the Witch of Atlas (402–3). The reference to the borrowing of the accoutrements of sailors, also speaks, covertly, of a homosexual recognition on behalf of the Tenor.[13] It is also interesting to trace the movement of the Tenor's gaze, which travels downward, from the neck to the knee, via the crotch where he imagines the Boy's penis to be, which is displaced on to the fringed part of the cummerbund which hangs down and swings.

Martha Vicinus argues, in a suggestive reading of *The Heavenly Twins* and turn-of-the-century theatrical male impersonation, that 'The Tenor and the Boy' suggests both 'man-boy-love' and lesbian

---

[13] See Marjorie Garber for a history of homosexual subculture amongst sailors in *Vested Interests: Cross-Dressing and Cultural Anxiety* (1992; London: Penguin, 1993), 57. Martha Vicinus also notes that the beautiful choirboy was by the 1890s a cliché among homosexuals as an object of desire. 'Turn-of-the-Century Male Impersonation: Rewriting the Romance Plot', in Andrew H. Miller and James Eli Adams (eds.), *Sexualities in Victorian Britain* (Bloomington and Indianapolis, Ind.: Indiana University Press, 1996), 187–213: 205.

desire. The rise of the male impersonator on the British stage, as a 'visual icon of the possibility of alternative sexual desire' in the late nineteenth century, coincided with the prevalence of the image of the New Woman to 'represent both an eloquent and luxurious sexual undecidability *and* a threatening homosexual potential—depending not so much on the intentions of the impersonator herself, as those of her audience'.[14] With her antecedent in the principal boy of the 1830s, male impersonators such as Vesta Tilley became public symbols of performed gender. Significantly, Vicinus sees a relationship between the sexually aware world of the theatre and the New Woman novels, particularly *The Heavenly Twins*, in which she argues that Angelica's direction of the Tenor's gaze to her body and self is highly staged: the Tenor remarks that her boy's costume looks as if it were for 'private theatricals' (418), and her flannel boating suit resembles Tilley's seaside dandy.[15] Certainly Angelica sees her cross-gendered performance as 'not a bit more marvellous in real life than it would have been upon the stage' and positions herself in the tradition of the male impersonator:

the same thing has been done before. George Sand, for instance; don't you remember how often she went about dressed as a man, went to the theatres and was introduced to people, and was never found out by strangers? And there was that woman who was a doctor in the army for so long—until she was quite old. James Barry, she called herself, and none of her brother officers, not even her own particular chum in the regiment she first belonged to had any suspicion of her sex, and it was not discovered until after her death, when she had been an Inspector General of the Army Medical Department for many years. And there have been women in the ranks too, and at sea. (456)

The sexologist Richard von Krafft-Ebing suggested that 'uranism' or sexual inversion, 'may nearly always be suspected in females wearing their hair short, or who dress in the fashion of men, or pursue the sports and pastimes of their male acquaintances; also in

[14] Vicinus, 'Turn-of-the-Century Male Impersonation', 187, Vicinus's emphasis. At the turn of the *twentieth* century male theatrical male impersonation became the focus of a number of novels by women including Sarah Waters's *Tipping the Velvet* (1998).

[15] Vicinus, 'Turn-of-the-Century Male Impersonation', 204. As Vicinus comments, the cover of the paperback edition, reproduced for the Michigan reprint, shows Angelica dressed in a boating suit, but without her boy's wig: 'Angelica's successful transvestism is undermined, as if it were too daring to illustrate in a cheap reprint' (204). The reader would not have mistaken the image for a boy: Angelica has a pre-Raphaelite face and flowing hair.

opera singers and actresses, who appear in male attire on the stage by preference'.[16]

Moreover, Vicinus argues seductively that the pervasive gender reversals, the allusions to food, warmth, and the Tenor's 'moral pedagogy', contribute to a 'Sapphic romance'. As in Barnes's *Nightwood* in which the transvestite quack doctor Matthew O'Connor 'teaches' Nora Flood about the 'third sex' as it pertains to her boyish lover Robin Vote, the Tenor and the Boy are also 'creatures of the night', who, constructed through fantasy and desire, have no place in the world.[17] The Tenor and Angelica's desires, cut off in this way, proliferate in a space outside of the law, only to be curtailed by the Tenor's tragic death. Vicinus reads the ending of the romance as an orgasmic culmination of these free-floating desires which simultaneously speaks of lesbian desire: 'At a time when a modern lesbian culture was just beginning to define itself publicly, the well-established contemporary male culture could have been a source of inspiration, however indirectly.'[18] Significantly Carroll Smith-Rosenberg in conversation with Vicinus suggests that Sarah Grand is wooing Angelica as the Boy through the Tenor 'as a means of speaking her own homosexual desire'.[19] There is certainly evidence in Gladys Singers-Bigger's journals that Grand was dabbling in a form of Sapphism in the power games she played with Gladys. Grand courted Gladys's very willing and fanatical affection with the promise of kisses, and Gladys in her turn hoped to marry Grand's son Archie in a bid to stay close to Grand (a hope that was cruelly dashed). Gladys obsessively recorded Grand's daily appearance and clothing in her journal, discussed the lesbian play *Mädchen in Uniform* with Grand, whose 'ejaculations of interest and encouragement were wordless and more like cries of pain', and expressed jealousy over other female admirers who gave Grand gifts such as cloisonné ash trays.[20] At

---

[16] Richard von Krafft-Ebing, *Psychopathia Sexualis* (1886; 12th edn., 1903). Quoted in Lucy Bland and Laura Doan (eds.), *Sexology Uncensored: The Documents of Sexual Science* (Oxford: Polity Press, 1998), 46–7.

[17] Vicinus, 'Turn-of-the-Century Male Impersonation', 206.

[18] Ibid. 206–7. As Vicinus states, with the advent of film in the early twentieth century, the theatrical male impersonator receded from view, and a new image rose to takes its place, which arguably had its genesis in European sexological catalogues of sexual identity and deviancy.

[19] Ibid. 206.

Grand's death her nurse placed in her hands a card from Gladys of 'the Heavenly Twins kittens'.[21]

The clashing of desires—man-boy/Sapphic/heterosexual—in and around *The Heavenly Twins* allows a reading of cross-gendering in this text which draws on nascent psychoanalytic theory (discussed more fully in later chapters). The impact of the Tenor's gaze contributes to Angelica's own sense of self-worth: she tells the Tenor that it 'was delightful to look at myself—an ideal self—from afar off with your eyes; it made me feel as if I could be all you thought me; it made me wish to be so' (457). Cross-dressing provides access to the (sexual female) ideal self that Angelica desires to be, and indicates that there is a more complex psychological explanation for her cross-dressing other than for reasons of masculine upward mobility. Her cross-dressing is consistently described in terms of pleasure. Since her relationship with her husband is avowedly celibate, it is possible to conjecture that the pleasure she experiences is an erotic release from repression:

I kept my disguise a long time before I used it . . . I don't think I had any very distinct notion of what I should do with it when I got it. The pleasure of getting it had been everything for the moment, and having succeeded in that and tried the dress, I hid it away carefully and scarcely ever thought of it—never dreamt of wearing it certainly until one night—it was quite an impulse at last . . . But having once assumed the character, I began to love it; it came naturally; and the freedom from restraint, I mean the restraint of our tight uncomfortable clothing, was delicious. I tell you I was a genuine boy. I moved like a boy, I felt like a boy . . . I used to like to play with the position and run the risk. (456)

This speaks of the transformative power of clothes, and questions the naturalness of gender itself. The sensuality of the language ('pleasure', 'delicious'), however, also suggests that the act is represented as other than a mere 'disguise'. Indeed, Angelica's relationship to her male costume is similar to that experienced by transvestites: the thrill of obtaining the clothing had been pleasurable in itself, and is subsequently kept closeted, and as such accrues fetishistic allure. The power and danger of the cross-dressing ('to

---

[20] Kersley, *Darling Madame*, 239. Grand shared a rare moment of prankish intimacy with Gladys over smoking: ' "Have a cig?" she asked and then as I looked up quickly, the love light in my eyes, she altered it chaffingly to "Have a fag?" and I reached out and touched her knee, worshipping the understanding amusement in her eyes . . .' (author's ellipsis, 253).
[21] Ibid. 330.

run the risk') increases Angelica's pleasure: 'I knew I was breaking a law of the land. I knew I should be taken before a police magistrate if I were caught masquerading, and that added excitement to the pleasure' (452). Outside of the law the male costume seems to be the source of sexual excitement in itself, and provides Angelica with the means by which to conceive of a glorified female sexual self ('an ideal self'), through the fetish of masculinity. It is this component that makes *The Heavenly Twins* not an anomalous text, but a proto-modernist work which anticipates the cross-gendering in the novels of Radclyffe Hall, Anaïs Nin, H.D., and Djuna Barnes. While the erotic nature of cross-dressing and the narcissistic value of the Tenor's love are dependent on one another, the coincidence of both elements are significant in terms of cross-gendered representation in female-authored fiction.

Ultimately the uncertainty about the status of 'The Tenor and the Boy' as text is replicated in the presentation of Angelica. Grand engages almost in a form of fetishistic disavowal: representation of female cross-gendering is at once avowed and officially foreclosed in the main body of *The Heavenly Twins*. Angelica's dangerous exper-iment which culminates in the death of the Tenor means that *The Heavenly Twins* text cannot finally endorse it. Once her 'disguise' has been discovered she is swiftly recuperated by her family, and by the novel itself. After the Tenor's death she even begins to feel the stirrings of maternal love in response to the grief felt by one of the choristers: 'All that was womanly in Angelica went out to the poor little fellow' (519). Suffering from 'nervous irritability' she feels compelled to cross-dress once more in her brother's clothes to savour 'the joy of perfect freedom from restraint' (530), and the 'exquisite sense of freedom which made the whole delight of the thing' (496), before taking up her position as dutiful wife to Mr Kilroy: 'Don't let me go again, Daddy, keep me close. I am—I am grateful for the blessing of a good man's love' (551).

THE UNWOMANLY TONGUE: SPEECH, WRITING, AND
TRANSVESTITURE IN *THE HEAVENLY TWINS*

Angelica's stutter speaks of a form of resistance that then manifests itself linguistically and verbally: her subsequent transvestiture is as a speech-writer for her husband. This is, as her husband recognizes,

a cruel curtailment; Angelica 'was headstrong, excitable, wild, original, fearless, and with an intellect large out of all proportion for the
requirements of the life to which society condemned her' (551).
Attempting to explain her cross-dressing she frames it in terms of a
self-contradiction that linguistically splits her consciousness:

> I see all the contradictions that are involved in what I have said and am saying,
> and yet I mean it all. In separate sections of my consciousness each separate
> clause exists at this moment, however contradictory, and there is no reconcil-
> ing them; but there they are. I can't understand it myself, and I don't want you
> to try. All I ask you is to believe me—to forgive me. (461)

Angelica appears to be saying that her separate identities exist as
fractured parts of discourse ('each separate clause exists at this
moment') that cannot be fused. Understanding is to be found somewhere between 'meaning it all' and 'I can't understand it myself',
but for the moment cross-gendering is inexpressible: it splits the
subject's consciousness. As her husband's speech-writer, the power
of her cross-dressing is diffused, but she still sees it as a transformative act: 'It was left for me to translate the principle into the vernacular' (534). Transvestism has been *trans*formed into linguistic
*trans*lation. In *The Beth Book*, Angelica becomes a writer in her
own right, joining Beth, who, notably, has read the cross-gendered
George Sand's *Historie de ma vie*.

Angelica's rebirth into speech and writing is strongly contrasted
with the reversal that Evadne experiences. One of the primary readers in the novel in a novel obsessed with reading—Teresa Mangum
speaks of the reader-protagonists 'fetishizing' the book, 'consciously demanding that it fill an unconscious desire for a sense of
unity and/or identity'—Evadne is a Darwinian in her ability to
interpret the marks of somatic traces of male perversion and
deviancy.[22] The epigraph (a quotation from Darwin in support of
Francis Galton on the subject of innate behaviour) presages the preoccupation with systems of 'reading' bodily characteristics through
physiognomy to determine character and sexual type. Evadne and
Dr Galbraith are both the amateur and professional exponents of
this science, elements of which were employed by early sexologists
to find some somatic trace for homosexuality. Those who are unable
to read in this way are given short shrift, and Evadne is vindicated in
her abhorrence of Sir Mosley when he infects Edith with syphilis.

[22] Mangum, *Married, Middle-brow, and Militant*, 102.

Galbraith scrutinizes Evadne according to the incipient science of psychoanalysis, but it is a method that bears the traces of Darwinism: while women are spiritually and morally advanced, they are seen ultimately as primitive and feral creatures, both intellectually and physically.[23] This theory enables a rigidification of the codes that regulate female behaviour. Evadne's father is a spokesman for law and order who resents the possibility of improvement in the position of women. When he realizes the extent of his daughter's wilfulness, he threatens to commit her to an asylum; ransacking her room for evidence of her deviancy, Mr Frayling finds books on pathology, anatomy, botany, and philosophy: 'He could not have been more horrified had the books been "Mademoiselle de Maupin," "Nana," "La Terre," "Madame Bovary," and "Sapho" ' (104). The paternal discourse in *The Heavenly Twins* teaches that when the traits of Victorian womanhood are in abeyance (such as piety, weakness, and vulnerability), unwomanliness, monstrosity, and masculinity rise to take their place.

But Evadne finds herself the subject of the very discourse that she excels in: she is 'an incomplete creature in a state of progression' (218). Her rebellion, which has its roots in reading, is interpreted as a sign of hysteria and she is consigned to dependence on her second husband Galbraith. When she refuses to live with her profligate husband Colquhoun, and, under familial pressure to do so, has to censor her 'unwomanly' tongue, the force of this vocal repression results in hysteria. As Elaine Showalter has documented, hysteria was a condition associated with the feminist movement, and considered to affect the most rebellious of women.[24] The fact that Evadne is figured as 'unwomanly' because of her opinions and speech, and is forced to repress both, make her a suitable candidate for hysteria. Hélène Cixous, in dialogue with Catherine Clément, has reversed the terms of the hysteria debate, converting hysteria into a form of suppressed rebellion, a means of assertion for women denied other social or intellectual channels of expression.[25] For fem-

---

[23] Certainly one of *The Heavenly Twins'* reviewers in the *Critic* thought so, saying that both Angelica and Evadne 'are hysterical and ill-balanced, and consequently selfish'. Quoted in Senf, p. xxiii.

[24] Elaine Showalter, *The Female Malady: Women, Madness, and English Culture 1830–1980* (1985; London: Virago, 1993), 145.

[25] Hélène Cixous and Catherine Clément, *La Jeune Née* (Paris: Union Générale d'Editions, 1975), 271–96. This stands in contrast to Clément who sees the hysteric's 'deviance' as carefully controlled and circumscribed by the social order.

inist critics, hysteria is a symptom of the dramatic social and cultural changes of the late nineteenth century.[26] Powerless, and lacking
sexual autonomy, the hysteric dramatized resistance through her
body, exaggerating the signs of femininity (vulnerability, sensitivity,
and passivity) while her illness enabled her passively to control and
exploit her limited situation. As Lyn Pykett argues, the 'discourse of
woman's affectivity' renders Evadne's hysteria as both 'withdrawal
and resistance'.[27] Angelica's form of resistance, first enacted
through the body, and then through a verbal transvestiture, is at
once more active and more devastating than the covert operations of
hysteria unconsciously performed by Evadne.

HERMAPHRODITES, ANDROGYNES, AND 'ROYAL MAUPINS':
FEMALE CROSS-GENDERING IN NINETEENTH-CENTURY
LITERATURE

Angelica's cross-gendering has its precursors in mostly popular and
sensation fiction, and French literature, influences that are acknowledged later in *The Beth Book* (1897) in which Beth's reading of
decadent (mostly French) literature including that of Théophile
Gautier is avowed and then disavowed. In the early nineteenth
century cross-gendering typically took the form of androgyny and
hermaphroditism in male-authored fiction. In Philip Cuisin's
Clémentine, Orpheline et Androgyne (1819) intersexual anatomy
seems 'responsible' for the female subject's behaviour which
includes cross-dressing and strenuous physical exercise. The eponymous protagonist of Honoré de Balzac's *Séraphita* (1834) and Henri
de Latouche's *Fragoletta* (1829) are both hermaphrodites who display 'lesbian' desire. The most notorious and influential of the

---

[26] Anorexia has been interpreted as another form of covert resistance, closely associated with hysteria, but seen as a peculiarly twentieth-century manifestation of it. See
Richard A. Gordon, *Anorexia and Bulimia: Anatomy of a Social Epidemic* (1990;
Oxford: Basil Blackwell, 1991). There is an anorexic subject in *The Heavenly Twins*,
who is treated with aversion therapy. The very real somatic changes of anorexia tend
towards masculinization, or, at least, a diminution of the signs of physical femininity,
such as amenorrhoea and lanugo (the growth of fine body hair). Many recent accounts
of anorexia speak of girls growing up with a secret though powerful fantasy of being a
boy—a 'tall long-legged prince' (ibid. 56). Gordon sees in the desire to escape womanhood (the 'purge of femaleness') the wish to achieve a 'masculine ideal' (57).

[27] Lyn Pykett, *The 'Improper' Feminine: The Women's Sensation Novel and the New
Women Writing* (London: Routledge, 1992), 175.

French novels was Gautier's *Mademoiselle de Maupin* (1835), whose cross-gendered subject disguises herself as Théodore de Sérannes to discover the true nature of men; in the process she is transformed into an adventurer. She has been read as both the phallic woman of the fantasies of male transvestites, and as a classic androgyne.[28] Allusions to *Mademoiselle de Maupin* in later novels, such as James Gibbon Huneker's *Painted Veils* (1920), for instance, became shorthand for the expression of the potential for perversity in women. For Jeanette Foster, who in 1958 compiled a descriptive and interpretative catalogue of lesbian (or 'sex variant') representation in nineteenth- and twentieth-century literature, Gautier's novel is a landmark text: it was the first inscription in modern fiction of a 'type' of female homosexual, 'the tall, wide shouldered, slim hipped figure endowed with perfect grace and with great skill in riding and fencing'.[29] While it can be argued that Foster is cataloguing *Mademoiselle de Maupin* according to a twentieth-century diagnostic classification, it is also possible to make the case that Gautier himself is drawing from an already familiar pattern of 'deviant' or 'variant' female sexual symbolizations. In a blurring of the boundary between fiction and scientific study, Radclyffe Hall cited Krafft-Ebing's case histories in *The Well of Loneliness*, and both Krafft-Ebing and Havelock Ellis referred to Flaubert's eponymous lesbian subject *Salammbô* (1862), Ernest Feydeau's *La Comtesse de Chalis* (1867), and *Mademoiselle de Maupin* in their works.[30]

Gautier and Balzac inscribe the link between lesbianism and masculinity, but in the 1890s the androgyne still persisted as the primary icon of female cross-gendering. What Sherrie Inness has called a

[28] See respectively: Peter Ackroyd, *Dressing Up, Transvestism and Drag: The History of an Obsession* (London: Thames and Hudson, 1979), 144, and A. J. L. Busst, 'The Image of the Androgyne in the Nineteenth Century', in Ian Fletcher (ed.), *Romantic Mythologies* (London: Routledge & Kegan Paul, 1967), 1–95, who glosses that it is not 'simply a question of male mentality in a female body: her mind and body alike possess something of both sexes so that she feels she belongs to the third sex' (41).

[29] Jeanette H. Foster, *Sex Variant Women in Literature: A Historical and Quantitative Study* (London: Frederick Muller, 1958), 60–1.

[30] Richard von Krafft-Ebing, *Psychopathia Sexualis, with Especial Reference to Contrary Sexual Instinct: A Medico-Legal Study*, trans. Charles Gilbert Chaddock (Philadelphia: F. A. Davis, 1892), 230 n. 1; Havelock Ellis, *Studies in the Psychology of Sex*, i. *Sexual Inversion* (London: The University Press, 1897), 78. When *The Well of Loneliness* was successfully defended in America against charges of obscenity, Morris Ernst cited *Mademoiselle de Maupin* as a book that was more scandalous, but which had not been found to be 'obscene'.

'definite pathology' was not constructed until the 1880s and 1890s, and the masculine lesbian became a recognizable 'type' in French literature at about the same time.[31] Sâr Josephin Péladan's work illustrates both of these modes: in *La Gynandre* (1891), the male protagonist encounters a group of 'Royal Maupins' who consciously affect masculinity in their names and dress. In *Le Vice suprême* (1884), the Princess d'Este's male characteristics (flat chest, narrow hips) are assimilated into an androgynous persona. In contrast, some female-authored fiction of the late nineteenth century transgressed from the cross-gendered woman as hermaphrodite and androgyne (whose deviant behaviour is ascribed to a biological substrate). In *Monsieur Vénus* (1884) and *Madame Adonis (1886)* by Rachilde (pseudonym for Marguérite Aymery Vallette, and herself a cross-dresser) the cross-gendered woman was conceived for perhaps the first time in terms of sexual autonomy (if one constructed on an axis of sado-masochism). In *Monsieur Vénus*, Raoule enjoys a cross-gendered eroticism that is maintained at the cost of her male lover's feminization (she forces him to cross-dress). In *Madame Adonis*, a woman who is having an affair with her lover's wife, cross-dresses to elude detection.

As Peter Farrer has catalogued, from the 1880s to the 1890s literary representation of *male* cross-gendering proliferated both at the high and low level with Rudyard Kipling in 'His Wedded Wife' (1888) and 'The Honours of War' (1911), Arthur Conan Doyle in *A Study in Scarlet* (1888) and 'The Story of the Man with the Watches' (1898), and Mark Twain in *Huckleberry Finn* (1884) and *Pudd'nhead Wilson* (1894), popularizing the idea of cross-dressing in particular. Twain, it is conjectured, after reading *The Heavenly Twins*, may have revised *Pudd'nhead Wilson* and *Those Extraordinary Twins*.[32] Moreover, masquerade was extended to include both the bodily transformation of sex and the magical transposition of souls between bodies of the opposite sex. Thomas Bailey Aldrich's 'Mademoiselle Olympe Zabriski' (1873) was the first story in English in which a man dressed as a woman plays a major role. Between 1889 and 1900 the English Society paper

[31] Sherrie Inness, 'Who's Afraid of Stephen Gordon?: The Lesbian in the United States Popular Imagination of the 1920s', *NWSA Journal*, 4.3 (Fall 1992), 303–20: 305.

[32] Rowlette argues that Twain did so because he thought the twins superfluous. In his marginal notes in his copy of *The Heavenly Twins* he wrote: 'Thus far the twins are valueless lumber, and an impertinent and offensive intrusion' (17).

Modern Society published several anonymous stories that featured a cross-dressed man in such tales as 'A Clifton Masculine Maid' (1891) and 'The Twins' (1900). Popular fiction typically took the form of parodies and satires of the French model, such as Archibald Gunter and Fergus Redmond's *A Florida Enchantment* (1892), a burlesque of Péladan and Rachilde, and the erotic *Gynecocracy* (1893), both contemporaneous with *The Heavenly Twins*. *A Florida Enchantment* employed the device of sex change as a magical transformation in which souls are transplanted into other bodies.[33]

In Britain and America there was far less of what one could call a 'tradition' in the narrative representation of female cross-gendered female behaviour. The French influence can, however, be detected in Mary Hatch's *The Strange Disappearance of Eugene Comstock* (1895) in which a cross-dressed lesbian villain, raised as a boy by a father who wanted a son, is immersed in the sensual delights of Paris. Caricatures of rebellious and transgressive women as masculine were also prevalent in such works as Elizabeth Lynn Linton's *The Rebel of the Family* (1880) and *The Autobiography of Christopher Kirkland* (1885). The closest literary precursors to Grand's novel are perhaps E. D. E. N. Southworth's American bestseller *The Hidden Hand* (1859), in which a young woman, with a birthmark in the shape of a hand imprinted on her palm, crossdresses at the beginning of the novel so that she can function in the world; and Theodore Winthrop's potboiler *Cecil Dreeme* (1861), the story of a man who falls in love with a cross-dressed woman. Florence Dixie's utopian *Gloriana; or, The Revolution of 1900* (1890), also makes an interesting parallel. The eponymous heroine cross-dresses as Hector D'Estrange to enter Eton and Oxford, and becomes an expert in women's rights. She trains a legion of Amazonian 'White Guards', and becomes a member of parliament and, once unmasked as Gloriana, eventually prime minister. Given this sporadic and impoverished history of female cross-gendering in British and American literature, *The Heavenly Twins* enjoys a peculiar and almost singular position (it also functions as such in Grand's oeuvre). The text does not provide a biological or psycho-

---

[33] Peter Farrer, '120 Years of Male Cross-Dressing and Sex-Changing in English and American Literature', in Richard Ekins and Dave King (eds.), *Blending Genders: Social Aspects of Cross-Dressing and Sex–Changing* (London and New York: Routledge, 1996), 123–32.

logical explanation for Angelica's behaviour, as was common in much 'cross-gendered' literature such as Cuisin's *Clémentine, Orpheline et Androgyne*. Rather, she is positioned as one of a long line of female passing women, which includes women who passed as sailors, George Sand, and Dr James Barry. In 1895 the *Lancet* published a series of letters recounting stories and biographical details of James Barry, but Angelica's fantasy narrative had already spoken of a pleasure in cross-dressing that was missing from the medical accounts of that behaviour.[34]

THE 'CULTURE OF INVERSION': MANNISHNESS AND
SEXOLOGY AT THE *FIN DE SIÈCLE*

The increase in the incidence of (mostly male) cross-gendering in literature coincided with the emergence of sexology at the *fin de siècle*. *The Heavenly Twins* was published at a time when ideas of sexual identity were undergoing 'enormous changes in definition, attitude, and self-presentation'.[35] Laura Doan asserts that we can talk of a 'culture of inversion' (or cross-gendering), at the end of the nineteenth century in which gender roles were in flux.[36] One of the most pervasive female images of this disruption was the New Woman. Sarah Grand, using the language of cross-gendering, claimed to have invented the phrase the 'New Woman' in *The North American Review* in 1894, to describe a type of woman who 'while retaining all the grace of manner and feminine charm, had thrown off all the silliness and hysterical feebleness of her sex . . . I never could have meant the vulgar creature who passes for the approved type of new woman. Woman was never meant to be developed

[34] Masquerade dominated the popular literature, theatre, and press until at least the 1930s. A number of popular titles on gendered impersonation appeared during this period, including Bram Stoker's *Famous Impostors* (1910). *Urania* magazine (1915–40), whose philosophy was that 'gender was a cultural construction which worked against the realization of an individual's potential', contained extracts from newspapers on cross-dressing, passing women, hermaphrodites, and transsexuals. See Emily Hamer, *Britannia's Glory: A History of Twentieth-Century Lesbians* (London and New York: Cassell, 1996), 69. James Barry remains a figure of interest; see Patricia Duncker's novel *James Miranda Barry* (1999) and Rachel Holmes's biography *Scanty Particulars* (2002).
[35] Vicinus, 'Turn-of-the-Century Male Impersonation', 187.
[36] Laura Doan, *Fashioning Sapphism: The Origins of a Modern English Lesbian Culture* (New York: Columbia University Press, 2001), 32.

man.'[37] But the New Woman image, which was widespread in Europe and America in the 1890s in magazines, journals, novels, and drama, was, despite Grand's protestations, heavily invested in the culture of cross-gendering.[38] As Joel Kaplan and Sheila Stowell have documented, the New Woman, in an age of taxonomic obsession, encapsulated a range of 'types', including the 'liberated bachelor girl, unmanageable wife, frustrated spinster, and street-corner demagogue'.[39] All of these 'types' were understood and 'read' through the sign of cross-gendering as represented through clothing, bodily cues, and language.

The Heavenly Twins was a response not only to the debate about male sexuality framed by feminist militancy, but also to changes in the understanding of female sexuality addressed by sexology. The period 1880–1914 saw a nationwide campaign to increase awareness about the possible dangers to women of the sexual life of the adult male.[40] The development of sexology arose in the 1880s initially as a response to growing concerns over sexual problems such as prostitution and venereal disease, and only later broadened its field to conceptualize the emergence of competing sexual identities.

A systematic theory of cross-gendered inversion was first envisioned by the German sexologist Karl Heinrich Ulrichs between 1864 and 1880. It was Ulrichs, an 'invert' himself by his own definition, who termed the phenomenon of a 'woman's soul encased in a male body' as 'uranism' (a word derived from Plato's category of 'urning'), and claimed that it resulted from 'psychic hermaphroditism'

[37] Sarah Grand, 'The New Aspect of the Woman Question', *The North American Review* (Mar. 1894).

[38] For an exposition of the social and cultural impact of the New Woman in Britain see Ruth Brandon, *The New Women and the Old Men: Love, Sex and the Woman Question* (London: Secker and Warburg, 1990), and in America see Carroll Smith-Rosenberg, *Disorderly Conduct: Visions of Gender in Victorian America* (1985; New York: Oxford University Press, 1986), 176–7; 245–96. For an analysis of the New Woman novels see Ann L. Ardis, *New Women, New Novels: Feminism and Early Modernism* (New Brunswick, NJ: Rutgers University Press, 1990). Feminism has recuperated the New Woman figure as a sign of anarchic sexual independence. See Elaine Showalter, *Sexual Anarchy: Gender and Culture at the Fin de Siècle* (1990; London: Bloomsbury, 1991), 38–9.

[39] Joel Kaplan and Sheila Stowell, *Theatre and Fashion: Oscar Wilde to the Suffragettes* (Cambridge: Cambridge University Press, 1994), 61.

[40] For a controversial and radical feminist account of this movement see Sheila Jeffreys, ' "Free from all Uninvited Touch of Man": Women's Campaigns Around Sexuality 1880–1914', in L. Coveney, M. Jackson, S. Jeffreys, L. Kaye, and P. Mahoney (eds.), *The Sexuality Papers: Male Sexuality and the Social Control of Women* (London: Hutchinson in association with the Exploration in Feminism Collective, 1984), 22–44.

in the first few weeks of embryonic life. According to the definition of uranism only the soul, not the body, was assigned to the other sex, and inversion was indicated primarily by sexual preference. Furthermore uranians were conceptualized as a 'third sex' whose gender traits were inverted. In modern terms Ulrichs's work is noteworthy for conceptualizing the split between the sexed body and gender. His ideas were popularized in Britain by Edward Carpenter during the period of the rise of the 'New Woman'; he used Ulrichs's theories to suggest a convergence of gender in 'intermediate' types: the feminization of men and the masculinization of women.

Stimulated by Ulrichs's work, another German sexologist Carl Westphal was the first to put sexual inversion on what Havelock Ellis has called 'an assured scientific basis'.[41] Westphal crucially produced a new diagnostic category, and a psychological, rather than anatomical, definition of homosexuality. The model of inversion remained fully functional: a homosexual woman was physically a woman and psychologically a man. This 'scientific' conception became a sexological commonplace, and the term 'sexual inversion' eventually widespread in Europe. In 1864 a woman wrote to Westphal for medical advice for her wish 'to be a man', which Westphal diagnosed as sexual inversion.

From the 1890s Magnus Hirschfeld became the foremost exponent of Ulrichs's belief that uranism was a biological variation of the sexual drive, arguing that the sexual instinct took a different form in men and women: *'male desire is directed towards activity, the female towards a passive experience.'*[42] The increasing biological determinism of the sexologists explains why it is so difficult for them to conceive of desire in women, cross-gendered or otherwise. Moreover, as Jane Rule has recognized, while Hirschfeld identified a feminine group of inverts, they could not be recognized as 'homosexual' since they presented no evidence of inversion of secondary sexual characteristics (enlarged clitoris, masculine hair distribution, deep voice, muscle development).[43]

---

[41] Havelock Ellis, *Sexual Inversion*, 25.

[42] Magnus Hirschfeld in *Sexual Anomalies and Perversions: Physical and Psychological Development and Treatment (A Summary of the Works of the Late Professor Dr. Magnus Hirschfeld Compiled as a Humble Memorial by his Pupils)* (London: Francis Aldor [1937]), author's italics, 55.

[43] Jane Rule, *Lesbian Images* (1975; London: Peter Davies, 1976), 33.

A movement away from a focus on sexual acts to the psychology of perversion was becoming the norm. The standard work of this new field was Richard von Krafft-Ebing's *Psychopathia Sexualis* (1886). It was the first medical classification of sexual disorders, and the first to describe sexual practices according to the categories of disease.[44] As Sander L. Gilman has shown, homosexuality now replaced masturbation as the 'exemplary sexual degeneracy'.[45] But it was a homosexuality concretized as inversion: within this model a woman loved another woman along an axis of heterosexuality which positioned one partner as 'inverted' in the form of her object choice (i.e. she loved like a man); homosexual preference and gender inversion were now locked together. An interest in the physical signs of inversion (i.e. masculinity in lesbians) predominated: Case 130, for instance, had 'coarse somewhat masculine features; a harsh, deep voice; and made rather the impression of a man in female attire than that of a lady, if one overlooked the bosom and the decidedly feminine form of the pelvis'.[46] Women who had sexual relations with other women were divided into four discrete types: masculine inverts who took a masculine role; women who attracted masculine lesbians but were themselves more feminine; cross-dressers; and 'degenerate' homosexuals who were virtually male. Women, like Case 130, who 'desired' masculine attire, were subsumed into a complex classificatory system as a composite of masculine attributes. Where these attributes were in evidence, sexual inversion was diagnosed:

In the inclinations of the amazon for manly sports, the masculine soul in the female bosom manifests itself; and not less in the show of courage and manly feeling. The female urning loves to wear her hair and have her clothing in the fashion of men; and it is her greatest pleasure, when opportunity offers, to appear in male attire.[47]

The female invert, to Krafft-Ebing's eyes, looks like a 'man in woman's clothes'. Sexual inversion is significantly broadened out by Krafft-Ebing: in each case study of female sexual inversion, he asso-

[44] As Havelock Ellis has summarized, Krafft-Ebing recognized four stages of congenital sexual inversion: (1) psychosexual hermaphroditism (2) homosexuality (3) effeminatio and viraginity (in which the whole psychic disposition corresponds to the 'abnormal instinct'), and (4) androgynia and gynandria (in which bodily form corresponds to 'abnormal instinct' and psychic disposition). *Sexual Inversion*, 31.
[45] Sander L. Gilman, *Difference and Pathology: Stereotypes of Sexuality, Race and Madness* (Ithaca, NY: Cornell University Press, 1985), 198.
[46] Krafft-Ebing, *Psychopathia Sexualis* (1892), 309.   [47] Ibid. 280.

ciates the invert with the refusal of conventional female roles. Such social perversion is seen to precipitate the development of sexual perversion. It was Krafft-Ebing's model which formed the ground for scientific work on homosexuality until the advent of Freudian psychoanalysis. As Gert Hekma has documented, at the turn of the century sexologists increasingly came to understand 'non-homosexual perversions as specific forms of hetero- or homosexual relationship drive.'[48] Albert Moll was behind this shift, and was instrumental in turning homosexuality into the only 'systematic aberration' of the heterosexual pattern.

In 1896 Havelock Ellis published *Sexual Inversion* in German (originally written in association with the homosexual writer John Addington Symonds) as the first of the *Studies in the Psychology of Sex* (it was published in Britain in 1897 shortly after Oscar Wilde was released from prison).[49] Ellis, according to his biographer Phyllis Grosskurth, had been 'seriously contemplating a book on inversion by the summer of 1892', which was precisely the time when he learnt of his wife Edith's relationship with another woman: he 'was still reeling from the shock over Edith and was obsessed with a desire to understand her behaviour' (the Ellises persuaded Symonds to include lesbianism).[50] While Symonds provided a case history of himself (as Case Z) and many of his friends, and Edward Carpenter also supplied histories, Edith Ellis, who is thought to be Case 36, furnished many of the contacts for the material on female inversion.

Ellis rejected the theory of 'urning', and like Krafft-Ebing believed in an innate foundation for inversion, firmly defined as being 'sexual instinct turned by inborn constitutional abnormality towards persons of the same sex'.[51] Dealing primarily with male

[48] Gert Hekma, 'A History of Sexology: Social and Historical Aspects of Sexuality', in Jan Bremmer (ed.), *From Sappho to de Sade: Moments in the History of Sexuality* (1989; London: Routledge, 1991), 173–93: 182.

[49] Phyllis Grosskurth comments that Ellis always regretted that *Sexual Inversion* was the first volume of *Studies in the Psychology of Sex*; for the second edition of *Sexual Inversion* in 1901, Ellis renumbered it as vol. ii. *Havelock Ellis: A Biography* (1980; New York: New York University Press, 1985), 184. The third edition was published in the United States in 1915. While Ellis accounted for Hirschfeld's *Die Homosexualität* (1914) and Freud's *Three Essays on the Theory of Sexuality* (1905), the findings of this edition went unchanged.

[50] Grosskurth, *Havelock Ellis*, 173.

[51] Ellis, *Sexual Inversion*, 1. But unlike Krafft-Ebing, Ellis did not believe that inversion could be 'cured' and 'was the first heterosexual investigator to grant [inverts] dignity as complete human beings'. Grosskurth, *Havelock Ellis*, 187.

inversion, women were confined to a single chapter in a presentation of only six cases. Ellis, who, building on Krafft-Ebing's categorization of female inversion, was 'as emphatic about the mannishness of the typical female invert as he had been reserved about the effeminacy of the male invert', consolidated the image of the female invert:[52]

when they still retain female garments these usually show some traits of masculine simplicity, and there is nearly always a disdain for the petty feminine artifices of the toilet. Even when this is not obvious there are all sorts of instinctive gestures and habits which may suggest to female acquaintances the remark that such a person 'ought to have been a man'. The brusque, energetic movements, the attitude of the arms, the direct speech, the inflexions of the voice, the masculine straightforwardness and sense of honour, and especially the attitude towards men, free from any association either of shyness or audacity, will often suggest the underlying psychic abnormality to a keen observer. Although there is sometimes a certain general coarseness of physical texture, we do not find any trace of a beard or moustache . . . In the habits not only is there frequently a pronounced taste for smoking . . . but there is also a dislike and sometimes incapacity for needlework and other domestic occupations, while there is often some capacity for athletics. No masculine character is usually found in the sexual organs, which are sometimes undeveloped.[53]

Although Ellis theoretically separated sexual inversion from cross-dressing, there is a conflation in his writing. He invokes sixteenth- and seventeenth-century women who were executed for dressing in male attire and using dildos, drawing comparisons between these women and the Countess Sarolta V, who was dressed in boys' clothes by her father, and married a woman (she was the subject of a report by Krafft-Ebing in *Psychopathia Sexualis*). Ellis did not categorize women's romantic friendships within the framework of sexual inversion, since many women who indulged in such friendships were easily assimilated into heterosexuality. 'Real congenital perversion' was recognizable by any morbid trait, such as neuropathic heredity, violence, or transvestism. The 'congenital' invert was a sexually threatening figure, rivalling men for women's love, and is distinguished from the 'pseudo-invert' who, while plain in feature, was marked with less masculinity, and was the object of the congenital invert's desire.[54]

---

[52] Paul Robinson, *The Modernization of Sex: Havelock Ellis, Alfred Kinsey, William Masters and Virginia Johnson* (London: Paul Elek, 1976), 11.

[53] Ellis, *Sexual Inversion*, 96–8.   [54] Ibid. 87.

As Jane Caplan has recognized, Ellis's dual model of inversion and homosexuality was thwarted by this 'organo-evolutionary understanding of sexuality'.[55] While Ellis ostensibly campaigned for a woman's right to sexual expression, his work was fuelled by a post-Darwinian ethos, which offered 'evidence' for the incontrovertible, physical differences between men and women.[56] Physiology was used as a basis for determining (sexual) character: while Ellis found that the man's body ('erect' and 'closely knit') predisposed him to be 'instinctively seeking action', the woman's body ('protuberant curves', 'unevenness') made her prone to a 'state of comparative repose' in which she found 'satisfaction in an attitude of overthrow'.[57] Degree of 'abnormality' in women is determined at the time at which the male sex hormone becomes operative in women; this can result in 'atrophy of the uterus, with changes in the ovaries, under–development of the labia and overgrowth of the clitoris, atrophy of the mammae, narrowing of the hips, broadening of the shoulders, with either marked muscular development or adiposity'.[58] But Ellis, like Krafft-Ebing before him, also associated inversion with feminism (and by implication the prevalence of the New Woman), thus suggesting a conflicting theory of inversion than the one of innateness. For Ellis there was a direct correlation between the growth of opportunities for women and the increase in the numbers of middle-class female inverts.

RECLAIMING THE (FEMALE) TRANSGENDERED AND
TRANSVESTITE SUBJECT FROM SEXOLOGY

The much-debated question of the influence of sexology on culture is complex.[59] It is understood that in the later nineteenth century

[55] Jane Caplan, 'Sexuality and Homosexuality', in Cambridge Women's Studies Group (ed.), *Women in Society: Interdisciplinary Essays* (London: Virago, 1981), 149–67: 155.

[56] For development of this see Margaret Jackson, 'Sexology and the Social Construction of Male Sexuality (Havelock Ellis)', in L. Coveney, M. Jackson, S. Jeffreys, L. Kaye and P. Mahoney (eds.), *The Sexuality Papers: Male Sexuality and the Social Control of Women* (London: Hutchinson in association with the Exploration in Feminism Collective, 1984), 45–68: 50.

[57] Havelock Ellis, *Man and Woman: A Study of Human Secondary and Sexual Characters* (London: Walter Scott, 1894), 31–2.

[58] Havelock Ellis, *Psychology of Sex* (1933; London: Heinemann, 1948), 196. This edition is a condensed version of *Studies in the Psychology of Sex*.

[59] For a very useful account of this question through the 'realm of the law' see Doan, *Fashioning Sapphism*, 31–63.

there was a rigid polarized gender system in place, and that sexology, arguably, worked to preserve that system. Some historians
argue that feminist agitation had created an atmosphere of anxiety
about the changing position of women, and the mutability of sex
and the fragility of sexual difference became the focus for a form of
masculine mobilization. Margaret Jackson thus asserts that the
development of sexology must be viewed against increased feminist
militancy, and that the sexologists shored up boundaries of sexual
difference against the onslaught posed by the desire of many women
for political and social change.[60] She agrees with Lillian Faderman
that sexologists 'provided a weapon against love between women'
when 'women's increasing independence threatened the social structure,' and with Nancy Sahli that the label 'lesbian' became 'syn-
onymous with female autonomy and commitment between women
because feminism and women's growing independence constituted a
threat to the established order.'[61] The New Woman also became a
repository for social fear: she was vilified as the embodiment of masculine desire for privilege and status, with much contemporary
satire portraying her drinking, smoking, wearing masculine attire,
and invading male territory. Victorian medicine and society warned
that if women were educated and sought employment outside
marriage, humanity itself would be threatened with imminent
degenerative collapse.

Jackson and others perhaps grant too much influence to the sexologists. The scientific discourses that were in circulation in the
1890s, that created a catalogue of cross-gendered attributes, both
arose out of, and contributed to, the debate about female sexuality,
and the position of women. The effects of sexology, however inva-
sive, took a long time to be felt, partly because the readership of sexological works was necessarily élite due to the covert dissemination
of *Sexual Inversion* in the early twentieth century (the first edition
was bought up by Symonds's literary executor Horatio Brown, and,
after the release of the second edition, George Bedborough of the
Legitimation League was arrested and tried for selling a copy of the

[60] Jackson, 'Sexology and the Social Construction of Male Sexuality', 50, 52.
[61] See Lillian Faderman, *Surpassing the Love of Men: Romantic Friendship and Love
Between Women from the Renaissance to the Present* (1981; London: The Women's
Press, 1985), *passim*. Nancy Sahli, 'Smashing: Women's Relationships Before the Fall',
Chrysalis, 8 (Summer 1979), 8–27.

book in 1898).[62] Preferring a reading of sexological influence that is
less deterministic, and more rooted in the complexities of the textuality of the case history, I agree with Jay Prosser that a reading of
these histories reveals that sexologists were cataloguing sexual
behaviours and identities as they emerged. Diagnosis did not wholly
determine identity: rather many of the subjects of the narratives
were already self-diagnosing. Prosser uses the example of Krafft-
Ebing's Case 164 who 'bewailed the fact that she was not born a
man', and notes the sexologist's mimicking of 'what was clearly the
subject's own prior diagnosis of h/erself'.[63] As Prosser argues, the
personal narrative written up as case history 'provided the clinician
with the pathognomonic signs of inversion'; it 'created the textual
space for the clinician not only to record but to perform the diagnosis, for the "disease" manifested above all in figures of speech'.[64] In
Prosser's terms, the subject's autobiography 're-presents' the body
sometimes as a fantasized self: the self that they wished they could
be through the transformation of clothes, appearance, and speech.
Ellis's Case D, for instance, who could never think of herself as
female, creates for herself a fantasy of male identification, in which
she casts herself as liberator: 'I was always the prince or the pirate,
rescuing beauty in distress or killing the unworthy.'[65] We might

---

[62] Although Biddy Martin draws attention to Aimée Duc's obscure novel *Sind es
Frauen?* (*Are They Women?*) (1901) which focuses on a 'group of women who identify
themselves in the newly available terms of the third sex, terms they attribute to Richard
von Krafft-Ebing'. *Femininity Played Straight: The Significance of Being Lesbian* (New
York: Routledge, 1996), 54. Significantly Martin finds most interesting not the masculine
Minotschka's nervous weakness, but the 'attribution to her of a psychic wound for which
[Minotschka's] phallic [walking] stick compensates and which only the complement of a
feminine woman can ultimately heal or cover up' (56). I will explore this observation
more fully in the subsequent chapters. Although Martin does not use the term 'fetishism',
her analysis of Duc's text employs fetishistic diction: Minotschka's return to Paris is 'a
fantasmatic identification with what has been lost or disavowed in the effort to define
feminine homosexuality against female afflictions' (65). Martin argues that both reading
Minotschka's 'butchness' as 'phallic imposture that cracks to expose the real woman
underneath', or 'her butch performances as strategic masquerades that allow her entry
into the male-defined realms of scholarship and exchange' are both flawed: 'Underneath
Minotschka's butch defenses is not "a woman" but a butch who has defended against a
range of things, including the qualities of vulnerability, dependence and attachment too
often associated with femininity and women' (67).

[63] Jay Prosser, *Second Skins: The Body Narratives of Transsexuality* (New York:
Columbia University Press, 1998), 145

[64] Ibid. 144.

[65] Havelock Ellis, *Studies in the Psychology of Sex*, ii. *Sexual Inversion* (New York:
Random House, 1936), 239.

argue that Angelica's narrative in 'The Tenor and the Boy' takes the form of a case history in which desire, motivation, and fantasy are closely self-examined by talking to a consoling and understanding figure.

Jay Prosser has usefully rescued the transsexual from these sexological accounts, arguing that the sexological category of inversion can be understood in modern terms not as exclusively homosexual, but as transsexual, or transgendered.[66] According to this theory Ulrichs's formulation of 'a man's soul enclosed in a woman's body' or vice versa recurred 'identically as the popular trope for transsexuality a century later in transsexual accounts'.[67] He states that the subject of Westphal's 1864 case, who specified that she wanted to be a man, 'has been recast as a founding moment for medical research into female-to-male transsexuality'.[68] It is the case that many of the invert's bodily traits were essentially cross-gendered characteristics. Krafft-Ebing's Countess Sarolta V, does, as Prosser argues, pose the greatest challenge to the equation of inversion exclusively with homosexuality, and 'reads as one of the most persuasive female-to-male transsexual narratives in sexology'.[69] By 1900 the category 'invert' began to disappear from medical texts to be replaced by 'homosexual'. In Freudian psychoanalysis, sexual inversion, as Prosser notes, appears as a myth, 'sexology's false construction of homosexuality'; he cites 'Psychogenesis of a Case of Homosexuality in a Woman' in support of this argument:

The mystery of homosexuality is therefore by no means so simple as it is commonly depicted in popular expositions—'a feminine mind, bound therefore to love a man, but unhappily attached to a masculine body; a masculine mind, irresistibly attracted by women, but alas! imprisoned in a feminine body' . . . the supposition that nature in a freakish mood created a 'third sex' falls to the ground.[70]

---

[66] Prosser notes that Havelock Ellis in *Sexual Inversion* 'crucially names both sexual inversion *and* homosexuality, suggesting strongly that they were *not* coextensive'. 'Transsexuals and the Transsexologists: Inversion and the Emergence of Transsexual Subjectivity', in Lucy Bland and Laura Doan (eds.), *Sexology in Culture: Labelling Bodies and Desires* (Oxford: Polity Press, 1998), 116–31: 120, Prosser's emphasis.

[67] Prosser, *Second Skins*, 143.   [68] Ibid. 140.   [69] Ibid. 146.

[70] Sigmund Freud, 'The Psychogenesis of a Case of Homosexuality in a Woman' (1920), *The Standard Edition of the Complete Works of Sigmund Freud*, trans. James Strachey *et al.*, 24 vols. (London: The Hogarth Press and the Institute of Psycho-Analysis, 1953–74), 18. 147–72: 170–1.

While cross-gendering continues to be articulated in Freud, it is refigured 'from gender identities, into phantasmatic and momentary sexual identifications'. Inversion is made into a figure for sexual object-choice: one loves like a man/woman.

But can the same recuperative strategy be performed on behalf of the female transvestite and fetishist? According to Robert Nye sexual fetishism existed as an anthropological, philosophical, and economical concept prior to the late nineteenth century, but was first documented and named by medical and psychoanalytic establishments in the 1880s and 1890s most notably in the work of Jean-Martin Charcot and Krafft-Ebing. The modern concept of fetishistic perversion formulated in French psychiatry was precipitated by cultural fears of a falling national birth-rate, a rising death-rate, and degeneracy.[71] But from the outset, female fetishistic perversion was rarely acknowledged. Gatian de Gaeton de Clérambault in *La Passion des étoffes chez un neuropsychiatrie* (1908) refused to believe in the existence of female fetishists, despite evidence to the contrary; this subsequently became a clinical commonplace.[72] Jann Matlock has suggested that throughout the first half of the twentieth century 'one detects an epistemological split between fetishism, increasingly classed as exclusively male, and transvestism, which included male and female variants'.[73] But if transvestism became, as Matlock suggests, 'the perversion psychiatrists were willing to leave to woman', this was only because it was not recognized as perversely fetishistic.[74]

[71] Robert A. Nye, 'The Medical Origins of Sexual Fetishism', in Emily Apter and William Pietz (eds.), *Fetishism as Cultural Discourse* (Ithaca, NY: Cornell University Press, 1993), 13–30: 13, 19. For example, Alfred Binet conceptualized fetishism within a framework of cultural crisis. See 'Le Fétichisme dans l'amour', *Revue Philosophique*, 24 (1887): 142–67, 252–74.

[72] Charcot and Valentin Magnan claimed that women concealed their perversions better than men, which might explain the low incidence of women presenting themselves for analysis. 'Inversion du sens génital et autres perversions sexuelles', *Archives de Neurologiel*, 3 (Jan.–Feb. 1882), 53–60, and 4 (July 1882), 296–322. Cross-dressing was outlawed by a Paris ordinance (1857), and by the *fin de siècle* the cross-gendered woman came to the attention of sexology through her arrest by the police.

[73] Jann Matlock, 'Masquerading Women, Pathologized Men: Cross-Dressing, Fetishism, and the Theory of Perversion, 1882–1935', in Emily Apter and William Pietz (eds.), *Fetishism as Cultural Discourse* (Ithaca, NY: Cornell University Press, 1993), 31–61: 34.

[74] Ibid. 34. Female cross-gendered behaviour was seen in terms of a woman's social rather than sexual role. This was partly because, given that women had a more restricted social position, cross-gendered behaviour was understood within the context of what was considered to be the perfectly natural desire to become a man. But inevitably female

The category of the transvestite became available in Hirschfeld's *Die Transvestiten: Eine Untersuchung über den Erotischen Verkleidungstrieb* (*Transvestites: The Erotic Drive to Cross-Dress*) (1910). Prior to this inscription a number of terms were applied to cases in which some form of cross-dressing was involved: some of the available terms, such as fetishism and sexual inversion were used. As Dave King has noted, some terms were grafted together, such as 'effemination with fetishism', and some entirely new terms coined such as 'gynomania' and 'psychical hermaphroditism'.[75] Within this discursive excess, however, there is scant evidence of female cross-dressing and of concepts of pleasure and eroticism being attached to female cross-gendering more generally. The references, where they appear, are isolated and sketchy. One of Westphal's earliest case histories was of a young woman, classed as sexually inverted, who enjoyed putting on her brother's clothes.[76] The 'abnormality', according to Westphal, was the result of hereditary degeneration and neurosis, and masculinity was connected with an inappropriate sex drive. In his study of 'Miss Z', Krafft-Ebing remarks upon her coarse masculinity (deep voice, short hair, masculine dress) ascribing to her a masculine character in spite of her assertion that she 'considers herself a woman in all respects' (and by his own logic, the fact of her well-developed breasts and female build). The operations of what is possibly fetishistic cross-gendering (as a child it was her 'greatest pleasure to put on boys' clothes') are obscured in the assimilation of this desire into characterological inversion.[77] Despite suggesting that some women may have beard or hair fetishes, Krafft-Ebing does not ascribe pathological fetishism to women. Moll distinguished cross-gendering in women who wore men's clothing because their occupation necessitated concealment of their sex, from other women who did so for 'impulsive reasons'; the latter were 'perverts' who had an orgasm

cross-gendered behaviour would exceed the limitations imposed upon it. Most interestingly, as Matlock points out, female transvestism is threatening because it suggests the potential commodification of male bodies, and undermines the fantasy of female modesty that the objects of fetishism are claimed to defend and promote (58).

[75] Dave King, 'Gender Blending: Medical Perspectives and Technology', in Richard Ekins and Dave King (eds.), *Blending Genders: Social Aspects of Cross-Dressing and Sex–Changing* (London and New York: Routledge, 1996), 79–98: 80.

[76] Carl Westphal, 'Die Konträre Sexualempfindung', *Archiv für Psychiatrie und Nervenkrankheiten*, 2 (1869), 73–108.

[77] Krafft-Ebing, *Psychopathia Sexualis*, 285.

when cross-dressed, and had no desire for 'normal intercourse'.[78]
Ellis, noting that Krafft-Ebing found no case of erotic fetishism in
women, believed, conversely, that it occurred occasionally, although
he recognized with Moll that the soldier's uniform was a peculiar
fetish for women.[79] But no model of psychic and behavioural motivation was drawn from this observation.

Importantly Hirschfeld, who coined the term 'transvestism',
recognized that women may derive 'sex gratification' from wearing
men's clothes.[80] Hirschfeld and Ellis worked to differentiate the
transvestite from the homosexual category, and Hirschfeld criticized
Krafft-Ebing who saw transvestism as nothing more than a variant
of homosexuality. For Hirschfeld, transvestism was 'the impulse to
assume the external garb of a sex which is not apparently that of the
subject as indicated by the sexual organs'.[81] In 1928 Ellis rejected
the term 'sexoaesthetic inversion' in favour of 'eonism' (named after
the Chevalier D'Eon), which was the only alternative term to transvestism to enjoy any currency, although it also covers what would
now be considered transsexualism (he objected to the term transvestism because it focused solely on the element of cross-dressing).
Ellis coined the term 'eonism' to account for those 'occasional cases'
of men and women 'who took pleasure in behaving and dressing like
the opposite sex and yet were not sexually inverted'.[82] Ellis asserts
that there is 'no true fetichism, the garment possessing no marked
dynamic erotic power in itself, or when worn by another person,
but only when worn by the subject himself; in some cases, moreover,
clothing played little or no part.'[83] Although Ellis cites Gutheil's
case of fetishistic female transvestism (discussed in Chapter 2),
he collapses the category into those who have adopted men's
dress to pass and earn a living, or those who are 'inverts'. The only
real theoretical challenge to this understanding of transvestism
came from psychoanalysis, which understood it as a disruption in
psychosexual functioning.

[78] Maurice Chideckel, *Female Sex Perversion: The Sexually Aberrated Woman As She
Is* (1935; New York: Brown Book Company, 1968). See also Albert Moll,
Untersuchungen über die Libido Sexualis (Berlin, 1897).
[79] Ellis, *Psychology of Sex*, 130.
[80] Magnus Hirschfeld, *Transvestites: The Erotic Drive to Cross-Dress*, trans. Michael
Lombardi-Nash (1910; Buffalo, NY: Prometheus, 1991).
[81] Quoted in Havelock Ellis, *Studies in the Psychology of Sex*, vii. *Eonism and Other
Supplementary Studies* (Philadelphia: F. A. Davis, 1928), 13.
[82] Ibid. 1.   [83] Ibid. 11.

Read against these accounts Angelica's cross-dressing in *The Heavenly Twins* seems unrecognizable. In the sexological accounts at the *fin de siècle*, female transvestism is an anomaly; the sexual and pleasurable aspects of that activity so forcibly present in Grand's novel, are repressed by the sexologists, or subsumed into the category of inversion. But what is so important about *The Heavenly Twins*, for this study of fetishism and cross-gendering in women's writing, is that it puts into discourse the textual operations of fetishism which circulate around the body of the cross-dressed woman in female literary modernism: namely avowal and disavowal. While Angelica is allowed almost unlimited access to her desires in 'the interlude', ultimately these are disavowed by the novel as a whole. Moreover Angelica in 'The Tenor and the Boy' represents, in a sense, the fantasized ideal of female transvestism as empowering, emancipatory, and sexually embellished. But in the novels of Radclyffe Hall, Anaïs Nin, H.D., and Djuna Barnes, and through the juxtaposition of the opposing discourses of sexology and Freudian psychoanalysis, Grand's inscription becomes highly compromised.

2

'A New Perverseness'
Female Cross-Gendering and Theories of Fetishism, 1915–1930

CROSS-GENDERED VISIBILITY AND INVISIBILITY, 1914–1918

In 1915 the cross-dressing writer Christopher St John (formerly Christabel Marshall), later a friend of Radclyffe Hall, anonymously published *Hungerheart: The Story of a Soul* to little public notice.[1] It has been largely ignored ever since, but it is being revived here as part of the tradition of early twentieth-century lesbian writing prior to *The Well of Loneliness*, and indeed, as a previously unattributed precursor to Hall's novel. St John began writing *Hungerheart*, a *roman à clef* which ends with her relationship with Edy Craig, at the turn of the century, and in many respects it is an important 'crossing' novel: one that crosses centuries, genders, and theories of sexuality. It also juxtaposes a series of lesbian signifiers that are evident in later fictions of cross-gendering by Hall, H.D., Barnes, and Nin, such as the fantasy of either being or desiring a heroic boy figure, the fetishization of the lesbian subject and/or her lovers in masculine accoutrements, and the desire to write.

Like Stephen Gordon in *The Well*, the protagonist is given a boy's name, John-Baptist—a reworking of 'St John'—by her father. The absent father, who takes on a mythic status in the imagination of the young child, is remembered as 'like my heroes, who were handsome and young'.[2] All she has left of her pretty dead mother is a fading photograph, and both her surrogate mothers die early in the book.

---

[1] Christopher St John affected a masculine appearance most of her life—she dressed in a man's suit to perform a drawing-room entertainment, and a photograph in Cicely Hamilton's *Life Errant* (London: J. M. Dent and Sons, 1935) shows Hamilton and St John dressed as George Eliot and George Sand respectively for a fancy dress ball in 1911.

[2] [Christopher St John], *Hungerheart: The Story of a Soul* (London: Methuen, 1915), 8. Further references will be cited in the text.

Like Stephen Gordon, her 'first love' is her housemaid Nennie, whose dismissal from the house sets in motion the narrative of unfulfilled desire that propels the whole novel. The fantasy world John-Baptist creates, in which she is cross-gendered as a heroic crusader boy, crumbles as she 'just had a hunger for Nennie's lap and her caressing hands and her delicious gay smile' (14). It is Nennie's maternal beauty—her 'beautiful hands, beautiful lips'—that reminds John-Baptist of Greek statuary (a common motif in H.D.'s work), and that fuels her desire to 'penetrate to a beauty uncorporeal and mystical, a beauty not to be seen but felt' (37). John-Baptist's early desire coincides with cross-gendered wishes: she had 'all sorts of wild dreams of going to sea' (15), and she feels wrong in her feminine clothes due to her strong build.[3] Lady Martha Ladde's 'beautiful manly brow' (82) entrances the adolescent John-Baptist, and the maternal Madame Pohlakoff entreats her not to lose her 'little-boy look' (112).

But the oscillation between gendered 'selves' is never fully resolved by the text: 'I was more of a woman—or of a man—than most girls of my age, and more of a child' (56). She at once is sorry that she was born a girl 'because for a girl apparently there was no human life' (58), but being excluded from the world of masculine action 'provoked in me no desire to be a boy, at least not the kind of boy I knew' (33). Similarly this ambiguity is replicated in the objects of her desire: Lady Martha Ladde encompasses both the maternal and the boyish in her name, and as David Trotter points out in one of the few readings of this novel, Giovanna Ludini both recognizes John-Baptist's desire and 'disavows' it.[4] Desire itself, which propels the text through the motif of hunger, is at once avowed and disavowed: 'It was *to love* I yearned more than to *be loved*, and I was entirely free from sexual instincts' (88). And yet she always wants to be the lover, and her language is tinged with a powerful sexuality: 'The touch of a hand would penetrate to my soul when words left me unmoved' (186). In the final sections of the novel she falls in love with Sally (Edy Craig), and they have a sexually ambiguous rela-

[3] Katharine Cockin argues that St John was influenced by sexological theory in her figuration of John-Baptist. *Edith Craig (1869–1947): Dramatic Lives* (London and Washington: Cassell, 1998), 23.

[4] David Trotter, 'Lesbians Before Lesbianism: Sexual Identity in Early Twentieth-Century British Fiction', in Billie Melman (ed.), *Borderlines: Gender and Identities in War and Peace, 1870–1930* (New York and London: Routledge, 1998), 193–211: 207.

tionship in which she wonders 'which was the husband and which was the wife in the *ménage!*' (219).

Lesbianism remains on the very edge of overt articulation, expressed covertly here through reading: 'Such strange ideas, such inexplicable emotions, seethed in my mind after some of this reading' (34). The text is constantly gesturing to something that lies just beyond it, to which it is inexorably propelled through avowed and disavowed desire. This is marked inter-textually in John-Baptist's own writing which is disfigured by her unspoken sexuality: 'the pleasure that I got out of writing was from the first mingled with pain and humiliation ... I hungered to produce, yet what I did produce turned me sick with its ineffectualness, and barrenness of invention' (92–3). These textual humiliations form part of the narrative of *The Well of Loneliness*.

Hungerheart was published the same year that D. H. Lawrence's *The Rainbow*, with its portrayal of lesbian 'shame', was banned. This marks a point of crisis in the presentation of lesbian relationships in fiction. Gertrude Stein's *Things As They Are* (1903), narrating the complex sexual relationships of three lesbian women, one of whom thanked God she 'wasn't born a woman', was written in 1903 but not published until 1951. Ellen Thorneycroft Fowler's *The Farringdons* (1900) and *The Story of Mary MacLane* (1902) present the female protagonists' romantic idealization of an older woman or fantasy figure without recourse to sexual symbolization. Meanwhile in the second decade of the century there was a predominant strain of pejorative accounts of lesbian behaviour in both male- and female-authored fiction which circulated around motifs of sterility, masculinity, and sickness; the most notable examples of this can be found in Henry Kitchell Webster's *The Great Adventure* (1916), Clemence Dane's *Regiment of Women* (1917), A. T. Fitzroy's sensation novel *Despised and Rejected* (1918), and Arnold Bennett's *The Pretty Lady* (1918), which diagnoses lesbianism as one aspect of wartime hysteria.[5]

[5] Although it should be noted that Laura Doan sees Fitzroy as challenging the discourses of sexual science, particularly Edward Carpenter's notion of the 'superior male Uranian'. *Fashioning Sapphism: The Origins of a Modern English Lesbian Culture* (New York: Columbia University Press, 2001), 154. Emily Hamer has documented that Una Troubridge read *Regiment of Women* to Radclyffe Hall, and Hall asked Dane whether she would adapt *The Well of Loneliness* for the stage; Hamer argues that *Regiment* deserves more critical attention, and that it is better thought of as a 'complex lesbian gothic novel written, at least in part, for a lesbian audience rather than as a lesbian horror story written in order to inculcate homophobia'. *Britannia's Glory: A History of Twentieth-Century Lesbians* (London and New York: Cassell, 1996), 86, 88.

But if female sexuality and cross-gendering were circumscribed, marginalized, and rendered virtually invisible (through anonymous publication) or notoriously visible (at a public trial) in literary works in the first decade and a half of the twentieth century, by the end of the First World War, as Laura Doan has put it, 'female bodies were everywhere "cross-dressed" in military or police uniforms'.[6] Caroline Howlett argues that by 1913 'femininity had lost its stability as a signifier in the heterosexual economy' as a result of the public profile of militant suffragettes who concealed hammers under their feminine clothing.[7] Masculine clothing, partially sanctioned by the war through the visibility of uniforms, was now taken up by many women as a signifier of social but also sexual liberation. In April 1918 Vita Sackville-West donned the land girls' breeches and gaiters, and 'went into wild spirits';[8] Doan has suggested that these masculine items 'were the catalyst for a radical life-changing moment that culminated in an entirely new sense of self and a headlong plunge into lesbian desire' with Violet Trefusis.[9] Sackville-West also occasionally cross-dressed as an ex-soldier 'Julian' when she met Trefusis. Her novel *Challenge* (1923), written with Trefusis, was a *roman à clef* of their love as Eve and Julian. Echoing Angelica in *The Heavenly Twins,* Vita found pleasure in the 'risk of being found out', as did the lesbian artist Gluck, who called herself Peter and in 1918 designed her own male costume: 'I am flourishing in a new garb. Intensely exciting. Everybody likes it. It is all black though I can wear a coloured tie if I like and consists of a long black coat, like a bluecoat boy's with a narrow dark leather belt.'[10] Male accoutrements, particularly those associated with uniforms, had a transformative affect, taking on the value of fetishes. But, as Doan

[6] Doan, *Fashioning Sapphism,* 66.

[7] Caroline Howlett, 'Femininity Slashed: Suffragette Militancy, Modernism and Gender', in Hugh Stevens and Caroline Howlett (eds.), *Modernist Sexualities* (Manchester and New York: Manchester University Press, 2000), 72–91: 77.

[8] Nigel Nicolson, *Portrait of a Marriage* (1973; London: Weidenfeld and Nicolson, 1990), 99. Bryher and H.D. also wore breeches in 1919 while in Cornwall.

[9] Doan, *Fashioning Sapphism,* 64. Rose Collis has documented that during the First World War a number of women were arrested for 'masquerading' in male uniform. *Colonel Barker's Monstrous Regiment: A Tale of Female Husbandry* (London: Virago, 2001), 55–6.

[10] Nicolson, *Portrait of a Marriage,* 105; Diana Souhami, *Gluck 1895–1978: Her Biography* (1988; London: Weidenfeld and Nicolson, 2000), 35. Gluck's portrait *Medallion,* of her self and lover Nesta Obermer, was used for the Virago edition of *The Well of Loneliness* used here.

explains, as the war ended the uniform lost its meaning as a 'sign of women's patriotism' and became 'at best a signifier of gender confusion and at worst an indisputable sign of the inappropriate appropriation of masculine power'.[11] Doan traces this signifying shift in the efforts of the London Metropolitan Police to denigrate the Women Police Service and its Commandant Mary Allen's insistence on a suitable masculine uniform: accusations of transvestism proved most detrimental to the WPS. In 1920–1 this resulted in the question of criminalizing sexual relationships between women entering official records of parliamentary proceedings for the first time.[12] A few months earlier Radclyffe Hall, also in the public eye, had won a slander action against Sir John Lane Fox-Pitt, a member of the council of the Society for Psychical Research; he had called Hall, who had delivered a paper on contact with her dead lover Mabel Batten, immoral.

But the visibility of the WPS members, particularly Mary Allen, 'played an important and daring role in pioneering a startlingly new and radical form of "female masculinity" '.[13] Whether the prevalence of the uniform 'accelerated the trend toward more masculine fashions for women' is much debated, and trousers were not generally worn by women in public until the Second World War.[14] But what is certain is that the war had released not only compatriotism amongst women, and a possibility to forge close, sometimes lesbian relationships, but also a range of sexual signifiers. As Doan convincingly argues, the uniform—love of which had been linked by the sexologist August Forel in *The Sexual Question* with female sexual inversion, and is remarked upon in *The Well*—allowed many women to make their lesbianism visible.[15] The uniform is perhaps the most iconic of all masculine dress appropriated by women. In one sense it provides a signifier of resemblance to other women within the same corps or 'body', or a sense of 'uniformity' or unity—an embodiment which fetishism seeks to achieve. In another sense it redistributes and partitions the body's surfaces—the medals, buttons, and belts emblazon the female body in a way that fetishism does. By the early 1920s a few women were even seeking to make their cross-gendering permanently visible, by physically masculinizing their bodies.[16]

---

[11] Doan, *Fashioning Sapphism*, 67.   [12] Ibid. 37.   [13] Ibid. 82.
[14] Ibid. 67, 84.   [15] Ibid. 76.
[16] In *Sexual Pathologie: Ein Lehrbuch Für Artze unde Studierende* (1922), Magnus Hirschfeld describes a female who had a bilateral mastectomy for this purpose.

'THE LOVELY GARNISH OF A BOY': BRYHER AND THE
'YES, NO' OF CROSS-GENDERING

Like *Hungerheart*, Bryher's autobiographical series, documenting
the dawning of her own literary consciousness through the cross-
gendered persona of Nancy, also reframes an understanding of the
inscription of the cross-gendered woman in *The Well of Loneliness*.
Moreover, both *Development* (1920) and *Two Selves* (1923), which
culminates in meeting a female poet (a thinly veiled portrait of her
friend and lover H.D.), inscribe the act of writing as specifically
cross-gendered. Bryher (born Winifred Ellerman, nicknamed 'Boy'
by H.D.) was an avid reader of sexology, and when she first made
contact with Ellis, at H.D.'s urging, it was to discuss cross-
dressing—Bryher had been researching what became her essay 'The
Girl-Page in Elizabethan Literature' (1920).[17] Like many of the subjects of sexology, Bryher had already 'self-diagnosed' inversion;
Ellis, when she visited him in spring 1919, said, using what we would
now recognize as the discourse of transsexuality, that it was possible
that she 'was a boy sort of escaped into the wrong body . . . just a
girl by accident'.[18] Bryher was also one of the first subscribers to the
British Journal of Psychoanalysis, and met Freud in 1927 through an
introduction from Ellis. It is, however, Ellis's sexological schema
that she uses in *Development* and *Two Selves* to present Nancy as a
child whose 'inner' self is a boy. Her 'surface' self is conventionally
feminine, while beneath this her masculine self resists and rebels; the
two selves oscillate through avowal and disavowal: 'Two Selves.
Jammed against each other, disjointed and ill-fitting. An obedient
Nancy with heavy plaits tied over two ears that answered ⟨⟨yes, no,
yes, no,⟩⟩ according as the wind blew. A boy, a brain, that planned
adventures and sought wisdom'; this boy-self 'crie[s] for conscious-

[17] Bryher used her ideas from this essay in her historical novel *The Player's Boy* (1953).
Diana Collecott usefully draws out the lesbian encoding of this text and Bryher's interest
in cross-dressed roles or the 'breeches parts'. *H.D. and Sapphic Modernism 1910–1950*
(Cambridge: Cambridge University Press, 1999), 241–4. Barbara Guest notes how Bryher
acted out her desire to be a boy in the historical fiction for which she is best known: 'a
lone boy, faced by danger, would conquer all. There was always a battle and there was
always a boy'. *Herself Defined: The Poet H.D. and Her World* (London: Collins, 1985),
115.
[18] Bryher, letter to H.D. (20 Mar. 1919). Quoted in Collecott, *H.D. and Sapphic
Modernism*, 186.

ness'.[19] What Susan Stanford Friedman has termed the 'organizing metaphor of duality', evident in Bryher's work, informs the work of all the women discussed here: it is the split between two modes of being, two structures of narration, and two conflicting desires ('yes, no') which, I argue, is the basis for fetishism.[20]

In *Two Selves* Nancy's discomfort in her body and gender—signalled through her ultra-feminine name, which by the turn of the century was used to refer to male homosexuals—is narrativized according to her desire to experience freedom through 'breeches and short hair' (48). In *Development* the wish to be a boy, which Stephen Gordon feels so vehemently, reads like the gender dysphoric testimonies of modern-day female-to-male transsexuals: 'She was sure if she hoped enough she would turn into a boy.'[21] Inversion theory is enlisted to explain Nancy's desire for masculine upward mobility: she has a 'boy's heart' encased in an unsuitable woman's body (162). The desire to be a boy is collapsed into the wish to write, and literature becomes an erotic stimulus: 'Lovelier than the opening petals of the almond, richer than a southern morning, impressions poured into the white and rounded vase of her imagination, clamorous and hot with sweetness' (18). Bryher conceives of the artist as male (always 'he'), and writing is a substitute activity for being a sailor (72). But writing also provides access to lesbian objects of desire: 'the loveliness of Helen' (19) and Shakespearean heroines, like Portia, with 'the lovely garnish of a boy' (13).

In *Two Selves* the writing process is thwarted by Nancy's gendered split: the two identities are incompatible ('as if a sharp sword were thrust into a golf bag for a sheath', 5) and she ultimately demands the healing influence of a friend, 'a placing together of two lives' (7). To be a boy is to travel and to experience adventure which are the prerequisites of Nancy's identity as a writer; to write, to be a published author, are the prerequisites for finding a friend; only with a friend will she be 'recognized as an individual', will her 'integrity' be restored (46). Writing is a cross-gendered act for Nancy because only through experiencing adventure as a boy can she forge a new language. She desires a friend to heal the split that

[19] Bryher, *Two Selves* (Paris: Contact, [1923?]), 5, 98. Further references are cited in the text.

[20] Susan Stanford Friedman, *Psyche Reborn: The Emergence of H.D.* (Bloomington, Ind.: Indiana University Press, 1981), 34.

[21] Bryher, *Development* (London: Constable, 1920), 7. Further references are cited in the text.

she detects in herself, and enable her to 'shoot ahead, be the thing she wanted' (124). At the end of *Two Selves* Nancy visits the H.D. figure who promises to be the friend that Nancy desires: 'A tall figure opened the door. Young. A spear flower if a spear could bloom. She looked up into the eyes that had the sea in them, the fire and the colour and the splendour of it. A voice all wind and gull notes said: "I was waiting for you to come" ' (126).[22] The poet's own gendered uncertainty ('a spear flower if a spear could bloom') makes her the ideal object of desire. The phallicism of 'shooting ahead', and the spear-like poet figure, are the corollary of Nancy's desire for masculinization, a female friend, and the stimulus to write. H.D. redeploys the same imagery in the figuration of her cross-gendered sister-lover (see Chapter 3).

'A MOST PECULIAR YOUNG WOMAN': SICKNESS AND
PERVERSION IN *THE UNLIT LAMP*

Like Frances McFall who refashioned herself as Sarah Grand for the publication of *The Heavenly Twins*, Marguerite Radclyffe-Hall remade herself as the androgynously named Radclyffe Hall with the publication of *The Unlit Lamp* (1924) about a homosexual woman who cannot free herself from her mother.[23] In her two subsequent works centring on homosexual women, both protagonists are known by male names: William (Wilhemina in 'Miss Ogilvy Finds Herself') and Stephen (*The Well of Loneliness*). She took her inspiration from a piece in *The Times* (19 April 1914) which cast elderly mothers preying upon the energy and life-blood of their unmarried daughters as emotional vampires. At the centre of the novel is a triangular relationship consisting of the boyish Joan Ogden, her

[22] Bryher recreates this scene in her memoir: 'It was my first real contact with an artist, and H.D. was the most beautiful figure that I have ever seen in my life, with a face that came directly from a Greek statue'. *The Heart to Artemis* (London: Collins, 1963), 191. As is emphasized throughout this work, particularly in the chapter on H.D., statuary and Artemisian imagery (of the white huntress) are pervasive encodings of cross-gendered lesbianism.

[23] Hall remarked: 'Had I remained *Marguerite* Radclyffe-Hall I am sure I should now never have written a word. I might have developed a complex.' From a version of an unfinished essay, quoted by Sally Cline, *Radclyffe Hall: A Woman Called John* (London: John Murray, 1997), 18, Cline's emphasis. To her friends and lovers she was known as 'John' from about 1908.

dependent but powerful mother Mary, and Elizabeth Rodney, Joan's teacher, and the object of her barely acknowledged lesbian desire. The mother's vampiric emotional feeding from the daughter destroys her relationship with Elizabeth, the rival for Joan's love, and ultimately destroys Joan. Hall's novel is 'perverse' in the sense that it does not allow for the free flow of desire but consistently re-roots it into vampirism, perverse fetishism, sickness, and death.[24]

The metaphor of vampirism is prevalent from the outset. India, where Colonel Ogden and Mary Ogden spent their early married life is the 'great vampire', and Mary's father died of a haemorrhage here.[25] But Mary, wiry and strong, had withstood the draining effects of the country, and had become something like a vampire herself: 'Her pathetic eyes were sunken and somewhat dim . . . and her drooping mouth was pale' (12). Returning to the deathly town of Seabourne, which wraps its octopus-like tentacles around each of its inhabitants (the novel was originally entitled 'Octopi'), Mary simulates the appearance of an invalid. She performs weakness and vulnerability, particularly for her daughter Joan who is 'so quick to respond to the appeal of illness'; the need to do this becomes a 'positive craving' (12). Mary's desires are perverted through this dramatization of herself as an invalid, so that even the most quotidian event, such as how and where her children are educated becomes a 'fetish' (15). She amasses objects around her fetishistically, 'useless things', such as empty bottles, worn out hair-brushes, discarded clothes, and bedroom slippers, things that have been close to her body, and now represent parts of it, in order to fill up the house so that 'the space was purely Mrs. Ogden' (233). She is consistently figured through her monstrous appetite, which, for Elizabeth, gives her the appearance of a 'starving dog', or a 'terrier on a scent' (21, 25): 'Starving, what for? She shuddered. Had Mrs. Ogden always been so hungry? She was positively ravenous, you could feel it about her, her hunger came at you and made you feel embarrassed' (21–2). Her need for blood manifests itself rebelliously when she serves her husband kidneys for breakfast that bleed over the plate, provoking Colonel Ogden into asking 'Do you think I'm a cannibal?' (28).

---

[24] See Elaine Showalter, *Sexual Anarchy: Gender and Culture at the Fin de Siècle* (1990; London: Bloomsbury, 1991), 179–82, for an account of the association of homosexuality and vampirism in turn-of-the-century literature.

[25] Radclyffe Hall, *The Unlit Lamp* (1924; London: Virago, 1981), 12. Further references will be cited in the text.

Joan Ogden, boyish and clever, is presented as the son and husband that her mother never had. Repulsed by her husband's bodily presence ('his masculine personality pervaded everything; the room reeked of it'), Mrs Ogden recasts herself as a 'virgin whose privacy had suffered a rude intrusion' (25). Against this loveless marriage, Mary redirects her fantasies towards her daughter's powerful presence: 'Joan was large-boned and tall for her age, lanky as a boy, with a pale face' (11), and has black hair, which is cut short during an illness.[26] Although boyish, like Stephen Gordon, she is not overtly presented as an invert, although the implication is that her sexual identity is 'other'. When Joan challenges her ultra-feminine sister Milly's (hetero-)sexual misconduct, the latter retorts: 'You stand there calling me names and putting on your high and mighty air as though I were some low creature that had defiled you; and why? Only because I'm natural and you're not. You're a freak and I'm just a normal woman' (161). The rest of Joan's family, and Elizabeth, understand her behaviour and her personal style only in masculine terms. Elizabeth often bypasses Joan's femininity: 'You'll be able to wallow in a bog of sentimentality and to pat yourself on the head because you're not as other men. *You* have a sense of duty, whereas I—You'll feel that your offering yourself as a sacrifice. Oh, I know it all, and it makes me sick, sick, do you hear? Positively *sick* . . . Perhaps you expect me to praise you, to tell you what a really fine fellow I think you' (169). On learning that she wishes to study medicine at Cambridge, her father ventriloquizes one voice from the sexological debate about the masculinization of women: 'It's positively indecent—an unsexing, indecent profession for any woman . . . Do you think you're a boy?' (110–11).

However, it suits Joan's mother's (sexual) purpose to recognize that her daughter 'was so like a boy—one felt that she was a son sometimes' (55). Instead of exhibiting repulsion towards her masculine daughter, as Anna does in *The Well*, Mary Ogden eroticizes Joan's masculinity and takes her first as the son she has lost, and then as a substitute husband: 'Joan's strong, young arms would comfort and soothe, and her firm lips grope until they found her

---

[26] Trevor Hope argues that this is significant, that it is through the 'discourses of disease and symptomaticity' that lesbian desire can be read. 'Mother, Don't You See I'm Burning? Between Female Homosexuality and Homosociality in Radclyffe Hall's *The Unlit Lamp*', in Elizabeth Wright, Mandy Merck and Naomi Segal (eds.), *Coming Out of Feminism* (Oxford: Blackwell, 1998), 123–53: 127, 132.

mother's; and Mrs. Ogden would feel mean and ashamed but guiltily happy, as if a lover held her' (13). While her mother entreats Joan to alter her masculine appearance, nevertheless she desires it in order to actualize the daughter-husband as a chivalrous, strong, and protective lover. This is also the quality that appeals to Elizabeth as we watch her through Elizabeth's eyes: 'Joan was so quiet, so reserved, so strong. Strong, yes, that was the right word, strong and protective' (21). From the outset Elizabeth is attracted to her pupil, with her coltish, athletic body and fine mind, whom she watches 'covertly' (23). To Joan, Elizabeth most closely resembles a tree: 'it must be the green dress. But her eyes are like water, all greeny and shadowy and deep looking . . . a larch tree just greening over' (34), a motif of resemblance which is also used in H.D.'s *HER* and Barnes's *Nightwood*, to characterize the lesbian lover or subject.[27] The words 'colt' and 'tree', lesbian encodings, are repeated throughout the text at key moments to signify unspoken desire between the women. It is through Joan's appearance, particularly her clothing, that Elizabeth first registers both her desire for Joan and her rivalry with Mrs Ogden:

Elizabeth felt hot; why in heaven's name make a fool of Joan like that . . . what possessed Mrs. Ogden to make her wear white? Joan looked too awful in white, it made her skin look yellow. Then the dress was too short; Joan's dresses always were; and yet she was her mother's favourite. Curious—perhaps Mrs. Ogden wanted to make her look young; well, she couldn't keep her a baby for ever . . . Elizabeth felt that she could dress Joan; she ought to wear dark colours, she knew exactly what she ought to wear. (36)

Both women's fantasies are united in Joan at this point: the mother's who wants her to remain in the close relationship of childhood, and the lover's who sees in her the growing woman in child's clothes. But Elizabeth also desires to inhabit the position of the mother. In an attempt to appeal to Joan, Elizabeth asks Joan if she likes her dress: 'Elizabeth wanted to say, "Do you think me at all beautiful, Joan?" But something inside her began to laugh at this absurdity' (36).

Elizabeth's beauty, however, is all in her hands: the first description of Elizabeth drifts down to 'her fine, long hands . . . folded idly in her lap; she had a trick of folding her hands in her lap' (19). Throughout her fiction hands are the most catalogued and fetishized part of the body for Hall.[28] The link between hands, inversion, and narcissism in sexology was established in Féré's *L'Instinct sexual* in the case of a girl who was sexually excited by kissing her own hands—a practice Féré called 'auto-fetichism'. Féré discusses narcissism in terms of splitting: for the girl the hand is not herself, but a fetish, an object which functions in the absence of the beloved.[29] Holding hands with her 'lover-like' mother, desperately trying to summon up some emotional response which she knows her mother desires, Joan feels repulsed by her mother's vampiric physicality, and yet tender towards her at the same time:

> To Joan there was an actual physical distaste for the handclasp, yet she dared not, could not let go. She was conscious in a vague way that her mother's hand felt different. Mechanically she began to finger it, slipping a ring up and down; the ring came off unexpectedly, it was loose, for the hand had grown thinner. Her mind seized on this with avidity; here was the motive she needed for love: her mother's hand, small and white, was thinner than it had been before, it was now terribly thin. There was pathos in this, there was something in this to make her feel sorry; she stooped and fondled the hand. (66)

This key scene between the mother and Joan in which the mother weakens herself to appeal to Joan arouses a strain of perversity in Joan herself. Unable to 'awaken her dulled emotions', nauseated by the feel of her mother's bloodless flesh, she detaches her mother's

---

[28] Sally Cline draws out the biographical importance of hands for Hall: her mother rebuked her by saying that her hands were just like her father's, and, discussing the nature of the possible sexual abuse by her stepfather Alberto Visetti, Cline suggests that is was his hands 'that stamped fear upon her mind' (32). In her early stories, as Cline documents, such as 'The Career of Mark Anthony Brakes' and 'The Woman in the Crêpe Bonnet', as well as in her unpublished novel 'Michael West', there are repeated references to abusive male hands (46). In her biography of Hall Una Troubridge stated that Hall always noticed people's hands, and they become reclaimed as an index of female beauty and lesbian desire, as in the case of her cousin Jane Randolph's lovely hands. In a widening of the importance of hands for Hall, Vera Brittain claims that while writing *The Master of the House* (1932), a study of the life of Christ as a young man, Hall had to 'seek radiological treatment for acute pain in the palms of both hands, accompanied by an angry-looking stain which after some days of endurance gradually faded'. *Radclyffe Hall, A Case of Obscenity?* (London: Femina, 1968), 81. Vita Sackville-West also remembered that Violet Trefusis had indexed her desire for Vita with her hands: she 'parted my fingers to count the points as she told me why she loved me. I hadn't dreamt of such an art of love' (Nicolson, *Portrait of a Marriage*, 100).

[29] Havelock Ellis refers to this case in *Studies in the Psychology of Sex*, vii. *Eonism and Other Supplementary Studies* (Philadelphia: F. A. Davis, 1928), 354.

hand from her body and redirects her emotional energy into that body part with a greedy desire which can find no other suitable object. From this point on, Joan's love for her mother is conducted through a fetish, that most perverse of objects.

This can be usefully compared with the most significant erotic moment between Joan and Elizabeth. In a highly symbolic scene in which Elizabeth attempts to rescue a woman who is on fire, the themes of desire (literally being on fire) and thwarted ambition come painfully to the surface in this novel which, in its title, registers the lack of any kindling of desire. The burning woman rushes towards Elizabeth and Joan, however, marking them out. The woman dies, and Elizabeth is left with a severely burnt hand. The roles between the women are reversed as Joan realizes that 'Elizabeth the dominating, the practical, was now as helpless as a baby. The thought thrilled her' (99). The mother/child relationship that had become eroticized by Mary is now inverted between Joan and Elizabeth; this presages a perverse seduction that turns on the image of Elizabeth's damaged hands:

They went slowly upstairs to the bedroom. Joan had been in the house before but never in that room; she paused instinctively at the door, feeling shy. Something told her that by entering this bedroom she was marking an epoch in her relations with Elizabeth, so personal must that room be; she turned the handle and they went in . . . Very gently Joan helped her to undress; it was a painful and tedious business. Joan noticed with surprise that Elizabeth's clothes were finer than Mrs. Ogden's; it gave her a pleasure to touch them. (99)

After this moment the relationship between teacher and pupil is lost forever and is replaced by 'something infinitely more intimate and interesting' (100). Elizabeth, at first, is unwilling to relinquish the old relationship. In Joan's own 'self-analysis' Elizabeth and her mother are intertwined ('Did she love Elizabeth and was that why she did not love her mother?' 69). In the next scene, Mary and Elizabeth's rivalry comes to the surface; Elizabeth, as caregiver and nurturer, displaces Mary Ogden, and accuses her of exploiting Joan's 'abnormally developed capacity for affection' (71), using the metaphors of vampirism that run throughout the text: 'She's consuming herself even now, and what will she do later on? Yet, how can she come to fruition if she's drained dry before she begins to live at all?' (72). After this confrontation, Mary's desires multiply: 'She was like a drug-taker from whom all stimulant has been suddenly removed; the craving was unendurable, dangerous alike to body and mind' (75), and she finds herself constantly losing ground to Elizabeth who finally gets her way in creating the desired image for Joan. The burning of Elizabeth's hands sets in motion the plot development for the middle section of the novel. Horrified by them, 'hideously seamed and puckered with large, discoloured scars' (109), Joan makes the decision to become a doctor. This announcement causes her father to have a stroke that marks his steady decline.

Lesbianism, which as Trevor Hope points out is 'never narratively realized in *The Unlit Lamp*', is encoded through tropes of appearance, the (sick) body and articulation.[30] The sexual love between Elizabeth and Joan is unspoken, reflecting a general inarticulacy in the novel itself. Colonel Ogden is literally struck dumb by Joan's announcement that she wants to be a doctor, and Mary is constantly struggling for words or repressing them with regard to her love for Joan:

there was so much that she felt she must say to Joan at that moment; the words tingled through her, longing to become articulate. She wanted to cry out like a primitive creature; to scream words of entreaty, of reproach, of tenderness. She longed to humble herself to this child, beseeching her to love her and her only, and above all not to let Elizabeth come between them. But even as the words formed themselves in her brain she crushed them down, ashamed of her folly. (102)

Heavy dashes cut off sentences at the precise moment of the articulation of desire, for example in Joan's exclamation to Elizabeth: 'Your beautiful hands! You were so proud of them—' (109), and Elizabeth's fantasized declaration: 'I did this thing, I found Joan and I gave her the best I had to give, freedom and—' (126). The delayed closure to this sentence, suggesting the sexual, is reinforced by the eroticism of the imagery of the 'clasped hands' as they walk silently home.

After living and working with Joan in close confines for several months, studying the intimate workings of the human body for Joan's examinations, the force of the repression of her feelings for Joan manifests itself through truncated sentences, and off-kilter syntax. In her attempt to negate her 'neurosis', there is an excess of neurasthenic diction ('dissatisfied', 'apprehensive', 'fanciful', 'nervy', 'overworking recklessly') which reaches a climax as the sentence, in which Elizabeth rejects psychoanalytic theories of the self, breaks down entirely: 'at last she broke—' (130). Her tirade against medicine as a study of 'the disgusting organs of our disgusting

[30] Hope, 'Mother, Don't You See I'm Burning?', 126.

bodies, to learn how and why they act, or rather how and why they don't act' speaks of her own repressed and unspoken desires, but ends again in linguistic fracture: 'it's because of you and your career, it's because I'm mad for you to have a future—I've been so from the first, I think—I don't care what you do if only you do something and do it well, if only you're not thrown on the ash-heap—' (130). This sentence, ending on an image of waste, stutters to a close with the short hyphen followed by a long heavy dash, suggesting that this is exactly where Joan's future lies. This speech reawakens in Joan the realization that Elizabeth depends on her: the tree imagery intimately associated with Elizabeth manifests itself deep within Joan's body ('Elizabeth had taken root in her and would blossom or fade, according to the sustenance she could provide', 130). Finally Elizabeth replaces her half-formed sentences with the pathetic and potent symbolism of her scarred hand which she stretches towards Joan, and to which Joan clings desperately, psychically detaching 'the hand' from Elizabeth's body, investing it with all hopes and fears ('I'm only afraid of your taking your hand away', 131). Using exactly the same manipulative strategies as Mary Ogden (she literally uses her hand), Elizabeth appeals to Joan's protective instincts, which are so closely associated with her sexual desires, as the chivalrous, manly lover. At this moment Elizabeth embodies the mother-lover through her scarred and frail hands. This interaction ends with Elizabeth proclaiming her desire that Joan make a home with her, and Joan's promise that she will break free of 'this detestable place'. In an obsessive repetition of this scene, Joan is on the verge of speaking but remains silent, and clutches at Elizabeth with an outstretched hand 'as though groping for protection'. The boundaries that demarcate the women (weak/strong, age/youth) are being eroded. Elizabeth asserts a 'different' part of herself that is young, rebellious, and life-loving, demanding of pleasure: her lesbian self.

In London Joan's own lesbian self is recognized and affirmed by Beatrice Lesway, a masculine Cambridge woman whose 'whole appearance left you bewildered; it was a mixed metaphor, a contradiction in style, certainly a little grotesque' (200), and whose name unsubtly signals her sexual identity. Beatrice can 'read' Joan, but Joan cannot read Beatrice properly: she has no idea what 'cravings, if any, tore her unfeminine bosom', and sees a battle of rival masculine and feminine forces staging itself on her 'untidy, art-serged body' (201). Similarly Richard Benson, who adores Joan's 'black, cropped hair, her beautiful mouth, and her queer, gruff voice' recognizes her as a precursor of the 'as yet unborn women, stimulating his imagination, challenging his intellect, demanding of him an explanation of themselves' (209). It is significant that Joan is the locus of other people's interpretations of her as 'unnatural', 'queer', 'a most peculiar young woman', 'a kind of heartless freak', and yet does not come to any self-realization. She does stop to consider her 'unusual' behaviour, but she conceptualizes it only in terms of convention and tradition, rather in terms of a sexual identity: 'I defy precedent. I'm Joan Ogden, a law unto myself, and I mean to prove it' (248). In a sense *The Unlit Lamp* articulates the very dividing line between literary text and sexology: Joan remains at once 'unexplained' through the extended tropes of inarticulation, and on the very cusp of explanation, through the discourse of perversion.

A significant feature of the perversion at work in *The Unlit Lamp* is an almost fetishistic relation to (masculine) clothes. In an effort to assuage the tension of working in close proximity with Elizabeth in such strained circumstances, Joan takes pleasure and 'relief' in her clothing and her appearance, brushing her short hair till it shines, and polishing her shoes: 'the more unhappy she felt the more care did she lavish on her appearance; it was a kind of bravado, a subtle revenge for some nameless injustice that fate had inflicted on her' (158). It is encoded as a secret sign to Elizabeth which she recognizes and approves, but which she does not articulate, through a 'new perverseness'. Their desires now become perversely embodied, at once unmentionable and materially present, a 'hungry, restless thing' that stands between them and makes them afraid of each other. Against this figuration of repressed and re-directed desire, Hall places the unchecked heterosexual desires of Milly, who 'couldn't help it' when she gave way to her impulses and had sexual relations with a man who works, significantly, in the 'circulating' library (his and Milly's desires are allowed freedom to circulate). She is cruelly punished for this sexual expression, first verbally by Joan and then by the text itself when she contracts consumption (she is literally consumed by her desires), and is reclaimed by Seabourne where she swiftly dies. Seabourne also strengthens its grip on Elizabeth, who starts to wither and age. Joan is perversely drawn by some 'miserable attraction' to the spectacle of Elizabeth's unguarded body: the grey hairs, the lines around her mouth, the puckered eyelids, the 'secret things about

Elizabeth', and the damaged hand which had grown a 'little less firm and smooth' (211). Desire, unable to find free expression, is covert, and secret, something that feeds on flaws and weaknesses and makes Joan flush with shame. Elizabeth's frustrations become impossible to bear as the 'pent-up unhappiness of years gushed out' and she murmured in a 'kind of ecstatic anguish': 'Oh! Oh!—Oh! Oh!', followed by the repeated incantation of Joan's name, and hysterical twitching in her legs.

Mary Ogden ultimately triumphs over the 'unsexed bluestocking' Elizabeth Rodney. She appeals to the 'chivalry and protectiveness' that had been such a part of her early relationship with Joan, and exerts a strong nostalgic sexual power by wearing a dove grey dress that reminds Joan of the pretty woman of her childhood. In a farewell letter to Joan, Elizabeth explains her love for Joan in precisely the discourse that has fuelled the novel (repression and redirection of natural desires): 'I managed to dam up the torrent, till it flowed away from its natural course; it flowed out to you, Joan' (260). At the end of the novel, when Joan has been reclaimed triumphantly by her mother, her only moments of 'sensuous enjoyment' occur when her mother is asleep: ' "All is as it should be," she thought dreamily, "and I know exactly why it is so, only I can't quite find the words. Somewhere at the back of my mind I know the why of everything" ' (283).

In the final section of the novel Joan, who is now twenty years older, and has lost much of the suppleness of her coltish body, and the liveliness of her mind (she has in many respects become her mother), confronts her author in the guise of the succeeding generation of New Women at Lymington. This is partly a fantasized pen portrait of Hall and Troubridge, who have bobbed hair and well-tailored clothes. One of them is dressed in riding breeches. They mock Joan for her feminizing touches to what is essentially a masculine form of dress: ribbon instead of a necktie, and a pearl brooch attached to her stiff collar. These women identify Joan as 'a kind of pioneer that's got left behind . . . the beginning of things like me' (284).

INVERTS AND PSEUDO-INVERTS: *THE WELL OF LONELINESS* AND SEXOLOGY

In Hall's short story 'Miss Ogilvy Finds Herself' (1926), a transitional text between *The Unlit Lamp* and *The Well of Loneliness*, female cross-gendering is enacted as a trans-historical sex change, in which Miss Ogilvy, at a loss to know how to employ herself after the end of the First World War, is drawn to an island off the Devon coast. Here she discovers prehistoric remains that provide access to a primitive age, in which she is retrospectively reincarnated as a pre-historic cave-dweller. The presentation of Miss Ogilvy, a lonely, middle-aged spinster of masculine manner and appearance, is informed by theories of inversion: she has a 'tall, awkward body with its queer look of strength, its broad, flat bosom and thick legs and ankles'.[31] Indeed, Hall saw the story as a precursor to *The Well of Loneliness*, her 'serious study of congenital sexual inversion'.[32] The story, how-ever, explores the notion that the invert predates sexological inscrip-tions. When Miss Ogilvy finds the bones of the prehistoric man, she is thrown into a trance-like state in which she, as the cave-dweller, impregnates a beautiful mate:

His speech was slow and lacking in words when it came to expressing a vital emotion . . . the word that he spoke had a number of meanings. It meant: 'Little spring of exceedingly pure water.' It meant 'Hut of peace for a man after bat-tle.' It meant: 'Ripe red berry sweet to the taste.' It meant: 'Happy small home of future generations.'[33]

It is clear that the word that is being searched for bears all the sym-bolic and literal resonance of the vagina and the womb. It is signific-ant that the word propels the man/Miss Ogilvy into a linguistic crisis. Hall's use of this mystifying mode is symptomatic of her struggle to articulate lesbian desire.

This struggle in both 'Miss Ogilvy' and *The Unlit Lamp* must be seen in context of the low incidence of both female cross-gendering and lesbianism in literature in the first decades of the twentieth cen-tury, perhaps due to the limited circulation of sexological works on inversion in Britain. But by the early 1920s in France, Romain Rolland's *Annette et Sylvie* (1922), Victor Margueritte's *La Garçonne* (1922), and Jacques Lacretelle's *La Bonifas* (1925) spoke of a growing relaxation in the conventions governing the expression of sexual behaviour. This took slightly longer to occur in Britain and America: as Jeanette Foster has documented, cross-fertilization

---

[31] Radclyffe Hall, 'Miss Ogilvy Finds Herself', in *Miss Ogilvy Finds Herself* (London: William Heinemann, 1934), 3.
[32] Radclyffe Hall, author's footnote, *Miss Ogilvy Finds Herself*.
[33] 'Miss Ogilvy', 26–7.

between continental and Anglo-American attitudes culminated in the translation after 1920 of a large amount of French fiction (including Proust and *La Garçonne*).[34] Radclyffe Hall, encouraged by her first love Mabel 'Ladye' Batten, read many French writers, including Colette, Zola, George Sand, Renée Vivien, and, as Sally Cline has noted, was influenced by the French-born Violet Paget (Vernon Lee) who presented female cross-dressing in her works.[35] After its ban, *The Well* continued to be printed in France.

Just prior to the publication of *The Well*, Woolf's *Mrs Dalloway* (1925) and Rosamund Lehmann's *Dusty Answer* (1927) gave more positive representations of sexual love between women, although the androgynous Geraldine Manners in *Dusty Answer* has a recognizable set of characteristics: short-haired and masculine in appearance, with a seductive allure for other women.[36] Coinciding with *The Well* was Woolf's *Orlando*, an encoded lesbian love letter to Vita Sackville-West. The two novels are intimately related, not just because Woolf was a defence witness at the trial which led to the banning of *The Well* (herself successfully negotiating scandal and prohibition with the more subtle, playful, and encoded *Orlando*), but because they speak divergently of the creative aspects of female cross-gendering. For Woolf, creative ability is the outgrowth of intersexual identity: the ability to slip effortlessly from one gender to another, and from one genre to another, allows for enhanced creative expression. In *The Well*, Stephen Gordon's writing is tainted by her inability to think herself beyond her own thwarted subject position; her writing bears the price of the investment in the theory of inversion. Bryher fictionalizes the writing process as a repression of her feminine self and a coming to consciousness of her boy-self. In *The Well* Stephen struggles with a similar split in her consciousness that has implications for her writing.

[34] Jeanette H. Foster, *Sex Variant Women in Literature: A Historical and Quantitative Study* (London: Frederick Muller, 1958), 240–1.

[35] Cline, *Radclyffe Hall*, 64.

[36] Also in 1927, George Moore published a short story, 'Albert Nobbs', in *Celibate Lives*, in which a girl passes as a male waiter in order to find employment; her sex is discovered only at death. The potential for desire (lesbian, heterosexual self-pleasuring) is completely subsumed by her full assumption of the masculine role, and Moore emphasizes that the utilitarian need to cross-dress negates any conscious pleasure in the act. If self-pleasuring is an impossibility in 'Albert Nobbs' sexual love enters the text merely as an aporia. In her encounters with Hubert, another passing woman, Albert learns that Hubert is married to another woman. She wonders if Hubert 'let the girl into the secret, or [left] her to find out when—'. *Celibate Lives* (London: Heinemann, 1927), 63.

In *The Well of Loneliness*, originally entitled 'Stephen', Radclyffe Hall embarked on her most systematic symbolization of the invert, making notorious and iconic a form of female cross-gendering.[37] Like Bryher, Radclyffe Hall was also an exponent of sexological theories of inversion, overtly supporting the theories of Havelock Ellis, and persuading him to write a preface for *The Well*.[38] This book was the one that she had been longing to write, and is a form of mythologized semi-autobiography: 'I admit, I did draw upon myself, I drew very ruthlessly upon myself' (an admission she later disavowed).[39] Michael Baker argues that it is a self that has been refashioned through Ellis and Krafft-Ebing; he suggests that in later life, when Hall professed to being a 'congenital invert', she read back into her own childhood and adolescence many of the traits she attributed to Stephen Gordon, radically changing her appearance in the 1920s. Her lover Una Troubridge was eager to promote this image, 'masculinizing' pictures of Hall as a young girl, presenting Hall as a tomboy in her own biography: Hall had 'not the countenance of a young woman but of a very handsome young man'.[40] In order to temper Troubridge's retrospective masculinization Baker desperately attempts to recover Hall's lost femininity: he observes that Hall's 'earliest photographs show an apparently normal little girl with strong features'.[41] Troubridge herself underwent a similar form of reinvention. She cropped her hair on meeting Hall, and altered her clothes; Baker states that her style was a 'soft imitation of John's severe style', but Cline suggests that she was always

[37] Several critics, including Doan, suggest that the title *The Well of Loneliness* is an ironic play on (indeed, I might suggest, an inversion of) the Cave of Harmony, a Soho nightclub founded in 1917 by the actress Elsa Lanchester and others, which Hall and Troubridge attended. Doan notes that Lanchester parodied the sexologists in a sketch 'Krafft-Ebing, Case #74B of Zurich'. *Fashioning Sapphism*, 136.

[38] This was perhaps a clever piece of marketing because Ellis's profile was high due to the publication in 1928 of *Eonism* as vol. vii of *Studies in the Psychology of Sex*. Significantly this included essays on narcissism, auto-eroticism, and on cross-dressing with the conclusion that transvestism is not related to homosexuality. As Jay Prosser notes, Ellis's introduction as 'framing device' suggests that *The Well* itself is a case history. *Second Skins: The Body Narratives of Transsexuality* (New York: Columbia University Press, 1998), 157.

[39] Hall quoted in Diana Souhami, *The Trials of Radclyffe Hall* (London: Weidenfeld and Nicolson, 1998), 154.

[40] Una Troubridge, *The Life and Death of Radclyffe Hall* (London: Hammond, 1961), 46.

[41] Michael Baker, *Our Three Selves: The Life of Radclyffe Hall* (London: Hamish Hamilton, 1985), 19.

boyish.[42] After Hall's death, Troubridge had Hall's clothes altered to fit her, which signifies not only a wish to embody her dead lover, but a desire to exist in some erotic relation to her, through clothes.

Esther Newton's reading of Hall's and Troubridge's dress, and the symbolization of Stephen Gordon is recuperative of lesbian-feminist insurgence: 'Cross-dressing for Hall is not a masquerade. It stands for the New Woman's rebellion against the male order and, at the same time, for the lesbian's desperate struggle to be and express her true self.'[43] According to this definition Newton argues that cross-gendering in *The Unlit Lamp* signifies the New Woman's modernity and aspiration to male privilege. In *The Well* the same mode of self-actualization enacts the signification of lesbian sexuality, which barely broke the surface of *The Unlit Lamp*. Laura Doan provides a convincing argument that masculine clothing was not necessarily *read* as denoting lesbianism in the 1920s, since a boyish if not mannish look was fashionable for women 'of all sexual persuasions', until at least the time of the trial of *The Well* when uncoincidentally a more feminine look became *à la mode*. From this moment, Doan argues, Hall's appearance became firmly linked with lesbianism, but prior to this it would have been seen as distinctly modern(ist) (Doan demonstrates how this look can be traced back to the New Woman of the turn of the century). The monocle, cigarette, and masculine cut of clothes were all signifiers that were 'up for grabs' in the early to mid-1920s but solidified as markers of deviant sexuality after 1928.[44] Doan suggests that 'cross-dressing was just as likely to be playful or erotically pleasurable as it was political' for women but does not expand on this point.[45]

Havelock Ellis—who took note of her modern look: monocle and shingled hair—corresponded with Hall, and she was fluent in theories of homosexuality having read widely from Krafft-Ebing, Iwan Bloch, Edward Carpenter, Magnus Hirschfeld (although she does not refer to his 1910 landmark work on transvestites).[46] She found Ellis most sympathetic to her own understanding of inversion, but it

[42] Ibid. 89; Cline, *Radclyffe Hall*, 112.

[43] Esther Newton, 'The Mythic Mannish Lesbian: Radclyffe Hall and the New Woman', in Estelle B. Freedman, Barbara C. Gelpi, Susan L. Johnson, and Kathleen M. Weston (eds.), *The Lesbian Issue: Essays from SIGNS* (Chicago: University of Chicago Press, 1985), 7–25: 20.

[44] See Doan, *Fashioning Sapphism*, 96–125.   [45] Ibid. 98.

[46] Ibid. 227 n. 118.

is in her father's copy of Krafft-Ebing that Stephen Gordon recognizes herself. Rebecca O'Rourke suggests that Case 131 (Countess Sarolta V) in *Psychopathia Sexualis* served as a model of Stephen.[47] Most significant is the role of the father in the development of Sarolta's cross-gendered behaviour (he taught her to hunt and ride and called her Sandor). Sarolta's prayer to God is very similar to Stephen's; and the denial of the sensuality of her own body certainly bears comparison. Hall understood that if inversion were congenital, then she was cleansed of blame; it was not an act of deviancy, but something in nature. Newton argues that the 'mannish lesbian' model, which emanated from the conflation of inversion and the New Woman in the cultural imagination, was symbolized by Radclyffe Hall, and subsequently adopted by many women who wanted to break out of the asexual paradigm of romantic friendship. Stephen's cross-gendered persona is a double symbol 'standing for the New Woman's painful position between traditional political and social categories, and for the lesbian struggle to define and assert an identity'.[48] Newton suggests that Hall had no alternative for her presentation of Stephen.[49]

As Newton remarks, Stephen Gordon's body is the somatic symbol of the femininity she rejects. The catalogue of her inversion bears very close comparison to that of Ellis. She is born 'narrow-hipped, wide-shouldered', bearing a strong resemblance to her father, who recognizes 'that indefinable quality in Stephen that made her look wrong in the clothes she was wearing'.[50] Stephen abhors the sight of herself with long hair and feminine accoutrements (23), and she indulges in what were perceived as masculine pastimes. She prefers the company of men and is erotically drawn to women. When she falls in love with Angela Crossby, she acquires a masculine wardrobe; on moving to London she has her hair

[47] Rebecca O'Rourke, *Reflecting on 'The Well of Loneliness'* (London: Routledge, 1989), 3.

[48] Newton, 'The Mythic Mannish Lesbian', 18.

[49] Martha Vicinus adds to this argument: Hall had '[Natalie Clifford] Barney's hedonistic lesbianism, [Renée] Vivien's self-created tragedy, Colette's theatrical affair with the marquise [de Belboeuf]'. But for Hall 'these women were either too secretive or too ostentatious and therefore too close to the heterosexual fantasies about the life of the deviant'. ' "They Wonder to which Sex I Belong": The Historical Roots of the Modern Lesbian', in Henry Abelove, Michèle Aina Barale, and David Halperin (eds.), *The Lesbian and Gay Studies Reader* (New York: Routledge, 1993), 432–52: 445.

[50] Radclyffe Hall, *The Well of Loneliness* (1928; London: Virago, 1991), 15. Further references will be cited in the text.

cropped, and becomes a 'voracious smoker' (210). In *Sexual Inversion* Ellis outlined the model for the 'pseudo-invert', who was not masculine, but not womanly enough to attract men; therefore she was understood to be a target for the predatory and insatiable congenital invert. Some critics, who simplistically map Hall's text against Ellis, have argued that Mary Llewellyn most closely corresponds to the pseudo-invert; others argue that she is as 'inverted' as Stephen.[51] The Parisian inverts who congregate around Valérie Seymour share signs of somatic masculinization: Pat's strong and heavy ankles, Margaret Roland's 'boy's voice on the verge of breaking' (355), Jamie's 'loose-limbed' body (363). As Terry Castle usefully points out, just as the bodies of these women are 'marked', so the text itself seems 'unbalanced and out of sync—"ill" in an almost endocrinal sense. Moments of joy are contaminated before they can even register on the psyche; yearning for freedom results in pain and scarification, a corrugation of the heart.' Castle notes that the 'deranged, infernal tour of the Parisian homosexual underworld', with the effeminate Brockett as a guide, and presided over by the collector of inverts, Monsieur Pujol, anticipates the 'caliginous, neo-Baudelairean scenery' of Djuna Barnes's *Nightwood*.[52]

As Alison Hennegan argues, however, the model of congenital inversion is not rigidly maintained: the figuration of Stephen's masculine traits 'will also bear social and psychological explanations'.[53] Stephen's masculine behaviour can be read as a result of the father's desire for a son, for example, or the mother's rejection

[51] Ruehl argues that Hall presented the relationship between the congenital and pseudo-invert 'far more rigidly than anything Ellis wrote'. 'Inverts and Experts: Radclyffe Hall and the Lesbian Identity', in Rosalind Brunt and Caroline Rowan (eds.), *Feminism, Culture and Politics* (London: Lawrence and Wishart, 1982), 15–36: 23. In contrast see Loralee MacPike, 'Is Mary Llewellyn an Invert? The Modernist Supertext of *The Well of Loneliness*', in Elizabeth Jane Harrison and Shirley Peterson (eds.), *Unmanning Modernism: Gendered Re-Readings* (Knoxville, Tenn.: University of Tennessee Press, 1997), 73–89. MacPike contests that Mary is 'part of an emerging new icon which came to full fruition only in the 1980s'; her strong sex drive and self-confidence blur 'the boundaries which sexology and Stephen Gordon so emphatically maintain' (77, 85).

[52] Terry Castle, *Noel Coward and Radclyffe Hall: Kindred Spirits* (New York: Columbia University Press, 1996), 52, 53.

[53] Alison Hennegan, Introduction, *The Well of Loneliness* (London: Virago, 1991), p. xv. Vera Brittain was one of the first critics to notice a representational ambivalence; as she wrote in *Time and Tide* in Aug. 1928, it 'raises and never satisfactorily answers . . . the question as to how far the characteristics of Stephen Gordon are physiological and how far they are psychological'. Brittain, *Radclyffe Hall*, 50.

of the daughter. In *The Well* there is a reminder that sexology did not account for the diversity of human expression and identity, and that it poses Stephen as anomalous even in terms of mannish lesbianism: as Stephen's governess tells her: 'You're neither unnatural, nor abominable, nor mad; you're as much a part of what people call nature as anyone else; only you're unexplained as yet—you've not got your niche in creation' (153). While Hall had a deep emotional investment in the model of sexual inversion, *The Well* provides other means of reading cross-gendered acts. She writes into her model of the invert a degree of frailty and ambivalence that 'exceeds' the overt text that espouses congenital inversion; she both avows and forecloses the pleasures that are generated through Stephen Gordon's body.

'YOU CREATED THE THING THAT I AM': THE POTENTIAL FOR FETISHISM IN *THE WELL OF LONELINESS*

By the 1920s the indexing of homosexuality in terms of sexual inversion was being seriously contested by psychoanalytic conceptions of sexual development with a radically different emphasis being put on the perverse as central to identity formation and culture itself.[54] Just prior to the publication of *The Well*, Sigmund Freud published 'Fetishism'. Pre-Freudian sexologists and psychoanalysts had theorized fetishism as a male sexual practice, but Freud, to use the phraseology of Lorraine Gamman and Merja Makinen, 'phallicized' fetishism, investing the mother with a phallus, as the fetishized object of desire.[55] Freud first addressed fetishism in 'Three Essays on the Theory of Sexuality', suggesting that the fetish (another part of the body like the foot or hair, or an inanimate object such as a piece of fur or clothing) is a substitute for the 'sexual object'.[56] The relation of the individual to the fetish is symbolic, and not always immediately explicable. Freud regards a 'certain degree' of fetishism

[54] See Chapter 3 for analysis of this challenge.
[55] Lorraine Gamman and Merja Makinen, *Female Fetishism: A New Look* (London: Lawrence and Wishart, 1994), 39.
[56] Sigmund Freud, 'Three Essays on the Theory of Sexuality' (1905), *The Standard Edition of the Complete Psychological Works of Sigmund Freud*, trans. James Strachey *et al.*, 24 vols. (London: The Hogarth Press and the Institute of Psycho-Analysis, 1953–74), 7. 135–243: 154. Further references to Freud's work, unless otherwise stated, are to this edition (*SE*).

as 'normal', but stresses that it becomes pathological when the 'fetish passes beyond the point of being merely a necessary condition attached to the sexual object and actually *takes the place* of the normal aim, and, further, when the fetish becomes detached from a particular individual and becomes the *sole* sexual object'.[57] In 'On the Genesis of Fetishism' (1909) Freud did mention female fetishists, but universalized the practice of clothes fetishism in order to neutralize it as a perversion: 'all women . . . are clothes fetishists . . . It is a question again of the repression of the same drive, this time however in the passive form of allowing oneself to be seen, which is repressed by the clothes, and on account of which clothes are raised to a fetish.'[58] During the process of the splitting of the ego, one aspect of the clothing is repressed while the other is promoted as a fetish. It is not a symbol, but merely related to the moment of repression by dint of circumstance. This is important for a recuperation of female fetishism because it shifts emphasis away from the symbolic meaning of fetishes, and on to the scene of fetishism, deflecting the associative taint of 'phallicism' away from female cross-gendering.

In 'Fetishism', the fetish is inscribed as the ultimate penile substitute because Freud believes that the little boy, who becomes a fetishist, recreates the mother as phallic because the horror of imagining her 'castrated' is too great. The little boy disavows the mother as castrated and uses the fetish to fixate on the moment before the horrifying revelation. This is why, Freud reasons, many of the fetish objects are shoes, boots, feet, velvet, or pieces of fur, because, more often than not, the revelation occurred when the little boy was peering up his mother's skirts. The fetish is used as a 'token of triumph' over the little boy's own possibility of castration; in this sense the fetish is 'fitted' to enable sexual satisfaction to take place.[59] Fetishism operates according to the laws of disavowal, and the ego splits along the line dividing avowal ('I know women do not have penises') from negation ('but I refuse to admit that this is the case'). Freud's conception of castration and disavowal was formulated solely in relation to the male body, its pleasures and desires, which forced him into a psychoanalytic impasse: fetishism did not occur in women.

---

[57] Freud, 'Three Essays', 154.

[58] See Louis Rose (ed.), 'Freud and Fetishism: Previously Unpublished Minutes of the Vienna Psychoanalytic Society', trans. Louis Rose, *Psychoanalytic Quarterly*, 57 (1988), 156.

[59] Sigmund Freud, 'Fetishism' (1927), *SE* 21. 147–57: 154.

That Freud's 'Fetishism' and *The Well* occur within one year of each other is significant, whether Hall read Freud or not. Hall's text, overlaid on to the 'perverse' *The Unlit Lamp*, and read through Freud, is a powerful denial of Freud's conclusion. In this reading the figure of the mother, as in Freud's theories, is central: the father's wish for a boy, and the mother's rejection of the daughter (and the narcissistic wound and splitting of the ego that occurs as a result) can be read as the cause and not the effect of Stephen Gordon's cross-gendering. Stephen's masculine clothing is in fact figured as a fetish through which sexual potency and narcissism are secured and promoted, against the debilitating effects of the withdrawal of the mother's love. Stephen's mother Anna is introduced as the 'arche-type of the very perfect woman' (7), and her beauty is glorified by both Stephen and by the text: the landscape around Stephen's home at Morton, with its 'swelling slopes', takes on the undulating form of the female (mother's) body and the house, which Stephen adores, is like 'certain lovely women' (7). Anna, who wants to fulfil her husband's desire for a son, grieves as she breast-feeds her daughter. Sir Philip, pitying Stephen, remarks on the perfection of her fingers and hands, and Anna, in a bid to recognize and extol this part of the body deemed perfect, kisses them. Stephen's subsequent cross-dressing can arguably be read in terms of reparation of this wound to the infantile sense of self, and her erotic relationship to hands can be traced back to this primal scene of the parents' validation of that perfect part of her imperfect body. It is through the parents' response to their masculine and unwanted child that it is possible to detect the intersection of sexological theory with psychoanalysis. Stephen's father longs for a son, and projects a fantasy that Anna maintains within herself. He is presented as indulging in some kind of disavowal of his own: when his daughter is born he christens her Stephen and encourages her in her masculine behaviour.[60] Her mas-culine body in fact enables both parents to perpetuate their fantasy that they have a son, although the fantasy is less clearly realized in

---

[60] Charlotte Wolff notes that the recognition that the mother would have preferred a male child has an 'injurious effect' upon the little girl. Indeed, these maternal responses 'strike at the heart of the daughter's being, and are an essential cause of the development of lesbianism'. *Love Between Women* (London: Duckworth, 1971), 119. Hall, in notes for an unpublished article about *The Well*, wrote that the 'invert's most deadly enemies are not infrequently his or her parents'. Quoted in Souhami, *The Trials of Radclyffe Hall*, 156.

Anna. Ultimately it is this masculine body that comes to be both cherished and loathed, and through which Stephen attempts to reclaim sexual pleasure and self-love which have been systematically denied.

Stephen, 'acutely responsive to beauty', worships her mother's aesthetic appeal, but finds in her only coldness, antagonism, and near-hatred, which fills her with a 'deep sense of her own short-comings' (11). The self-loathing emanates from the beautiful Anna's response to her daughter who so closely resembles her father:

It would seem to Anna that she must be going mad, for this likeness to her husband would strike her as an outrage—as though the poor, innocent seven-year-old Stephen were in some way a caricature of Sir Philip; a blemished, unworthy, maimed reproduction—yet she knew that the child was handsome. But now there were times when the child's soft flesh would be almost distaste-ful to her; when she hated the way Stephen moved or stood still, hated a certain largeness about her, a certain crude lack of grace in her movements, a certain unconscious defiance. (11)

Anna cannot forget the son of her dreams and of her husband's fan-tasies, and she looks at Stephen, who is a flawed copy of her hus-band, with regret. Stephen, unable to discern the reason for her mother's sadness, nevertheless responds to it. She senses that she is different and demands an explanation of it: 'But what was she? Her thoughts slipping back to her childhood, would find many things in her past that perplexed her. She had never been quite like the other small children' (99). Rebecca O'Rourke remarks that this recognition of difference is 'both indexed against her mother and removes her from her'.[61] Her father affirms the difference which makes her look 'wrong' in her feminine clothing, and unlike Anna. Stephen's sense of identity is henceforth factored against her parents and projected on to a sartorial field. As she remembers later: 'she had always been lonely and discontented, she had always been trying to be someone else—that was why she had dressed herself up as young Nelson' (99).

Hall presents Stephen's subsequent desire to protect those she loves as emanating from the need to protect and conserve Anna's beauty which she herself lacks. She responds much like a lover, admiring her mother's form and physique ('Stephen would stand just a little behind her, thinking how gracious and lovely she was',

[61] O'Rourke, *Reflecting*, 49.

29); her gaze is often directed through her father's and the identification between father and daughter substantiated:

> she too would stand looking at Anna, and sometimes she must catch her breath
> in surprise at the fullness of that calm beauty. She never got used to her
> mother's beauty, it always surprised her each time she saw it; it was one of
> those queerly unbearable things, like the fragrance of meadow-sweet under the
> hedges.
>   Anna might say: 'What's the matter, Stephen? For goodness' sake darling, do
> stop staring!' And Stephen would feel hot with shame and confusion because
> Anna had caught her staring. (32)

Stephen's response to Anna is imbued with some ill-defined sexual
feeling: it is the erotic and troubled mother–daughter relationship of
The Unlit Lamp, but in reverse. In *The Well* it is the mother who
reacts with revulsion at the close physicality of the daughter: 'So
that the girl should not wake and kiss back, she would kiss her
lightly and quickly on the forehead' (81). Moreover, Anna is fiercely
jealous of Stephen's relationship with Sir Philip; she imagines that
her husband and daughter are 'enleagued' against her, that Stephen
has taken her husband from her, and supplanted her in his affections. A 'straightforward' psychoanalytic explanation does not have
to be forcibly extracted from the text: Stephen, as Jean Radford
glosses, can be read as identifying with the loving parent and his
masculinity, and as defending against her mother's response. Taking
the linguistic chain of 'convert-invert-pervert' explored in the first
chapter, she 'converts' anger into idealization, and takes the mother
as love object. In Lacanian terms, she takes the loved one's (her
father's) desire as her own ('But for his sake she must also love the
thing that he loved, her mother', 84).

After the death of Sir Philip (who has taken Stephen's 'secret' to
his grave), and Anna learns of her daughter's sexuality, the 'physical
repulsion' she has felt for Stephen is vindicated. As Radford
observes, Anna can now rationalize her inability to love due to the
fact that she has an unnatural daughter; the mother's testimony
poses Stephen's inversion as cause, and her failure of maternal love
as effect. In fact Hall leaves the issue open-ended; while Anna's
vindication depends upon a congenital explanation that is to some
extent upheld in the narrative, Hall also allows for the possibility that Stephen is unable to 'take up a feminine position' because
her mother is repelled by her at an early age and withdraws her

love.[62] But Stephen blames both her parents, not just her mother: 'it was you and my father who made this body' (204), 'by your passion you created the thing that I am' (237). In this accusation are two conflicting implications: that Stephen is the product of hereditary congenital defect *and* unconscious parental fantasies. It is the ambivalence of Stephen's presentation that enables a 'fetishistic' reading of the text to emerge: in the oscillation between two opposing discourses there is produced a figure of instability and undecidability.

The pivot on which this oscillation moves is Stephen's body. Since she cannot love it, she can gain no physical satisfaction from it. Psychoanalysis teaches that if object-love relationships are not secure, then sexual gratification cannot take place. Whatever provides this security opens the way for the genital orgastic process, and narcissism is the 'libido-cathexis' of the ego from early libidinous object gratification, that is, 'from the security the infant derives, in the sense of being important enough to be loved'.[63] Stephen wishes that her body was as beautiful as her mother's, and because it is not it becomes a thing to be at once pitied and hated. But she converts this into a 'perverse' pride in her masculine figure, and she takes up body-building and fencing to enhance her muscularity. It is her strange but handsome appearance that attracts Angela Crossby and Mary Llewellyn.

'SHE DID NOT KNOW THE MEANING OF HERSELF':
RETHINKING FEMALE FETISHISM THROUGH TERESA DE
LAURETIS AND ELSA B.

Stephen's cross-dressing presents simultaneously with her developing interest in her body. More than a mere outward manifestation of sexual inversion, Stephen's transvestism takes on many different aspects and fulfils a number of functions, one of which is to sustain a fragile

---

[62] Jean Radford, 'An Inverted Romance: *The Well of Loneliness* and Sexual Ideology', in Jean Radford (ed.), *The Progress of Romance: The Politics of Popular Fiction* (London: Routledge & Kegan Paul, 1986), 96–111: 101.

[63] Sandor S. Feldman, 'On Homosexuality', in Sandor Lorand and Michael Balint (eds.), *Perversions, Psychodynamics and Therapy* (1956; London: The Ortolan Press, 1965), 71–96: 78.

sense of self. This function of cross-dressing is also intimately related to Stephen's desire to project her identity. When her mother attempts to impose her own soft and expensive feminine dresses upon Stephen, the latter rejects them, claiming that her body and face are ill-suited to them, and sees in her mother the confirmation and reflection of this fact:

But Stephen had seen that fleeting expression, and she stood very still when her mother had left her, her own face growing heavy and sombre with anger, with a sense of some uncomprehended injustice. She wrenched off the dress and hurled it from her, longing intensely to rend it, to hurt it, longing to hurt herself in the process, yet filled all the while with that sense of injustice. But this mood changed abruptly to one of self pity; she wanted to sit down and weep over Stephen, on a sudden impulse she wanted to pray over Stephen as though she were someone apart, yet terribly personal too in her trouble. Going over to the dress she smoothed it out slowly; it seemed to have acquired an enormous importance; it seemed to have acquired the importance of prayer, the poor, crumpled thing lying crushed and dejected. (71–2)

In this passage Hall presents Stephen's psychic motivations for her transvestism. While she wants to wear the clothes that her mother has chosen for her because she desires the mother and wants to be loved by her, the clothes make her look grotesque. Stephen's dresses accrue all the bitterness that is directed towards Stephen by her mother, and the father's secret desires for a son, and take on aspects of Stephen's 'lost' femininity.[64] As Stephen projects on to this dress her rejected femininity, the narration splits ('she wanted to sit down and weep over Stephen'), and she can only react to the dress as a facet of her self ('the poor, crumpled thing lying crushed and dejected').

Splitting is a defensive process which occurs when ego-integrity is threatened; following Gillespie, it is understood to describe the ego in sexual perversions, particularly fetishism. According to Freud the ego of the fetishist is split inasmuch as the attitude towards the object allows one to disavow castration anxiety, which another part of the ego admits. Since the splitting process has occurred at a moment of sartorial and somatic dysphoria, it would follow, given

---

[64] See Robert Dickes, 'Parents, Transitional Objects and Childhood Fetishes', in S. A. Grolnick and L. Barkin (eds.), *Between Reality and Fantasy* (New York: Jason Aronson, 1978), 307–19, for an analysis of how parental responses affect the development of their children's fetishism.

that the fetish is chosen for its metonymic relation to the moment of repression rather than a metaphoric aspect, that fetishism, which functions in order to protect the ego, should operate within a sartorial and somatic field. Since a struggle over an item of female clothing has precipitated the split, it follows that Stephen turns to masculine clothing in order to repair the damage.

Stephen aims to please her mother by wearing feminine clothing, but when she comes of age she chooses tailor-made masculine clothes, and Anna is forced to withdraw. When she falls in love with Angela she becomes more anxious about her appearance to the point of over-indulgence and narcissism; she spends hours before a mirror, cataloguing her faults and advantages, and nurturing an incipient clothes fetishism, indulging herself in the things that Joan Ogden could not allow herself:

She would wear a black tie—no, better a grey one to match the new suit with the little white pin stripe. She ordered not one new suit but three, and she also ordered a pair of brown shoes; indeed she spent most of the afternoon in ordering things for her personal adornment. She heard herself being ridiculously fussy about details, disputing with her tailor over buttons; disputing with her bootmaker over the shoes, their thickness of sole, their amount of broguing; disputing regarding the match of her ties with the young man who sold her handkerchiefs and neckties—for such trifles had assumed an enormous importance. (135)

For Stephen, as for Joan, these objects take on a sexual significance because they have been purchased with her lover in mind, and she 'would feel little shivers of pleasure creeping' (135) into her body; the split narrativized in the confrontation with Anna is reproduced here in the phrase 'she heard herself'.

Throughout the novel Stephen's cross-dressing is used to attract other women. As a child she cross-dressed for Collins, the housemaid, who is her first object of desire. She revels in Collins's admiration of her dressed as the young Nelson; if Collins responds with less than excessive admiration she would 'tear off the clothes she so dearly loved donning, to replace them by the garments she hated' (16). Stephen wonders later whether her childhood transvestiture had been anything more than some sort of 'inadequate childish protest', which she had nevertheless enjoyed (99). At a moment of conflict and unhappiness with Angela she buys more clothes for herself, including an ornate man's dressing gown and a pair of white crêpe de Chine pyjamas.[65] In competition with her childhood adversary Robert Antrim for Angela's affections, her moment of extreme consumerist extravagance is both a means of signalling to Roger that she is worthy manly competition, and of gaining access to her acquisitive lover. The act gives her a 'fleeting satisfaction', but leads to deep self-loathing:

That night she stared at herself in the glass; and even as she did so she hated her body with its muscular shoulders, its small compact breasts, and its slender flanks of an athlete. All her life she must drag this body of hers like a monstrous fetter imposed on her spirit. This strangely ardent yet sterile body that must worship yet never be worshipped in return by the creature of its adoration. She longed to maim it, for it made her feel cruel; it was so white, so strong and so self-sufficient; yet withal so poor and unhappy a thing that her eyes filled with tears and her hate turned to pity. She began to grieve over it, touching her breasts with pitiful fingers, stroking her shoulders, letting her hands slip along her straight things—Oh, poor and most desolate body!

Then she, for whom Puddle was actually praying at that moment, must now pray also, but blindly; finding few words that seemed worthy of prayer, few words that seemed to encompass her meaning—for she did not know the meaning of herself. (187–8)

Stephen is presented ambivalently in this passage, which reveals Radclyffe Hall's own uncertainty about her creation and the status of fictional fantasy itself. The anger that turns to pity also turns to self-love as Stephen's fingers travel from her breasts and shoulders downwards to her thighs in a masturbatory movement that is also a

---

[65] The incidence of whiteness (white pyjamas which clothe Stephen's white body) is noteworthy in the light of Cassandra Laity's study of a homoerotic code of decadence employed by H.D., which includes imagery of white Greek statuary (see Chapter 3). *H.D. and the Victorian Fin de Siècle: Gender, Modernism, Decadence* (Cambridge: Cambridge University Press, 1996). In Djuna Barnes's short story 'Dusie' (1927), a cross-gendered woman dresses in a man's white dressing-gown (see Chapter 4). Valérie Seymour is dressed in white when Stephen meets her for the first time, and as a child Stephen tells her mother that the 'white smell' of flowers reminds her of her (28). The lure of silk pyjamas was compelling for Hall's circle. Her friend Naomi 'Mickie' Jacob recalled Hall in her final illness: 'John was in bed, immaculate as always, her hair shining and sleek, her pyjamas the last word in silk elegance. I always told her that her pyjamas roused the spirit of furious envy in me!' *Me—and the Swans* (London: William Kimber, 1963), 127. Vita Sackville-West bought her lover Evelyn Irons a suitcase full of men's silk pyjamas. Victoria Glendinning, *Vita: The Life of Vita Sackville-West* (London: Weidenfeld and Nicolson, 1983), 242. Angela Crossby is reminded of Stephen when she has to endure 'flaccid' embraces from her husband dressed in *pink* pyjamas: the allusions to his impotence and effeminacy contrast with Stephen's potency and manliness.

gesture of self-protection and reparation.[66] This is the body that Stephen has in effect created: while born already endowed with masculine characteristics, she has enhanced her muscularity to the stage where it is not only white, strong, and self-sufficient, but also, as Teresa de Lauretis notes, phallic.[67] According to de Lauretis's influential reading, she wishes to mutilate it because it bears the mark of 'castration', and therefore is 'inadequate' to signify and bear the subject's desire. She argues for 'the very effectiveness of castration as a psychic structure' since it figures 'the internalized prohibition or inaccessibility of the first (lost) object of desire that is the mother's body.' Therefore castration anxiety is composed of 'allowing access to desire itself, the phallus representing at once the mark of difference and lack, the threat of castration, and the signifier of desire'.[68] In the case of Stephen Gordon, it is not the paternal phallus, but, as de Lauretis argues, a fetish which 'signifies at once the absence of the object of desire (the female body) and the subject's wish for it'.[69]

[66] Compare this with what Emily Apter has called 'narcissistically defined female fetishism' in Zola's *Nana* (1880) with reference to Nana's scene before the mirror in which she fondles parts of her body while kissing her reflection. *Feminizing the Fetish: Psychoanalysis and Narrative Obsession in Turn-of-the-Century France* (Ithaca, NY: Cornell University Press, 1991), 47.

[67] Teresa de Lauretis, *The Practice of Love: Lesbian Sexuality and Perverse Desire* (Bloomington, Ind.: Indiana University Press, 1994), 241.

[68] Ibid. 212, 216.

[69] Ibid. 222. See also Judith Halberstam's reading against de Lauretis in *Female Masculinity* (Durham, NC, and London: Duke University Press, 1998), 102–6. Halberstam 'vigorously' resists de Lauretis's reading which sees Stephen's lesbian desire as 'always a melancholic attempt to make up for her masculinity that is not male and femaleness that is not feminine', believing that such a reading 'confirms the most conservative attempts to shore up the essential and historical relations between masculinity and men and condemns masculine women once more to the pathos of male mimicry' (102). Halberstam re-reads *The Well*'s mirror scene in terms of Stephen's 'disidentification with the naked body' (106). This interpretation is important and persuasive, but it over-reads the 'liberating' aspects of Hall's representation and does not attend to the fissures and discontinuities in the text, which as I argue are part of the discourse of fetishism. See also Jay Prosser's reading of this scene (*Second Skins*, 155–69), which sees Hall eschewing psychoanalytic theory (which she does *overtly*, but not *covertly*), noting that the one reference to a psychoanalyst (Sandor Ferenczi) is in one of Brockett's cruel jokes. But I would argue that it is not the case that in referencing psychoanalysis in this way (through a Freudian 'joke') Hall refuses psychoanalysis, but that she at once avows and disavows it. Prosser reads Stephen as 'transgendered' rather than as a fetishist, and while there is much to be admired in this interpretation Prosser again over-reads Stephen, downplaying the narrative instabilities of her figuration through the conflicting discourses of fetishism and inversion, and ignoring the later mirror scene involving Mary. Melanie A. Taylor also argues that the 'transgender aspects' of the characterization of Stephen Gordon need to be accounted for, in order to show how theories of inversion 'failed to distinguish between cross-gender identification and same-sex desire'. While this certainly

She succumbs to the attraction of masculine clothing ('Nor could she resist the lure of pyjamas made of white crêpe de Chine', 221), because it signifies her desire for both the body she desires for herself as subject (her own body) and object (her lover); masculine clothes at once fetishize the female body beneath the clothing and enhance her allure as a lover. In the passage quoted above it is possible to discern the same processes at work that were evident in Stephen's moment of sartorial unease. In this case her hatred for her own body precipitates a splitting process as she begins to contemplate her body as something distinct from herself; she must love it in order to return it to herself.

In the early 1920s a 34-year-old woman called Elsa B. bearing marked similarities to Stephen Gordon, presented herself in a mixture of feminine and masculine clothing before the sexologist Emil Gutheil, not for treatment but so that she could have documentation to permit her to wear men's clothing in public. As for Stephen Gordon, female clothing is 'the signal for a bitter struggle' for Elsa B.[70] Contemporaneous with Hall's novels, Gutheil's report can be used to extract from them a more comprehensive theory of female fetishistic cross-gendering. Gutheil notes that Elsa's primary and secondary sexual characteristics are of normal appearance, but that she has a 'male type of walk' and urinates in a standing position.[71] As a child she played with boys' things and became attached to a winter coat resembling a hussar's uniform; she developed a pronounced aversion to feminine clothing during her adolescence. A desire to cross-dress manifested in her early teens, and she began to cross-dress fully in her early twenties.

Elsa B. displays characteristics and attitudes that Gutheil interprets as indicative of female assimilation of masculinity. She remembers that at 8 years old she noticed her brother's penis and was envious of it for its difference; she dreamt at the time that she had a penis, and in reality would masturbate in the position of a male

---

does need to be addressed, I think Taylor's reading of Stephen's substitution of her own (female) body for the (male) body that has been lost, which is a simple 'inversion' of de Lauretis's model, is misleading. ' "The Masculine Soul Heaving in the Female Bosom": Theories of Inversion and *The Well of Loneliness*', *Journal of Gender Studies*, 7.3 (Nov. 1998), 287–96: 287, 292.

[70] Emil Gutheil, 'Analysis of a Case of Transvestism', in *Sexual Aberrations: The Phenomena of Fetishism in Relation to Sex*, ed. Wilhelm Stekel, trans. S. Parker (London: John Lane, The Bodley Head, 1930), ii. 281–318: 281.

[71] Ibid. 281.

during coitus. Her closest relationship is with her elderly landlady whom she calls 'mother', and in her fantasies she sees herself as father of a family, having penetrative sex with a wife. Her sexual interest is directed towards women but she has not had any direct sexual contact. The most significant aspect of this case report, however, is the woman's testimony which asserts that her cross-dressing is sexually motivated and fulfilling, with fetishistic aspects:

As regards clothing, I may say that simply putting on men's clothing gives me pleasure. The whole procedure is comparable to that of tense anticipation of pleasure which subsides in relief and gratification as soon as the transvestiture is complete. I even experience lustful satisfaction in dreams of this act . . . It affords me downright sexual pleasure. Simply putting on my suit can provoke an orgasm . . . The transvestiture has a far greater pleasure-value in my eyes than any intercourse, and I could easily forgo the latter in favor of the former.[72]

Cross-dressing first occurred at the age of 14 in a suit belonging to her brother, producing sexual relief. In childhood wearing the hussar's coat gave her feelings of superiority for the first time in her life, which suggests that the transvestism, as with Stephen Gordon, may be connected with repairing a narcissistic wound. Her stepfather had told her that she was ugly and she believed him, but cross-dressed she felt that she looked handsome, like her father. The fetish (masculine clothing) does not only deflect interest away from the castrated body, but alleviates anxiety about an old wound to the ideal self inflicted by the mother (or the father).

Gutheil certainly understands Elsa to have a mother fixation when she reveals that her mother had not wanted a baby girl, and had neglected her. She experienced an orgasmic sexual response in fantasies of a mother figure, and the language used to describe the feeling employs the same figures of speech as the first part of the previous passage: the slipping on of masculine clothes is similar to a mother figure 'lovingly slipping her hands' down Elsa's head and face, or over her cheeks, to the extent that she would feel these fantasies 'so intensively that I could almost sense them physically and a shudder of delight would run through me'.[73] It is possible that Elsa's transvestism became a psychic and sexual necessity because of the narcissistic wounds inflicted upon her in infancy, and that transvestism enabled her both to alleviate the anxiety felt when attention was directed towards her body, and to allow her to enjoy and

---

[72] Ibid. 284, 289.   [73] Ibid. 287.

fetishize her femininity beneath the male clothing. Gutheil recognizes that the root of Elsa's fetishism lies in an infantile narcissistic wound:

> Her mother turned away from her in earliest infancy, neglected to satisfy her need for affections and soon gave her to understand that she was not wanted because a boy had been desired. But what was the difference in the girl's eyes? Her first answer was: the clothes. But, regardless of what the real difference may have been, she did not want to be a girl. When, later, her stepfather kept telling her she was ugly, she resisted the humiliation doggedly, long before she realized what may have been the basis for it. She simply wanted to be pretty ... the feeling of femininity and the sense of personal ugliness soon injured her infantile narcissism to such an extent that her healthy psychic orientation was repressed.
>
> One day she recognized the real basis of sex differences and then it first dawned upon her why she could not achieve her mother's love. Her infantile mind was then convinced that the only attribute which attracted a mother's love was the possession of a certain physical adnexa.[74]

This recognition was first formulated, Gutheil reasons, in penis envy and the castration complex: Elsa meted out various castrative retributions against her brother (a nail in his food, an accident that required a nasal operation, for example). But when it became clear that she would never grow a penis, she 'disappeared in the developing fiction of her own maleness'. Gutheil, of course, means the penis when he speaks of 'physical adnexa', but if we substituted, following de Lauretis, 'a body that could be loved' we reach a better understanding of female cross-gendered behaviour.

Gutheil remains beholden to the laws of a phallic sexual economy. He cannot understand the masculine accoutrements, used as fetishes, by Elsa, as anything other than penile substitutes. As a consequence, the logic of his interpretation fails: Elsa's transvestism results in both symbolic sexual contact with the father, *and* the impetus to seek a mother substitute as a love object. The problem, again, is that Gutheil does not really consider female transvestism as a genuine form of fetishism. He believes, ultimately, that it is a form of 'compulsion neurosis' in which the 'patient's desire for the genital of the other sex is displaced to the clothing'.[75] If the physical

---

[74] Gutheil, 'Analysis of a Case of Transvestism', 307.   [75] Ibid. 318.

adnexa that Elsa lacks is understood to be a feminine body that is loved, then the reaction to herself in male clothing and the fantasies of a loving mother make sense: she believes that vanity plays a large part in her life and visualizes herself as a 'rather handsome male' when cross-dressed. Most significantly, she associates being hand-some with being virile, and in Elsa the fetishization of a beautiful body, as with Stephen Gordon, allows her to experience deep satis-faction. Oppression is lifted from her, and sexual pleasure is allowed to take place, not because she now believes that she is in possession of a penis, but because the assumption of masculine clothing allows her to relish the handsome male that she has become, and as a consequence to rediscover and love the body beneath the clothing. If we rephrase the terms of the equation, female transvestism becomes a means of glorifying the *sexual* female body.

MANIPULATING THE FETISH: WRITING AND (DIS)EMBODIMENT

Expanding on, and deviating from, de Lauretis's theory of the les-bian fetish, this section explores the linguistic nature of splitting and its effect on embodiment. Throughout *The Well* the splitting process is accompanied by a failure of language: 'Language is surely too small to contain those emotions of mind and body that have some-how awakened a response in the spirit' (320). Indeed, the lack pre-cisely of words with which to know and come to terms with herself, reinforces the proposal that female fetishistic cross-gendering is understood by these women writers to be a specifically sexual and *textual* process. This is enforced through the pervasive imagery of hands as a writerly tool, a sexual instrument, and a lesbian fetish in *The Well*, which significantly widens the meaning of this symbol as it appears in *The Unlit Lamp*. The struggles that Stephen confronts in her writing, the split she experiences between invert and artist, throws into relief, in this very oscillation, the fetishistic nature of fic-tion writing for the 'inverted' writer. It is significant that writing functions for Stephen in much the same way as her transvestism, by at once drawing attention to her 'lack' (of the female body, not the penis) and providing a means whereby that lack can be addressed. Stephen is encouraged in the appreciation of 'all literary beauty' by her governess Puddle, who, like Beatrice Lesway, has a masculine

appearance with none of the suppleness and beauty of Joan's and
Stephen's bodies: 'it seemed square all over—square shoulders,
square hips, a flat, square line of bosom; square tips to the fingers,
square toes to the shoes' (65). Like Beatrice, Puddle has a specific
function: to allow the lesbian subject to recognize herself, and to
encourage her to write 'with a curious double insight', which will
enable her, evasively, to capture 'queer hopes, queer longings, queer
joys and even more curious frustrations':

Writing, it was like a heavenly balm, it was like the flowing out of deep waters,
it was like the lifting of a load from the spirit; it brought with it a sense of relief,
of assuagement. One could say things in writing without feeling self-conscious,
without feeling shy and ashamed and foolish—one could even write of the days
of young Nelson, smiling a very little as one did so. (68)

Writing for Stephen is a sexual, if not fetishistic process: it is
described in terms of 'relief' and 'assuagement', connotative of both
the sexual and reparative nature of sexual fetishism. It is also significant that Stephen should be reminded of her childhood and her
early transvestiture as young Nelson: cross-gendering and writing
hold the same power of erotic release, and the fusion of the two is a
corollary to Bryher's intimate relation between inversion and creativity. The implication in the passage quoted above is that fiction is
particularly suited to the expression of sexual fantasy, and therefore
is susceptible to the vicissitudes of desire and subject-formation. It
is in this sense that *The Well* is a fetishistic text: in Hall's self-
promoting fantasy, the ambivalence which generates Stephen
Gordon has implications for the production of the text itself. In its
oscillation between its adherence to inversion theory on the one
hand, and its narrative of female fetishism on the other, it offers
itself to be read as radically split. The split is enmeshed in the story
of Stephen as fiction-writer: the price of the seduction by sexology
is that Stephen's writing must suffer.

Writing and sexology are brought together in the figure of Sir
Philip. It is through his secret marginal notes to texts by Ulrichs, that
he not only 'reads' his daughter, but also quantifies her and makes
her into his own case history. (This contrasts poignantly with
Stephen's 'non-comprehension' of 'Why am I as I am—and what
am I?', 152). The father also encourages Stephen in her own 'queer
compositions' (78), spending hours closeted in his study, ousting
the mother—who notices that Stephen and Sir Philip's hands are

similar—discussing the 'smell and the essence of books' (78). After Sir Philip's death Stephen cannot write, but she returns to writing in earnest after her estrangement from both Angela Crossby and her mother; her first novel is born out of her attachment to her home and all that it had come to signify to her. Writing soon becomes painful for Stephen when the playwright Brockett, co-opting the clothing motif, tells her that her second novel is a failure, without any emotional centre, like a dress hung on a dummy. (Brockett, in contrast, is an emotional vampire, who 'fed his genius on live flesh and blood', 235). The implication that she has been merely playing with words, while ignoring the 'body' of the work cuts to the core of Stephen's anxiety about her own body/text: she feels that her heart which will not bleed any more is a 'dry, withered thing' (235). Her first novel 'The Furrow' has literally written itself on and into her body, which is now a mass of heavy (textual) lines: the 'strong rather massive line of the jaw looked aggressive these days by reason of its thinness. Faint furrows had come between the thick brows' (210). In accordance with this new body, she has further masculinized her appearance by smoking and cutting her hair very short ('In a mood of defiance she had suddenly walked off to the barber's one morning and had made him crop it close like a man's', 210). Stephen ascribes the failure of her writing to lack: 'there's something wrong with it. I mean that my work could be much more vital; I feel it, I know it, I'm holding it back in some way, there's something I'm always missing' (216). The lack is specifically that of a loved (sexual) body:

Why have I been afflicted with a body that must never be indulged, that must always be repressed until it grows much stronger than my spirit because of this unnatural repression? What have I done to be so cursed? And now it's attacking my holy of holies, my work—I shall never be a great writer because of my maimed and insufferable body—(217)

Stephen's writing fails because of her fractured sense of self—for Stephen, who is paradigmatic of the modernist 'woman writer', unity is a crucial idea in traditional concepts of creative success and healthy embodiment. Could her text in all its disunities actually be proto-modernist? This is reflected in the text of *The Well* itself which is at certain points off-kilter, repetitious, and obsessive; this is evident in the very last section of the novel which has an hallucinatory feel, conveyed in the repeated ellipses, the final splitting of the subject ('No, assuredly this was not Stephen Gordon who stood there unmoved by such pitiful sobbing', 445), and the motifs of atrophy.

It is only through her relationship with Mary that Stephen is restored to herself both physically and in her writing. (It is worth noting that in Mary's own writing—the letter to Stephen—she writes of those things 'a less privileged pen had best left unwritten—loyalty, faith, consolation, devotion; all this and much more she wrote to Stephen', 341). Returning to her writing, after having known sexual and loving fulfilment, Stephen writes from a different perspective, with 'wholeness', and for Mary: 'love was the actual source of her effort' (346). Mary is pretty and feminine enough to offer Stephen the narcissistic empowerment that she craves, and to return Stephen's body to herself. Stephen is able to play out her own failed mother–daughter relationship as part of being 'all things' to Mary: 'father, mother, friend and lover'. But Mary is also the mother to Stephen, as a 'perfect woman', the fantasized Anna (318). What Mary finds sexually alluring in Stephen *is* her body. In an important scene which takes place after Stephen and Mary have returned to Paris from their Orotavan honeymoon, Mary enters Stephen's bedroom 'quite without fear or restraint or shyness', which gives her 'a warm little glow of pleasure', to find Stephen brushing her short hair:

Seeing Mary in the glass she did not turn round, but just smiled for a moment at their two reflections. Mary sat down in an arm-chair and watched her, noticing the strong, thin line of her thighs; noticing too the curve of her breasts—slight and compact, of a certain beauty. She had taken off her jacket and looked very tall in her soft silk shirt and skirt of dark serge. (323)

This repairs the damage of the earlier mirror scene: it is the same body, but one that is viewed through the desiring eyes of Mary, an inversion, as it were, of the former gaze. This is a moment of simultaneity in which the lovers' gazes collide: Stephen desires Mary who desires a Stephen who can desire herself. The fetish of masculinity (the 'heavy silk masculine underwear', and the masculine shirts which Mary finds in Stephen's wardrobe) is both what entrances the lover and what signifies her own desire.[76] Indeed, the lover, in this

[76] Hall's letters to her lover Evguenia Souline are full of intricate details about clothing—about what she is wearing ('I say to myself that I dress for you'; 'I wanted to ask you this morning whether you thought my white collar was clean enough to wear a second time and what stock I should put on'), and detailed advice about what Souline should wear, mainly for health reasons, but also to please her ('Don't laugh, but I often

case sustains and finds some fetishistic pleasure in the masculine woman: Mary perversely insists on looking after Stephen's clothing, sewing on buttons and darning her socks, despite the fact that no such imperfections exist in Stephen's wardrobe. When they go shopping, it is Mary who stares at the 'temptations' on offer in the shop windows, and picks out Stephen's scarves and neckties. As Hall's letters to her lover Souline suggest, Hall believed that the congenital invert was defined not solely by mannish dress style, or by behaviour, but by the object of her desire.[77] Could it then be the case that by sustaining Stephen's clothes fetishism, Mary in turn becomes a fetishist?

Restoring her body to herself means being loved by a feminine and beautiful woman, and this is what Stephen desires in her mother and Angela Crossby (whose name suggests gender 'crossing'). Like Anna, Angela is consistently described as delicate, white, and vulnerable in her beauty, the one for whom Stephen indulges her love of feminine accoutrements. Their first meeting precisely replicates the erotic scene in *The Unlit Lamp* when the sight of Elizabeth's damaged hand arouses Joan. When Stephen first encounters Angela a dog has bitten her hands, and she is sucking the blood from her fingers (in another echo of *The Unlit Lamp* with its pervasive vampire motif).[78] Hall in *The Well* manipulates the symbolism of the hand as a sexual object in order to convey a sexuality that has been

think about your cloths [*sic*]. As far as possible you should always wear collars like the one on the black coat you had at Bagnoles—an upright collar, even higher than that one—and I liked the silver clasp, it was right . . . How I do adore to have the dressing of you'). She buys clothes for Souline like her own, and performs Mary's ministrations for Stephen, putting away Souline's 'crêpe de chine combination', and preparing her stockings. She feels the same tidiness about her books: 'I can't see it go out with a button undone, with its left shoe off and its face & hands dirty!' References to Souline's beautiful hands are also numerous. *Your John: The Love Letters of Radclyffe Hall*, ed. Joanne Glasgow (New York and London: New York University Press, 1997), 67, 26, 43, 85.

[77] See Joanne Glasgow, introduction, *Your John: The Love Letters of Radclyffe Hall*, 10.

[78] Naomi Schor has assessed the 'erotic charge' of wounds to the hand. See 'Female Fetishism: The Case of George Sand', *Poetics Today*, 6.1–2 (1985), 301–10. In both *Hungerheart* and her essay 'Close-Up' (1949) Christopher St John recounts her first meeting with Edy Craig who was busy mending a mitten and 'did not put it down before shaking hands, with the result that I was pricked by her needle. Cupid's dart, for I loved Edy from that moment'. *Edy: Recollections of Edith Craig*, ed. Eleanor Adlard (London: Frederick Muller, 1949), 16–34: 19. Pain is an essential part of the fictionalized relationship between the women in *Hungerheart*.

systematically circumscribed.[79] Hands signal both pleasure and disgust. Anna is displeased by the young Stephen's 'curiously strong' fingers which feel like Sir Philip's (30), while Stephen longs for the touch of Anna's cool, pure hand; Stephen implores Angela to hold her hand tighter because she likes the feel of her fingers, and buys her a pearl ring to match the cool white of her hands; in contrast Stephen's hands are 'sunburnt and weather-beaten' (165), bony and masculine: 'they had never been skilful when it came to illness; strong they might be, but rather inept; not hands wherewith to succour the wounded' (271); Collins notices the young Stephen's dirty nails and she blushes at the reproach; while Brockett's unpleasantly feminine hands make Stephen feel a 'queer little sense of outrage' (227). The first thing Valérie Seymour notices about Stephen is her 'tell-tale fingers' (246) that have been stained by smoking (two lesbian signifiers here collide in Valérie's expert gaze). The paucity of Stephen's relationship with Angela is finally symbolized through the imagery of empty hands, while at the end of the novel Stephen is accused by 'those terrible ones' of indeterminate gender, pointing at her with their 'shaking, white-skinned effeminate fingers' (446). However, hand imagery also signals the onset of Mary and Stephen's sexual relationship, as language fails: 'Stephen bent down and kissed Mary's hands very humbly, for now she could find no words any more . . . and that night they were not divided' (316, Hall's ellipsis).

[79] An edition of *The Well* (Pocket Books, 1964) had depicted on its cover a green hand reaching up to clasp a descending blue hand. Michèle Aina Barale notes that the placement of hands (vertical not horizontal) hints at sexual inequality in terms of dominance and submission. The thrusting green hand has its index finger extended while the descending blue hand has its index finger separated from the rest of the hand forming a 'V' and suggesting invagination. Barale remarks: 'what we are invited to infer is that the unseen genitals of one of these missing fingers . . . has genitals more male than female'. 'Below the Belt: (Un)Covering *The Well of Loneliness*', in Diana Fuss (ed.), *Inside/Out: Lesbian Theories, Gay Theories* (New York: Routledge, 1991), 235–57: 241. In Constance Fenimore Woolson's sexually ambiguous short story 'Felipa' (1876), about a young girl who dresses in boys' clothes and is obsessed with an older, beautiful woman, similar imagery is used: 'The child caught the descending hand and kissed the long white fingers.' Joan Myers Weimer (ed.), *Women Artists, Women Exiles: 'Miss Grief' and Other Stories* (New Brunswick, NJ, and London: Rutgers University Press, 1988), 150. (This story also anticipates motifs found in many of the novels under discussion here: the injured Felipa takes great joy in being nursed by her beloved; her 'second self' is a dog, and she makes a crude doll which looks like a 'fetich'; see *Nightwood*; she is a 'queer thing' who has a special relationship with trees; see *HER*; she obsesses over her beloved's beauty and wishes to be like her, despite her 'ugliness'.)

Judith Roof argues that lesbian sexuality in a mainstream system is a 'point of the failure of and return to a heterosexual system, that is defined not as male/female, but as male and not male', in which the fetish persistently reappears in order to maintain this system. Roof notes that in the heterosexual system the fetish is the signifier of 'no difference', in that it provides something to see in heterosexually phallic terms.[80] Roof warns that the hand as fetish is close to Freud's notion of the penis substitute, as a visual sign of both the presence and absence of the penis on women. As she notes, its persistent presence as part of the woman's body, as 'intimate participant in sexual activity', defends against its obvious exclusion.[81] The hand in *The Well*, however, is not the Freudian penile substitute, but a fetish that works like Stephen's masculine clothing/body—a part of the body used to mark difference between lovers and signal attraction. If the lesbian fetish is often an object or sign with connotations of masculinity or active sexuality, this is not because it is a substitute for the lacking penis, but because, as de Lauretis argues, 'such signs are most strongly pre-coded to convey both to the subject and to others, the cultural meaning of sexual (genital) activity and yearning toward women'. Such signs can effectively deny the subject's female body, but can also resignify her desire for it through the symbolization of its prohibition.[82]

Stephen's early desire for the housemaid Collins can now be read through the tropes of fetishism. This desire is stimulated by Collins chiding Stephen for her dirty fingernails; Stephen then furiously scrubs them clean and parades her sore 'plump red fingers' in front of the maid. This desire becomes inextricably linked with her early cross-dressing as the young Nelson, which Stephen performs to impress Collins, who, in her turn 'plays up' to Stephen and indulges her in her fantasy of being a boy. Both hands and cross-dressing are associated with physical maiming, one of the recurrent motifs of the novel. As in *The Unlit Lamp* in which Elizabeth's maiming provokes Joan's desire, Stephen, who wants to relieve some of Collins's burden of suffering from housemaid's knee, first of all fantasizes 'that in some queer way she was Jesus, and that Collins was kneeling and kissing her hand, because she, Stephen, had managed to cure her by

---

[80] Judith Roof, *A Lure of Knowledge: Lesbian Sexuality and Theory* (New York: Columbia University Press, 1991), 65.
[81] Ibid. 64.   [82] De Lauretis, *The Practice of Love*, 263.

cutting off her knee with a bone paper-knife and grafting it on to her own'. Significantly this fantasy of dismemberment of the loved one, and rememberment of the loved one in oneself is a 'mixture of rapture and discomfort' for Stephen (18). She then physically attempts to take on the symptoms of housemaid's knee by scraping her knees along the floor until they are red and swollen (like her fingers). Hall suggests that Stephen, who is read by others as 'blemished, unworthy, maimed' (11), converts this into a means of accessing a desire which 'she could never quite put into words' (20). As in *The Unlit Lamp*, tropes of articulation and silence play an important part in *The Well*: 'they were silent'; 'there was so much that might not be spoken between them'. Around such phrases desires cluster and await expression.

When Stephen, who has just acquired a new set of tailor-made clothes, comes to Angela's aid after her hands have been bitten, she misreads this promiscuous woman as a child-like girl who seemed to be like 'some rare, pale flower without blemish or stain' (130).[83] Stephen is enraptured by her very white skin, and her 'amazingly blonde' hair which is almost silver, and which she wears short 'like a mediaeval page': 'it was straight, and came just to the lobes of her ears, which at that time of pompadours and much curling gave her an unusual appearance' (129). In the sense that Angela is, in Stephen's fantasized version of her, interchangeable with the mother, this lover–mother relationship is an interesting twist on that in *The Unlit Lamp*. The maiming of Angela's hands kick-starts the relationship between the two women which reaches an erotic, but perverse, climax combining the imagery of clothes and damaged hands: Angela who has just returned to Upton is found by Stephen unpacking her feminine clothes and is 'all but snowed under by masses of soft, inadequate garments. The bedroom smelt strongly of Angela's scent, which was heavy yet slightly pungent' (175). In this ultra-feminine space Angela addresses the problem of their relationship: that Stephen is not a man. Stephen castigates herself

---

[83] Leslie J. Henson reads Angela's characterization as the stereotypical 'faux femme': 'the feminine woman who gets involved with other women but isn't "really a lesbian" '. As a feminine woman, but also as a working-class woman who has worked as a dancer and a prostitute, 'the text offers a classic sexological denial of femme desire. Thus, Angela allows herself to be swept away only because "Stephen's need was now hers, by sheer force of its blind and uncomprehending will to appeasement" '. ' "Articulate Silence[s]": Femme Subjectivity and Class Relations in *The Well of Loneliness*', in Laura Harris and Elizabeth Crocker (eds.), *Femme: Feminists, Lesbians, and Bad Girls* (New York and London: Routledge, 1997), 61–7: 62.

for being unable to 'protect' Angela ('Then would come the most poignant suffering of all, the deepest, the final humiliation. Protection—she could never offer protection to the creature she loved . . . She could neither protect nor defend nor honour by loving; her hands were completely empty', 152). Angela prepares Stephen for her ultimate betrayal by confiding her life story, which is shot through with details of physical deprivation, most notably the damage done to her hands from bleeding chilblains. The imagery of hands and blemishes multiplies at the end of the chapter culminating in encoded sexual release: one of Angela's tears makes a 'small, dark blot' in Stephen's coat sleeve; Angela's face is 'marred by weeping; it looked almost ugly, splotched and reddened as it was by her weeping' (182). The failure of language combines with sexual desire in a precursor to Stephen's sexual relationship with Mary, and, as in *The Unlit Lamp*, scarring and the erasure of beauty set the scene for erotic release: 'And because of that pitiful, blemished face, with the pitiful weakness that lay behind it, the unworthiness even, Stephen loved her so deeply at that moment, that she found no adequate words' (182). Instead of words, Stephen places the pearl ring, which reminds her of the purity of her mother's diamonds, on 'the hand that used to bleed in the winter' (182). It is a restoration of beauty to the damaged body, and a signifier of the protection that as a lover she is capable of offering, but in the end, with Mary, which she is unable to provide. The imagery of blemishes pertains additionally to Stephen whose body is inscribed as maimed and ugly. Throughout the novel she speaks of wishing to harm herself given that in the eyes of God she has already been branded with what she imagines is the mark of Cain: 'there are so many of us—thousands of miserable, unwanted people, who have no right to love, no right to compassion because they're maimed, hideously maimed and ugly—God's cruel; He let us get flawed in the making' (207). When Valérie Seymour is drawn to her, it is not for her talent or intellect but for her 'outward stigmata of the abnormal' (247). While an ambulance driver in France she receives a shrapnel wound that leaves a long livid scar that becomes inflamed during moments of passion.[84] After she is wounded, she and Mary Llewellyn form a close

---

[84] One of Hall's early sonnets, 'The Scar', provides the key to understanding this motif: 'Upon my life I bear one precious scar: | Each night I kiss it, till anew it bleeds, | And tell each drop of blood, as hallowed beads | Are told by those dear few who faithful are. | To me it seems to beautify, not mar, | My inner self, for from that deep wound leads

attachment that provides Stephen with the sexual satisfaction and the indulgence of the body that she has craved.

But this satisfaction is short-lived. As Stephen's commitment to her writing forces them apart she 'gives' her friend Martin Hallam to Mary. Significantly it is while Stephen is writing the book that intended 'to get born', that Mary's health suffers. Unlike Mary who offers 'loyalty, faith, consolation, devotion' through her writing, Stephen only gives half of herself when she is writing, and Mary's longing for her increases: as Stephen reads her work her 'deep, husky voice' prompts Mary to kiss her hand or the scar on her cheek; while Stephen lies exhausted by Mary (caught between the need to 'save herself for her work', and the desire to 'give herself wholly to Mary'), Mary is ill with unfulfilled desire. Martin suggests a curiously authorial intrusion in which Hall has written herself into the text as a brother, cross-gendered twin, or double to Stephen: his name 'Hallam' crucially encodes Hall's name with the additional ontological 'am'. Like Stephen he is bony with a 'loose-limbed figure that slouched from much riding' (420), and also bears a scar from the war. (In a cross-fertilization of imagery from Elizabeth's figuration in *The Unlit Lamp*, he is closely associated with trees.) Moreover he is in love with Mary (although there is an implication that he loves her because she is loved by Stephen). Significantly he pre-empts Stephen's physical relationship with Mary when he talks symbolically about the 'twisted and crippled' trees which have enormous courage, and, in a poetic echo, take their birds with them to heaven when they die: 'And in death they were not divided' (93).

In Freudian terms, as Radford observes, Stephen, at the end of the novel, re-enacts a renunciation, one originally imposed on her by her mother, but she also 'reverses' it. Her love for Mary has reunited her with her mother in the sense that she has become the 'good' mother, and the imagery of fecundity which began the book is also present at its close; Stephen is possessed by all the inverts of the world: 'Her barren womb became fruitful—it ached with its fearful and sterile burden. It ached with the fierce yet helpless children who would clamour in vain for their right to salvation' (446).[85]

| A path to gained respect, my secret needs | Quenched by the bleeding of that fountain are.' *A Sheaf of Verses* (1908; Windsor: Gaby Goldscheider, 1985), 108.

[85] Radford, 'An Inverted Romance', 105.

But ultimately the fantasy of cross-gendering and of enduring love and sexual satisfaction with Mary has been curtailed by Hall: the invert is not worthy of Mary's love. The ambivalence with which Hall presents Stephen is evident in this closing off of erotic possibilities for Stephen. This is finally indicated in the invocation of the 'voice', 'into which those millions had entered', a voice which is finally rooted in the 'very entrails' of the body (447). Throughout *The Well*, Hall insinuates that what is missing from Stephen's writing is precisely the openness of sexual expression ('there was something else that distracted, something she was longing to put into words yet that shamed her so that it held her tongue-tied', 215). In a final collapse between protagonist and author, the text that Stephen has been writing during the breakdown of her relationship with Mary, written with her pen 'dipped in blood', and to which she intends to give voice, is *The Well of Loneliness*.

AFTERMATH

Radclyffe Hall avowed and disavowed fetishistic practice in cross-gendered women through the overdetermination of the figuration of Stephen Gordon and the metaphors of splitting and absence/presence she employed in *The Well*. But in her 'official' public statements on the subject of female cross-gendering she exerts more control over how she perceived her own brand of female cross-gendering. This meant that if her primary goal of gaining acceptance of female sexual inversion was to be achieved, and moreover if the book were to be saved from charges of obscenity, then the sexual element would have to be marginalized if not extinguished altogether. As Hall's representative had pronounced in court, *The Well* dealt with 'what is known and tabulated as inversion—a physical disability . . . [The novel's] theme is not perversion . . . The theme is inversion, and indeed, it deals with a disability laid upon certain members of humanity for which they are not responsible . . . But perversion, a deliberate thing done of free will and a totally different matter, is not the subject-matter of this book.'[86]

---

[86] Doan, *Fashioning Sapphism*, 89–90. Privately to her lover Souline, Hall stresses that she must not think that they are *'perverted'*. *Your John*, 51, Hall's emphasis.

Hall could not manage this in *The Well*, but she made every effort to deny 'perversion' (i.e. sexual pleasure) in the trial, and she very publicly denounced the activities of the cross-dressing Valerie Arkell-Smith when she went on trial just a year later for falsifying a marriage registry.[87] Arkell-Smith, who had cross-dressed from a young age, been treated as a boy by her father, as an adult passed in her role as Colonel Barker, and married another woman. She told her wife Elfrida Haward, who first knew her as a woman, that she was a man who had been 'acting as a woman for family reasons. I made some excuse about it being my mother's wish, and she believed it.'[88] As for Angelica in *The Heavenly Twins*, cross-dressing is an addictive pleasure; and, as Rose Collis reports, she obsessively had her photograph taken wearing dress suits and her signature uniform. According to Hirschfeld, as Collis notes, 'the inclination to be photographed in the costume favoured by them is widespread among transvestites'.[89] Notably the feature that Elfrida is most drawn to in 'Bill', as she calls Barker, are her hands: 'No one who ever saw them would forget them. They were beautiful hands, the kind that Velasquez painted—lissom, slender, with the smoothest knuckles I have ever seen.'[90] Elfrida, who publicly declared that her honeymoon was 'perfectly normal', is contradicted by Barker who claims 'never have I had unnatural instincts, never have I in the slightest been a sexual pervert'.[91] However, Hall thought that Barker was precisely a pervert and not an invert because she appeared to be cross-dressing for financial gain: 'I would like to see her drawn and quartered ... a mad pervert of the most undesirable type.'[92] She particularly despised her 'mock war medals' and her wounds, which in Stephen Gordon's facial scar and uniform she had countenanced. Although Hall was concerned that coming so close after *The Well* trial, Barker could set back the cause of same-sex marriage, it is probable from this statement that she would also not publicly endorse the range of pleasures that Elsa B. clearly enjoyed. After *The Well*, Hall never wrote about lesbianism or cross-gendering again.

---

[87] At the trial when Barker appeared in women's clothes, the *Daily Mail* remarked that she looked like a man dressing as a woman. See Doan, *Fashioning Sapphism*, 94.

[88] Collis, *Colonel Barker's Monstrous Regiment*, 78.

[89] Ibid. 111.   [90] Ibid. 90.   [91] Ibid. 95.   [92] Ibid. 150.

3

'I am Her'
The Cross-Gendered Woman as Fetish Object
in H.D.'s *HER*

TRANSITIONING FROM SEXOLOGY TO FREUD

The Well of Loneliness covertly and fetishistically stages the debate
between sexology and psychoanalysis, but the transition from sexology to psychoanalysis is more visible in both the relationship
between Havelock Ellis and Sigmund Freud, and their relationships
with Bryher and her lover H.D. As her novel *HER* dramatizes, H.D.
became familiar with psychoanalysis through her friend Frances
Gregg—the model for Fayne Rabb—before 1911.[1] Her first personal
encounter with sexology was in 1919 when she had several meetings
with Havelock Ellis, who confirmed her feelings of sexual 'ambivalence'.[2] Her lover Bryher, who was writing about the girl-page in
Elizabethan drama, had first consulted him about cross-dressing
and transvestism. It was with him that she and Bryher travelled to
Sapphic Greece in 1920, and to him that H.D. related her 'jellyfish'

---

[1] Diana Collecott usefully draws out the connections between Frances Gregg and
Fayne Rabb. *H.D. and Sapphic Modernism 1910–1950* (Cambridge: Cambridge
University Press, 1999), 66. Frances, like Fayne was a cross-dresser; travelling with
Llewellyn and John Cowper Powys in Italy in 1912 she was arrested for transvestism.
John Cowper Powys recorded, without naming her, that the 'feelings that this beautiful
girl in boy's clothes excited in me rose like flames'. *Autobiography* (1934; London:
Macdonald, 1967), 406. In Gregg's short story 'Male and Female' the Gregg character
draws attention to her 'gender trouble' which always made her friends cast her 'in male
roles in their amateur plays'. Bronte Adams and Trudi Tate (eds.), *That Kind of Woman:
Stories from the Left Bank and Beyond* (London: Virago, 1991), 210–29: 210. In her novel
The Mystic Leeway Gregg speaks of gender confusion: 'male and femaleness in sexual
matters is remarkably inconclusive and fluid'. *The Mystic Leeway*, ed. Ben Jones
(Ottawa: Carleton University Press, 1994), 94.
[2] Collecott points out (206) that H.D. signed herself 'Hyacinth' in her letters to Ellis;
Fayne is also likened to Hyacinth in *Asphodel*: 'a strong boy not a pimp'. *Asphodel*, ed.
Robert Spoo (Durham, NC, and London: Duke University Press, 1992), 55. Further ref-
erences will be cited in the text.

experience in the Scilly Isles.[3] She was familiar with *Sexual Inversion*, and it partially influenced her first novel *Paint It Today*. But it was clear that, as friends had warned her, Ellis was unsuitable for H.D. Freud correctly summarizes the problem in *Tribute to Freud*: 'He records so many funny things that people do but never seems to want to know why they do them' (148). This marks the transition from sexology to psychoanalysis. Her interest in analysis was renewed during the post-war years and greatly expanded in the 1920s through Bryher, an early advocate and financial supporter of psychoanalysis. In the period 1931–2, H.D. underwent at least three sessions with Hanns Sachs, and twenty-four with Mary Chadwick; eventually frustrated with Chadwick's inability to 'follow the workings of my creative mind', Hanns Sachs suggested that she work directly with Freud.[4]

During the year prior to their meeting, H.D. began to read intensively in the subject and her own prose from the period 1927–35 began to 'display a clinical interest in her own writing-subject'.[5] As Susan Stanford Friedman has documented, Freud worked with H.D. on her unresolved feelings about her bisexuality, and problems she was having with her writing, and part of this 'cure' in 1933 included 'therapeutic writing of events'; she returned to him in 1934 after another breakdown in her writing.[6] Friedman has suggested that H.D.'s writer's block was 'at least partially the result of the vulnerability she felt as a woman in a man's world'; her letters to Bryher in 1933 and 1934 reveal that the image of literary men plagued her and frustrated her ability to write: 'I keep dreaming of literary men, Shaw, Cunninghame, Grahame, now Noel Coward and Lawrence

[3] Ellis is in fact 'unsympathetic' to the experience, 'or else he did not understand or else he may have thought it was a danger signal'. H.D., *Tribute to Freud* (1956; Boston: David R. Godine, 1974), 130. Further references will be cited in the text. The 'jellyfish' experience occurred in H.D.'s room on the Scilly Isles: she had the impression of being 'submerged' in an aqueous environment (the wallpaper in the room was covered in palmtrees, coral-plants, and sea-flowers and she felt the impulse to 'let go' into a 'sort of balloon, or diving bell'). A description of this occurs in the 'Advent' notebook, quoted in Kenneth Fields, Introduction, *Tribute to Freud*, p. xxxi.

[4] Sachs had advised H.D. to continue analysis with a man, 'preferably one superior' to herself. *Tribute to Freud*, 150.

[5] Dianne Chisholm, *H.D.'s Freudian Poetics: Psychoanalysis in Translation* (Ithaca, NY: Cornell University Press, 1992), 22.

[6] Susan Stanford Friedman, *Psyche Reborn: The Emergence of H.D.* (Bloomington, Ind.: Indiana University Press, 1981), 30–1. The volume that Freud wanted her to commit to paper was *Bid Me to Live*; it helped 'break the clutch' that hindered the natural flow of her writing.

himself, over and over. It is important as book means *penis* evidently and as a "writer," only, am I equal in uc-n [unconscious], in the right way with men. Most odd.'[7] In *HER* H.D. fictionalizes both the debilitating influence the male artist could exert upon female creative energy and the internalized split between art and femininity. At the end of the novel we leave Her on the brink of a creative breakthrough. Creativity is something that is nurtured by the mother in *HER*, so it is significant that part of Freud's 'cure' for writer's block was to bring to consciousness her 'mother-fix': 'F. says mine is absolutely FIRST layer, I got stuck at the earliest pre-OE stage, and "back to the womb" seems to be my only solution.'[8] Despite the fact that Freud believed that art was an exclusively masculine preserve, both Chisholm and Friedman have argued that the non-sequential, non-logical, free-associational techniques of Freudian analysis were key factors in the production of H.D.'s literary texts. Freudian analysis aided H.D. in the adaptation of dream interpretation and symptom analysis towards the articulation of desire and writerly aspiration.[9] More importantly, as Claire Buck states, the 'central insight which H.D. takes from psychoanalysis is that the self is a text to be read'.[10]

But if Freud helped H.D. to cure herself of her writer's block, it is unlikely that he enlightened her about her sexual 'ambivalence'. Freud, who understood perversion as central to culture, circumvented understanding of the operations of 'perverse' female sexuality. He made radical departures from sexological modes of conceptualizing sexual behaviour, constantly seeking to dispel both the spectre of the invert and of biological determinism from his texts, and yet cross-gendering in women in Freudian theory is a 'stage' which girls pass through on their way to becoming women, envisaged solely in terms of penis envy and the masculinity complex.

[7] H.D., letter to Bryher, 15 May 1933. Quoted in Friedman, *Psyche Reborn*, 37.

[8] H.D., letter to Bryher, 23 Mar. 1933. Quoted in Friedman, *Psyche Reborn*, 132.

[9] Chisholm, *H.D.'s Freudian Poetics*, 5; Friedman, *Psyche Reborn*, 67.

[10] Claire Buck, *H.D. and Freud: Bisexuality and a Feminine Discourse* (Hemel Hempstead: Harvester Wheatsheaf, 1991), 99. After Freud, H.D.'s analysis continued again in London in 1936 and 1937 with Walter Schmideberg, who was a member of Freud's circle; after the Second World War she spent six months in a clinic in Switzerland suffering from a nervous breakdown brought on by 'war shock'. She returned in 1953 to have two operations; convalescing at a 'nervenklinik' in Küsnacht near Zurich she met Erich Heydt, an analyst associated with Medard Boss's school of existential psychoanalysis in Zurich. Friedman, *Psyche Reborn*, 20. It was at Küsnacht that she wrote *Tribute to Freud*.

Any sexual motivation for cross-gendered behaviour is neutralized by the logic that, since women are already castrated, they cannot undergo the vicissitudes of the castration complex, such as fetishism. This model of female masculinity had massive implications for the (mis)understanding of female sexual behaviour in the early twentieth century.

Freud revolutionized the way sexual behaviour was conceptualized, and confronted the problems upon which sexology had run aground, by offering a method of social adaptation which invaded the public consciousness with great rapidity. While sexological works were only available to élite groups in the first few years of the twentieth century, Freudian psychoanalytic concepts took hold in the popular imagination through the wider dissemination of the works, and the cross-fertilization of Freudian ideas in the mass media, business, and politics. In differentiating himself from the sexologists, Freud conceptualized sexual perversions in terms of 'normal' sexual development, and introduced the idea, against the tenets of sexology, that homosexuality is acquired rather than congenital. For Ellis the exclusive sexual interest that man felt for a woman was a biological law, but for Freud it was merely the provocation for intense inquiry. Freud worked retrospectively from heterosexuality to hypothesize radically that sexual abnormality is not a perversion of the normal, but rather that normality is the residual category after other sexual possibilities have been eliminated or impeded. Each man and woman was potentially bisexual and 'polymorphously perverse': complete masculinity and femininity were only achieved as the result of repression, sublimation, and disavowal: the libido is illimitable, purposeless, and objectless, and requires the interjection of psychic processes to contain it within certain boundaries.

Freud first promoted his ideas on bisexuality in 'Three Essays on the Theory of Sexuality' (1905). If, Freud reasons, there is no heterosexual attraction ordained in nature, then there can be no gendered sex, and there cannot, at the outset, be masculinity or femininity in a psychological sense. The theory of bisexuality is potentially liberating, ostensibly aiming to deconstruct fixed ideas of masculinity and femininity: it is no longer a matter of divining a woman's essence, but of trying to theorize how the female child with bisexual inclinations becomes a woman. However, Freud's theory is, under further scrutiny, one directional and serves to affirm the predominance of masculinity in both genders. Psychical hermaphroditism ('which presupposes that the sexual object of an invert is the opposite of that of a normal person') cannot be substantiated: it is only in homosexual women that complete 'character-inversion' can be discerned; in men 'the most complete mental masculinity can be combined with inversion'.[11] While sexual role was no longer paradigmatic of male gender role, both sexology and psychoanalysis refused to distinguish women's sexual behaviour from their cultural gender role.

Sarah Kofman, whose reading of Freud is very important for this study, suggests that Freud's theory of bisexuality was elaborated to counter accusations made by female psychoanalysts.[12] It also allows him to exhibit his own fetishism: to endow the little girl with the ultimate signifier of masculinity; like a fetishist he is incapable of recognizing the difference between infants, because, 'as we all know, it is not until puberty that the sharp distinction is established between the masculine and feminine characters'. While he does highlight differences, the 'auto-erotic activity of the erotogenic zones is, however, the same in both sexes . . . So far as the auto-erotic and masturbatory manifestations of sexuality are concerned, we might lay it down that the sexuality of little girls is of a wholly masculine character'.[13] This masculine character is determined by the fantasy that she once possessed a penis, and that it was taken from her; this also extends to the idea that the mother possesses a penis that has also been taken. Freud pioneered the view that male fetishism develops to allay anxiety provoked by the sight/idea of the castrated mother. When the little girl first glimpses the little boy's penis, Freud believes she is 'overcome' by envy which culminates 'in the wish, which is so important in its consequences, to be boys themselves'.[14] The clitoris is a substandard penile 'substitute', a 'mutilated organ'.[15] In a footnote appended to 'Three Essays' in 1924, Freud has to invent a phase subsequent to the oral and anal

---

[11] Sigmund Freud, 'Three Essays on the Theory of Sexuality' (1905), *The Standard Edition of the Complete Works of Sigmund Freud*, trans. James Strachey *et al.*, 24 vols. (London: The Hogarth Press and the Institute of Psychoanalysis, 1953–74), 7. 135–243: 142. Further references will be to this edition (*SE*).

[12] Sarah Kofman, *The Enigma of Woman in Freud's Writings*, trans. Catherine Porter (1986; Ithaca, NY: Cornell University Press, 1985), 13–14.

[13] Freud, 'Three Essays', 219.   [14] Ibid. 195.

[15] Sigmund Freud, 'On the Sexual Theories of Children' (1908), *SE* 9. 205–26: 217.

organizations in order to accentuate the primacy of the penis: the phallic stage. While the 'leading erotogenic zone' in the little girl is the clitoris, its 'masculine' pleasures must be renounced if she is to become a woman.[16] At this stage three paths lie before the adolescent girl: that of 'normal' femininity, of neurotic hysteria, and of masculine overcompensation. In the hysteric, what she has sufficiently repressed will lead to neurosis: the 'hysterical crisis reinstates in woman her lost, overly repressed masculinity,' which she does not wish to renounce. The normal path differed from the neurotic/hysteric path only by a difference in the force of repression. Freud traces the development of the little girl to the point at which her libido is directed from the mother towards the father and the desire for the penis is replaced by the desire for a child, a transformation which has a biological imperative: the future of the species depends on the recognition of the vaginal zone. A girl who refuses to suppress her clitoral activity will adopt a 'posture of masculine overcompensation' or become homosexual: she stubbornly clings to masculinity and to the hope of 'getting a penis some time'.[17]

In 'Psychogenesis of a Case of Homosexuality in a Woman' (1910), which formulates many of Freud's ideas on female sexuality—the masculinity complex, penis envy, and the theory of infantile bisexuality—Freud can find no correspondence between the degree of 'physical hermaphroditism' and 'psychical hermaphroditism'; indeed, the subject of this case history, while tall and sharp of feature and somewhat intellectual, bears 'no obvious deviation from the feminine physical type'.[18] Freud emphasizes that it is not the absence or presence of physical signs of masculinity, but behaviour towards the love object, that is the determining factor in homosexuality. Freud's new conceptualization, however, bears the residue of the model of inversion: his subject plays the 'masculine part' in her renunciation of narcissism, and in her masculine anaclitic overvaluation of the object.[19] Lesbian desire is traced to the daughter's pre-Oedipal desire for merging with the phallic mother, the

---

[16] Freud, 'Three Essays', 220–1.

[17] Sigmund Freud, 'Female Sexuality' (1931), *SE* 21. 221–43: 229–30. Kofman, *Enigma of Woman*, 124, 143–5.

[18] Sigmund Freud, 'The Psychogenesis of a Case of Homosexuality in a Woman' (1920), *SE* 18: 145–72: 154.

[19] Ibid. 154. In the case history of 'Dora', the subject's desire for Frau K. is 'masculine' or '*gynaecophilic*'. 'Fragment of an Analysis of a Case of Hysteria ("Dora")' (1905 [1901]), *SE* 7. 1–122: 63.

powerful mother she loved before she learned of her mother's castration, and is a negative and reactive choice. His theory of castration rests on the supposition that the male child believes that if the father has already castrated the mother, then he may castrate him for desiring her. This predisposes the son to homosexuality. Heterosexuality in the male is maintained precisely at the cost of the male perception of female worth. If we extend Freud's logic, as Kofman does, heterosexuality serves as the reassurance against castration anxiety.[20] In homosexual women the transition from the mother to the father leaves them 'resentful and embittered', and they renounce womanhood altogether seeking 'another goal' for their libido. In 'Psychogenesis' Freud invokes sex change as a corollary to unstable gender identity (based on what he perceives as the 'masculinity complex' in women) and deviant object choice: 'what actually happened was the most extreme case. She changed into a man and took her mother in place of her father as the object of her love.'[21] Freud finds the problem of how a young girl successfully changes the object of her love and achieves full femininity completely intractable.

In 'On Narcissism' (1914), Freud sees woman's nature emanating not from a deficiency or lack, but from her self-sufficiency and 'unassailable libidinous position'.[22] What is attractive is not only her beauty, but also the preservation of her original narcissism which man has lost. In later essays, such as 'The Infantile Genital Organization' (1923), Freud has retrogressively to discount all he has granted here. He confiscates her enviable libidinous position and invokes beauty as merely, as Kofman puts it, a 'supplementary garment' worn to conceal the repulsiveness of her sexual organs.[23] In 'Some Psychical Consequences of the Anatomical Distinction Between the Sexes' (1925) Freud makes a more concerted effort to ascertain the differences of female development, and recognizes that the Oedipus complex must be partially displaced in order to acknowledge that it has 'a long prehistory and is in some respects a

---

[20] Kofman, *Enigma of Woman*, 84–5.

[21] Jay Prosser reads this as a signifier of the subject's 'transgendered' status, and that this illustrates Freud's investment in the sexology that he disavowed. 'Transsexuals and the Transsexologists: Inversion and the Emergence of Transsexual Subjectivity', in Lucy Bland and Laura Doan (eds.), *Sexology in Culture: Labelling Bodies and Desires* (Oxford and Cambridge: Polity Press, 1998), 127. The second point is valid, but the first perhaps takes Freud too much at his word.

[22] Kofman, *Enigma of Woman*, 52.   [23] Ibid. 212.

secondary formation'.[24] But, as Kofman states, with this late disclosure comes the discovery that woman is radically other.[25] In this context it makes sense that Freud should invent the phallic phase (1924): 'the primacy of the phallus *had* to cover up and finally abolish the surprising, frightening, and fascinating character of female sexuality in its difference.'[26]

Freud wrote 'Female Sexuality' in 1931, two years prior to meeting H.D. Here he builds on the evidence of 'Anatomical Distinction' to posit an active element in the female child's behaviour towards her mother: he discovers that the attachment to the mother lasts longer than he expected (sometimes into the fifth year), and indeed that some women are 'arrested' at this stage. Freud's final statement on female sexuality the following year is presented in his lecture 'Femininity', in which he finally attempts to solve 'the riddle of the nature of femininity'.[27] He is forced to abandon any notion of a developmental parallelism, and to admit that the little girl has no reason to envy the boy his activity and aggressiveness, and that she may wish to have the mother's child, or even impregnate her. Freud attempts to determine how the female child changes both her erotogenic zone and her object, how she progresses from the masculine to the feminine phase 'to which she is biologically destined', and what constitutes the 'specific factor' which is not present in little boys. This factor is penis envy: the little girl's love is directed to the 'phallic mother'; when she discovers that her mother is castrated, she renounces her as love object. Perversely this means that not only is the girl more fetishistic than the boy in her disavowal of her mother's castration, but that 'as a result of the discovery of women's lack of a penis they are debased in value for girls just as they are for boys and later perhaps for men'.[28] Freud establishes culture's rejection, negation, and denigration of femininity as natural law.

The girl now turns to her father; it is a reaction to the repression of clitoral activity and the supposed desire for a penis, and is seen as a residual result of the castration complex. But the struggle

---

[24] Sigmund Freud, 'Some Consequences of the Anatomical Distinction Between the Sexes' (1925), *SE* 19. 241–58: 251.

[25] Kofman, *Enigma of Woman*, 21.   [26] Ibid. 134.

[27] Sigmund Freud, 'New Introductory Lectures on Psycho-Analysis, Lecture 33: Femininity' (1933 [1932]), *SE* 22. 112–35: 113.

[28] Ibid. 127. This contradicts Freud's previous statements about the potential for female fetishism: while the little girl may disavow her own castration, there is no reason to disavow the mother's.

to repress the clitoris and transfer her love means that she remains in the Oedipal period for a considerable time. As a consequence, 'the formation of the super-ego must suffer'.[29] If Freud finds it difficult to explain how the young girl changes her love object it is because he has consistently clung to her primary identity as a 'little man' through the oral, anal-sadistic, and phallic stages. It is no surprise then that as a little man she is so attached to the mother. If the girl is disappointed in her relation with the father, it is likely that she will regress towards the earlier stage of masculinity. The behaviour of lesbians is invoked to bear this out: they play the parts of mother and child as often as they assume the roles of 'husband and wife'. What separated the lesbian from the heterosexual 'normal' woman is finally a 'constitutional factor'; appealing to biology in this way amounts to saying that a woman takes herself to be a man when she is in fact already almost a man.[30] Because the renunciation of the mother and pre-Oedipal activity is difficult and protracted, the heterosexual woman belatedly overcomes these vicissitudes and is located in an unstable position and in permanent conflict with her repressed masculinity. She will choose a man as love-object who bears some resemblance to the man she wished she could be as a little girl. By the time the young woman has come to terms with her femininity, she is incapable of change: she frightens psychoanalysts with her 'psychical rigidity and unchangeability'.

Freud wrote and presented the lecture on 'Femininity' during the years that he was analysing H.D. In adulthood he had noted that women may turn to writing, or indeed to psychoanalysis to sublimate their penis envy: women's 'hostile bitterness' never completely evaporates and is 'clearly indicated in the strivings and in the literary productions of "emancipated" women'.[31] It was to Freud that H.D. turned to help her to come to terms with her bisexuality, and to cure the mechanism that had blocked her writing the prose in which she explored her sexual ambivalence.

---

[29] Ibid. 129.   [30] Ibid. 130. See Kofman, *Enigma of Woman* 204–5.
[31] Sigmund Freud, 'The Taboo of Virginity' (1918 [1917]), *SE* 11. 191–208: 205.

'I HAVE ENDEAVOURED TO WRITE STRAIGHT':
THE STATUS OF H.D.'S PROSE

In recent years H.D.'s prose has gradually been accorded the same amount of critical attention as her poetry. Before her death, H.D.'s fiction and other prose works suffered from authorial suppression and critical neglect; since the posthumous publication of the semi-autobiographical fictions *Paint It Today*, *HER*, and *Asphodel*, feminist criticism has conferred upon H.D.'s unpublished prose a special status as overtly expressive of lesbian desire. All three works obsessively return to her desire for Frances Gregg, her engagement to Ezra Pound, the loss of Gregg, marriage to Richard Aldington, her affair with Cecil Gray and the birth of their daughter Perdita, the losses in the First World War, her near-fatal attack of influenza, and the arrival of her saviour and lover Winifred Ellerman (Bryher). *Paint It Today* (composed 1921 and unfinished), encompassing the years 1912–19, begins with H.D.'s trip to Europe with Gregg and her mother, and ends with meeting Bryher; *Asphodel* (composed 1921–2) is a fleshed out account of those events; while *HER* travels back to events in Philadelphia. 'Madrigal' was to form the fourth book, but this surfaced as her autobiography *Bid Me to Live (A Madrigal)* (1960).

Susan Stanford Friedman's work on H.D.'s published and unpublished prose provides an indispensable theoretical frame for the analysis undertaken in this chapter: her understanding of H.D.'s literary career as structured according to a psycho-textual split between prose and poetry, has implications for this study of fetishistic female cross-gendering.[32] Friedman casts H.D.'s fiction as the mode which narrates 'her experience of modernity', particularly her experience of a 'multiply split, gendered subject'.[33] Friedman theorizes H.D.'s palimpsestic fictional oeuvre as a process of autobiographical self-fashioning which was an outgrowth of modernism itself: the narratological drive of autobiography accentuated modernity's destruction of the unified self, splitting the authorial self from the authored self.[34] This split spills over into the literal production

---

[32] Susan Stanford Friedman, *Penelope's Web: Gender, Modernity, H.D.'s Fiction* (Cambridge: Cambridge University Press, 1990), 5.

[33] Ibid. 64, 80.   [34] Ibid. 70, 82.

of H.D.'s prose works, in H.D.'s self-sustained distinction between 'H.D. Imagiste', and the multiple authors of her prose: Edith Gray (early short stories), J. Beran ('The Suffragette'), Helga Dart (*Paint It Today*), Helga Doorn (one of the names on the frontispiece of *HER*), Alex Dvorat and D. A. Hill (an anagram of Hilda) and Delia Alton (*Majic Ring, The Sword Went Out to Sea, White Rose and the Red, The Mystery, Magic Mirror,* and *Bid Me to Live*).[35] As Delia Alton, the most prolific of H.D.'s prose-personae (the name is a combination of elements from Hilda and her married name Aldington), she also wrote an extended commentary on the development of her own writing in 1948–50 in which the distinction between author and text is elided. In the proliferation of prose-writers it was as if H.D. herself did not want her poetry contaminated by the swarming selves of the prose.[36]

In Friedman's analysis, H.D.'s poetry and prose exist in a strictly dichotomous relation: compared with the 'contained and ordered' discourse of her poetry, the prose is the 'language of excess, of plenitude'; while the poems are 'individuated, separated', the prose remains 'bonded, bound' to the Mother.[37] Friedman argues that, curiously, H.D. did not openly explore figurations of female sexuality in her poetry (a form Hélène Cixous identified as suitable for *écriture feminine*) but chose semi-autobiographical prose as the 'discourse of female desire'.[38] While I would take issue with this schematic reading which places H.D.'s poetry in an unnatural position within the parameters of 'male modernism', the terms of Friedman's argument, which poses the posthumously published

[35] Ezra Pound took credit for the *nom de plume* of 'H.D.' H.D., *End to Torment: A Memoir of Ezra Pound With the Poems from 'Hilda's Book' By Ezra Pound*, ed. Norman Holmes Pearson and Michael King (Manchester: New Directions, 1979), 18. H.D. believed in the constructive and transformative power of names. She says that her father found her name in the dictionary: 'What would I have been, if my initial had come at the beginning and he put his finger on Alice?' *The Gift* (1969; New York: New Directions, 1982), 8. (This last clause contains a veiled accusation to her father concerning the death of Alice, her half-sister.)

[36] Friedman has also argued for the use of male masks in the prose, most notably in *Hedylus* and *Nights*: both Hedyle and Hedylus the male poet are 'textual projections of H.D.'s divided self'. *Penelope's Web*, 255.

[37] Friedman, *Penelope's Web*, 6, 26. Susan McCabe takes issue with the neatness of this division in ' "A Queer Lot" and the Lesbians of 1914: Amy Lowell, H.D., and Gertrude Stein', in Joyce W. Warren and Margaret Dickie (eds.), *Challenging Boundaries: Gender and Periodization* (Athens, Ga., and London: University of Georgia Press, 2000), 62–90: 72.

[38] Friedman, *Penelope's Web*, 25.

prose in a liminal relation to the poetry and to modernism more generally, and argues for the different function of prose, as opposed to poetry, is compelling. Semi-autobiographical fiction for H.D. enables the exploration of fantasized subjectivity and sexuality: in other words it is more susceptible to the operations of fetishism.

H.D.'s prose has certainly been read critically as more intimate and personal than her poetry, which had been revered for its 'crystalline' self-sufficiency: 'one feels, in the midst of this burning subjectivism, this consuming Narcissism, that it would be a relief to come oftener upon a simple narrative statement or a connected bit of dialogue.'[39] This view of her prose is substantiated by H.D. herself, who asserted that H.D. the poet could not have written the Delia Alton novels because she was not 'intimate' enough to tell such personal stories; writing to Norman Holmes Pearson about the authoring of *Bid Me to Live*, she deferred to Delia Alton: 'I presume the book is by *Delia Alton*. I, as H.D., could never have done it or the other later ones.'[40] The authorial 'I' of the poet stands in proud contradistinction to the other self/selves of the prose. Previously she had commented to Imagist poet and novelist John Cournos: 'I do not put my personal self into my poems. But my personal self has got between me and my real self, my real artist personality. And in order to clear the ground, I have tried to write things down— in order to think straight, I have endeavoured to write straight.'[41] In H.D.'s analysis the prose provides an opportunity to discard psychic baggage, to work through fantasized scenes. In order to write 'straight' (*read* heterosexual) poetry, H.D. would write straight (*read* prosaic) fiction: she would vent her queerness in her prose.

That H.D. gave her fiction a therapeutic purpose before she met Freud in the early 1930s is significant in the light of H.D.'s formal engagement with psychoanalysis which was motivated by her writer's block. Dianne Chisholm understands H.D.'s identification with Freud as being a dramatic way of curing herself of 'the blocks and gaps that infect the telling of her life story'.[42] In the same way that Anaïs Nin turns to psychoanalysis in order to convert her diary

[39] Conrad Aiken, quoted in Friedman, *Penelope's Web*, 28.

[40] H.D., letter to Norman Holmes Pearson, 14 Sept. 1959. Quoted in Friedman, *Penelope's Web*, 44.

[41] H.D., letter to John Cournos, 9 July [1919?]. Quoted in Friedman, *Penelope's Web*, 34.

[42] Chisholm, *H.D.'s Freudian Poetics*, 4.

into fiction, so H.D. found a way, through analysis, to trace the sources for her own creativity back through lines of maternal descent.[43] The early semi-autobiography of *HER* narrativizes both the desire for reintegration with the mother and a self-conscious preoccupation with splitting and doubling which makes it susceptible to fetishism.

'I AM HER GART PRECISELY': LANGUAGE, FETISHISM, AND IDENTITY

The writing of *HER* took place in 1927, the same year that Freud published 'Fetishism', and before H.D. underwent analysis. While Fayne gives Her (short for Hermione) some German psychoanalytic texts, psychoanalysis is figured as something that is 'missing' from an understanding of human behaviour:

She could not know that the reason for failure of a somewhat exaggeratedly-planned 'education,' was possibly due to subterranean causes. She had not then dipped dust-draggled, intellectual plumes into the more modern science that posts signs over emotional bog and intellectual lagoon ('failure complex,' 'compensation reflex') to show us where we may or where we may not stand.[44]

Since psychoanalytic practice and discourse had not yet infiltrated the Philadelphia of the novel ('In those days those astounding Freudian and post-Freudian volumes had not yet found their way into the common library', 18), psychoanalysis exists as the repressed in the text. For instance, the narrator avows and disavows Freudian interpretation of sister-in-law Minnie's appropriation of the word 'father': 'Words that had not (in Philadelphia) been invented, beat about them: Oedipus complex . . . The word "father" as Minnie spoke it, reversed itself inward, tore at the inner lining of the thing called Her Gart' (15). Minnie's appropriation of this familial term is regarded by Her as a theft which also disrupts her own sense of self: 'It stole from Her a presence that left her (no one else had)

---

[43] This is fully explored in *The Gift*.

[44] H.D., *HER* (1981; London: Virago, 1984), 4. Further page references will be cited in the text. *HER* was first published under the title *HERmione* (New York: New Directions, 1981). I am using the Virago edition because H.D. never intended that the title should read *HERmione*, as is shown by the original title-page (reproduced in Friedman, *Penelope's Web*, p. xvii). H.D. used upper-case letters *HER*, as I will use here throughout when referring to the title of the novel.

alone and that again stole from her a presence: . . . the half of herself that was forever missing' (16). This is not a question of castration anxiety; what is stolen is not phallic, but an image of the twin
sister that is both her lover and her ideal self: 'the thing that would
have had that other hound, twin hounds, fleet-footed' (16). Her
reasons that if her father is 'father' to the detested Minnie (on to
whom Her 'projects' parts of her rejected feminine self) then the
image of the 'twin-self sister' would be 'blighted'. This image of the
twin-self sister is what is fetishized because it represents an ideal,
beautiful self that has been lost or submerged.

The psychoanalytic phrases which float in and out of *HER* are
ones that are most closely associated with the Freudian construction
of lesbian identity: 'Her Gart was then no prophet. She could not
predict later common usage of uncommon syllogisms; "failure complex," "compensation reflex," and that conniving phrase "arrested
development" had opened no door to her' (3); similarly she 'had not
been able to predict "cerebralism," "narcissism," nor cerebral-erotic
affinities' (17). The language of psychoanalysis, distinct and alien,
erupts into the text of *HER*, suggesting other concepts of character
formation. The influence of psychoanalysis upon H.D. has been
much discussed, but I would like to support Friedman and
DuPlessis's supposition that H.D. was probably influenced by
Freud's theories of narcissism, which find expression in the 'lyrical
and linguistic fusions' of Fayne and Her.[45] However, it is important
to note that while the twinning/doubling motif might recall Freud's
idea that narcissism is a component of lesbian desire, the pervasive
cross-gendering and de-feminization of both female figures defend
against the possibility that narcissism could be redeployed as signi-
ficatory of megalomania, infantilism, and arrested development. In
HER masculinity, projected on to Fayne by Her, acts as a fetish that
fleetingly manages and negotiates the fantasized introjections of the
female lover.

It is in the absence of resonant phrases culled from psychoanalysis that Her constitutes her own sense of identity which, in the
attempt to negate subject/object splitting, inevitably becomes tau-
tological: 'Her Gart went round in circles. "I am Her," she said to

---

[45] Susan Stanford Friedman and Rachel Blau DuPlessis, ' "I Had Two Loves
Separate": The Sexualities of H.D.'s *HER*', in Susan Stanford Friedman and Rachel Blau
DuPlessis (eds.), *Signets: Reading H.D.* (Madison: University of Wisconsin Press, 1990),
205–32: 218.

herself; she repeated, "Her, Her, Her." Her Gart tried to hold on to something; drowning she grasped, she caught at a smooth surface, her fingers slipped, she cried in her dementia, "I am Her, Her, Her" ' (3). The reiteration of the name 'Her', signifying self-identity at the level of the possessive, suggests that the process of the enunciation of a self that is integral to itself ('I am Her Gart precisely') is not only thwarted but will lead to madness: 'She was drowned now. She could no longer struggle. Clutching out toward some definition of herself, she found that "I am Her Gart" didn't let her hold on. Her fingers slipped off; she was no longer anything . . . what was she?' (4).

In her rejection of polarized categories of gender (this will inevitably culminate in her union with the boyish Fayne Rabb), Her can almost envisage the possibility of another complexly gendered position: 'she felt psychic claw unsheathe somewhere, she felt herself clutch toward something that had no name yet' (8). To anchor herself firmly she clings to 'trivial vestiges' and these objects and words take on the value of fetishes; so Her invests objects with enormous significance and reveals a synecdochic relationship to the body: 'In that red lock, was the whole of Minnie Hurloe' (19). The constant repetition of self-declarative phrases ('I am HER'; 'I am Her Gart precisely'; 'I am Hermione') is like a 'weight holding her down, keeping her down. Her own name was ballast to her light-headedness' (33). In the self-declarative statement 'I am Her' is resistance to subject–object splitting: the repeated inculcation of 'her/Her' acts like a fetish, staving off anxiety engendered by language itself. The word 'Her' stands in for both self and object, and like a fetish disavows difference, and fractures the sentence, as meaning oscillates. Her also figures herself as 'the word AUM', and this 'frightened her' because it signifies spiritual transcendence: 'She tried to forget the word AUM, said "UM, EM, HEM" '; she was 'clearing her throat trying to forget the word . . . I am the word . . . the word was with God . . . I am the word . . . HER' (H.D.'s ellipses, 32).[46]

Her's struggle to self-conceptualize according to a different gender economy is also a facet of her difficulty with writing; the reason she cannot get words on to a page is because the words split off from

---

[46] Janice S. Robinson suggests that 'Aum' is a variation of 'Om', 'a mantra used in Hinduism, Sikhism, and Lamaism in mystical contemplation of ultimate reality'. *H.D.: The Life and Work of an American Poet* (Boston: Houghton Mifflin, 1982), 16.

meaning, as 'Her' splits off from the inculcation 'I am Her Gart precisely'. Splitting precipitates the operations of fetishism: in *HER* fetishism is not rendered so much at the level of behaviour, as at the level of representation; in her rejection of femininity and her self-recognition in Fayne Rabb, Her's identity is both textual and sexual. She cannot commit ultimately to George Lowndes because she comprehends their relationship to be a masquerade; she cannot write because her relationship to language is similarly experienced as mimicry (a 'new variant on the old dialogue', 40). When she talks she feels as if she speaks 'words from a child's primer, words for a beginner, a Slav, a Russian, a Hindu learning to speak English' (93), or words from a play: words that 'had been written for her, she was repeating words that had been written' (94–5).

But words, while her 'plague', are also her 'redemption' (67), and are accessed through her mother. The father is associated with science, and an incipient psychoanalysis, but Her is not his natural successor, or indeed his natural daughter, having recently failed a paper on conic sections in mathematics at Bryn Mawr. In one encounter, Carl Gart reinstates the inequality of the father–daughter bond: 'Hermione has some odd way of seeing . . . she had failed him. "I mean—what were you saying, daughter?" He called her daughter like a Middle West farmer, like someone out of the Old Testament, like God saying *daughter I say unto you arise*. He called her daughter out of some old, old volume . . . she left the room . . . defeated' (H.D.'s ellipses and italics, 100). Her turns to her mother Eugenia who is presented as a creative force: it is she who critiques Her's mode of expression ('George Lowndes is teaching you, actually *teaching* you words, telling you what to say', 95), and who says that it will 'kill' her if she marries George. It is also Eugenia's suggestion, in response to Her's meditation on her beauty ('Your throat looks so pretty coming out of that ruffle. . .like a moonflower. You're soft like a moonflower', H.D.'s ellipses, 80), that Her pick up the pen, but Her initially feels the masculine side of her parentage 'too terribly in me' (80). Remembering the night she gave birth to Her, however, Eugenia's words 'had more power than textbooks, than geometry, than all of Carl Gart and brilliant "Bertie Gart" as people called him. Bertrand wasn't brilliant, not like mama' (89).

As Friedman and DuPlessis have argued, the name 'Her' has 'different valences' in Her's relationships with Fayne Rabb and George Lowndes. With George, 'Her', as pronoun and as object case of 'she', signifies her 'object status within conventional heterosexuality', and as an objectified decorative spectacle. With Fayne, 'Her' slips between pronoun and possessive pronoun to signal a fusion, one that generates two selves, 'subject and object indistinct'.[47] As Fayne's name signals from the outset, Her's desire for complete assimilation with the female lover will be doomed to failure: Fayne merely 'feigns' or simulates the mirrored double which Her fantasizes, which she projects on to Fayne via the fetish of masculinity.[48]

In her relationship with George, Her needs him in order to project a sense of self that is posited according to female development: 'She wanted George as a child wants a doll, whose other dolls are broken. She wanted George as a little girl wants to put her hair up or to wear long skirts' (63). The heterosexual relationship is desired by a split-off part of Her ('some uncorrelated sector of Her Gart') that requires 'othering': 'She wanted George to define and to make definable a mirage, a reflection of some lost incarnation, a wood maniac, a tree demon, a neuropathic dendrophil'; significantly, Her wants George to 'make the thing an integral, herself integrity' (63). And so the hands that will soothe Fayne Rabb, here reach towards George 'like the hands of a drowned girl' (63) imploring him to 'incarnate Her' (64). She is ultimately forced to rethink her self-identity in the light of George's incursions ('I am in the word TREE. I am TREE exactly', 73).[49]

But the distinction made by Friedman and DuPlessis does not take into account Her's attempt to objectify George: 'Hermione knew she must formulate George Lowndes. It was going to be very difficult to formulate George, to concentrate enough to get an image of George' (44). But he does ultimately elude her; speaking in 'harlequin' language and wearing 'harlequin' clothes, Her wonders

[47] Friedman and DuPlessis, ' "I Had Two Loves Separate" ', 212.

[48] Rachel Blau DuPlessis draws out the full range of meanings of Fayne's name: feign/fain (gladly, willingly)/fay (fairy or faith). The last suggests Fayne's unfaithful behaviour when she has a sexual relationship with George. DuPlessis also notes that on the title-page of the typed MS of *HER*, H.D. correlated the coded names with actual people, beginning with Hermione/the poet. Fayne is the only character not decoded. 'Romantic Thralldom in H.D.', *Contemporary Literature*, 20.2 (Spring 1979), 178–203: 180.

[49] Friedman has pointed out that Her's identification with a tree is a 'playful transformation' of Pound's 'Hilda's Book' in which the female figure is repeatedly imaged as a tree. *Penelope's Web*, 118. Compare this with Joan's likening Elizabeth to a tree in *The Unlit Lamp*, and the encoding of Djuna Barnes's lover Thelma Wood in *Nightwood* (see Chapter 4).

whether there is actually 'a George at all': 'he loomed again beautiful, constructed, made' (69). Her cannot maintain her own performance in the heterosexual relationship which engenders her as decorative spectacle, as essential femininity, and she feels uncomfortable in the feminine attire she wears to please George:

She knew that the hat was wrong, had sensed from the beginning that the hat was badly chosen. Something underneath me, that isn't me, wanted George all the same to like me. I am playing not false to George, not false to Fayne. I am playing false to Her, to Her precisely. Her became an external objectified self, a thin vibrant and intensely sincere young sort of unsexed warrior. (187)

The levels of conflicting identities and subjectivities finally settle on the image of the cross-gendered warrior. Being dressed for a party she is asked to move gracefully, but Her can only pirouette 'woodenly': 'How did one move, if one might be at a party? Hermione stood frozen, stiff with terror, a studio mannequin hung with blue silk. Where now would all this lead her?' (114). She perceives her body, particularly her hands, as part objects: 'My hand is like a wax doll in a toy shop. I seem to have been set here like a doll in a window, set upright with a wax hand curved on its wax-wrist joint around a doll teacup' (151). As a doll she is a spectacle of commodified femininity.[50] In *Tribute to Freud* H.D. relates a dream in which she finds herself partially cross-dressed in evening wear; this dream, imparted to Freud, expresses many of the anxieties about female identity that are enacted in *HER*:

I tell him last night's dream: hotel, stranger, dark (or in-the-dark) young man in the hall, he passes the open door and sees me. I wear a rose-colored picture-gown or ball-gown. I am pleased that he sees me and pose or sway as if forward to a dance. In a moment, he has caught me, I am lost (found?), we sway together like butterflies. He says, 'You *do* know how to dance.'

Now we go out together but I am in evening-dress, that is, I wear clothes like his. (I had been looking at some new pictures of Marlene Dietrich, in one of the café picture-papers.) I am not quite comfortable, not quite myself, my trouser-band does not fit very well; I realize that I have on, underneath the trousers, my ordinary underclothes, or rather I was wearing the long party–slip that apparently belonged to the ball-gown. The dream ends on a note of frustration and bewilderment. (H.D.'s emphasis, 180–1)

---

[50] The doll is a pervasive motif in *Nightwood*, connoting rather the failure of lesbian love (see Chapter 4).

The transition to men's evening dress suggests a certain discomfort with the ultra-feminine ball-gown; but the masculine attire does not fit and she feels physically uncomfortable, insinuating that the vacillation between masculinity and femininity might not be resolved. This is not a fantasized scene of fetishistic transvestism—H.D. retains her female undergarments beneath her masculine clothes—but a performance of gender anxiety. Freud's analysis of the dream is not reproduced. This scene might be contrasted with that in the 'Murex' section of *Palimpsest* in which Friedman reads Helen's elaborate ritual of dressing in a shimmering blue dress for a romantic evening with Rafton as signalling her 'assumption of femininity' and the 'repression of her "masculine" intellect'.[51] H.D. associates the male figure with Ezra Pound who was the model for George Lowndes in *HER*.

THE BOY HUNTER AND TWIN SISTER-SELF: THE PATH TO WRITING

Her's inability to '*love* George Lowndes properly' is contrasted with her attraction to Fayne Rabb. Already having lost a biological sister in infancy, *Her* rejects her closest 'sister' Minnie; it is clear from the erotic cadences of her description that the sister she craves will take on aspects of a lover: 'A sister was a creature of ebony strung with wild poppies or an image of ivory whose lithe hips made parallel and gave reflection of like parallel in a fountain basin' (10). The psycho-sexual benefits of narcissism cannot be found in the heterosexual relationship.[52]

The image of the twin sister-lover recurs throughout H.D.'s poetry and prose. In *Paint It Today*, Midget longs passionately for a 'girl child of her own age, a twin sister', a yearning that is satisfied in adulthood when she meets Josepha.[53] Friedman has summarized

---

[51] Friedman, *Penelope's Web*, 244.

[52] Otto Rank records a version of the Narcissus myth as related by Pausanius which has implications for this passage: Narcissus became inconsolable after the death of his twin sister, but when he discovered the reflection of his own image in the water, he was comforted, taking solace in the perfect resemblance of himself to the beloved sister. *Beyond Psychology* (New York: Dover, 1958), 98.

[53] H.D., *Paint it Today*, ed. Cassandra Laity (New York and London: New York University Press, 1992), 6. In 1934 Frances Gregg wrote to H.D. that she 'wanted the original woman who poked her head through the womb of time. You are it, and I am your still born twin'. Quoted in Barbara Guest, *Herself Defined: The Poet H.D. and Her World* (London: Collins, 1985), 180.

that in *Mira-Mare* Alex and Chris are androgynously named twins; in *Nights* (1935), written while H.D. was consulting Freud, Natalia and Helforth are bonded as 'psychic twins', while 'Nat' (a masculinized Natalia) and Neil are 'this terrible Siamese-twin'.[54] In 'Narthex' (1928), where Gareth is the 'intellectual almost-twin', twinship is a trap, not a liberation as it is in *HER*, which inhibits Raymonde's creativity.[55]

H.D. employs similar motifs of twinning, combined with mirroring and entwining, in the rendering of lesbian desire in *HER*. Her is already split off from herself, already contains a twin within herself: her mind is 'separated like amoeba giving itself another amoeba, a sort of birth, a sort of twin repeating itself' (120). Hence, it is possible to read Fayne as that which Her desires to make herself whole. Before she meets Fayne, Her is surprised to be able to turn the front of her head, and look 'into the back of her head as a child may do, astonished to find things turned round in a mirror' (75). This falsifying and multiply doubled image suggests that Her is undergoing a perverse form of the mirror stage. In retrospect she knows that this mode of perception 'related back to an odd girl' (76), whose name is 'Itylus', who makes things 'click into place'.[56] The repeated incantation from Swinburne ('my sister, O singing swallow') speaks of Her's desire for a sister-lover. Cassandra Laity has fully documented the intertext of Swinburne's poems in *HER* which includes 'Faustine', 'Itylus', and 'Before the Mirror', and comprises what Friedman has termed a lesbian erotic code. 'Before the Mirror' inspired by Whistler's painting 'The Little White Girl', in which the subject gazes into a mirror, connotes an erotic portrait of female narcissism. The lesbian vampire of 'Faustine' inflects Fayne and Her's kiss with a decadent sexuality, while 'Itylus' which provides the 'O sister' mantra signals the repeated desire for a lost twin.[57]

[54] Friedman, *Penelope's Web*, 264, 271. Quoting from H.D. *Nights* (1936; New York: New Directions, 1986), 27.

[55] Friedman, *Penelope's Web*, 275, 262. See *Kora and Ka (Mira-Mare)* (Dijon: Imprimerie Darantière, 1934), and 'Narthex', in Alfred Kreymborg, Lewis Mumford, and Paul Rosenfeld (eds.), *The [Second] American Caravan: A Yearbook of American Literature* (New York: Macaulay, 1928), 225–84.

[56] Itylus' mother kills him mistaking him for her sister-in-law's eldest son. Zeus turns him into a nightingale. This nightingale is reimagined in *HER* as Swinburne's swallow.

[57] Cassandra Laity, *H.D. and the Victorian Fin de Siècle: Gender, Modernism, Decadence* (Cambridge: Cambridge University Press, 1996), 35–42; Friedman, *Penelope's Web*, 120. Collecott points out that significantly Swinburne's favourite novel was Gautier's *Mademoiselle de Maupin*, and that Bryher was familiar with it when she wrote

The line 'Oh swallow my sister' is bowdlerized by Eugenia: 'It would be far better Hermione if you would try to *swallow* this nice bacon' (124). This shift of meaning initiated by the mother emphasizes the incorporation of the loved one desired by Her: she might literally want to *swallow* or eat the lover. The word 'swallow' and the name 'Faustine' are also used in *Paint It Today* with reference to Midget's beloved Josepha.

Consulting a ouija board, Her is told that she will meet a 'boy in a tunic'. The boy is Fayne Rabb. Cross-gendering is prevalent throughout H.D.'s poetry ('Amazon', 'Hymen'), and prose, creating a cluster of erotic images: the hunter, the male or female statue, and cool white hands. In 'Hymen' (1921) the maidens of Artemis mournfully prepare their sister for the rites of marriage as if for death. The prose voice intones: '*they are boyish in shape and gesture. They carry hyacinths in baskets, strapped like quivers to their backs. They reach to draw the flower spays from the baskets, as the Huntress her arrows.*'[58] This 'Artemisian discourse', as Friedman calls it, is also adopted by Bryher in her memoir *The Heart to Artemis*, and at the end of *Two Selves* when Nancy confronts the poet and fantasized object of her desire: 'A tall figure opened the door. Young. A spear flower if a spear flower could bloom.'[59] In *Paint It Today*, Josepha calls Midget a 'white sword flower'.[60]

The relationship between Fayne and Her is figured as encapsulating a similar moment of recognition that pre-dates their meeting: ' "I'm glad I waited in this corridor." "Oh—then you recognize me?" "*Recognize* you? But I always knew you." ' (139). The word 'Her' assumes different meanings when it is substituted for Fayne's name: 'I know her. Her. I am Her. She is Her. Knowing her, I know Her. She is some amplification of myself like amoeba giving birth, by breaking off, to amoeba. I am a sort of mother, a sort of sister to Her'

her essay 'The Girl-Page in Elizabethan Literature', and it 'may have been an intertext for her novel *The Player's Boy* as well as H.D.'s *Her*' (51); Swinburne also makes reference to Henri de Latouche's novel *Fragoletta* in his poem of the same name. H.D. was influenced by the hermaphrodite of Balzac's *Séraphita*, an image of 'wholeness' (51). Interestingly, John Cowper Powys, in love with Frances Gregg, wrote a poem (first line 'Shall I not be really cruel to you?') shortly after they met which used Swinburnian imagery. Ben Jones notes that in this poem 'Frances is marked as fetish, as the desired object that can be subdued'. 'Surprised by Frances: Travel and Recognition in *The Mystic Leeway*', *The Powys Journal*, 5 (1995), 35–53: 44.

[58] H.D., 'Hymen', in *Collected Poems 1912–1944*, ed. Louis L. Martz (Manchester: Carcanet Press, 1984), 104. H.D.'s italics.

[59] Bryher, *Two Selves* (Paris: Contact, [1923?]), 126.   [60] *Paint It Today*, 25.

(158). Since amoeba breed precisely by splitting, it is possible to read Her's conception of her desire for Fayne in terms of fetishism; what Her fetishizes in Fayne is her similarity (reflecting an illusion of 'integrity'), which is incorporated under the auspices of difference (the fetish of masculinity: the boy in the tunic, Pygmalion, Itylus). The idea that Her wishes to mother Fayne is displaced through the reintroduction of the nominal 'Her', suggesting that Her desires to birth herself anew through an introjection of the loved one.

Fayne, however, is granted sufficient autonomy to counter Her's appropriation and to exceed Her's fantasy of the twin sister-self. Largely occluded through the narrative of Her's memory of her presence at Nellie Thorpe's gathering (Fayne is a distorting convex mirror), she enters the text cross-dressed as Pygmalion, a role which presages the relationship between the two women as that of male sculptor to female sculpture (Her as Hermione is 'out of *The Winter's Tale*', 32), creative subject to created object.[61] Significantly, Fayne in her guise of Pygmalion, makes Her speak using her hands. Her's hand in her relationship with George, signalling her lack of sexual autonomy, is 'something apart, weighted, a weight of broken-off hand flung down, sunk, smudged out' (84). Fayne's hand by contrast is thrusting and sexual:

A hand swift, heavy; small, heavy swift hand. A hand thrust out and the hand (as it were) was thrust from behind a curtain. 'All this room, I've been saying is like a curtain.' The words were (as it were) dragged out of her long throat by a small hand, by a tight hand, by a hard dynamic forceful vibrant hand. The hand of Fayne Rabb dragged words out of the throat of Her Gart. 'The whole thing comes right perfectly. I mean it is true that man is a shadow (what is that Greek tag?) I mean man being a shadow or a spirit or a bit of fire or something holding together a corpse. You are, aren't you?'

The hand let go dynamically. 'Am—what, Hermione?' 'You are—you make me see the transience in everything. You are conscious aren't you that Fayne Rabb is nothing?' 'I am, little blasphemer, conscious of none of any such thing. I am of *great* importance.' 'You are and you just aren't; don't joke about all this. I mean I see (through you) the meaning of—of—' 'Eternity?' 'No-oo—not that exactly.' 'Maternity?' 'Oh horrible—' 'Paternity?' 'Fayne—are you really still there?'

'I am, Miss Her Gart. And I am not . . .' (H.D.'s emphasis, 144–5)

---

[61] In her poem 'Pygmalion' (1916), H.D. is the sculptor making 'image upon image for my use'. *Collected Poems*, 49.

The emphasis on hand movements in this passage is continued throughout *HER*; the first sentence with its enclosing syntax closing down on the word 'small' suggests the encompassing nature of this imagery. The hand is 'shorthand' for lesbianism, decadent eroticism, and masturbation. The image of Her's cool, white hands intersects with the memory of Fayne, connoting a self-pleasuring eroticism: Her 'with hands stretched like some suppliant across the dead body of its child or slain lover', remembers the 'hypnotizing fingers' that had soothed her temples, the 'white marble' of her head (181). In her relationship with George her hand feels dismembered, lifeless, and anerotic (63, 84, 151, 189). The hand, as in *The Well*, is a fetishized object of desire, manipulated by the text to convey explicit erotic responses. Like the tree image, the cool white hands and long fingers figure in Pound's 'Hilda's Book': 'Saint Hilda pray for me | Lay on my forehead | Cool hands of thy blessing.'[62] Significantly, as Barbara Guest attests, on the cover and title-pages of H.D.'s copy of *Sea Garden*, her lover Frances Gregg had claimed this image with a hand-written poem, mimicking H.D.'s Imagist style, on Hilda's hands.[63] In *HER* the cool white hands are subversively transfigured into instruments of lesbian love. The white hand also appears in the poem 'Hyacinth' (1924): 'I think of chaste, slight hands, | veined snow.'[64] Laity observes that marked or 'veined' white hands are a synecdoche for decadent sexuality (masturbation, homoeroticism), particularly as configured through the decadents' fixation with Grecian statuary.[65]

In their union Fayne and Her discourse on the problematic nature of lesbian desire. In an extended meditation following the long extract quoted above, Fayne explains the distinction between identification and narcissistic enclosure (conveyed syntactically through the enclosing hands): 'Drawn to you I am repulsed, drawn away

---

[62] Ezra Pound, '*Sancta Patrona Domina Caelae*'. H.D., *End to Torment*, 83–4.

[63] Guest, *Herself Defined*, 81 n. 1. As well as this poem, Gregg also transcribed 'Hermaphroditus', an important figure of the cleavage of male and female for both H.D. and Gregg.

[64] *Collected Poems*, 201.

[65] Laity, *H.D. and the Victorian Fin de Siècle*, 77. As Diana Collecott has pointed out Bryher also employs 'the transformative whiteness of the erotic body'; significantly the colour white is located at a 'point of completion and transformation' (37). Rachel Blau DuPlessis points out that in *Helen in Egypt* whiteness is 'often an image of the integrated self, the place where prismatic colors fuse'. 'Romantic Thralldom', 197. Dora in Freud's case history reflects on Frau K's 'adorable white body'. 'Fragment of an Analysis of a Case of Hysteria', 61.

from you, I am negated. You are not myself but you are some pro-
jection of myself' (146). This fear of negation is borne out in Her's
conception of Fayne which is at worst illusory ('You are and you just
aren't'). Fayne is doubly threatened in Her's retrospective narrative
which constructs Fayne as fetishized fantasy object: her image as a
cross-dressed boy in a tunic survives in the text as a split-off part of
Her which she desires to make her whole, to concretize 'the word
HER, precisely'. Fayne ultimately attempts to reassert her power, as
Robin does in Barnes's *Nightwood*. In *HER*, Fayne re-enacts her
Pygmalion role, but Her refuses the implications: 'Curtains part as
I look into the eyes of Fayne Rabb. "And I—I'll make you breathe,
my breathless statue." "Statue? You—*you* are the statue" ' (H.D.'s
emphasis, 163).[66]

The desire for 'integrity' is also performed through the speech-act
itself. Fayne stimulates Her's production of language by forcibly
extracting words from her throat, and words become 'projections of
things beyond one', phrasing which deconstructs the 'one-ness' of
Her's desired self-possession through her incarnated lost twin,
revealing the oppositional 'two-ness' of her union with Fayne. Even
though Her reproduces the same mimetic discourse through Fayne
as she did through George ('Why do you say yes Fayne, why do you
say, no Fayne? Have you no reality, no voice, no articulate self?',
177), Her is able to see 'through' Fayne, that is through her eyes,
which in a fore-echo of *Nightwood*, are 'two lenses of an opera
glass' (146).[67] This allows her to see George Lowndes in a new
dimension, and to confront him when he refuses to help her with her
writing; she is now able to say that 'Love is writing' (149). This statement also repairs the relationship with the mother who desired her
daughter to take up the pen to relieve 'looking odd and worried and
distracted and not right here' (80).

Her rejects the notion that she is seeking her mother in Fayne ('oh
horrible'), and the novel itself seems to stand as a statement against
Freud's later insistence that H.D.'s dreams spoke of a desire for union

---

[66] Chisholm notes that in her assumption of both parts in Pygmalion she plays both
the male and female part in love, and understands this 'vacillation' between roles as con-
tributing to Her's illness *H.D.'s Freudian Poetics*, 81.

[67] This image is inverted in *Nightwood*: 'The louder she cried out the further away
went the floor below, as if Robin and she, in their extremity, were a pair of opera glasses
turned to the wrong end, diminishing in their painful love'. *Nightwood: The Original
Version and Related Drafts*, ed. Cheryl J. Plumb (1936; Normal, Ill.: Dalkey Archive
Press, 1995), 55.

with the pre-Oedipal phallic mother. H.D. wrote in *Tribute to Freud* that if one could stay with the mother there would be no 'break in consciousness', which in Freud's view was symptomatic of an infantile regression to subject and object fusion (33). Friedman and DuPlessis argue that *The Gift* attests to Freud's possible influence in convincing H.D. that her love for Frances Gregg and Bryher had been unconsciously activated by her desire for fusion with the mother.[68] In *Tribute to Freud*, Freud also explains H.D.'s desire to be a boy as a component of her desire for integration with the mother (120). Freud's theory of female development interprets the hostility the little girl feels towards her mother as emanating from the 'fact of her castration'; 'her mother's preference for her son' merely 'reflects the unconscious residue of her own penis envy.'[69] But, as Friedman has usefully outlined, H.D. rejected Freud's collusion in making biological difference the reason for ambivalent mother–daughter relationships, and preferred to understand the bond in terms of patriarchal distortion: 'the mother has sometimes acted on behalf of men' to injure her daughter psychically. To repair the connection with the mother as an element of her creative identity, H.D. can be seen to be using Freud's diagnosis of her desire for integration with the mother to convert her from the wounding and wounded woman to an 'ideal mother-symbol who is free to nourish her daughter'.[70] This may also account for the equivocal figuration of the mother in *HER*; while she is the upholder of patriarchal norms (she objects to Her's involvement with George Lowndes, but insists on marriage when she realizes the depth of Her's feelings for Fayne), she is also a powerful creative force (her narrative of Her's birth is valorized by Her over and above 'Gart's' achievements), who wants to nurture her daughter's own repressed literary skills. But while it is arguable that H.D.'s subsequent prose revalidates mother-love, in *HER* the sister-lover assumes partial responsibility for Her's creative output. In *HER*, the desire is not for fusion with the pre-Oedipal mother but for the incorporation of a female twin that Her feels she has lost; only through integration can sexual and creative potency be restored. While Fayne 'feigns' her suitability for the task (she is combative and

---

[68] Friedman and DuPlessis, ' "I Had Two Loves Separate" ', 219.

[69] Precisely what discussions of H.D's sexuality took place in consultation with Freud is not entirely clear from *Tribute to Freud*. Friedman conjectures what Freud might have said in *Psyche Reborn*, 133–5. See also 142.

[70] Friedman, *Psyche Reborn*, 142.

disloyal), her image stimulates Her's creative output; the novel ends with Fayne in Her's workroom.

The family unit fails Her and she must turn to other means of validation. In *Tribute to Freud*, one of the female masks that H.D. adopts is that of Mignonne, whose 'body did not fit it very well':[71]

> It was small, *mignonne*, though it was not pretty, they said. It was a girl between two boys; but ironically, it was wispy and mousy, while the boys were glowing and gold. It was not pretty, they said. Then they said it was pretty—but suddenly, it shot up like a weed. They said, surprised, 'She is really very pretty, but isn't it a pity she's so tall?' The soul was called Mignon, but, clearly, it did not fit its body. (106–7)

The shift from the feminine to the masculine version of the name suggests that the failure of 'them' to validate the girl's beauty has resulted in fragmentation or splitting; while the feminine name denotes the unloved body, the male name represents the child's inner being. In *HER*, Her's beauty, her feminine self is restored through both sexual and creative fulfilment.

Although her family is equivocal about Her's beauty, Fayne's recognition of it is sexually stimulating for Her: 'She felt fibre tighten and sinew harden' (178). Her also seems to experience sexual relief through the enjoyment of Fayne as a boy. Whereas Her had felt 'smudged out' in a rough and humiliating sexual encounter with George, she is pleasantly stimulated by the memory of Fayne as Pygmalion and the boy-hunter:[72]

> *Curled lips long since half kissed away* came right in the white face. The mouth was straight now, the mouth of a boy hunter . . . Across the shoulders there was a strap holding arrows. Marble lifted from marble and showed a boy. 'You might have been a huntress.' '. . . You were so exactly right as that Pygmalion.' Her bent forward, face bent toward Her . . . Long ere they coined in Roman gold your face—your face—your face—your face—your face—Faustine. (H.D.'s emphasis, 163–4)

As Laity has shown, the Swinburnian inter-text provides the erotic code for this sequence: the curled lips are those of the lesbian vampire Faustine who is fused in Her's consciousness with the marble

---

[71] Mignon is from Goethe's lyric 'Kennst du das land'; it is the only female mask in *Tribute to Freud*.

[72] Lin Knutson reads the encounter with George as rape. 'Arrested Moments: Communitas and Liminality in H.D.'s *HER*', *Sagetrieb*, 15.1/22 (Spring and Fall 1996), 35–50: 43.

statues of *fin de siècle* decadence. Moreover, erotic desire enables Her to write; she does not experience the fragmentation of identity that Bryher expresses in *Two Selves*, but discovers her creative centre through sister-love.

In ultimately rejecting George, Her vocalizes her love for Fayne in phrases that suggest, for George at least, narcissism: 'Anyhow I love—I love Her, only Her, Her, Her' (170). Feminist readings of *HER* have valorized the 'celebratory' nature of the fusion of Fayne and Her which produces multiple selves, but if subject and object, first and third person are both 'Her/her', then this fusion threatens to create an 'impossible' space, a space of irrecoverable 'mythic unity'.[73] The desire for integration of the loved one, for the merging of subject and object, which has failed due to Fayne's infidelity with George, precipitates a collapse of difference that leaves Her on the brink of insanity. In a sense fetishism has failed: taken out of a homosexual frame of reference, the fetish of masculinity cannot negotiate the split between self and fetishized object, and the distinction collapses.

Her's breakdown is first understood in terms of 'hysteria', the definitive female physical and mental disorder; when asked by her nurse what had caused her illness, Her 'can't say that there was anything special' other than that she was 'to marry George Lowndes' (201).[74] Her collapse is also linguistic: significantly her primary physical symptom is a sore throat—'Words made runnels in the throat, different shapes like frost on nursery windows' (193)—indicating that Her's illness has its roots in childhood (the nursery), and has been caused by her desire for identificatory wholeness, the fusion of signifier and signified, subject and object. Language, specifically writing, 'was what started things' (198): 'The thing she realized in that moment, that fraction of waiting, was lost. Nothing could bring the thing back, no words could make the thing solid and visible and therefore to be coped with. Solid and visible form was what she had been seeking. I will put this into visible language' (213).

After her breakdown, Her is more concerned with feet than with hands: 'Now standing on her feet, she realized that she liked her

---

[73] Helen McNeil, Introduction, *Her* (London: Virago, 1984), p. xi.

[74] Chisholm notes that *HER* can be read alongside Freud and Josef Breuer's *Studies on Hysteria*, and Freud's 'Dreams and Hysteria' and 'Hysterical Phantasies and Their Relation to Bisexuality'. Her acts out her delirium with 'paraphasia', and mixing of language is also one of the 'symptoms' of 'Anna O' H.D.'s *Freudian Poetics*, 76–8.

feet' (221), and 'Now her feet seemed to be filled with memories and the soles of her swift feet' (224). The word 'feet' also suggests the metrical feet of poetry, the stamping out of a rhythm: 'Her feet were pencils tracing a path through a forest' (223). She steps out into a world covered in white snow and makes her mark upon it while everything 'had been erased', and before it 'would be written on' (222); she is the Creator, and she writes '*Art thou a ghost my sister white sister there, art thou ghost who knows . . .*' (223). Just as the first symptom of her illness was words making 'runnels' in her throat, she stamps on a runnel in the ice, the ice cracks, and she thinks of Fayne.

Fayne is intimately instrumental in this process of drawing 'Her out of Her' and this ultimately defends against the risk that H.D. takes: that Her will register lesbian love as narcissistic enclosure, as the sublimation of the object. But, at the end of *HER*, H.D. registers that Her's restoration to health is aided by her inability finally to objectify herself, and she does this through Fayne ('Call the thing Fayne Rabb', 216). The 'visible language' denotes the 'crystalline' formation of the Imagist poetry that is the immediate creative outgrowth of the events of *HER*.

'LESBIAN LAYERS': *PAINT IT TODAY* AND *ASPHODEL*

In *Paint It Today*, the Fayne-figure Josepha is also intimately involved with the Hermione-figure Midget's creative awakening, and the same theme—the desire for a twin sister—appears in a more inchoate form. The subject in this fragment is more radically split as Miss Defreddie/Midget. Midget is the lesbian self, the self that 'had broken from all humanity, had fought and won, was a flaming banner. Josepha had called her a white sword flower.'[75] The text breaks off with only the title of the succeeding section: 'White Althea', which was going to be about Bryher. Fayne and Her enter a new individuated relationship in *Asphodel*, a novel that has a problematic status in H.D.'s oeuvre. Written in the 1920s, as Robert Spoo documents, it is one of the earliest surviving fragments of sustained experiments in autobiographical fiction. From one perspective it is an early version of *Bid Me to Live (A Madrigal)*: in 1959 H.D. told

[75] *Paint It Today*, 25.

Norman Holmes Pearson that '[Madrigal] Phoenix-ed out of *Asphodel* that was put far away & deliberately "forgotten" '; from another it is a 'sequel' to *HER* which was composed after it, but was set earlier in H.D.'s life. In support of the latter there is evidence that she revised *Asphodel* around 1926–7, but marked it for destruction.[76] Friedman argues that H.D. found it difficult to complete the narratives of lesbian desire, and catalogues *HER*, *Asphodel*, and *Paint It Today* on a sliding scale of sexual expression, the latter representing the 'lesbian layer'.[77] *Asphodel*, read against *Madrigal*, presents scenes that are repressed or partially obscured in the later text; while *Paint It Today* restores to both *Asphodel* and *Madrigal* the narrative of the sister-lover.[78]

The motifs of cross-gendering and hand imagery continue into *Asphodel* as Fayne, Her, and Fayne's mother embark on a trip to Europe; Her identifies herself and Fayne with a statue of Joan of Arc, the 'girl who was a boy' (9), and compares her lover to Joan: 'Jeanne d'Arc was more beautiful than Fayne, though I'm afraid her hands weren't pretty' (13). *Paint It Today* redeploys the same marbled hand imagery. Midget's gaze first rests upon 'the shoulders, a marble splendour', the 'hand, small, unbending, stiff with archaic grandeur'; Midget recalls statues in the Louvre, particularly that of Hermaphroditus, which, in a revision of the Pygmalion myth, she brings to life in her mind.[79]

The fear of merging with the mother is more pronounced in *Asphodel*: she has no desire to 'creep back into our mothers, be born that way' (51), and is horrified by Fayne's incestuously close relationship with her mother (53). In *Paint It Today*, Midget imagines herself as Orestes poised over the mother with a knife: 'She was defeated. She was not Orestes. She was a girl. Yet she was not

[76] H.D., letter to Norman Holmes Pearson, 14 Oct. 1959; H.D., letter to Bryher, 18 Apr. 1949. Quoted in Robert Spoo, Introduction, *Asphodel* (Durham, NC: Duke University Press, 1992), pp. x, xiii.
[77] Friedman, *Penelope's Web*, 23–5, 212. Diana Collecott argues that H.D.'s 'entire oeuvre can be read as a creative dialogue with Sappho' (3). Collecott's statement that in her prose on Sappho H.D. employs a 'rhetorical strategy of denying yet affirming, of making present and making absent at one and the same time' which 'can be related to the status of lesbian desire in the cultural codes of the present century' (33), can also be related to the discourses of fetishism as I examine in this chapter.
[78] Friedman, *Penelope's Web*, 179, 190–1.
[79] *Paint It Today*, 9. Laity traces the connection between Midget as a 'sister of Charmides' and Oscar Wilde's poem of statue-love ('Charmides'). *H.D. and the Victorian Fin de Siècle*, 69.

Electra, the sister.'[80] In *Asphodel*, Hermione longs to 'cut, as it were the cord', to start a life with Fayne which sustains them both individually:

> I don't want to be (as they say crudely) a boy. Nor do I want you to so be. I don't feel a girl. What is all this trash of Sappho? None of that seems real, to (in any way) matter. I see you. I feel you. My pulse runs swiftly. My brain reaches some height of delirium. Do people say it's indecent? Maybe it is. I can't hear now, see any more, people . . . That's all the division I can ever have between them . . . Hermione. (H.D.'s second ellipsis, 53)

In this rejection of theories of lesbianism (inversion and woman-identified loving), Her finds herself without the means to articulate their relationship. The sensual and sensory 'I see you. I feel you' does not hold, as an erotic hysteria takes over and 'division' threatens. The reassertion of her identity is spurious since this is a patronymic handed down by the grandfather who read Shakespeare: 'that's not me . . . I'm something different' (53).

The relationship founders on Fayne's inability to commit to Her and her subsequent marriage; Fayne's unsuitability for heterosexuality is again indexed in hand imagery: 'Fayne Rabb lifted her little hand but it was not the hand of Fayne Rabb. It was the hand of something other separated forever now from Fayne Rabb' (79). In Her's consciousness, Fayne is removed from the person who had 'sturdy knees wound about with straps that held together sandals . . . Wide breadth of strong and sturdy shoulders' (80). While the wedding dress brings out Fayne's 'firm little breasts' and 'perfect narrow hips', she looks 'odd'; Her views Fayne's transformation from sturdy Amazon to a 'parody of womanhood' with horror (86, 97). The final indignity is perpetrated by the mother-in-law: the bridal glove with the finger 'cut off at the knuckle' to allow access to the ring-finger signals the castration of Fayne's lesbian sexual instrument (86).[81] The sister is 'all smudged out' (echoing Her feeling 'smudged out' by George in *HER*, 84), the marble of the decadent statue has been 'buried beneath obscene filth of lava, embers, smouldering ash and

---

[80] *Paint It Today*, 44.

[81] In *The Gift*, the father also has a pair of gloves with the fingers cut off, 'so that he could manage all those little screws that were so important on his instruments' (41). H.D. remarks that people told her she had hands like her father.

hideous smoke and poisonous gas' (118).[82] Her must await the witchy Morgan-le-Fay figure of Beryl (Althea in *Paint It Today*) to save her from her own broken marriage, with the promise of a visit to Greece, to contemplate cool white statuary, to see her through illness and pregnancy. Beryl also introduces her to a 'sort of superior intellectual psycho-analysis' (185); H.D. herself thought of *Asphodel* as 'without the daemonic drive or the *daemon* that (or who) was released by ps-a [psychoanalysis]'.[83]

'LITTLE-PAPA' AND HELEN: ESTABLISHING ARTISTIC IDENTITY IN *TRIBUTE TO FREUD*

When H.D. attended sessions with Freud in Vienna in the early 1930s it was for her own linguistic crisis. What form the treatment took is not clear, but Chisholm makes the case that H.D.'s identification with Freud, and the transference that she achieved with him, cured her of the writer's block that affected her autobiographical narratives.[84] *Tribute* itself is less a homage to Freud, and more another autobiographical narrative: perhaps her most self-exploratory. Chisholm argues that Freud actually participated in H.D.'s writing; 'it is his scene of transference which enables the recall of the "writing on the wall" memory'; he helps to interpret it and affirms H.D.'s image of herself as a prophetess.[85] This is borne out by H.D.'s dream in which she is 'salting' her typewriter, seasoning her writing with Freudian desire and significance.[86] This rather glorifies Freud's involvement: H.D.'s dream, as related in *Tribute to Freud*, seems to be an expression of resentment (148), and, in a rare burst of anger at Freud, she recalls that she 'was rather annoyed with

---

[82] As Collecott notices: 'recuperated from the bridal gown for lesbian passion, whiteness also represents lesbian resistance' (37). She cites Midget in *Paint It Today* who, as she listened to her mother's plans for marriage annihilating her desire for a 'white lover', is herself 'steel white'. *Paint It Today*, 41–2.

[83] H.D., letter to Norman Holmes Pearson, 19 Oct. 1959. Quoted in Friedman, *Penelope's Web*, 141.

[84] Chisholm, *H.D.'s Freudian Poetics*, 4.

[85] Chisholm, *H.D.'s Freudian Poetics*, 10–11. The 'writing on the wall' experience consisted of hallucinations H.D. had in a hotel in Corfu in 1920, caused by mysterious flickering lights, which projected images of classical Greek figures and icons on to her wall. The recollection of these experiences forms a large part of her analysis with Freud.

[86] Chisholm, *H.D.'s Freudian Poetics*, 11.

the Professor in one of his volumes. He said (as I remember) that women did not creatively amount to anything or amount to much, unless they had a male counterpart or a male companion from whom they drew inspiration' (149). She wonders whether the dream was in fact proof of his 'infallibility', but as H.D. herself said 'the Professor was not always right' (18). Having become dissatisfied with her role as imagist, she adapted the techniques of dream interpretation and symptom analysis to help articulate desire and aspiration.

We first become aware of Freud, if in a covert and circumscribed way, in H.D.'s work with the writing of *HER* in 1926–7. *Tribute to Freud* can be read 'over' *HER* as a palimpsestic text, first in the struggle with Freud over the primacy of the mother, and second, in the obsession with twinning and duality. The fetishistic desire for a twin in *HER* is explored and analysed in *Tribute to Freud* and forms the basis for understanding H.D.'s ambivalent relationship with her mother. H.D. recognizes that the mother's body is the locus of castration: this is the foundation of a form of fetishism that manifests itself both linguistically and narcissistically.[87] *Tribute to Freud* resolves the linguistic breakdown of *HER* that dramatizes the absence of a 'self-signifying language'. Her's linguistic crisis is one of identity; her desire for Fayne Rabb is based on the idea that she is the twin sister whom she has lost; Her's breakdown is precipitated by fetishism that results in her inability to recognize differentiation between object and subject, self and other. In *Tribute to Freud* H.D. confronts these very issues: she speaks of her obsession with duality and her desire for a twin sister. But in *Tribute to Freud* she learns to write again; and, as Chisholm points out, she 'materializes maternal fantasy' in the most general Freudian sense ('Writing was in its origin the voice of an absent person').[88]

In order to access the mother, H.D. must negotiate with and confront the father in transference through Freud. H.D. calls him 'little-papa' and she associates her father's object-filled study with Freud's

---

[87] Madelon Sprengnether remodels castration as being severed from the mother, and the mother's body as the locus of division; her body, therefore, already contains 'the lack that fuels desire', and is itself the symbolic. *The Spectral Mother: Freud, Feminism, and Psychoanalysis* (Ithaca, NY: Cornell University Press, 1990), 234.

[88] Chisholm, *H.D.'s Freudian Poetics*, 102. Freud, 'Civilization and its Discontents' (1930 [1929]), *SE* 21. 57–145: 91.

room, the scene of her analysis (19). A sequence in which she is remembering a 'tall, bearded figure . . . appear from the Ark-like door of the outdoor study' (21) slips into a reverie of her father walking down the steps and seamlessly into a vision of Freud, the Professor, sitting quietly, 'like an old owl in a tree' (22).[89] Freud was insistent that H.D. 'had not made the conventional transference from mother to father, as is usual with a girl at adolescence. He said he thought my father was a cold man' (136).

H.D.'s dream of the Princess, and Freud's interpretations of it, form a useful means of examining H.D.'s resistance to Freud, the little-papa. The dream features a Princess who looks for a baby that is in water beside H.D. in a low basket: 'The Princess must find the baby. I know that she will find this child. I know that the baby will be protected and sheltered by her and that is all that matters' (37). Freud wonders if it is H.D. who is the baby (Moses) or the on-looking child (Miriam). H.D. rejects the first theory out of hand but will later entertain it more thoroughly, and projects this dream on to a possible memory from childhood:

There is the little girl with her doll in her father's study. She has come to her father's study to be alone or to be alone with him. Her brother's interests are more lively and exterior and her brother does not enter readily into her doll-family games. He should be the dolls' father or the dolls' doctor, who is called in occasionally. But this does not interest him. He has soldiers and marbles and likes to race about, outdoors and indoors. Here in our father's study, we must be quiet. A girl-child, a doll, an aloof and silent father form this triangle, this family romance, this trinity which follows the recognized religious pattern: *Father*, aloof, distant, the provider, the protector—but a little un-get-at-able, a little too far away and giant-like in proportion, a little chilly withal; *Mother*, a virgin, the Virgin, that is, an untouched child, adoring, with faith, building a dream, and the dream is symbolized by the third member of the trinity, the *Child*, the doll in her arms. (H.D.'s emphases, 38)

H.D. subversively corrects this version of the family romance. She counters the assertion of the father being a cold man with the recollection of him taking the children out to buy them a box of ani-mals (136), and she remembers that on her father's desk was the

---

[89] The father is also associated with D. H. Lawrence; H.D. confuses her father's birth-day with Lawrence's death-day, and she associated the dream of a photograph of Lawrence with a similar one of her father (140). As an old man the father is also linked with Havelock Ellis (139).

sacred *ankh*, a symbol of life. Her identification of him with Freud, the 'mid-wife of the soul', goes further to challenge Freud.[90]

Chisholm argues that it is the dead mother, not the supposedly cold rationalist father, whom H.D. searches for, whom she would recover in transference, and whose suppressed creative energy she would validate. The quest for the mother is not as one-directional as Chisholm intimates: the devotion that was withheld in favour of the brothers exacerbated the separation process and enforced in the daughter the idea of the castrative power of the mother's body. H.D. associated Vienna with her mother from the outset: Helen Wolle had honeymooned there and was perhaps already 'sheltering the child, a girl, that first child that lived such a very short time' (16). But she disavows that she is seeking her mother: 'Mother? Mamma. But my mother was dead. I was dead; that is the child in me that had called her mamma was dead' (17). Associating the stove in the corner of Freud's room with *The Nürnberg Stove*, a book her mother had liked, she is dismissive of the symbolism and the conscious connection: 'why take up time going into all that, anyway?' (17). When Freud suggests that he is the mother in transference she repeats her disavowal of the mother's importance: 'All this seemed almost too simple at the time. My mother was dead; things had happened before her death, ordinary as well as incredible things, that I hadn't told her' (30).[91] H.D. admits that she 'did not want to face' her mother's death (31), and expresses a combination of resentment, jealousy, and desire when faced with her memory. She recounts the impression that there was not enough of her to go around: 'About *her*, there is no question. The trouble is, she knows so many people and they come and interrupt' (33); and the overwhelming feelings of resentment of her mother's preference for her brother: 'If I stay with my brother, become part almost of my brother, perhaps I can get nearer to *her*' (33). In a dream she contemplates a photograph of her father and his older brother, who 'was by far the more attractive. But I looked into the reflecting surface and I looked out at myself.' H.D. identifies with the younger, less attractive brother, seeing herself superimposed on his image; it is a scene at the mirror in which she

[90] Angela Moorjani interprets the maternal or 'matric' in the father as 'an instance of the "female fetishism" that was thought not to exist'. *The Aesthetics of Loss and Lessness* (London: Macmillan, 1992), 130.

[91] Freud told H.D. he was uncomfortable in the role of the mother: 'it always surprises and shocks me a little. I feel so very masculine' (147).

confronts her likeness to her father but also her inferiority.[92] H.D.'s brothers are remembered as 'golden boys' who are favoured by her mother; in comparison she feels small, plain, and forgotten: 'I do not always even understand the words my brother uses. He is a big boy and known to be quaint and clever for his age. I am a small girl and small for my age and not very advanced. I am, in a sense, still a foreigner' (26). This sense of exclusion and marginality exacerbates the infantile narcissistic wound: 'I was not, they said, pretty' (101). In analysis H.D. suffers a 'slight embarrassment' at being 'almost too tall' and is relieved to hear that Freud had an analysand who was 'considerably taller' (20). Being too tall does not invest her with feelings of superiority and pride; rather she feels as if her body 'did not fit'.

H.D. remembers from childhood that she had no idea of the power that she could enlist, that she could 'throw her small weight into the balance of conventional behaviour by following her mother and leaving her brother to his fate' (29). Her brother's fate is to become a scientist like his father (he is the 'little professor'); H.D.'s choice might then be to follow her mother who has taken a more creative path: '*She* has bound music folios and loose sheets on the top of our piano. About *her*, there is no question' (33). H.D. wished that she could paint like her mother (117) and recognizes that her creative impulse has been inherited through the distaff side of the family (121). Freud suggests that the dance-dramas that she uncharacteristically acts out for Bryher in Corfu 'were really a sort of display or entertainment for my *mother*' (176). The mother will hence be remembered in song and music, but there is a discordant note: in the guise of Mignonne/Mignon, H.D. finds herself in song to discover that 'the tune is missing' (107). *Tribute to Freud* explores the psychic manifestations of this lack which is a wound inflicted by the mother.

H.D. desires reintegration with the mother and a re-establishment of the earliest possible bond: 'I want a fusion or a transfusion of my mother's art' (151); that is, she wants the creative blood of her mother to flow in her own veins, she wants to recreate the amniotic relationship of the womb in which her mother's body nourished hers, and she wants to be *trans*formed through this *trans*fusion. But

---

[92] Claire Buck notes that identification with the father legitimates desire for the mother. *H.D. and Freud*, 107.

all she feels is 'overburdened and lost' (163). Her mother's creative impulse had in reality been largely suppressed or marginalized: she was self-conscious about her singing voice, and a mirror that she had painted was exiled from the public space of downstairs to a small private room upstairs. Significantly the only detail H.D. can recall about the mirror-painting is a narcissus: this was clearly a mother's warning about the dangers of self-reflection, and the memory causes H.D. to wonder whether her two previous books were 'too self-centred or "narcissistic" to satisfy my heart' (151). H.D. can only get near her mother through illness (a fact which may shed light on Her's hysteria) and she imagines and craves a return to symbiosis: '*If one could stay near her always, there would be no break in consciousness*' (33). H.D. envisions herself as only half-complete and associates the lapses of perception, which *HER* dramatized so painfully, as emanating from the loss of the mother's body. But fusion with the mother is not wished for entirely unproblematically, indeed she experiences a fear of the womb that is expressed through the metaphor of being buried alive. She is captivated by both an engraving called 'Buried Alive' in Freud's house and thinks of herself as the subject of the image, and also by Lawrence's *The Man Who Died*; the latter is a cause for resentment since she herself had wanted to write *Pilate's Wife*, a 'story of the wounded but living Christ, waking up in the rock-tomb' (142). Freud draws out the meanings of the fear of enclosure: 'psycho-analysis has taught us that this terrifying phantasy is only a transformation of another phantasy which had originally nothing terrifying about it all but was qualified by a certain lasciviousness—the phantasy, I mean, of intra-uterine existence.'[93] This oscillation between fear and desire for the mother makes the maternal fantasy fetishistic, in its signification of the disavowal of the lack inscribed by separation from the mother. This lack is not expressed as penis envy but as the desire for a twin.

'THERE WERE TWO OF EVERYBODY (EXCEPT MYSELF)':
TWINNING AND DUALITY IN *TRIBUTE TO FREUD*

In the light of the expressed wish for reintegration with the mother's body as a source of creativity, the preoccupation with twinning and

[93] Sigmund Freud, 'The Uncanny' (1919), *SE* 17. 217–56: 244.

duality must be seen as an outgrowth of ambivalent prenatal fantasies. H.D. has a cross-gendered desire to be her brother in order to get closer to her mother; that wish is articulated in the archetypal fairy tales of 'Little-Brother, Little Sister': 'One is sometimes the shadow of the other; often one is lost and the one seeks the other, as in the oldest fairy tale of the twin-brother-sister of the Nile Valley' (29). She fantasizes that she and D. H. Lawrence are twins, which is suggested in her conscious recognition of his inversion of her initials H.D./D.H. She imagines that Osiris and Isis (the 'twins in the old fairy story') have an 'atmosphere' and an impact upon her life (143), that one is incomplete and meaningless without the other (150). H.D. speaks of duality as a controlling force in her life:

There were two's and two's and two's in my life. There were the two actual brothers . . . There were the two half-brothers; there were the two tiny graves of the two sisters (one of those was a half-sister but there were the two or twin-graves). There were the two houses, ours and our grandparents' in the same street, with the same garden. There were the two Biblical towns in Pennsylvania, Bethlehem where I was born, and Philadelphia, where we moved when I was eight. There were for a time in consciousness two fathers and two mothers, for we thought that Papalie and Mamalie (our mother's parents) were our own 'other' father and mother, which, in fact, they were.
There were two of everybody (except myself) (31–2).

The twoness of people and of things has an alienating effect on the oneness of H.D.; she does not have a twin, a sister, or a corresponding part. Oneness, in H.D.'s philosophy, is not a mark of integrity and wholeness, but a sign of alienation and otherness. She desires a twin for her self, perhaps the sister her mother was carrying in Vienna, and remembers that people used to say that she and Frances Gregg looked like sisters.

While H.D. desires undifferentiated twoness, divisive duality precipitates the break in consciousness that she imagines emanates from the separation from the mother's body. She envisions the 'tripod' as the symbol of a new form of expression and thinking, a figure of 'prophecy, prophetic utterance or occult or hidden knowledge; the Priestess or Pythoness of Delphi sat on the tripod while she pronounced her verse couplets, the famous Delphic utterances which it was said could be read two ways' (51). While threeness—the trinity of mother/father/child—is briefly imagined, dualisms are later restored. The writing on the wall can be read 'in two ways': either it is a suppressed desire for forbidden 'signs and wonders', an expression of megalomania, or it is merely an extension of the artist's mind, a 'dangerous symptom' (51). *Tribute to Freud* also has a dual structure, and offers two ways of reading, in the documentation of her analysis in 'Writing on the Wall', and her rewriting of the events in 'Advent'.[94] She also begins writing the notes for *Tribute to Freud* on 19 September, a day sacred to St Januarius, a name associated with Janus who 'faced two ways' (100). In analysis H.D. describes her mind as having 'tugged two ways' and suggests to Freud that he might call it 'ambivalence'; her uncertainty over the enunciation of the term emphasizes its dualistic etymological root: 'do you say am-*bi*-valence? I don't know whether it's pronounced ambi-*valence* or am-*bi*-valence' (87). The latter pronunciation which lays stress on 'bi-' echoes Freud's diagnosis of H.D as the 'perfect bi-', both boy and girl. Being perfect in Freud's analysis is to be whole; according to this logic and to Friedman's gloss of it, H.D.'s bisexuality did not create a split, but rather redressed the castrative wound.[95] Friedman, as Buck has argued, finds this analysis too compelling: female sexuality is maintained at the cost of the illusion of integrity.[96] What is missing from Friedman's account is fetishism; in order for the female body to be 'whole', castration (the loss of the female body that was once loved) must be disavowed.

H.D.'s am-bi-valence—avowal and disavowal—of the wish to return to the womb is expressed through dualisms, most notably the 'jelly-fish experience of double ego' in which a 'bell-jar or half-globe as of transparent glass spread over my head like a diving-bell and another manifested from my feet, so enclosed I was for a short space in St. Mary's, Scilly Isles, July 1918, immunized or insulated from the war disaster' (116). H.D. first assembled her thoughts on this experience in *Notes on Thought and Vision* (1919), in which she

[94] As Buck has explained, 'Writing on the Wall' was written in 1944 and published as *Tribute to Freud* in 1956. In 1948 H.D. assembled the notes made at the time of the analysis as 'Advent'; it was left in manuscript until 1974 when it was incorporated into *Tribute to Freud*. 'Freud and H.D.: Bisexuality and a Feminine Discourse', *m/f*, 8 (1983), 53–66: 54. Friedman has read 'Advent' (which is in journal form) as less formal than 'Writing on the Wall', and more anchored in her original record. Where the original *Tribute* is more Freud based, 'Advent' is more free-associational and concerned with the mother. *Penelope's Web*, 299, 315–16.

[95] Friedman, *Penelope's Web*, 310–11. In literary terms poetry is also seen as 'perfect' compared with prose. Aldington spelled this out to her: 'Prose? No! You have so precise, so wonderful an instrument—why abandon it to fashion another perhaps less perfect?' Quoted in Guest, *Herself Defined*, 100.

[96] Buck, 'Freud and H.D.', 58, 63–4.

invests the jellyfish 'overmind' with the attributes of the womb.[97] It is worth comparing H.D.'s use of the bell-jar image with that of Anaïs Nin who speaks of a glass bell encasing a miniature castle that sits on her desk. The glass bell similarly reminds her of her father and she imagines herself inside it.[98] In Nin's short story 'Under a Glass Bell', Jeanne lives in a house covered by a glass bell in which she has retreated to live with her brothers; the house is full of mirrors which she wanted to smash so that she could 'be one'.[99] It is evident that H.D. 'could not stay' in her bell-jars, that she had to reintroject the 'double-ego'. The bell-jars that she visualizes encasing her feet and head could actually be convex lenses, like those fitted to her father's telescope. She fears that she will be scrutinized and annihilated under the gaze of psychoanalysis, just as her father and grandfather had examined matter through telescopes and microscopes: 'If I let go (I, this one drop, this one ego under the microscope-telescope of Sigmund Freud) I fear to be dissolved utterly' (116). The fragility and instability of 'one ego' is again underscored; while the double convex lenses of the bell-jars form a protective shell, they also signify that a split has occurred. She begins to see the world through a split in subjectivity, 'through my double-lens; it seemed everything had broken but that. I watched snow-flakes through a magnified pane of glass' (118). The double lens recalls the specific structure of the gaze between the two women in *HER* which constitutes a paradox: the double lens, while 'two', also constitutes 'one': the mutual, one-directional gaze of female lovers.

The bell-jar is also an object from H.D.'s childhood: one encased a stuffed snow-owl which her father gave to her as a gift with the proviso that it remained in his study. The associations are multiple: H.D. thought of Freud as a wise old owl, which also connotes the figure of Pallas Athené on his desk, which Freud, unlike the father, gives to H.D. without a codicil: 'It was a little bronze statue, helmeted, clothed to the foot in carved robe with the upper incised

[97] H.D., *Notes on Thought and Vision and the Wise Sappho* (San Francisco: City Lights Books, 1982), 18–19.

[98] Anaïs Nin, *The Diary of Anaïs Nin*, i. *1931–1934*, ed. Gunther Stuhlmann (New York: The Swallow Press and Harcourt, Brace and World, 1966), 181.

[99] Anaïs Nin, *Under a Glass Bell* (1947; London: Penguin, 1978), 40. In *The Bell Jar* (1963) Sylvia Plath dramatized the ambivalent (deathly and protective) aspects of the bell-jar; significantly descent into madness is precipitated by the narrator's failure to enter creative writing school.

chiton or peplum. One hand was extended as if holding a staff or rod. "She is perfect," he said, "*only she has lost her spear.*" I did not say anything' (H.D.'s italics, 68–9). The loss of the spear is the mark of her castration, which is an interpretation H.D. leaves unspoken.[100] But the implications are clear: the bell-jar re-encases the figure of Pallas Athené, restores her to herself, covers over the marks of castration. In that the 'jellyfish' experience will be analysed as a fantasmatic return to prenatal fusion, we might wish to read this sequence of associations as recognition of the mother's body as the site of castration, and the locus of am-bi-valence: the gift confirms that Freud 'knew I loved Greece. He knew that I loved Hellas' (69), but also that he was exploiting the chain of signification: Hellas—Helen—the mother Helen Wolle. Pallas Athené is also invoked in the memory of a friend Renée Athené, with whom she performed cross-dressed as a hero in school plays.[101] This in turn precipitates a recollection of Frances Gregg, the model for Fayne Rabb: 'Still later, my friend Frances Josepha, with whom I first came to Europe, showed me beautiful photographs of herself in Greek costume; she had been a boy or youth in some play' (186). Freud is resistant to H.D.'s memories of these female friends; he interrupts her memory of Renée, reprimanding her for making notes before the sessions, as if her thoughts were somehow prescripted, and pre-analysed. H.D. remains undeterred: 'I went on with Renée' (185).

The chain of association is compelling and almost comes full circle. It is significant that it is through Bryher's encouragement that H.D. persists in her vision of the bell-jars:

We were in the little room that Bryher had taken for her study when I felt this impulse to 'let go' into a sort of balloon, or diving-bell, as I have explained it, that seemed to hover over me . . . When I tried to explain this to Bryher and told her it might be something sinister or dangerous, she said, 'No, no, it is the most wonderful thing I ever heard of. Let it come.' . . . I was enclosed. I felt I was safe

[100] In her poem 'The Master' H.D. composed a rebuttal to Freud which resonates with the line 'woman is perfect'. *Collected Poems*, 455. Claire Buck critiques Friedman and DuPlessis's reading of the poem as an unproblematic celebration of female perfection and sexual autonomy, in their essay 'Woman is Perfect: H.D.'s Debate with Freud'. Buck rightly warns that such a reading has not taken into account the role of castration in the vicissitudes of language and subject formation. 'Freud and H.D.', 53–66.

[101] Pallas Athené and the idea of castration are also invoked during the writing on the wall visions. H.D.'s face feels stiff as if, like one of Athené's enemies, she has been turned to stone by the Gorgon; she also wonders whether she is, rather, Perseus wielding 'the ugly weapon of the Gorgon's severed head, because Athené (or was it Hermes, Mercury?) had told him what to do' (52).

but seeing things as through water. I felt the double globe come and go and I could have dismissed it at once and probably would have if I had been alone . . . It was being with Bryher that projected the fantasy. (130)

This appears to be a fantasmatic recreation of the 'subaqueous' realm of the womb; both Freud and H.D. coupled Bryher with Helen Wolle.[102] As Friedman has documented, Bryher, whose encouragement has a sexual ambi-valence in 'let it come', was not only present during H.D.'s 'psychic experiences' at Corfu and the Scilly Isles— she named herself after one of them after visiting them with H.D. in the first flush of love—but she was also a vital component in the completion of the writing on the wall.[103] Bryher acted as protector to H.D.'s child and saviour to H.D.: 'she would take me to a new world, a new life, to the land, spiritually of my predilection, geographically of my dreams' (40–1).[104]

'SHE IS ONLY A BOY': BEYOND FREUD

Freud is dismissive of H.D.'s relationships with women. In response to H.D.'s statement that she had been infatuated with Frances Gregg and 'might have been happy with her', he said 'No—biologically, no' (152). His response to Bryher is framed by inversion theory: 'She is *only* a boy . . . It is very clear' (170), and this remark is thought to provoke memories of her youngest brother whom she loves with a 'delirium of devotion' (171). Freud and H.D. discuss lesbianism briefly, and Freud, prompted by H.D., explains why psychoanalysis has ignored and misunderstood the female homosexual for so long:

The Professor speaks of the mother-layer of fixation being the same in girls and boys, but the girl usually transfers her affection or (if it happens) her fixation to her father. Not always. The Crete mother-goddess is associated with the boy or youth in the wall-painting of the crocus fields. We talk of Aegina too. The Professor went on about the growth of psychoanalysis and how mistakes were

---

[102] When H.D. tells Freud of the Scilly Isles experience, 'the transcendental feeling of the two globes or the two transparent half-globes enclosing me, I said I supposed it was some form of pre-natal fantasy. Freud said, "Yes, obviously; you have found the answer, good—good" ' (168).

[103] Friedman, *Psyche Reborn*, 132.

[104] Bryher had also fictionalized her concern with duality in *Two Selves*, which was completed with H.D.'s help during the years the women travelled to California and Egypt (see Chapter 2).

made in the beginning, as it was not sufficiently understood that the girl did not invariably transfer her emotions to her father. (175)

Freud interprets H.D.'s friends 'Joan and Dorothy' as 'substitutes, rivals for my mother's love' (137), but H.D. corrects him in her text: the women were 'devoted to each other', not to her. In Freud's view, a component of H.D.'s unconscious desire for the mother is the strong wish to be a boy: she would appropriate her younger brother's clothes, she was a 'hero' in school-plays, and had fantasies of girls in 'Elizabethan doublets'; in the Princess dream Freud saw a 'mother-symbol' and H.D.'s overwhelming desire to be a boy, or to be as important as the golden boys in her mother's eyes: 'But the Professor insisted I myself wanted to be Moses; not only did I want to be a boy but I wanted to be a hero' (120). During the writing-on-the-wall vision she wonders whether she is perhaps Perseus, the hero 'fighting for Truth and Wisdom' (52).

Her is resistant to implications that her relationship with Fayne is born of desire for the mother ('Oh horrible'). Given H.D.'s ambi-valence towards her mother in both *Tribute to Freud* and *HER*, it does not make any sense to theorize her position wholly in terms of a 'mother-fix' that is necessarily resolved in a desire for reintegration with the mother. The mother must be transformed through analysis into a source of her creativity. The desire for the cross-gendered woman in *HER* is a performance of fetishism that protects the subject from the psychic damage that the withdrawal of the mother's love has impelled. The hysterical illness suffered by Her is the corollary of a failure of a 'self-signifying' language. In her desire for Fayne Rabb, Her staged an introjection of the lost twin as a means of allaying the anxiety of a narcissistic wound: her love for Fayne is an expression of her desire for an ideal self.

What is perhaps missing from H.D.'s discussions with Freud is a detailed analysis of narcissism. In 'On Narcissism' Freud, in his differentiation between primary and secondary narcissism, pathologizes homosexuality as perverting what is 'the libidinal complement to the egoism of the instinct of self-preservation, a measure of which may justifiably be attributed to every living creature'.[105] Secondary narcissism, superimposed upon primary narcissism, signifies a withdrawal of the libidinal instincts from exterior objects to the

---

[105] Sigmund Freud, 'On Narcissism: An Introduction' (1914), *SE* 14. 69–102: 73–4.

ego.[106] In *HER*, H.D. entertains almost all of the variants of Freudian narcissistic object-choice, including loving according to 'what he himself is', 'what he himself was', 'what he himself would like to be', and as 'someone who was once part of himself'.[107] The relationship between her and Fayne is premised on the possibility that Fayne, imaged as an amoebic twin, was once part of Her: her desire for Fayne is precisely fetishistic because she exists to some extent as a lost piece of herself on to which she projects fantasies of reincorporation. In *Tribute to Freud* and H.D.'s other prose works the female subject finds a state of being that disavows the 'break in consciousness' that emanates from separation from the mother's body. In her relationship with Bryher, however, H.D., contra Freud, presents the erotic bond between them in terms of duality: 'We were always "two women alone" or "two ladies alone," but we were not alone' (50). This 'fixes' the divisive duality that has preoccupied her: they are two and yet intimately related, 'not alone'.

Reading Freud through Her's and H.D.'s narrative revises some theoretical connections between narcissism and lesbian desire. The erotics of *HER*, coupled with the introspections of *Tribute to Freud* on the desire for the mother, indicate that lesbian desire may be both anaclitic and narcissistic. Reading *Tribute* alongside *HER* we might reach the conclusion, in a resolution of duality, that the two 'paths' are actually one: I desire one who is like me and who also fills the Mother position constructed as an ideal. But even this is not the complete story given the ambivalence concerning the mother: again, reading *Tribute* back into *HER*, placing a 'Freudian' narrative upon it, we may arrive at the fetishistic components of Her's love for Fayne: it is a disavowal of the mother's body as the site of castration. De Lauretis argues that in lesbian perverse desire, the fantasmatic object (what is fetishized) 'is the female body itself, whose original loss in a female subject corresponds . . . to the narcissistic wound that the loss of the penis represents for the male subject'.[108] In *HER*, the fantasmatic object is a lost female twin resignified in cross-gendered performance, whose original loss is also a narcissistic wound, a mark of castration engendered by separation from the mother. The fetish of masculinity serves as the sign of prohibition,

---

[106] Ibid. 75.   [107] Ibid. 90.

[108] Teresa de Lauretis, *The Practice of Love: Lesbian Sexuality and Perverse Desire* (Bloomington, Ind.: Indiana University Press, 1994), 231.

difference, and desire; that is, as a sign of the internalized prohibition or inaccessibility of the first lost object of desire (the mother's body), of the difference between lovers which saves them from being subsumed into narcissistic self-enclosure, and of the desire for the other woman. What one woman desires in another is a part or the whole of the female body, but while Her recognizes that Fayne may be her lost twin sister-lover, that 'she is Her', the anxiety that this disavowal might engender is allayed through outward manifestations of difference (Fayne's appropriation of masculinity). De Lauretis intimates that the fetish performs a reciprocal function: that it is what both 'lures' and signifies 'desire for the female body', and what lures the lover, what the lover desires.[109] Her desires the masculine girl, not because of the masculinity complex which refuses castration, but precisely fetishistically in which the mother's body as the site of castration can be disavowed.

What *Tribute to Freud* allows is a healing of the break in consciousness which contaminates linguistic production as dramatized in *HER*. The am-bi-va-lent mother–daughter relationship and the obsession with duality, splitting, and twinning are confronted, if not 'wholly' cured. After analysis H.D. returned to prose-writing and in *The Gift* she addresses her recovery, retelling the story of her maternal descent, regaining possession of the repressed and suppressed musical, artistic, and linguistic gifts from her mother and grandmother.[110] She recovers from the writer's block that afflicted her in the early 1930s that can be traced back to the linguistic crisis enacted in *HER*. The inability to differentiate between subject and object, between self and other in *HER* was expressed partially through her fetishized desire for Fayne Rabb, the masculine girl, the signifier of both sameness and difference. In *Tribute to Freud* she can conceive of oneness again, of being self-possessed as a woman writer: 'You might say that I had—yes, I had something that I specifically owned. I owned myself' (13).

---

[109] De Lauretis, *The Practice of Love*, 243.

[110] When Hilda as a child asks her mother 'can ladies be just the same as men?', Helen answers 'Why yes, ladies write books of course, lots of ladies write very good books'. *The Gift*, 12. She also finds a twin for herself by playing on her brother's name Gilbert, and the story of Jack and Jill; she translates 'Jill' via the title of a book she remembers, *Gil Blas*: 'If I were Jill, I would be Gil, we would be "twins" ' (39). She and Gilbert later debate whether Aladdin is a girl or a boy—H.D. insists he is a girl: 'Is it only a boy who may rub the wishing-lamp?' (57).

4

'She is Myself'
Djuna Barnes's *Nightwood* and the Exhaustion of Female Fetishism

I AM HER/SHE IS MYSELF: TRANSITIONING FROM H.D.
TO DJUNA BARNES

In the intimacy of their inter-textuality Djuna Barnes's *Nightwood* (1936) and H.D.'s *HER* form an ambivalent pairing; they present similar figurations of fetishistic desire but they diverge in the broader implications of that figuration. This is most apparent in the inversion of Hermione's declaration of lesbian (narcissistic) identificatory desire for the cross-gendered woman—'I am Her'—into the 'She is myself' of *Nightwood*. While Her's fetishization of Fayne is solipsistic and internalized, Nora Flood's fetishized desire for Robin Vote is paradigmatic of the fetishistic nature of the text itself. Her's desire for Fayne is self-sustaining, Nora's for Robin is death driven: *Nightwood* is the most extreme statement of female fetishistic cross-gendering. For Barnes sexuality is a search for an image of the self, a twin or confirmation of identity, reinforcement of sameness under the disguise of difference, which is ultimately thwarted by the force of its own representation. In *Nightwood* female cross-gendering as a sexual and textual performance of fetishism is 'exhausted'.

Carolyn Allen has noted that *Nightwood* may be read as a 'theoretical fiction, or as a fiction of theory—a narrative that produces theory as well as story'.[1] While it disavows sexological theories of inversion and psychoanalytic theories of homosexuality, it avows an understanding of lesbian desire as an eroticization of sameness. There are obvious concerns over this conceptualization of lesbian

---

[1] Carolyn Allen, *Following Djuna: Women Lovers and the Erotics of Loss* (Bloomington, Ind.: Indiana University Press, 1996), 24.

desire which positions women who love women in an infantile and narcissistic position; but Allen argues that *Nightwood* 'rewrites' sameness through its refusal of the psychoanalytic terms of narcissism and its oscillatory 'scripting of differences between women lovers'.[2] Allen, in a similar methodological move to my own, sets the novel 'in conversation' with Freud's 'On Narcissism' to illustrate that Barnes writes what is absent in Freud's work, namely, the maternal position. While I agree with the phenomenology of Allen's critique, I detect in *Nightwood* an anxiety that Allen does not overtly acknowledge: the language of the novel does not simply, as Allen argues, defend against the threat of 'egoistic boundary loss' by posing 'voluntary anxiety' as a defence, but poses boundary loss, the merging of self with the other/lover as what is ultimately desired and fetishized. I argue that the oscillation between difference and sameness speaks of an anxiety about the presentation of a form of lesbian desire, an anxiety that is rendered as fetishism.

In *The Well of Loneliness* Stephen Gordon signifies on her body, through masculine clothing, her desire for the lost female body. In *Nightwood* a very different process is a work, but it is still a form of fetishism: the fetishism that the masculine woman accrued to herself in *The Well* is projected outwards in *Nightwood*; it is the text itself that fetishizes the cross-gendered female. Nora's desire for Robin, while shifting between recognition of sameness and difference, is ultimately, through another oscillation between absence and presence (what is absent or denied but fantasmatically wished for), and the operations of narcissism, the grounds for a subtextual exposition on the nature of female fetishism itself. If masculinity is the fetish that secures the desire of the lover, this implies that the fetish, detached from its subject, generates some kind of reciprocity of mutuality; the fetish is the 'lure' that in turn is fetishized by the subject's lover. As in *HER*, Barnes suggests that desire for the selfsame must be mediated by difference to ward against narcissistic enclosure. In this schema female cross-gendering is the fetish which protects against self-annihilation. Teresa de Lauretis states that 'the major public discourses on lesbian sexuality available in [the twentieth century] are discourses of sexual indifference—of inversion,

[2] Allen, *Following Djuna*, 19.

of masculinity complex, of lesbianism as pre-Oedipal fusion, psychosis, hysteria, bisexuality, or oscillation between masculinity and femininity—and they are all inadequate to the task'.[3] *Nightwood*, in its inability to avow any of these alternatives, but with its inability to find 'adequate' expression for lesbian desire, forces the cross-gendered woman into what I term an 'impossible' position.

Fetishism operates in *Nightwood* through the cross-gendered persona of Robin and via her absence both from her lover and in the text itself. As Allen has illustrated, Nora's 'retrospective narrative of desire' (her confession to Matthew O'Connor in 'Nightwatch') meditates and obsesses upon this loss of the lover. This loss produces in Nora a form of female fetishism: while the object of her desire is absent and longed for, she must evoke her presence through speech and the narrative of her desire. The text also registers this loss: Robin is granted very little interiority and the novel is predominantly composed of dialogue about her, the central piece being Nora's narrative: Robin is 'always the second person singular.'[4] For

[3] Teresa de Lauretis, *The Practice of Love: Lesbian Sexuality and Perverse Desire* (Bloomington, Ind.: Indiana University Press, 1994), 75.

[4] Djuna Barnes, *Nightwood: The Original Version and Related Drafts*, ed. Cheryl J. Plumb (Normal, Ill.: Dalkey Archive Press, 1995), 107. Further references to this edition will be cited in the text. References to Plumb's editorial will be cited in the notes. I am using this edition because my reading includes close examination of what remains of the drafts of the novel. All that is now extant of the two earlier versions of *Nightwood* (sent to publishers in 1932 and 1934) are 72 pages of fragments and a draft and published (emended) version of 'Run, Girls, Run!' which Barnes identifies as 'early mss of "Nightwood" '. The fragments consist of the first 4 pages of 'Watchman, What of the Night?' which were later discarded, 5 pages from 'Largo', some of which corresponds to the published 'Go Down, Matthew', and about 50 pages probably from the second version, including one page from 'La Somnambule' (none of which appears in the finished chapter of the same name), and the rest from 'Go Down, Matthew', very little of which appears in the published text. *Nightwood*, ed. Plumb, 241–2. Djuna Barnes told Hank O'Neal that she was anxious that no one should see early versions of *Nightwood* after her death, but she was loathe to destroy all of the drafts. *'Life is Painful, Nasty and Short . . . In My Case It has Only Been Painful and Nasty': Djuna Barnes 1978–1981, An Informal Memoir* (New York: Paragon House, 1990), 72. Plumb's version is the first scholarly edition of the text. This edition, which practises 'fidelity to the typescript', and is based on Barnes's third revision, 'preserves and presents the original voice, unmuted by the fear of censorship', before T. S. Eliot's interventions at Faber and Faber. *Nightwood*, ed. Plumb, pp. 149, xxv. Perhaps in light of *The Well of Loneliness* trial, T. S. Eliot wanted to emphasize the 'poetic' rather than the 'psychopathic' elements of the novel. Preface, *Nightwood* (London: Faber and Faber, 1985), 5. Barnes thought the New Directions hardback edition 'not sufficient'. O'Neal, *'Life is Painful'*, 58.

Joseph Frank, Robin, even in her absence, is the 'central figure—the figure around which the situation revolves'.[5]

'WHERE NO MODERN WRITER EVER GOES': TEXTUAL INSTABILITY AND THE DRAFTS OF *NIGHTWOOD*

It is not certain when Barnes began to write *Nightwood*, but Cheryl Plumb speculates that it could have been as early as 1927, during her break-up with her lover Thelma Wood in Paris.[6] One of the early titles for the work was 'Anatomy of the Night', which reflects the concern with the workings of the (sexual) body. Barnes wrote the first and second full versions at Hayford Hall in Devon in the summer of 1932 and 1933, but could not at first get it accepted by any publisher on the grounds that

they all say it is not a novel; that there is no continuity of life in it, only high spots and poetry—that I do not give anyone an idea what the persons wore, ate or how they opened and closed doors, how they earned a living or how they took off their shoes and put on their hats. God knows I don't.[7]

This is not strictly true—Barnes obsessively delineates Robin's appearance, her clothes, and the contours of her body, at the expense of her interiority and speech—but this statement does encapsulate the style of *Nightwood*. Cheryl J. Plumb describes it as 'daring in subject matter and verbal experiment', and Suzanne C.

---

[5] Joseph Frank, *The Widening Gyre: Crisis and Mastery in Modern Literature* (1963; Bloomington, Ind.: Indiana University Press, 1968), 32. Donna Gerstenberger warns against reducing *Nightwood* to the story of Robin Vote as she believes Franks does. 'The Radical Narrative of Djuna Barnes's *Nightwood*', in Ellen G. Friedman and Miriam Fuchs (eds.), *Breaking the Sequence: Women's Experimental Fiction* (Princeton: Princeton University Press, 1989), 129–39: 134. However, Barnes's friend Emily Coleman, who transcribed her conversations with Barnes on the problems of structuring the novel, objected to so much emphasis on O'Connor when to her mind the real subject of it was Robin, and her relationship with Nora. See Emily Coleman, letter to Djuna Barnes, 5 Nov. 1935, 'The Letters of Djuna Barnes and Emily Holmes Coleman (1935–1936)', ed. G. C. Guirl-Stearley, *The Missouri Review*, 22.3 (1999), 105–46: 110. The novelist Emily Coleman was instrumental in *Nightwood* becoming published: she wrote to T. S. Eliot to persuade him of its merits. Detailed correspondence between her and Barnes, now in the University of Maryland libraries, charts the progress of the novel.

[6] *Nightwood*, ed. Plumb, p. ix.

[7] Djuna Barnes, letter to Emily Coleman, 20 Apr. 1934. Quoted in *Nightwood*, ed. Plumb, pp. x–xi.

Ferguson is dazzled by its 'verbal pyrotechnics'.[8] Emily Coleman urges Barnes's prospective editor T. S. Eliot to recognize that the distorting images of *Nightwood* 'make you know something you did not know before'.[9] She recognizes the quality that makes *Nightwood* so radically different from other modernist texts: 'Can you read that and not see that something new has been said about the very heart of sex?—going beyond sex, to that world where there is no marriage or giving in marriage—*where no modern writer ever goes?*'[10] The rhetoric that took Barnes 'where no modern writer ever goes' is one of obfuscation and elusiveness, of, as Karen Kaivola has noted, the 'force of desire'. The effort to 'say something new' (the mantra of modernism) must necessitate a new form of expression: in this sense Barnes's narrative style is very similar to that of James Joyce, a writer she knew and respected.[11] Like Anaïs Nin (although Barnes would not welcome the comparison), Barnes was attempting a new form of narrative: in order to render the complexity of the love and jealousy of one woman for a 'girl who resembles a boy' but who also is 'myself', Barnes needed to find a new idiom.

What is most interesting about Emily Coleman's observations of *Nightwood*, is that to her it seems fissured from within, because there is no consistent point of view. Barnes's 'deadly introversion', which was 'almost pathological', has a textual manifestation: 'In this book you believe one thing half the time, and another—the opposite thing—the other half.'[12] Charles Henri Ford made a similar observation of a draft of 'Bow Down'; as Barnes recorded, Ford,

[8] Cheryl J. Plumb, *Fancy's Craft: Art and Identity in the Early Works of Djuna Barnes* (London: Associated University Presses, 1986), 13; Suzanne C. Ferguson, 'Djuna Barnes's Short Stories: An Estrangement of the Heart', *The Southern Review*, 5.1 (Jan. 1969), 26–41: 27.

[9] *Nightwood*, ed. Plumb, p. xxi.

[10] Coleman's emphasis. This is from a draft of a letter to Eliot that Coleman may have sent to him in a different form; she draws Eliot's attention to several passages, including the description of Frau Mann and of Robin ('The woman who presents herself as a picture forever arranged') and the 'terrible ten pages of the jealous life'. Quoted in *Nightwood*, ed. Plumb, p. xxi.

[11] Karen Kaivola, *All Contraries Confounded: The Lyrical Fiction of Virginia Woolf, Djuna Barnes, and Marguerite Duras* (Iowa City, Ia.: University of Iowa Press, 1991), 60. As Kaivola has noted (62), the title of *Nightwood* resonates with the 'Night Town' episode in *Ulysses*. The echo, however, goes beyond the titular: at the centre of both texts is the figure of the transvestite, Leopold Bloom in 'Night Town', Robin Vote and Matthew O'Connor in *Nightwood*.

[12] Quoted in *Nightwood*, ed. Plumb, p. xvi.

echoing the text's own internal fragmentation, 'has torn it to pieces as a work as a whole—says it has no plot (which does not so much matter) but has also no design—is written in different styles—does not hold together'.[13] (Barnes's language echoes the fragmentation of her text in her own broken syntax.) Modern critics have theorized this split nature of *Nightwood*: Carl Herzig argues that Barnes desires 'both to be "in" the world . . . and to step back from the world', and that her work is structured by a dualism of extreme opposites (human/animal, above/below, day/night, male/female); Louis F. Kannenstine believes that this leaves Barnes in a dynamic 'middle position'.[14] For Kannenstine, the figures in Barnes's fiction are struggling to become 'one unqualified whole, either one thing or the other, but they are blocked by the recognition of their duality, their inescapably fractured being'.[15] Alan Singer has identified a particular structuring device (the 'duplicity of the lie') that 'intrinsically jeopardizes . . . concept of form by its implementation of a split *telos*'.[16] As Singer argues in his exposition on metaphor in *Nightwood*, the middle position between dualities (which I argue is the locus of the fetish) is a denial of the authority of the 'literal/figurative dualism' that is found in 'conventional' novels.[17] Kaivola similarly speaks of *Nightwood* in terms of a 'radical split' (between culture and destruction, language and experience).[18] The nature of the production of *Nightwood* and Barnes's structuring motifs (both narrative and characterological) render the text as fetishistic, formed in the throes of a radical split.

While writing the final draft, Barnes concurred with Coleman's wish to erase obvious psychologizing from the novel. In 'The Possessed', eventually the final chapter, Barnes felt that the 'action' spoke for itself, without any narratorial embellishment: 'when they see each other Robin goes down with the dog, and thats [*sic*] the end. I do not go any further than this into the psychology of the

[13] Djuna Barnes, letter to Natalie Clifford Barney, 30 May 1933. Quoted in Phillip Herring, *Djuna: The Life and Work of Djuna Barnes* (1995; London: Penguin, 1996), 182.
[14] Carl Herzig, 'Roots of Night: Emerging Style and Vision in the Early Journalism of Djuna Barnes', *The Centennial Review*, 31.3 (Summer 1987), 255–69: 257; Louis F. Kannenstine, *The Art of Djuna Barnes: Duality and Damnation* (New York: New York University Press, 1977), 109.
[15] Kannenstine, *Art of Djuna Barnes*, p. xv.
[16] Alan Singer, 'The Horse Who Knew Too Much: Metaphor and the Narrative of Discontinuity in *Nightwood*', *Contemporary Literature*, 25.1 (Spring 1984), 66–87: 69.
[17] Ibid. 72.   [18] Kaivola, *All Contraries Confounded*, 67.

"animal" in Robin because it seems to me that the very act with the dog is pointed enough.'[19] In fragments from 'Go Down, Matthew', excised from the published text, Barnes wrote: 'What sense is there in saying the girl went wrong at twenty, that she wore a bowler hat by preference when but eight months old and showed a liking for kissing her grandmother's ⟨bottom⟩ [left elbow]; it's not that she did so that needs explanation', it's what it seemed like while she was about it.'[20] This passage is significant because it not only attests to Barnes's distaste for the exposition of motivational psychology, but in that it also provides a clue to an eroticism that survives, partly as a disavowal, into the published text: Nora's incestuous love for her cross-gendered grandmother.

The drafts of the novel unveil the ruptures in the body of the published *Nightwood* text; excisions surgically performed on it by Emily Coleman, T. S. Eliot, and Barnes herself, removing psychological explanations and more overt references to lesbian sex and sexuality, make it radically unstable and susceptible to a form of fetishism by the reader to fix meaning in order to interpret. The representation of Robin Vote is paradigmatic of this reading process: she is the object of obsession both within the text and therefore without. Nora's narrative, addressed to Matthew O'Connor, attempts to regain narrative control over the disruptive movement of Robin in and through the text.

'HOW CAN THIS BE, THAT I COULD LOVE A WOMAN?':
INVERSION AND PSYCHOANALYSIS IN BARNES'S FICTION

Nightwood is a sick text obsessed with the physical and sexual body written during a period when psychoanalysis was gaining rapid ground as a cultural discourse. All of its major characters suffer from sensory damage or hystericized symptoms. Robin sleepwalks and Felix Volkbein is blind in one eye. The characters are also soul-sick

---

[19] Djuna Barnes, letter to Emily Coleman, 11 July 1935. Quoted in *Nightwood*, ed. Plumb, p. xv.

[20] The word in angle brackets has been crossed out and the words in square brackets have been written in ink over the top in a fragment of 'Go Down, Matthew'. *Nightwood*, ed. Plumb, 273. Even though Barnes is being playful here, the bowler hat is a key item in the costume of cross-gendered female sexual deviance: see Liza Minnelli's performance of Weimar decadence as Sally Bowles in *Cabaret* (1972), and Sabina's erotic performance for Tomas in Milan Kundera's *The Unbearable Lightness of Being* (1984).

or mentally ill: Nora is suffering from a 'derangement in her equilib-
rium', Jenny Petherbridge has a form of kleptomania, O'Connor
speaks distractedly of anguish and loss, and Felix and Robin's son is
suffering from an unspecified mental disorder. O'Connor's late-
night discussions with Nora Flood, as many critics have suggested, is
reminiscent of a therapy session. Critics of *Nightwood* and the discourses of sexual science have usually read the novel as a parodic
commentary on sexological theories of inversion and psychoanalytic
theories of homosexuality, in contrast with *The Well of Loneliness*,
which is often described in these accounts as a secondary sexological
work.[21] Similarly, *Ladies Almanack* (1928), Barnes's wickedly satiri-
cal dedication to Natalie Clifford Barney's lesbian coterie of left
bank Paris, has been read as a critique of existing theories of lesbian
sexuality, and as a lampoon of *The Well*.[22] Carolyn Allen, observing
that 'there is no single identity position or causal explanation for
women who take women lovers', recognizes in Dame Musset a parody of the theory of inversion.[23] She

had been developed in the Womb of her most gentle Mother to be a Boy, when
therefore, she came forth an Inch or so less than this, she paid no Heed to the
Error, but donning a Vest of a superb Blister and Tooling, a Belcher for tippet
and a pair of hip-boots with a scarlet channel (for it was a most wet wadding)
she took her Whip in hand, calling her Pups about her, and so set out upon the
Road of Destiny.[24]

For Evangeline Musset phallic lack is as much the manifestation of
sexual expertise (she is 'wide famed for her Genius at bringing up by
Hand and so noted and esteemed for her Slips of the Tongue' and
doing it, moreover, 'without the Tools for the Trade', 9, 8), as it is
the mark of castration.[25] Barnes, while envisioning the possibilities

---

[21] Leigh Gilmour compares *The Well* and *Nightwood*, and maintains that *Nightwood*
did not prompt an immediate lesbian readership 'because it was presented neither
through a medical discourse nor in terms of narrative realism'. 'Obscenity, Modernity,
Identity: Legalizing *The Well of Loneliness* and *Nightwood*', *Journal of the History of
Sexuality*, 4 (Apr. 1994), 603–24: 614.

[22] See Susan Sniader Lanser, 'Speaking in Tongues: *Ladies Almanack* and the
Discourse of Desire', in Mary Lynn Broe (ed.), *Silence and Power: A Reevaluation of
Djuna Barnes* (Carbondale, Ill.: Southern Illinois University Press, 1991), 156–68.

[23] Allen, *Following Djuna*, 5.

[24] Djuna Barnes, *Ladies Almanack* (1928; Elmwood Park, Ill.: Dalkey Archive Press,
1992), 7. Further references are cited in the text.

[25] Frann Michel has noted that *Almanack* is a mockery of the 'psychoanalytic focus
on castration'. Barnes implies that castration is not simply loss of the male member since
the penis is a mere adjunct to the testicles (7). 'All Women Are Not Women All: *Ladies*

of female inversion (Musset challenges her disappointed father with the question 'Am I not doing after your very Desire?', 8), is ultimately condemnatory of sexological theory and the concept of the masculinity complex: 'For near to a Man or far from a Man, she will not be of him!' (53). Barnes would rather entertain the possibility that the first lesbian ('the first Woman born with a Difference') was hatched from an egg dropped unceremoniously from heaven (26).

Nightwood has been read as a more serious engagement with sexological and psychoanalytic constructions of female sexuality. Andrea Harris sees in Matthew O'Connor 'a biting parody of the figure of the sexologist'.[26] As she points out, *Nightwood* takes place in the 1920s 'when the shift to homosexuality had already been made', but Barnes uses the term 'invert' throughout, rather than homosexual, because 'she sees sexuality as interrelated with gender or sex role'.[27] *Nightwood* more subtly parodies sexual discourse and the category of inversion through using inversion as a linguistic effect. As Harris argues, *Nightwood* employs chiasmus, the rhetorical figure of inversion, to inscribe the invert.[28] Matthew O'Connor, who listens and then responds to Nora's impassioned pleas, is perhaps the most 'inverted' speaker in the novel, as Harris explains: 'Matthew uses the term "invert" to describe a state of vacillation or a blurring and confusion of genders within the subject rather than a simple predominance of feminine over masculine or masculine over feminine.'[29] I would add to Harris's reading that this vacillation is precisely what makes *Nightwood* open to the operations of fetishism. In this sense, interpretation is fetishism in the attempt to fix that which, as Suzette Henke has observed, is modelled on 'infinite semiosis, on a wilderness of sliding signifiers that refuse to be pinned down and rattle with echoes of undefined meaning, shadows

Almanack and Feminine Writing', in Mary Lynn Broe (ed.), *Silence and Power: A Reevaluation of Djuna Barnes* (Carbondale, Ill.: Southern Illinois University Press, 1991), 170–82: 177.

[26] Andrea L. Harris, *Other Sexes: Rewriting Difference from Woolf to Winterson* (Albany, NY: State University of New York Press, 2000), 63.

[27] Ibid. 163 n. 2.   [28] Ibid. 64.

[29] Ibid. 82. Harris uses the example of O'Connor's speech about the cultural importance of the invert, which I discuss later, to illustrate the use of an asymmetrical chiasmus (85–6). As Harris explains: 'because "the third sex" subverts binary oppositions by being a conjunction of masculine and feminine, it challenges the structure of binary opposition that shores up the world of the day, discourse, and structures of power, and is not recognizable, or "does not exist," in these contexts' (93).

of psychic states indefinitely deferred'.[30] O'Connor's cross-dressed metaphor of 'dressing the unknowable in the garments of the known' is, finally, what *Nightwood* fails to do.

Carolyn Allen suggests that Barnes enters into a discussion with Freud's theories of narcissism. Jane Marcus invites us to read Matthew, the gynaecologist who 'analyses' Nora, as a 'parodic Freud', precisely the Freud of the Fliess letters. Marcus sees Nora as Dora, the lesbian patient who chooses as a doctor a transvestite whose 'womb envy' is so pronounced that it 'parodies Freudian penis envy mercilessly'.[31] Allen argues that *Nightwood* attends to the 'psyche rather than to the social surround and to the psyche's encounter with others'.[32] While Radclyffe Hall offers an etiology for Stephen's cross-gendered identity (if one that incorporates both the psychoanalytic and the congenital aspects of homosexuality and cross-gendering), in *Nightwood* Barnes is not interested in providing a fictionalized case history of Robin Vote, or any of the other characters, as we saw from one of the drafts. Indeed as Frank notes, characterization *per se* is rendered problematic in a work where the so-called central character 'has not yet attained the level of the human'.[33] T. S. Eliot stressed in his preface to the Faber edition of *Nightwood* that it is 'not a psychopathic study', that we must read illness as a metaphor for loss of control, while in a draft, O'Connor equates telling the truth with a case history, as a 'bad idea . . . all the ⟨sensation⟩ [FACTS] of life but none of the ⟨facts⟩ [SENSATIONS]—what is the use!'[34] The transposition of the terms is significant: it constitutes a Freudian slip that speaks of the disavowal of psychoanalysis in *Nightwood*.

As Barnes stated to Coleman, she wished not to explain the motivations of her characters. For instance she supported Coleman's

[30] Suzette A. Henke, '(En)Gendering Modernism: Virginia Woolf and Djuna Barnes', in Kevin J. H. Dettmar (ed.), *Rereading the New: A Backward Glance at Modernism* (Ann Arbor: University of Michigan Press, 1992), 325–41: 331.

[31] Jane Marcus, 'Laughing at Leviticus: *Nightwood* as Woman's Circus Epic', in Mary Lynn Broe (ed.), *Silence and Power: A Reevaluation of Djuna Barnes* (Carbondale, Ill.: Southern Illinois University Press, 1991), 221–50: 230. Elizabeth Dolan Kautz inverts this relationship noting that it is O'Connor who is prostrate like a patient while Nora asks the questions. 'Gynaecologists, Power and Sexuality in Modernist Texts', *Journal of Popular Culture*, 28.4 (Spring 1995), 81–91: 88.

[32] Allen, *Following Djuna*, 13.   [33] Frank, *The Widening Gyre*, 32.

[34] Fragment of 'Go Down, Matthew' in *Nightwood*, ed. Plumb, 273. Words in angle brackets have been crossed out, and words in square brackets have been written in over the top.

suggestion to omit any narratorial and authorial extemporizing on the psychic implications of Matthew O'Connor's cross-dressing in a flannel nightgown; in a draft Barnes had added that 'for a night dress is our mother'; Coleman advised against the inclusion on the grounds that it was 'a bit smarty'.[35] With this in mind Barnes systematically closes down opportunities for the reader to interpret from the psychoanalytically rich field of childhood experience and trauma. Hedvig dies after giving birth to Felix, but, this trauma aside, his early developmental history is ostensibly withheld: 'At this point exact history stopped for Felix who, thirty years later, turned up in the world with these facts, the two portraits and nothing more ... What had formed Felix from the date of his birth to his coming to thirty was unknown to the world' (8). Details of Nora's childhood and adolescence, apart from a glancing reference to the fact that Matthew O'Connor delivered her as a baby, are almost entirely excised from the published text. In the draft of 'Go Down, Matthew', Catherine's childhood and development are sketched in (Catherine is the Nora figure). She was 'set up at twelve months and photographed, with my mother holding onto my bow at the back, kneeling down behind my chair so that she wouldn't be in the picture'.[36] This echoes the predominant motif of the doll as fetish in *Nightwood*. After her first romantic/sexual experience with a woman she remarks: ' "How can this be, that I could love a woman?" And that was the first thought about it and the last because after that there was no difference at all, only just love.'[37] There is a pencil line through this latter portion of text, as if Barnes could not face the idea of there being no signifiers of difference in lesbian love. In early drafts, allusion is made to the fact that Robin is, like Felix, an orphan. Frank reads Robin's awakening from her cataleptic state by Felix and Matthew O'Connor as 'the act of birth', since we have no knowledge of her life before that moment.[38] Felix and Robin's child, a congenital imbecile, is also a psychological lacuna, and one of Barnes's more extreme statements concerning reading childhood experience as the basis for adult psychology.

---

[35] Emily Coleman, letter to Djuna Barnes, 27 Aug. 1935. Quoted in *Nightwood*, ed. Plumb, 197.

[36] This bears comparison with Her's self-conceptualization as a doll: 'I seem to have been set here like a doll in a window'. H.D., *Her* (1981; London: Virago, 1984), 151.

[37] *Nightwood*, ed. Plumb, 298, 306.   [38] Frank, *The Widening Gyre*, 33.

'A TALL GIRL WITH THE BODY OF A BOY':
THE IMPOSSIBILITY OF ROBIN VOTE

Coleman's observation that Barnes entertained two contradictory points of view in the drafts of *Nightwood* is borne out in the published version. It is my contention that the text is split from within by its inability to manage successfully the figuration of Robin Vote, the masculine woman who has no history, few origins (we know only that she is American), and is the locus for others' desires, fetishized by her lovers and by the text itself. A symptom of this is in the composition of the novel: Barnes entertained divergent modes of conceptualizing the masculine woman, and inevitably rendered her as what I am terming an 'impossible', or excessive, subject.

Precursors of Robin are found in Barnes's early short stories. In *Nightwood* the infantile qualities become prevalent in Robin's figuration, and the doll takes on a more symbolic aspect as a fetish; in 'Dusie' (1927), published the same year that Barnes began *Nightwood*, the lesbian is characterized as a child-like cross-gendered woman who plays with toy soldiers and dolls:

Then she would lie over, her knees up, her head down, laughing and crying and saying, do you love me? to every woman, and every woman answered that they loved her. But it did not change her, and suddenly she would shout: Get out, get out of my room! Something in her grew and died for her alone.

When they were gone, thrown out, she would sit up in bed and amuse herself with the dolls they had brought her, wooden animals and tin soldiers, and again she would cast them from her with cunning energy.[39]

The narcissistic seeking of women to love her, the inverted solipsism of her actions ('for her alone'), and the expulsion of symbolized objects (dolls, animals, soldiers) is played out again by Robin Vote, as is the iconography of the masculine 'invert': Dusie is 'tall, very big and beautiful, absent and so pale. She wore big shoes, and her ankles and wrists were large.'[40]

Traces of Robin can also be found in a draft of 'Run Girls, Run!' as La Pirouetta, 'the dog-faced Girl' who 'took to loud barking'

---

[39] Djuna Barnes, 'Dusie', in Carl Van Doren (ed.), *Americana Esoterica* (New York: Macy-Masius, 1927), 78.

[40] Ibid. 75.

until she awoke the 'Bird of her Soul' and gave birth to Leda 'who
⟨xx⟩ turned out to be boy . . . studying his own hand, palm up, in a
manly effort to discover a trace of herself!'[41] It is noteworthy, given
the exploration of hands in previous chapters, that this complexly
gendered person looks for a trace of herself on the lesbian instrument of the hand. The transmogrification into a dog survives into
Nightwood, as does the bird in appellatory form in 'Robin'. In the
published version the character Hazel calls herself Gavin and wears
'galligaskins', and was 'no more girl than the pout of her breeks
would suggest'.[42] In this text Leda undergoes contortions in order
to ascertain how 'he' is made: 'never having heard that there's nothing much on the back, nearly dislocated his neck saying ⟨⟨Where is
the other?⟩⟩'. This misrecognition of individual sovereignty and
integrity, and the search for the lost part of the self, is a major obsession in *Nightwood*.

Another model for Robin Vote, avowed and disavowed by Barnes,
is Barnes's lover, the handsome and boyish silverpoint artist Thelma
Wood, with whom she had a passionate and destructive eight-year
relationship in Paris in the 1920s: Barnes called *Nightwood* 'my life
with Thelma'.[43] In 1936 Barnes wrote to Emily Coleman that the
title of her novel had changed from 'Bow Down' to 'Anatomy of the
Night', to 'Through the Night', to 'Night Without Sleep', to
'Nightwood', which was both an avowal and disavowal of Thelma's
name: 'Nigh T. Wood' ('low, thought of it the other day. Very
odd').[44] In a final disavowal of Thelma, Barnes later told Hank
O'Neal that the title was taken from William Blake's poem 'The

---

[41] *Nightwood*, ed. Plumb, 250. The word in angle brackets is illegible and has been
crossed out.

[42] Corrected text (in Barnes's hand) of 'Run Girls, Run!', *Caravel*, 2.5 (Mar. 1936).
Reprinted in *Nightwood*, ed. Plumb, 259.

[43] Djuna Barnes, letter to Emily Coleman, 14 Dec. 1935. Quoted in *Nightwood*, ed.
Plumb, p. vii. Herring follows Barnes's lead in his reading of Robin as Thelma. *Djuna*,
156–70. Lynn DeVore argues, however, from a reading of Barnes's foreward to Baroness
Elsa von Freytag Loringhoven's unpublished memoirs, that Robin is 'fundamentally'
based on the eccentric and artistic Baroness. DeVore is influenced by the description of
the Baroness as boyish and small-breasted with a body 'that gives her the appearance
of *death in reverse*'. 'The Backgrounds of *Nightwood*: Robin, Felix, and Nora', *Journal
of Modern Literature*, 10.1 (Mar. 1983), 71–90: 79–80, DeVore's italics. Barnes tried to
write a biography of Elsa, who committed suicide in 1927.

[44] Djuna Barnes, letter to Emily Coleman, 23 June 1936. Quoted in *Nightwood*, ed.
Plumb, pp. viii, ix. Barnes indulged in another disavowal: refusing to label her relationship with Thelma as lesbian, she stated that she 'just loved Thelma'.

Tyger' ('Tyger, Tyger, burning bright | In the forests of the night') and had nothing to do with Thelma's surname.[45]

Thelma Wood's inscription in the text is the trace element of an erotic code that Barnes ultimately wished she had eliminated: this is another metaphorical link with H.D.'s *HER* in the image of the self/lover as a tree. Thelma's name also seeps into the figuration of Nora Flood: 'though her skin was the skin of a child, there could be seen coming, early in her life, the design that was to be the weather–beaten grain of her face, that wood in the work; the tree coming forward in her' (46).[46] Kenneth Burke argues that this description of Nora encodes her 'predestination' to 'perversion'; certainly Thelma survives in the 'wood' that penetrates (as in the American vernacular for the male erection—'to get wood'), and becomes part of the lover's body.[47] Significantly in her mother's copy of *Nightwood*, Barnes deleted the phrase 'that wood in the work; the tree coming forward in her', but it has subsequently appeared in every edition.[48] Similarly, Matthew O'Connor, in his monologue on the nature of the night and of night creatures, speaks of the female homosexual who looks 'dark and muted', and who desires to be completely 'flat with the floor . . . utterly blotted out and erased so that no stain of her could ache upon the wood' (80). There is an erotic relation between the woman and the wooden floor that encrypts Barnes's desire for Thelma, and Nora's for Robin. Thelma survives, however, as one of the trees of the 'nightwood'. The chapter 'Where the Tree Falls' dramatizes the effect of Robin's absence upon the child Guido, while O'Connor speaks of the tree of night as being, in sexual terms perhaps, the 'hardest tree to mount'. His description of this tree draws from the code of lesbian eroticism (hands and sexual sap): the tree 'sweats a resin and drips a pitch against the palm' (72).

[45] O'Neal, *'Life is Painful'*, 104. Andrew Field is mistakenly convinced that Eliot suggested the title, and that Barnes accepted it because of its 'unwitting secret watermark of Thelma's name in it'. *The Formidable Miss Barnes: A Biography of Djuna Barnes* (London: Secker and Warburg, 1983), 212.

[46] The name Wood is echoed in Nora's surname Flood. This was brought to my attention by a slip or typo in Dianne Chisholm's, 'Obscene Modernism: *Eros Noir* and the Profane Illumination of Djuna Barnes', *American Literature*, 69.1 (Mar. 1997), 167–206: 180, which referred to 'Nora Wood'.

[47] Kenneth Burke, 'Version, Con-, Per-, and In-: Thoughts on Djuna Barnes's Novel *Nightwood*', in *Language as Symbolic Action: Essays on Life, Literature and Method* (Berkeley: University of California Press, 1968), 247.

[48] *Nightwood*, ed. Plumb, 193.

Elsewhere, as Georgette Fleischer has pointed out, 'wood becomes a hybrid form of flesh, particularly women's flesh', for example in Frau Mann's 'tan bark in her walk' and the flex of her calf which is 'as solid, specialized and as polished as oak'.[49] The tree as a symbol of lesbian sexuality is also overtly evident in 'Dusie': 'She has a strong bodily odor, like sleep and a tree growing.'[50]

Described as 'a tall girl with the body of a boy' (43), Robin ostensibly displays the somatic signifiers of inversion, and these masculine attributes are the most dominant aspects in her physical representation: the 'hipless smoothness of her gait' (61), the tendency towards dressing in boys' clothes (Nora 'would find her standing in the middle of the room, in boy's clothes, rocking from foot to foot', 122), the broad shoulders, large feet, and short hair (43).[51] Miriam Fuchs suggests that her white pyjamas suggest 'her sacred dimension while her later tendency to wear young men's clothes on the streets of Paris' links her to Adonis.[52] The white pyjamas also connect her with a lesbian encoding utilized in *The Well of Loneliness* and *HER*.[53] Her name, suggesting feminism and suffragism in her surname 'Vote', also connotes clothing ('robin-g'). Most importantly Robin is a sexual being, using her cross-gendered persona to attract a succession of women.

[49] Georgette Fleischer, 'Djuna Barnes and T. S. Eliot: The Politics and Poetics of *Nightwood*', *Studies in the Novel*, 30.3 (Autumn 1998), 405–35: 417. Fleischer makes the interesting point that after giving birth Felix finds Robin 'in the pod of the curtain, her chin so thrust forward that the muscles in her neck stuck out' which is an image suggesting female genitalia 'reminiscent of one of the erotic orchids being approached by a woman's hands in the silverpoint drawings of Thelma Wood' (417). The hand in the drawing is bulbous, claw-like and misshapen, the two visible fingers separated from the thumb in a vaginal 'V' shape.

[50] 'Dusie', 78.

[51] Emily Coleman suggested that Barnes might not want to overemphasize Robin's childish masculinity: she advises a change from 'her boy's legs' to merely 'her legs'. Emily Coleman, letter to Djuna Barnes, 27 Aug. 1935. Quoted in *Nightwood*, ed. Plumb, 193. The passage appears on p. 41 of the Dalkey Archive edition.

[52] Miriam Fuchs, 'Dr. Matthew O'Connor: The Unhealthy Healer of Djuna Barnes's *Nightwood*', in Anne Hudson Jones (ed.), *Literature and Medicine*, ii. *Images of Healers* (Baltimore and London: Johns Hopkins University Press, 1985), 125–34: 127.

[53] Laura Winkiel, following Jane Marcus, usefully observes that the scene in which we first see Robin 'seems to conflate two images of Marlene Dietrich in *Blonde Venus* (1932): the first is the scene in which Lola Lola abandons her flight from the law and her husband and gives up her child. She surrenders in a hotel room filled with plants and unseen, chirping birds. The second image is the famous Paris cabaret scene in which Lola Lola sings in a white tuxedo.' 'Circuses and Spectacles: Public Culture in *Nightwood*', *Journal of Modern Literature*, 21.1 (Summer 1997), 7–28: 22.

Some critics have, however, also argued for Robin's essential and constructed femininity: they point out that she is a mother (if one who rejects and abandons her child), and is remembered by Nora as dressing to the 'chimes of cosmetic bottles and cream jars; the faint perfume of hair heated under the curling irons' (52).[54] When Felix first sees and falls in love with her she is figured in the aspect of a hysteric in a faint: 'half flung off the support of the cushions from which, in a moment of threatened consciousness she had turned her head, lay the young woman, heavy and dishevelled' (34). In her relationship with Nora she is both wayward male child and husband, who rejects the motherly and wifely protection that Nora offers; at other moments she is the femme to Nora's butch, the vulnerable young woman who has to be led from the circus ring. But Barnes explains to Coleman the seeming ambiguity of Robin's sexuality in terms of contemporary mores:

Robins [*sic*] marriage to Felix *is* necessary to the book for this reason (which you can not know, not having lived with a woman having loved her and yet circulated in public with that public aware of it) that people *always* say, 'Well of course those two women would never have been in love with each other if they had been *normal*, if any man had slept with them, if they had been well f———— and had born a child'. Which is ignorance and utterly false, I married Robin to prove this point, she had married, had had a child yet was still 'incurable'.[55]

The incurability of Robin's homosexuality is underscored by the suggestion that, in a moment of rare access to Robin's consciousness, she fantasizes while she is pregnant: 'There was something commensurate in the heavy body with the weight in her mind where reason was inexact with lack of necessity. She wandered to thoughts of women, women that she had come to connect with women' (43).[56]

---

[54] See Carolyn Allen, 'The Erotics of Nora's Narrative in Djuna Barnes's *Nightwood*', *SIGNS*, 19.1 (Autumn 1993), 177–200: 186.

[55] Djuna Barnes, letter to Emily Coleman, 8 Nov. 1935. Quoted in *Nightwood*, ed. Plumb, pp. xvii–xviii.

[56] Andrea L. Harris attempts to unpick the complexities of Robin's gender and sexual identity: ' "She" is not simply a woman who, seeing herself as masculine, wants to be a man, which would imply a resolution of the conflicts between sex, gender, sexual practice, and desire. Rather, Robin is . . . a girl/prince: a female (her sex), who resembles a feminine male (her gender), who is sexually involved with both men and women (her sexual practice), and who loves women (her desire). These incongruous identifications exist side by side, and the tension between them is never resolved in a simple formula such as "Robin is a man in a woman's body". Robin is *not* a man in a woman's body but a woman who loves women, who seems masculine, and whose very body and self-presentation also seem masculine' (*Other Sexes*, 87–8). This explanation is perhaps too neat: it does not go far enough to illustrate Robin's radical 'impossibility'.

While *Ladies Almanack* ironically and comically ridicules theories of inversion, *Nightwood*, to accentuate Robin's 'incurability', conspires in the figuration of the active masculine lesbian as invert. Robin's inversion is not rendered unstable by the red herring of her being a wife and mother, but rather by the intersection of other modes of representation. The text, pushing Robin to the limits of representation, subjects her to the bestial: she is incarnated as various animals, can communicate with the lion at the circus where she first meets Nora, and finally becomes 'one' with a dog in the devastating climax of the novel. Like the invert, she is inscribed as the manifestation of congenital defect: 'Such a woman is the infected, carrier of the past—before her the structure of our head and jaws ache—we feel that we could eat her, she who is eaten death returning, for only then do we put our face close to the blood on the lips of our forefathers' (36). One of the primary motifs in *Nightwood* is the bestial constitution of human nature; as infected throwback, Robin, a 'beast turning human' (36), is a creature on the verge of (male) sexual maturity: she has temples 'like those of young beasts cutting horns' (113).[57] But also encoded into this passage is Robin as a sexual deviant infected with congenital illness, and as a sexually active lesbian who can be cunnilingually 'eaten'. T. S. Eliot removed other references to cunnilingus, but this one survived perhaps because it is more ambiguous; but the metaphor of cannibalism and vampirism should alert us to the 'perverse' meanings of this passage.[58] Robin, 'outside the human type', is also outside gender categories. She is, as O'Connor recognizes

a wild thing caught in a woman's skin, monstrously alone, monstrously vain; like the paralysed man in Coney Island . . . who had to lie on his back in a box, but the box was lined with velvet, his fingers jewelled with stones, and

---

[57] Bonnie Kime Scott catalogues Barnes's bestiary including drawings from *Ryder* (1928) and *The Book of Repulsive Women* (1915) showing women with hooves, horns and tails. *Refiguring Modernism*, ii. *Postmodern Feminist Readings of Woolf, West, and Barnes* (Bloomington, Ind.: Indiana University Press, 1995), 71–122. Barnes's last published work was *Creatures in an Alphabet* (1982).

[58] Margaret Vandenburg argues that Eliot's excisions make sexual inversion 'more pathological and tragic than transgressive and redemptive'. 'Aryan *Mundus* and Sexual Inversion: Eliot's Edition of *Nightwood*', *Prospects: An Annual of American Cultural Studies*, ed. Jack Salzman, 23 (Cambridge: Cambridge University Press, 1998), 329–55: 330. Vandenburg traces the inversions of the Bakhtinian carnivalesque, best illustrated in Robin: 'She was always holding God's bag of tricks upside down' (343). In the 'final ritual of inversion' Robin becomes dog/God (333).

suspended over him where he could never take his eyes off, a sky-blue mounted mirror, for he wanted to enjoy his own 'difference.' (121)

O'Connor's association of Robin with the man who 'wanted to enjoy his own difference' (note that the word 'difference' is marked off in the text with inverted commas), suggests that Robin remains different only unto her self, that she does not require an 'other'.[59] The implication that enjoyment of one's alterity is a process of death (the box suggests a coffin), impacts upon Nora's negation of Robin's ultimate difference, manifested in a desire for fusion and integration that can only result in annihilation. Kaivola argues that the animal kingdom invoked by Barnes is a 'place uninscribed by history', a realm prior to discourse.[60] As a *somnambule* Robin emanates from this preconscious realm, exuding the smell of death and corruption as she sleeps.

The early short stories 'The Rabbit' (1917), the tale of a man who undergoes a form of 'sex change' in order to repress his 'femininity', and 'A Night Among the Horses' (1918), dramatize precisely the anxiety that *Nightwood* so exhaustively and painfully explores; that the idea of a sovereign and unified self, threatened by the divisive nature of desire, succumbs to annihilation. In 'A Night Among the Horses', as Plumb observes, Freda is characterized as doll-like and mechanical ('that small fiery woman, with a battery for a heart and the body of a toy'); she is also described as sexually monstrous (a 'little beast', a 'praying mantis').[61] As Ferguson explains, the animal, like the doll, 'represents an impasse' in characterological individuation in Barnes's writing: because her characters 'are unable to reconcile their instinctive and violent revulsion against any intrusion upon the perfectly autonomous self with their equally strong and instinctive need for love, they remain outside human provenance, dangerous to themselves and to others, estranged'.[62] A similar

---

[59] For an enlightened discussion of how Robin and Matthew O'Connor 'function as privileged objects of desire, as the other (o)' for Nora, Felix, and Jenny see Elisabeth Bronfen, 'Wandering in Mind and Body: Death, Narration and Gender in Djuna Barnes' Novel *Nightwood*', *Amerikastudien*, 33.2 (1988), 167–77: 171. I do not agree, however, with Bronfen's assertion that Robin needs the 'projected desire of the others to give her a sense of personality' (173). As I argue, Robin cannot be read in such 'psychological' terms.

[60] Kaivola, *All Contraries Confounded*, 69.

[61] Plumb, *Fancy's Craft*, 56; Djuna Barnes, 'A Night Among the Horses', in *Spillway* (London: Faber and Faber, 1962), 44, 48. The stories first appeared in a somewhat different form in *A Book* (1923) and were also issued in *A Night Among the Horses* (1929).

[62] Ferguson, 'Djuna Barnes's Short Stories', 32.

process of annihilation is devastatingly dramatized in the short story 'Cassation' (1925) in which Gaya wants to inhabit a pre-Oedipal realm with her mentally disabled child, Valentine, where there is 'no father, no mother, no sisters, no brothers—only you, only you!' The 'wild' quality of her speech is emptied of meaning.[63] As Plumb suggests, Gaya asserts 'only the existence of a perceiving "I," which, lacking external reality, is only *vacancy*'.[64] In her reintegration with Valentine, she regresses to a subhuman mode of existence, disavowing consciousness and individual identity, and destroying the contractual obligations of human life.[65] Gaya's love becomes self-consuming, as Nora's threatens to be. These early stories speak of a deep-rooted anxiety that is reiterated in *Nightwood*: that the entry into the Symbolic, the accession to full humanity, is fraught with difficulty. It is impossible for Robin: an attempt is made to bring her into the realm of desire, into the Symbolic, but she cannot make herself comprehensible. Nora loves her, but misapprehends her, and she eventually reverts to her former position as a beast. This position of 'impossible alterity' is compounded by the mode of her representation, which is fetishistic.

Robin is fetishized not only by Nora but also by the text itself, which creates her as a figure of undecidability. She is unknowable as a textual representation and as a 'character'. Felix underscores this point:

'Strange, I had never seen the Baronin in this light before,' the Baron was saying, and he crossed his knees. 'If I should try to put it into words, I mean how I did see her, it would be incomprehensible, for the simple reason that I find that I never did have a really clear idea of her at any time. I had an image of her, but that it is not the same thing. An image is a stop the mind makes between uncertainties. (93)

In this passage, what Felix has to say about Robin's image can be equated with the value of the fetish that similarly symbolizes the 'stop' between the uncertainties of castration and corporeal/psychic integrity. But to 'call a stop between uncertainties' is to perceive human beings in the 'halt position of the damned';[66] Kannenstine glosses that this is the 'middle position' from which 'syntheses of dualities become possible'; rather, it is the position of the fetish

---

[63] 'Cassation', *Spillway*, 29.   [64] Plumb, *Fancy's Craft*, 68.   [65] Ibid. 69.
[66] 'A Night Among the Horses', 46.

which negotiates between narratives of avowal and disavowal.[67] As a fetishized object Robin exists at one remove from being 'known'; as Singer notes, as a picture 'forever arranged' she is an 'ideality', 'epistemologically self-sufficient', the 'prick of desire'.[68]

The unknowability of Robin is also experienced in interpretation and is intensified by the way in which she appears textually as an absent centre. Her speech, and her consciousness and subjective experiences, are rarely recorded, and where there is a concession to interiority, there is ultimately only emptiness and silence: she 'thought her unpeopled thoughts' (43). She first exists as an object of contemplation for Felix, as he observes her in a fainting fit, and later asleep; throughout the rest of the novel her movements are described as being those of a *somnambule*, someone who is caught between two realms of waking and sleep, consciousness and unconsciousness. As James Baird recognizes, Robin, in her state of inarticulacy, is a manifestation of the unconscious.[69] Even when conscious, she rarely emits words, and gesture and movement define her: 'She put her hand against his chest and pushed him [Felix], she looked frightened, she opened her mouth but no words came' (44). When she does speak it is excessively, shouting or 'cursing like a sailor' during childbirth (44); she asks of Felix 'Why talk?' (45), in a perfect articulation of her unsuitability for the realm of language. With Nora there is a brief exchange of words of introduction, which indicates both an avowal and disavowal of identity: 'After a pause the girl said, "I'm Robin Vote." She looked about her distractedly. "I don't want to be here." But it was all she said; she did not explain where she wished to be' (49); later, Robin's body, turned away from Nora, 'spoke of some awful silence' (52). In her cataleptic state Robin is a physical manifestation of the unconscious, and therefore a remnant of primitivism: Barnes likens her to the woman in Henri Rousseau's painting *A Dream*, in which the female figure is depicted against jungle imagery (34). The intersection of Robin's symbolization as primitive animal and *somnambule* make her a potent symbol of the realm of unlimited fantasy and desire.[70]

---

[67] Kannenstine, *The Art of Djuna Barnes*, 109.

[68] Singer, 'The Horse Who Knew Too Much', 82.

[69] James Baird, 'Djuna Barnes and Surrealism: "Backward Grief" ', in Kenneth H. Baldwin and David K. Kirby (eds.), *Individual and Community: Variations on a Theme in American Fiction* (Durham, NC: Duke University Press, 1975), 160–81: 177.

[70] Baird reads Nora's desire for Robin as 'physical longing for identification with Robin's beast-like innocence' (178). It is worth noting that Joseph Breuer considered somnambulism to be a symptom of hysteria. 'Case 1. Fräulein Anna O', in *The Standard*

Robin is endlessly described analogously, as a displacement: as Victoria Smith has put it, 'she signals desire in that she becomes nothing more than a series of metaphors and metonymies'.[71] Matthew O'Connor tells Nora that Robin is the 'eternal momentary . . . always the second person singular' (107), and it could be argued that she is also, most crucially, singular unto herself. It is in the simultaneity of all these positions (first, second, and third person) that she exists as a fetishized object of impossibility. As O'Connor remonstrates with Nora, Robin is unable to 'put herself in another's place', because she is herself the 'only position': 'she can't do anything in relation to anyone but herself' (122). If Robin is the only position, then the implication is not merely that she is self-absorbed to the point of pathological narcissism, but that she occupies a site of enduring but fantasmatic wholeness. If we recall that the fetish is in Marjorie Garber's terms 'a figure *for* the undecidability of castration, which is to say, a figure of nostalgia for ordinary "wholeness"—in the mother, in the child', then it can be argued that Robin is herself thus fetishized. She occupies the position of the phallic mother, not because of any fantasized penile endowment, but because she is imagined to be autonomous. Fetish objects (accoutrements of her masculinity, her bestiality) allow privileged access to her.[72]

The conception that Robin occupies a position of fantasmatic wholeness, supported elsewhere in the text, is augmented by Felix's recognition that Robin subsumes and neutralizes difference within her own body:

he felt that he was looking upon a figurehead in a museum, which though static, no longer roosting on its cutwater, seemed yet to be going against the wind; as if this girl were the converging halves of a broken fate, setting face, in sleep, toward itself in time, as an image and its reflection in a lake seem parted only by the hesitation in the hour. (36–7)

Edition of the Complete Works of Sigmund Freud, trans. James Strachey *et al.*, 24 vols. (London: The Hogarth Press and the Institute of Psycho-Analysis, 1953–74), 2. 21–47: 22. Further references will be to this edition (*SE*). Freud notes that the state of sleep is like illness 'in implying a narcissistic withdrawal of the positions of the libido on to the subject's own self'. 'On Narcissism: An Introduction' (1914), *SE* 14. 69–102: 83.

[71] Victoria L. Smith, 'A Story Beside(s) Itself: The Language of Loss in Djuna Barnes's *Nightwood*', *PMLA (Publications of the Modern Language Association of America)*, 114.2 (Mar. 1999), 194–206: 200.

[72] Marjorie Garber, *Vested Interests: Cross-Dressing and Cultural Anxiety* (1992; London: Penguin, 1993), 121.

The imagery of this passage works to convey the idea that Robin is almost impossibly doubled, that she occupies a position that is at the limits of signification. Felix's inability to put into words how he sees Robin, because it would be 'incomprehensible', is paradigmatic of the experience of reading and interpreting *Nightwood*. As Martin Bock has phrased it 'the language of *Nightwood* hovers between denotation and connotation; it simultaneously creates meaning but denies paraphrase. The text, in a sense, competes with and subverts itself.'[73] The image of the face which sets itself 'toward itself' implies a gesture of inconceivable contortionism, an image that cannot be 'imagined'.

The final sentence significantly invokes the image of Narcissus, in love with his own reflected image in a lake, whose self-obsession simultaneously creates the illusion of corporeal/psychic wholeness, and stimulates the impossible desire to separate oneself from one's body (she is described elsewhere as 'monstrously vain', 121). This is extended further when Robin assumes aspects of Echo, spurned by Narcissus, and doomed to a bodiless existence as a mere repeater of other people's words: 'Robin, unseen, gave back an echo of her unknown life' (51).[74] Like the face that sets itself toward itself, the ability to give back an echo of one's life suggests an incontrovertible, but unimaginable split that simultaneously emanates from and is reincorporated by her body. That Robin is herself the only position, that she 'can't do anything in relation to anyone but herself', that she is Narcissus incarnate, suggests that she is fetishized as an illusion of fantasmatic wholeness sustained by the pyrotechnics of the text itself. That she is a mere illusion is substantiated by Barnes's exasperated, but ultimately obfuscating, explanation of this passage: 'This seems too plain to me that I don't know how to make it plainer. Robin has been mentioned as Somnambule, sleepwalking in life, it has been more than hinted that she feels "without home"; her very nature makes her incomplete . . . in short the face of one who is sleeping, that face and that sleep seeking itself . . . in time . . . and time takes time.'[75] Barnes's statement that Robin's nature is incomplete

---

[73] Martin Bock, *Crossing the Shadow-Line: The Literature of Estrangement* (Columbus, Oh.: Ohio State University Press, 1989), 82.

[74] As Juliet Mitchell notes, Echo is the 'absolute *other*' in relation to Narcissus. *Psychoanalysis and Feminism* (London: Allen Lane, 1975), 39.

[75] Djuna Barnes, letter to Hildesheimer, 17 July 1959. Quoted in *Nightwood*, ed. Plumb, 219, Barnes's ellipses.

points to (mis)readings of her in the Symbolic. Moreover, the break-down of Barnes's syntax and diction at the end of the 'explanation' suggests that Barnes could not sufficiently 'explain' Robin outside the text as well as in it.

The recurrence of images of doubling and twinning in *Nightwood* is suggestive of a profound preoccupation with concepts of identification, narcissism, and desire. Felix recognizes his animal-other in a lion that 'somehow turned toward him a face like his own' (11). Nora understands that Matthew O'Connor cross-dresses in order that he may 'lie beside himself' (69); when he encounters Felix he 'threw off his unobserved self' (92). In a dream-like sequence, Nora experiences an illusion of Robin as a fantasy of self-perpetuating selves (the multiplying double shadows falling from a statue):

Waking she began to walk again, and looking out into the garden in the faint light of dawn, she saw a double shadow falling from the statue, as if it were multiplying; and thinking perhaps this was Robin, she called and was not answered. Standing motionless, straining her eyes, she saw emerge from the darkness the light of Robin's eyes, the fear in them developing their luminosity until, by the intensity of their double regard, Robin's eyes and hers met. So they gazed at each other. As if the light had power to bring what was dreaded into the zone of their catastrophe, Nora saw the body of another woman swim up into the statue's obscurity, with head hung down, that the added eyes might not augment the illumination; her arms about Robin's neck, her body pressed to Robin's, her legs slackened in the hang of the embrace. (56)

This passage plays with the image of the double to almost halluci-natory effect, the result of which is a teasing ambiguity: it is unclear whether Nora sees Robin in the statue or in the multiplying shad-ows; this proliferation of Robins is symptomatic of both Nora's anxiety and the textual obsession with Robin. Similarly 'the inten-sity of their double regard' is typically equivocal: while this refers to the gaze between Nora and Robin, the construction of this para-graph allows for the possibility that Robin, as a multiple self, is capable of double vision, of empowering Nora to look at her. The entry of Jenny Petherbridge into the 'zone of their catastrophe' breaks the multiply doubled nexus between Nora and Robin, and Nora wishes that 'the design would break and melt back into Robin alone' (57).

Nora recognizes that she has been 'loved by something strange', and that she came close to 'othering' Robin: a 'shadow was falling

on her—mine' which 'was driving her out of her wits', a threat
which makes her 'fate colossal' (128–9). Nora's desire is that she will
be able to 'come between and save' Robin, but since she is a mere
'shadow in her dream', it remains a fantasy (121). Nora speaks of a
coming 'between', but this is a misapprehension of both her position
and Robin's: Robin is indivisible.[76] However, Nora ultimately
understands the reality of her own position as Other: 'myself echo
struggling to answer' (121). O'Connor exclaims that a 'man is whole
only when he takes into account his shadow as well as himself'
(101), and Robin's inability to absorb Nora's shadow declares her
own peculiar singularity. Barnes has created precisely an 'impossible' or linguistically excessive position for Robin: she is 'outside the
"human type" ' (the word 'type' here denoting, linguistically, the
printed word) and the 'only position' (sexually and ontologically).
This means that Nora's love for Robin is also 'impossible': 'Only the
impossible lasts forever; with time, it is made accessible. Robin's
love and mine was always impossible, and loving each other, we no
longer love. Yet we love each other like death' (116). It is not the case
that their love is impossible because they exist on the same side of
desire; it is impossible because Barnes has conceived of Robin as
ultimately excessive in her integrity.

NOR HER: THE OTHER WOMAN

Nightwood fictionalizes Nora's 'impossible' desire for Robin in
terms of the fetishization of her radical alterity, but Nora is not conceived in terms of her utter difference. In an early fragment, the
character Catherine (a prototype of Nora) is dismissive of love as
complementarity: 'Suppose I had been that idiotic thing people call
the complement of herself?'[77] In the published version her name

---

[76] Miriam Fuchs notes that Robin is a 'deadly spillway for Felix, Nora and Jenny, who
draw their notions of self through her'. 'Djuna Barnes: "Spillway" into Nightmare', *The
Hollins Critic*, 18.3 (June 1981), 2–9: 5. One might add that she is deadly because she is
resistant to being othered: she casts no identificatory reflection. Fuchs argues that
Miranda in Barnes's play *The Antiphon* (1958) points to the hopelessness of believing in
a spillway, of 'pouring oneself into another's identity', when she repudiates her mother's
desire for metamorphosis (8). See *The Antiphon* in *Selected Works of Djuna Barnes*
(London: Faber and Faber, 1962). Augusta's desire to be Miranda manifests in dressing
in Miranda's clothes (198).

[77] Fragment of 'Go Down, Matthew'. *Nightwood*, ed. Plumb, 297.

change is significant, connoting a disavowal of the feminine ('nor her'), and yet an avowal of excessive emotion ('flood').[78] Nora's position in relation to Robin's masculinity is not one of marked femininity. She is described, like Robin, as being 'broad and tall' with the infantile quality that Robin also possesses ('her skin was the skin of a child', 46). Like Robin she exists on the periphery of society 'outside and unidentified', 'one of those deviations by which man thinks to reconstruct himself' (48). In the latter sense she is the archetypal Other. But she is also figured as Robin's mother-lover, and Robin herself envisions Nora as a Madonna figure (122). The nurturing aspects of Nora's behaviour towards Robin speak of her desire: 'the body of Robin could never be unloved, corrupt or put away. Robin was now beyond timely changes, except in the blood that animated her. That she could be spilled of this, fixed the walking image of Robin in an appalling apprehension on Nora's mind,— Robin alone, crossing streets, in danger' (51). Nora even rationalizes Robin's infidelity in terms of her being protected by the 'successive arms of women' (57). Nurturance, however, has an ultimate corollary: Nora's supreme desire is that the two lovers will be unified in death.

Nora (mis)recognizes her own self in Robin. Self-identification poses problems in conceptualizations of lesbian desire. The eroticization of sameness between women is the unfavourable correlative of psychoanalytic constructions of female homosexuality: that female sexuality, detached from the theory of inversion, can only be understood in terms of narcissism and identification, and not desire for the other. Discourses of sexual science and psychoanalysis have a tendency to pathologize homosexuality as a self-enclosing collapse into a love of itself. Gender theory has subsequently emphasized the importance of theorizing 'sexual difference within homosexuality'.[79] In order to write *Nightwood* out of reinstating an account of female homosexuality as a desire for the self-same, feminist and queer critics have attended closely to the intrusion of difference in the union between Robin and Nora. Allen argues that the women merely 'play out' conventional hegemonic scripts (that of

---

[78] I am grateful to Ros Ballaster for suggesting the double meaning of Nora's name as 'nor her' in a graduate supervision, Oxford, 1998.

[79] Judith Butler, *Bodies that Matter: On the Discursive Limits of Sex* (New York: Routledge, 1993), 240.

wife and husband, mother and child, for instance).[80] She also asserts that the novel's 'scripting of differences' between women lovers becomes not 'sameness' but 'resemblance', a formulation that Allen reads back into Freud's 'On Narcissism'. Both resemblance, and the risks intrinsic to the similarity between lovers, is eroticized in Nora's retrospective narrative, Allen argues; one such risk is the threat of ego boundary loss. According to this reading, while Barnes figures the relationship between Nora and Robin predominantly in terms of sameness, the incorporated signifiers of inversion and other strains of alterity in the encoding of Robin simultaneously reinstate difference. The circulation of power through the various performances of sexual scripts ensures that sameness can be invalidated in the production not of 'narcissistic identification nor radical alterity', but a 'doubled subjectivity of resemblance'.[81] It is thus argued by Allen that Nora, recognizing her own self in Robin, seeks to intersect the affirmation of sameness with constructions of difference, and that this becomes the focus of her retrospective obsession with Robin.

But rather than assume that Nora's recognition of the self-same in Robin is self-evident, Nora's declaration of identificatory anguish ('She is myself. What am I to do?', 108) is a moment of 'misrecognition' which negates Robin's position within the text as impossible subject. Allen, in her refusal to acknowledge Robin's 'radical alterity', conspires in Robin's negation. Nora's misrecognition enforces in Nora not a need to reimpose difference because she has run the risk of self-enclosure, but precisely the opposite. It engenders in Nora the desire for a complete integration with Robin, propelling them both towards death: 'Love becomes the deposit of the heart, analogous in all degrees to the "findings" in a tomb. As in one will be charted the taken place of the body, the raiment, the utensils necessary to its other life, so in the heart of the lover will be traced, as an indelible shadow, that which he loves' (50). In the early stages of their relationship Nora and Robin 'were so "haunted" of each other that separation was impossible' (49–50). But the nature of their involvement (Robin's subsequent detachment from Nora, Nora's obsession with Robin) creates in Nora a desire for eternal merging: 'Nora would wake from sleep, going back through the tide of dreams into which her anxiety had thrown her, taking the body of Robin down with her into it, as the ground things take the corpse, with minute persistence, down into the earth, leaving a pattern of it on the grass, as if they stitched as they descended' (51). This is the desire for incorporation, a complete assimilation of the loved one, laid bare, and the movement of that desire is towards (sexual) death. The going down is not only a descent into the ground, but a descent to the lovers genitals.[82] Their embraces are 'agonized' and an attempt at fusion: the 'two heads' in 'four hands' is suggestive of a composite body (52). Nora recognizes that 'there was no way but death' because only in death would Robin belong to her in ultimate union. Nora imagines that in resurrection 'we come up looking backward at each other', which is an inversion only possible in death and rebirth (52).

As the classic Freudian fetishist disavows sexual difference and constructs the fetish as a memorial to the recognition of castration, so Nora as fetishist disavows the difference between herself and Robin. She is at least aware on some level (avowal), as Bronfen puts it,

> that what she is doing to Robin is disfiguring and eternalising her, in an act of fixage that reduces her to a pure reflecting image, a depersonalised body, a hieroglyph, a dead sign. She understands that ultimately the fascination in this desire for an identity of their bodies in a center of erotics and death is that it cannot and must not be fulfilled, because Robin will not stay.[83]

In this scenario, Robin's signs of difference become fetish objects. Nora does not imagine that she would receive the same reflection of perceived wholeness in a heterosexual relationship: 'A man is another person—a woman is yourself, caught as you turn in panic; on her mouth you kiss your own. If she is taken you cry that you have been robbed of yourself' (119). Alan Singer argues that Robin's negation sustains the other characters' desire, and that she must be denied because she is inaccessible to them.[84] But this is to misrepresent the specificities of Nora's relation to Robin; it is rather the case,

---

[82] Erin G. Carlston, who also points this out, suggests that the text also 'goes down, like Robin, not into semiotic bliss, but into animalism and then silence'. *Thinking Fascism: Sapphic Modernism and Fascist Modernity* (Stanford, Calif.: Stanford University Press, 1998), 79.

[83] Bronfen, 'Wandering in Mind and Body', 174.

[84] Singer, 'The Horse Who Knew Too Much', 70.

as Shari Benstock usefully phrases it, that Robin is 'misread by Nora into conformity' in order to sustain her own self-concept.[85] While T. S. Eliot urged Barnes to excise the more flagrant references to both male and female homosexuality in the published text, Nora's fetishistic desire for Robin is covertly sexual. The following passage did not survive whole into the published version:

> Look for the girls also, in the toilets at night, and you will find them kneeling in that great second confessional, the one the Catholic church forgot—over the door Dames, a girl standing before her [girl], her skirts flung back one on one, while between the columns the handsome head of the girl made boy by God, bends back, the posture of that head volts forth the difference between one woman and another—crying softly between tongues, the terrible excommunication of the toilet[86]

This passage is significant because it spells out the precise meaning of 'bowing down' as sexual, and it establishes the more masculine partner ('the girl made boy') in the active position of the provider of sex, but maintains dissimilarity between these women ('the posture of the head volts forth the difference') in the explosion ('volts') of sexual pleasure. O'Connor meditates further on the desire for the invert:

> what is this love we have for the invert, boy or girl? It was they who were spoken of in every romance that we ever read. The girl lost, what is she but the Prince found? The Prince on the white horse that we have always been seeking. And the pretty lad who is a girl, what but the prince-princess in point lace—neither one and half the other, the painting on the fan! We love them for that reason. We were impaled in our childhood upon them as they rode through our primers, the sweetest lie of all, now come to be in boy or girl, for in the girl it is the prince, and in the boy it is the girl that makes a prince a prince—and not a man. They go far back in our lost distance where what we never had stands waiting; it was inevitable that we should come upon them, for our miscalculated longing has created them. They are our answer to what our grandmothers

[85] Shari Benstock, *Women of the Left Bank: Paris 1900–1940* (1986; London: Virago, 1994), 258. Although I take issue with Benstock's statement that Robin is Nora's 'denied, suppressed' self. Again, this reading denies Robin's radical alterity.

[86] *Nightwood*, ed. Plumb, 262. Labelled as 'discarded pages from early copy of "Nightwood" ', this corresponds to p. 80 of the Dalkey Archive edition. The excision begins after 'confessional' and ends at 'crying between tongues'. At the side of the text a line with a cross beside it runs from 'while between the columns' to 'between one woman and another'. What appears to be the word 'girl' (in square brackets) is handwritten above the first 'her'.

were told love was, and what it never came to be; they, the living lie of our centuries. (114-15) [87]

Judith Lee suggests that O'Connor's 'version of the fairy-tale romance is a "child's dream" because in ignoring the dichotomy between masculine and feminine it ignores the obstacles posed by sexual difference. The prince-princess in the tale symbolizes not androgyny (the resolution of sexual difference) but narcissism (the rejection of sexual difference).' O'Connor teaches, as *Nightwood* teaches, that love and desire lead 'not to an experience of wholeness but to the discovery that such an experience is irrecoverable'.[88] Nora's narrative, then, does not speak of establishing difference in the context of resemblance, but of the vicissitudes of desire. The fetishization of Robin allays the anxiety engendered by her position of radical alterity and her refusal to be assimilated by Nora. Nora's love for Robin attempts to re-establish a bond that has been lost, and, through that bond, a self that was once loved. Felix recognizes that Robin had 'an undefinable disorder, a sort of "odour of memory," like a person who has come from some place that we have forgotten and would give our life to recall' (100); and Nora's 'impossible' desire for Robin is based on the idea that she is a figure from childhood, from a place that has been forgotten.

FETISHISM AND FAMILIAL DISRUPTION: (M)OTHERS, GRANDMOTHERS, AND DOLLS

It is significant that O'Connor assumes that the desire for the invert emanates from childhood. Robin's inversion does not produce a masculine identification that is adult and sexual; rather she is seen by Nora as resembling a male child who plays with toys. Indeed, the 'girl who resembles a boy' is a fetish created by Nora ('our miscalculated longing has created them'): 'I saw her always as a tall child who had grown up the length of the infant's gown, walking and

---

[87] Published editions invariably read: 'And I, who want power, chose a girl who resembles a boy' (114). This sentence continued 'and once men who were children' but this has been emended on the first and second typescripts in Barnes's hand. *Nightwood*, ed. Plumb, 177.

[88] Judith Lee, '*Nightwood*: "The Sweetest Lie" ', in Mary Lynn Broe (ed.), *Silence and Power: A Reevaluation of Djuna Barnes* (Carbondale, Ill.: Southern Illinois University Press, 1991), 207–18: 209.

needing help and safety' (121). Robin is pathologically infantilized: when she delivers her son she cries 'like a child who has walked into the commencement of a horror' (44); she has a 'childish face' (43); and Nora thinks of her as 'my lover and my child' (129).[89] The erotics of the child's relationship with the mother come to the fore in this passage in which Nora recalls her physical struggles with Robin in which she would hold 'her by the hair, striking her against my knees, as some people in trouble strike their hands too softly; and as if it were a game, she raised and dropped her head against my lap, as a child bounces in a crib to enter excitement' (125). Robin is miming some form of cunnilingual activity, while Nora holds on to her head; Robin is the masturbating child. O'Connor identifies love between women as 'insane passion for unmitigated anguish and motherhood' (66), and Nora desires to be the mother of Robin: O'Connor recognizes that she 'should have had a thousand children' and Robin 'should have been all of them' (85). The central anxiety of *Nightwood* is expressed through the illusion of wholeness and integrity, which can be traced back to a desire for pre-Oedipal merging with the mother. O'Connor speaks of this concern:

> How more tidy had it been to have been born old and have aged into a child, brought finally to the brink, not of the grave, but of the womb; in our age bred up into infants searching for a womb to crawl into, nor be made to walk loth the gingerly dust of death, but to find a moist, gillflirted way. (83)

Nora's desire to merge wholly with Robin and her introjection of Robin as a child speaks of this anxiety. Moreover, if the fetish signifies ultimately a nostalgia for wholeness, this wholeness resides in the relationship between mother and child. Nora's fetishization of Robin as a male child signifies her desire for complete integrity.

But while the desire for pre-Oedipal union is paramount in *Nightwood*, the act of mothering is rendered unstable. Felix's father Guido, in a symbolic identification with his masculine and militaristic wife Hedvig, is figured in terms of a dubious fecundity and maternity; he is 'heavy' with blood and 'had been small, rotund, and haughtily timid, his stomach protruding slightly in an upward jutting slope that brought into prominence the buttons of his waistcoat and trousers, marking the exact centre of his body with the obstetric line seen on fruits' (3). Clowns, watched by Nora and Robin,

---

[89] Kenneth Burke notes that Robin's development is a 'symbolic return to the infantile' ('version, Con-, Per-, and In-' 244).

'were rolling over the sawdust, as if they were in the belly of a great mother where there was yet room to play' (49). Felix and Robin are both orphans, and when Robin gives birth she behaves as if 'she had lost something', and later rejects the child: 'I didn't want him!' (44–5). Matthew O'Connor also has his own claims on maternity; he is a transvestite, a fantasmatic incarnation of the phallic mother of psychoanalysis, and a gynaecologist who 'births' Nora: 'I brought her into the world and I should know' (45).[90] He also, as Martin Bock notes, 'delivers Robin from her fainting sleep', into a second birth.[91] But as Erin G. Carlston points out, O'Connor is also an abortionist.[92] He is therefore paradigmatic of a motif of sterility which runs alongside the theme of 'deviant' mothering: this is best illustrated in Mademoiselle Basquette and the image of the figure-head who are missing their lower halves.

The mother is bypassed in favour of the grandmother, an eroti-cized presence who is intimately connected with Robin through her cross-gendered figuration in Nora's dreams, and in Nora's 'incestu-ous' desire for both women. Sexual desire for the grandmother is more explicit in the drafts ('showed a liking for kissing her grand-mother's ⟨bottom⟩') but survives into the published text.[93] Nora, identifying with her father ('dreaming through my father') has two dreams about her grandmother; in the second the grandmother appears 'tangled in the grave grass'; in the first she is sexually preda-tory, 'dressed as a man, wearing a billycock and a corked moustache, ridiculous and plump in tight trousers and a red waistcoat, her arms spread saying with a leer of love, "My little sweetheart!" '(56). The grandmother also reappears though references to the tale of Little Red Riding Hood, of which Nora thinks when she sees O'Connor cross-dressed in his bed, as the beast, dressed in the grandmother's clothes, who will 'eat' the little girl. As Mary Lynn Broe suggests, the dreams intimate that 'erotic control' lies not with the mother, but with the cross-gendered grandmother; this is a transgression of age,

[90] As Plumb notes, Coleman suggests the deletion of the association between O'Connor cross-dressed in a flannel night gown and a mother figure. *Nightwood*, 197.
[91] Bock, *Crossing the Shadow-Line*, 79.   [92] Carlston, *Thinking Fascism*, 52.
[93] In the second typescript Barnes retained the phrase 'Nora had loved her grand-mother more than anyone of her family' but it is deleted in the first typescript and from subsequent editions. This corresponds to p. 55 of the Dalkey Archive edition. Coleman suggested deleting this line because of the difficulty of the phrase 'an expansive decaying splendour' that followed 'grandmother'. Emily Coleman, letter to Djuna Barnes, 27 Aug. 1935. Quoted in *Nightwood*, ed. Plumb, 194–5.

power, gender, and female desire, making '*permissible*' Nora's desire
for Robin.[94] In the second dream Nora summons Robin to a room
that she does not recognize as her grandmother's room, but which is
'nevertheless saturated with the lost presence of her grandmother'
(55); it is a welcoming of Robin into the body of the grandmother
herself: 'The architecture of dream had rebuilt her everlasting and
continuous, flowing away in a long gown of soft folds and chin laces,
the pinched gatherings that composed the train taking an upward
line over the back and hips, in a curve that not only bent age but fear
of bent age demands' (56). The desire for Robin to enter the grandmother's room is thwarted because it is 'taboo' (55). The figure of the
sexually predatory cross-dressed grandmother leads to a dream
association with the 'disfigured and eternalised' Robin, which also
creates a textual association that finds ultimate expression in 'Robin
is incest' (129). Nora's love for Robin is incestuous not only because
of Nora's fantasmatic alliance of her lover with her grandmother, but
because Nora conceives of Robin as, alternatively, her own child.[95]

The instability of the act of mothering, and the establishment of
alternative patterns of familial relationships finds symbolization in
the statue in the house that Nora and Robin share, of a 'tall granite
woman bending forward with lifted head, one hand . . . held over the
pelvic round as if to warn a child who goes incautiously' (50). This
figure is ambiguous: it seems to speak both of fecundity and of
sterility (in the warning to a child). This finds further expression in
Robin's giving Nora a doll, an act which Nora interprets as symbol-
izing impending loss: 'We give death to a child when we give it a
doll—it's the effigy and the shroud; when a woman gives it to a
woman, it is the life they cannot have, it is their child' (118).[96] Just
as she had once held her own son 'high in her hand as if she were
about to dash it down', Robin holds the doll she has given Nora
('Our child') 'high above her head, as if she would cast it down, a
look of fury on her face'; she subsequently destroys the doll in a fit
of anger (122–3). O'Connor sees the doll as the emblem of the
invert:

Mary Lynn Broe, 'My Art Belongs to Daddy: Incest as Exile, The Textual
Economics of Hayford Hall', in Mary Lynn Broe and Angela Ingrams (eds.), *Women's
Writing in Exile* (Chapel Hill, NC: University of North Carolina Press, 1989), 41–86: 71.

Kaivola has termed Nora's desire to recover the lost closeness with her grandmother as 'impossible': Robin takes the place of the grandmother but she remains
inaccessible (89).

The doll is a recurring motif in *Ryder* and the play *The Dove*.

The last doll, given to age, is the girl who should have been a boy, and the boy who should have been a girl! The love of that last doll was foreshadowed in that love of the first. The doll and the immature have something right about them, the doll because it resembles but does not contain life, and the third sex because it contains life but resembles the doll. The blessed face! It should be seen only in profile, otherwise it is observed to be the conjunction of the identical cleaved halves of sexless misgiving! (123)

To destroy the doll is to break a bond, but it also suggests the erasure of identity; this is because dolls accrue power depending on who gives and who receives, and become fetishized due to their symbolic representation of human beings. The doll is, as Dianne Chisholm terms it, 'a lifeless fetish of aborted desire'.[97] If the doll also takes on aspects of death and sterility, and is a symbol of the child the lesbian couple cannot have, then Nora's desire for complete integration with Robin and her fetishization of her as a male child can be understood as a remnant of pre-Oedipal cravings that is ultimately death driven.

The doll is passed by Robin from lover to lover, from Nora to Jenny Petherbridge, a fetishist, who collects objects and people. Jenny's desire for Robin is explained in terms of her acquisitive personality: Matthew O'Connor calls Jenny a 'squatter', a 'looter', a 'bird snatching the oats out of love's droppings' (83, 85), stealing and simulating that which she does not have. Her speech is mimicry ('the words that fell from her mouth seemed to have been lent to her', 59), and she mimetically assumes the symbolic features of the lover: in Jenny's home Nora finds evidence of Robin's habitation, objects that seems to acquire fetish value, like the objects that are amassed by a kleptomaniac, including a doll sitting against a pillow, and a photograph of Robin as a baby, which Nora recognizes as 'the one that she had told me was lost' (118). Robin and Jenny Petherbridge represent 'the two halves of a movement'. This is not doubling (while Robin inclines backwards, Jenny leans forwards), but the failure of complementarity that is indicative of death. It is a movement

that had, as in sculpture, the beauty and the absurdity of a desire that is in flower but that can have no burgeoning, unable to execute its destiny; a movement that can divulge neither caution nor daring, for the fundamental condition for completion was in neither of them; they were like Greek runners, with

---

[97] Chisholm, 'Obscene Modernism', 184.

lifted feet but without the relief of the final command that would bring the foot down,—eternally angry, eternally separated, in a cataleptic frozen gesture of abandon. (61)

Here is the equation of lesbian desire with the death drive, and an illumination of the morbidity of the desire that Nora experiences.

'SAVED BY SEPARATION': TEXTUAL AND PHYSICAL DISMEMBERING AND REMEMBERING

Jenny is a study in dismemberment, figured in terms of separate body parts that will not fit together. Only in a metaphoric hall of mirrors did she appear 'like a single personality' (65): 'She had a beaked head and body, small, feeble, and ferocious, that somehow made one associate her with Judy; they did not go together. Only severed could any part of her have been called "right" ' (58). Jenny finds a counterpart in Caroline of Hapsburg, who is re-membered by O'Connor to have been dis-membered, and parts of her body 'put in three utterly obvious piles?—her heart in the Augustiner church, her intestines in St. Stefan's and what was left of her body in the vault of the Capucines' (135). O'Connor comments that Caroline was 'saved by separation', but the text's overriding philosophy does not validate this belief.

Dismemberment is also a motif of Barnes's other work, perhaps played out to most startling effect in a short dramatic piece 'Madame Collects Herself' (1918). Madame Zolbo is made up of the body parts of former lovers: the hair of a dead male singer, blood from an anarchist, an index finger from a general, and a piece of skin from a baron. She believes literally in the Shavian philosophy that 'a woman's only what a man, or men, make her'.[98] In a fit of jealousy her beautician Monsieur Goujon tries to kill Madame, but is thwarted because he cannot find the 'real' her: as his assistants remove the male appendages, Madame disappears and a blonde canary rises up towards the ceiling. Goujon cages her, but she is restored to her magnificent self. This almost unperformable play is a premature critique on psychoanalytic theories of the masquerade and gendered embodiment: what is it that precisely makes the woman?

---

[98] Djuna Barnes, 'Madame Collects Herself', in *At the Roots of the Stars: The Short Plays*, ed. Douglas Messerli (Los Angeles: Sun and Moon Press, 1995), 62.

Dismemberment is one of the key configurations by which fetishism is engendered in *Nightwood*. The fetish is a part object that substitutes for and represents wholeness, and *Nightwood* obsesses on the instability of bodies. As I have already suggested, the impetus for wholeness is all-consuming in *Nightwood*, and is figured most decisively and grotesquely upon the body of Frau Mann, the trapeze artist and denizen of the nightwood, who has become identified with her costume to such an extent that the 'stuff of the tights was no longer a covering, it was herself; the span of the tightly stitched crotch was so much her own flesh that she was unsexed as a doll' (12). Nora had wished for a process of sexual assimilation between herself and Robin which would have 'moulted our parts, as figures in the waxworks are moulted down to their story, so we would have broken down to our love' (130). Nora's love for Robin is narcissistic and fetishistic in the sense that Nora demands an erasure of difference in the fusion of their bodies, in the 'moulting' of separate parts.

The loss of Robin to other women inflicts psychological and physical damage upon Nora which is experienced as 'complete and dismembering' (a syntactic oxymoron which significantly denotes *Nightwood*'s schizoid mode). Her absence is experienced as loss of a body part: 'Robin's absence, as the night drew on, became a physical removal, insupportable and irreparable. As an amputated hand cannot be disowned . . . so Robin was an amputation that Nora could not renounce. As the wrist longs, so her heart longed, and dressing she would go out into the night that she might be "beside herself" ' (53). That Nora experiences the loss of Robin in terms of castration is significant: Nora demands Robin's presence because she craves undifferentiated wholeness. It is in this sense that Robin is a fetish; she is a signifier of presence that defends against the absence or loss that Nora fears. This is not phallic lack, but the loss of the body of the loved one and the reflection of an ideal, unified self.

The disembodied and embodied hand is both a signifier of lesbian sexuality and a fetish object in *Nightwood* as it is in *The Well of Loneliness* and other 'lesbian' texts. In *Ladies Almanack*, the tongue was glorified as a sexual instrument and it finds some endorsement in the 'crying between tongues' (where 'tongue' is a sexual verb) quoted in the excised section of text in which O'Connor describes lesbian cottaging. But in *Nightwood* the hand is privileged: the sexuality of hands, more evident in the drafts, stands as a signifier of

lesbian desire. Barnes was persuaded to excise passages that relate
to the movements of Nora's hands in the final chapter: the phrase
'with a quick involuntary gesture Nora put her hands on the fore
parts of her legs, bending' is supplanted by merely 'Nora bent'
(138).[99] Robin's hands are the most catalogued part of her body:
when Felix first sees her, the narrator remarks that, in her faint, her
hands 'long and beautiful, lay on either side of her face' (34). This
gesture of self-containment is replicated by Catherine (the Nora
figure) in an early draft: 'I put my ⟨two⟩ hands beneath [her] ⟨that⟩
head to hear something between us.'[100] Felix takes note of Robin's
idiosyncratic way of experiencing objects:

> When she touched a thing, her hands seemed to take the place of the eye. He
> thought, 'She has the touch of the blind who, because they see more with their
> fingers, forget more in their minds.' Her fingers would go forward, hesitate,
> tremble, as if they had found a face in the dark. When her hand finally came to
> rest, the palm closed, it was as if she had stopped a crying mouth. Her hand lay
> still and she would turn away. At such moments Felix experienced an unac-
> countable apprehension. The sensuality in her hands frightened him. (40)

Robin's hands are simultaneously reticent, commanding, protective,
and potentially violent; her movements anticipate both her later
nocturnal lesbian encounters that are often anonymous ('as if they
had found a face in the dark'), and her behaviour with Nora. The
hand which stops the crying mouth might either be closed in mur-
derous anger—suffocation—or closed across the mouth in a gesture
of assuagement. The 'sensuality' of Robin's hands, which Felix finds
so disturbing, suggests that the hands take on a number of potentially sexual functions. Felix later notices that her hand seemed
'somehow older and wiser than her body', an observation which
speaks of Felix's anxiety about her sexuality and his own potency:
'looking at her he knew that he was not sufficient to make her what
he had hoped' (41).[101] (Homo)sexuality is conveyed by the position-
ing of her hands; the attraction of Robin for Jenny's 'niece'—in that
distortion of familial relations in *Nightwood* she is in fact no relation—is signalled through her hand gestures, which communicate a

[99] *Nightwood*, ed. Plumb, 185.

[100] Ibid. 293. From draft of 'Go Down, Matthew'. Word in square brackets has been
handwritten in over the crossed-out word in angle brackets.

[101] That she has a susceptibility to corruption and perversion is intimated by her
choice of reading matter. Felix finds her annotated copy of the memoirs of the Marquis
de Sade (44).

burgeoning sense of her own sexuality: 'She had been playing, but the moment Robin entered she ceased and sat, staring under her long-lashed eyelids at no one else, as if she had become prematurely aware' (62).[102] Barnes was clearly anxious to downplay the eroticism which she saw conveyed in the hands of this doll-like child. Jenny is transfixed by 'every movement of Robin's hand' as it touches her hand and strokes her hair (65), and she forces her body into Robin's embrace: 'Robin's hands were covered by Jenny's slight and bending breast, caught in between the bosom and the knees' (66). Jenny's own hands cannot sufficiently disclose her desire for Robin: 'There was a trembling ardor in her wrists and fingers as if she were suffering from some elaborate denial' (58). The way in which these hand movements are described (in terms of sexual desire and 'denial') substantiates a reading of the fetishistic nature of the desire Robin engenders. The fetish is a signifier of presence that protects against the possibility of absence and loss; in the nightwood, where hands grope for faces in the dark, where Robin uses her hands instead of her eyes, presence has been officially validated.

As in *The Well* and *HER*, the hand performs a multiple function as fetish: as an ungendered sexual object and a writerly tool. The narrative of Nora's desire for Robin is manifested textually in the obsessive letters she writes to Robin. Her pleading 'If I don't write to her, what am I to do?' (106), which is a syntactic echo of the identificatory plea 'She is myself, what am I to do?', speaks of the compulsive need to restore the body of the loved one. Against O'Connor's urging that she 'rest now, put down the pen', she supplicates that 'I've got to write to her . . . I've got to' (106). In *Ladies Almanack*, both Evangeline's hand and tongue are privileged as sexual and writerly instruments; as Plumb glosses, the tongue that plays upon the handful that 'had been she indeed' is metaphorically the spirit of the artist.[103] In a further echo of H.D.'s 'love is writing', writing provides access to the beloved.[104]

The dream of the grandmother, in which Nora desires to touch the plume and the inkwell, anticipates Nora's final compulsion to

---

[102] The phrase 'her two small wax-like hands tender with the new life in them cupped up in her lap' appeared in other published editions such as that of Faber and Faber, between 'sat' and 'staring'. But Barnes indicated that she wished it excised in her own copy and this was upheld in the New Directions third edition (1949). *Nightwood*, ed. Plumb, 163.

[103] Plumb, *Fancy's Craft*, 100.

[104] *Her*, 149. In *The Antiphon* 'love is death'. *Selected Works*, 196.

write to Robin which is not just a means of 'constructing the self'
but of recreating the loved one through language, fictionalizing the
beloved.[105] Writing and narration are more fetishistic practices.
Nora's narrative, relayed to Matthew O'Connor, is riven by pain
and loss, recollected as melancholia. But it is through melancholia,
which operates along similar lines to fetishism—through disavowal—that Nora can introject the loved one, restore, re-member,
the lost one to herself through narrative. Freud noted that both the
fetishist and the melancholic adopted similar ways of both keeping
and giving up the object whose loss they could not withstand.[106] As
Judith Butler explains in her re-reading of Freud's 'Mourning and
Melancholia':

> If in melancholia a loss is refused, it is not for that reason abolished.
> Internalization preserves loss in the psyche; more precisely, the internalisation
> of loss is part of the mechanism of its refusal. If the object can no longer exist
> in the external world, it will then exist internally, and that internalisation will
> be a way to disavow the loss, to keep it at bay, to stay or postpone the recog-
> nition and suffering of loss.[107]

Nora's narrative, and her desire to write to Robin, are the last desperate attempts to incorporate the loved one through fetishistic
melancholia. But the novel itself can not sustain this attempt: the
operations of dismemberment which occurred as part of the

---

[105] Jane Marcus draws on Barnes's personal history (her grandmother Zadel Barnes
was a writer) to explain the dream (246). As Phillip Herring notes, Zadel's breasts were
the subject of cartoons in letters to Djuna—a letter of 9 July 1905 shows a sketch of a
woman with her breasts distended to resemble penises. One of Barnes's rare and surviving letters to Zadel of this period shows a stick-woman with a pen between her legs.
'Djuna Barnes and Thelma Wood: The Vengeance of *Nightwood*', *Journal of Modern
Literature*, 18.1 (Winter 1992), 5–18: 7.

[106] See Sigmund Freud, 'Fetishism' (1927), *SE* 21. 152–7, and 'Splitting of the Ego in
the Process of Defence' (1940 [1938]), *SE* 23. 275–8.

[107] Judith Butler, *The Psychic Life of Power: Theories in Subjection* (Stanford, Calif.:
Stanford University Press, 1997), 134. Butler's reading allows her to see 'gender as a kind
of melancholy, or as one of melancholy's effects' (132), crucially emending her view in
Gender Trouble (1990) to address 'the question of how certain forms of disavowal and
repudiation come to organize the performance of gender' (145): 'Drag thus allegorizes
heterosexual melancholy, the melancholy by which . . . a feminine gender is formed
(taken on, assumed) through the incorporative fantasy by which the feminine is excluded
as a possible object of love, an exclusion never grieved, but "preserved" through height-
ened feminine identification' (146). Adam Phillips in his commentary on Butler's piece,
notes that 'there is a kind of intellectual melancholy in the loss of a third sex that never
existed and so can never be mourned; this third, irrational sex that would break the spell
(or the logic) of the two, and that is one of the child's formative and repressed fantasies
about himself or herself' (158).

wrenching of 'Nightwood' from the multiplicity of the drafts, finally become part of Barnes's overarching vision which seeps into every layer of representation and rhetorical device in the text. There is no sustaining vision of wholeness—as is so devastatingly presented in the book's final chapter, 'The Possessed'.

EXHAUSTION

In 'The Possessed', Robin's radical alterity is confirmed as she undergoes canine transmogrification. Arriving at her private chapel, Nora is confronted with the diverse aspects of Robin's excessive representation as male child, invert, and beast:

On a contrived altar, before a Madonna, two candles were burning. Their light fell across the floor and the dusty benches. Before the image lay flowers and toys. Standing before them in her boy's trousers was Robin. Her pose, startled and broken, was caught at the point where her hand had reached almost to the shoulder, and at the moment Nora's body struck the wood, Robin began going down, down, her hair swinging, her arms out. The dog stood, rearing back, his forelegs slanting, his paws trembling under the trembling of his rump, his hackle standing, his mouth open, his tongue slung sideways over his sharp bright teeth, whining and waiting. And down she went, until her head swung against his; on all fours now, dragging her knees. The veins stood out in her neck, under her ears, swelled in her arms, and wide and throbbing, rose up on her hands as she moved forward. (139)[108]

There is no linguistic communication here, as each woman, and the dog, respond to and mimic physical movement (Nora's crashing to the floor is shadowed by Robin's for instance). It is appropriate that Robin should confront Nora before an image of the Madonna, with whom Robin has identified Nora; O'Connor tells Nora that 'You almost caught hold of her, but she put you cleverly away by making you the Madonna' (122). Judith Lee has argued that as such Nora is herself inviolable; while Robin occupies the space between the human and the bestial, Nora is positioned between the human and the holy. Lee observes that as the Madonna, Nora 'provides a barrier for Robin against her own "non-Being", she would face were she

---

[108] Plumb notes that the first English edition (Faber, 1936) and all subsequent editions up to New Directions (1961) have 'fingers' instead of 'hands'. *Nightwood*, 185. The Dalkey Archive edition adheres to changes Barnes made to the version in the *Selected Works* (Farrar, Strauss, and Cudahy, 1962).

to recognize the difference within herself between her identity' as subject and other, between the self she narcissistically creates and 'the self she must be'.[109] She absorbs difference and counteracts Nora's claim upon her by forcing her into an inviolable position. In trying to (m)other Robin, Nora is herself (m)othered.

In this final encounter, Robin's identification with the dog is complete: the veins 'swell' and 'throb' in her neck and arms enacting a phallicization of her entire body as she assumes a position 'on all fours'. Nora's dog is terrified by what it sees in Robin and is 'backed into the farthest corner' as Robin lunges at it barking as she does so, 'in a fit of laughter, obscene and touching' (139). The encounter ends with Robin 'lying out, her hands beside her, her face turned and weeping' and the dog lying down beside her 'his head flat along her knees' (139). The novel ends here and the final union is not between Nora and Robin, but between Robin and Nora's dog. (Thelma is also finally encrypted into the 'wood' of the floor.) Other versions of this chapter have a greater eroticism and phrasing which have been altered by Barnes, at Coleman's suggestion, in order to mute the overtly sexual passages. Barnes had been particularly bemused and angered by responses to 'The Possessed'; despite her assertions to the contrary, it was assumed that Robin was copulating with Nora's dog. To Chester Page, she insisted: 'The dog is *not* being romantic towards Robin! It is furious at the mystery of her drunkenness, a kind of exorcism of what it does not understand.'[110] In a different version the dog's symbolic role is more delineated: 'the dog, the model of what she was to do stood there.'[111] Critics, however, remain unconvinced by Barnes's disclaimers: Herring notes the occurrence of bestiality in *Ryder* and Field relates that in a draft of *The Antiphon* the epigraph read: 'This is my story, its crying of woman and a Dog'; while she had once inscribed a copy of *Nightwood* as 'Memories of a Dog Boy'.[112] The sexual frame of reference had already been cultivated: the 'angel on all fours' who administers cunnilingus (81) finds a sinister counterpart in Robin's

---

[109] Lee, *'Nightwood'*, 214.

[110] Mary Lynn Broe (ed.), *Silence and Power: A Reevaluation of Djuna Barnes* (Carbondale, Ill.: Southern Illinois University press, 1991), 362.

[111] *Nightwood*, ed. Plumb, 185. 'The dog stood rearing back' has been emended from continuing 'the dog, the model of what she was to do' by Barnes on the two carbon typescripts.

[112] Herring, *Djuna*, 168; Field, *The Formidable Miss Barnes*, 226.

identification with Nora's dog. Coleman was more concerned with Nora's own possible sexual stimulation and advised that Nora, putting her hands on 'the upper parts of her legs', would have to be excised: 'It isn't that publishers wouldnt [*sic*] like it—it is that *you do not want that idea there* yourself.'[113]

Carolyn Burke documents that after reading *Ulysses* and discussing the 'voice of the eunuch' with Joyce, Barnes's writing from *Nightwood* on became 'haunted' by the possibility of 'imagining a way out of sexual dichotomies'.[114] *Ladies Almanack*'s playfulness was a ruse that masked a real anxiety: precisely the struggle to imagine a way out of such dichotomies. In *Almanack* Barnes settles for displacing one myth (penis envy) by creating another (lesbian genesis). In *Nightwood* the central conflict for Barnes was the representation of lesbian desire. The multiplication of positions for Robin (invert, hysteric, male child, husband) was not merely a radical and an ingenious play of sameness and difference, but a manifestation of her fetishized position of wholeness. Moreover, the whole text operates on disavowal, the discourse of fetishism: *Nightwood* suggests that while the ultimate desire is for wholeness, that wish leads only to annihilation. At the close of the novel that fear of extinction is fully realized.

Djuna Barnes, in her exhaustive search for a way out of sexual dichotomies, was exhausted by *Nightwood*: she was reported as saying that she had been frightened by it and had not been able to write anything afterwards.[115] Coleman recorded that 'Eliot said he shd think Djuna would not write again—he felt the pressure so great in this; as though she had writen [*sic*] herself out'.[116] After

---

[113] Emily Coleman, letter to Djuna Barnes, 27 Aug. 1935. Quoted in *Nightwood*, ed. Plumb, 210, Coleman's emphasis. The passage concerned is on p. 138 of the Dalkey Archive edition, from 'Nora bent'. The 'sliding' of Robin towards the dog remains, however, despite Coleman's insistence that it must come out, because Barnes replied that she could not change it; she omitted 'mistress'.

[114] Carolyn Burke, ' "Accidental Aloofness": Barnes, Loy, and Modernism', in Mary Lynn Broe (ed.), *Silence and Power: A Reevaluation of Djuna Barnes* (Carbondale, Ill.: Southern Illinois University Press, 1991), 67–79: 73. See also Djuna Barnes, 'James Joyce', in *I Could Never Be Lonely Without a Husband: Interviews*, ed. Alyce Barry (1985; London: Virago, 1987), 295.

[115] Malcolm Lowry, letter to Herr and Frau Clenens ten Holder, 26 Apr. 1952. Malcolm Lowry, *Selected Letters*, ed. Harvey Breit and Margerie Bonner Lowry (1965; London: Penguin, 1985), 312.

[116] Quoted in Miriam Fuchs, 'The Triadic Association of Emily Holmes Coleman, T. S. Eliot, and Djuna Barnes', *ANQ: A Quarterly Journal of Short Articles, Notes, and Reviews*, 12.4 (Fall 1999), 28–39: 35.

1936 she published only one play and a handful of poems before her death in 1982. Critics have spoken about *Nightwood* as a metafiction about the 'crisis of modernism', the most obvious signifier of which is O'Connor's lapse into silence and his last prophecy: 'Now . . . the end—mark my words—now *nothing, but wrath and weeping!*' (136).[117] This is compounded by the exhaustion of Robin and Nora's dog at the end of the novel, which Fuchs calls the 'rest of a hunted beast, bred of exhaustion of the human spirit'.[118]

Nightwood, in its struggle to imagine a way out of sexual dichotomies, implicitly engages with problems met and shelved by Freud, that would not be addressed until the advent of Lacanian psychoanalysis. In its confrontation of the moment of fundamental and irreducible division, and the desire for wholeness, *Nightwood* is unique and frightening in its vision. In a sense Barnes had spelt out the limits for the female modernist representation of sexuality, and by extension for female fetishism.

[117] Charles Baxter, 'A Self-Consuming Light: *Nightwood* and the Crisis of Modernism', *Journal of Modern Literature*, 3.5 (July 1974), 1175–87: 1176, 1186.
[118] Fuchs, 'Djuna Barnes: "Spillway" into Nightmare', 6.

5

'Becoming Djuna'
Anaïs Nin's Diaries and Fiction

BECOMING DJUNA BARNES

If Djuna Barnes demonstrated the limits of fetishistic female cross-gendering in a negative engagement with psychoanalysis and sexology, Anaïs Nin, whose writings (both diary and fiction) constitute a continuous stream of self-analysis, resituates the fetishes of masculine femininity within a psychoanalytic frame and in so doing suggests a wider fetishization of the accoutrements of gender itself. She does this through her 'masculine' women Sabina and Lillian, but also through the 'feminine' Djuna. This naming of her 'feminine' woman is perhaps inappropriate given Barnes's obsession with the masculine woman and the strain that she puts on the very categories of gender. It is an identification Barnes repudiated—she resented that Nin had used a name that she felt was the signifier of her originality—and she declined any invitation to meet Nin.[1] But for Nin, Barnes was a persistent point of reference: she is mentioned in *A Spy in the House of Love* and also appears in a fantasized cleavage with Nin herself as the neglected and reclusive writer Judith Sands (a name which suggests George Sand) in *Collages*. If Barnes was 'haunted' by *Nightwood*, then so too was Nin: she wrote an unanswered letter to Barnes telling her that she thought the novel was the 'most beautiful thing I have ever read about women, and women in love', that it 'touched, illumined, awakened' her, and that she wanted to install herself in Barnes's fictional milieu.[2]

Nin restages the hoped for encounter with Barnes in *Collages* (1964). Dr Mann, who has translated the Barnes figure, Judith

---

[1] Nin insisted that she had not heard of Barnes when she wrote her early novels, and that she found the name 'Djuna' in an anthology of Welsh names. She thought that it was male because of its use in a Sherlock Holmes story. *Conversations With Anaïs Nin*, ed. Wendy DuBow (Jackson, Miss.: University Press of Mississippi, 1994), 206.

[2] Anaïs Nin, *The Diary of Anaïs Nin*, ii. 1934–1939, ed. Gunther Stuhlmann (New York: The Swallow Press and Harcourt, Brace and World, 1967), 239–40.

Sands, into Hebrew, writes a letter to Sands telling her that she has
given birth to him: 'I feel you once described a man who was me
before I knew who I was, and it was because I recognized him that I
was able to recognize myself.' He tells her that no other writer
knows 'that at times men behave like women and women like men,
and that all these distinctions are mock distinctions, and that is why
your doctor put on a wig when he wanted to talk about his loves'.[3]
He urges her to publish again to restore his fragile sense of self, but
she fears public exposure, and keeps her new manuscript under her
bed. Nin puts in Sands's mouth her own fear that publication will
irrevocably fracture her sense of self: Sands is anxious that people
will steal her image and 'expose it to the world, distorted of course',
and that others will 'resuscitate parts of me which I have already
buried' (163). To encourage her to publish, Mann takes her to an
exhibition of Tinguely's 'Machine that Destroys Itself', which is
made up of broken, discarded objects (in an echo of Nin's short
story 'Ragtime'), constructed to resemble a printing press with a roll
of paper that spills out the names of artists and writers. The
machine then operates in reverse, and the paper rolls 'backwards,
perversely, and swallowed the names in a desperate inversion' (166).
When the machine is sabotaged and catches fire, one of the few
names preserved on the list is that of Judith Sands. Sands takes this
as a positive sign that her name will live on, and she retrieves her
manuscript from beneath her bed, and begins to read: it is the beginning of *Collages*. This final transmutation of Nin into Sands, was
precisely the kind of over-identification that both Barnes and Nin
feared: that their public selves would experience irrevocable fragmentation.

'UNTRANSMUTED, UNTRANSFORMED, UNTRANSPOSED':
PSYCHOANALYSIS AND NIN'S DIARY

This identification with Djuna Barnes, if denied by Barnes herself,
enabled Nin to connect with women writers in a way that she had
not been able to do in the 1930s and 1940s. Transcribing women's
lives in her diary stabilized her writing, and helped her to negotiate

---

[3] Anaïs Nin, *Collages* (1964; London; Virago, 1993), 158–9. Further references will be
cited in the text.

the split between her diary and her fiction. But it had not always been this way. In the early phase of her career, Anaïs Nin epitomized the 'neurotic' writer of Freud's imaginings, self-diagnosed and subsequently formally recognized as such by a succession of analysts. Unable to 'convert' her diary writing into fiction, Nin underwent a Freudian analysis in order to enable her to do so.[4] Freudianism exerts a pernicious influence on Nin's diary writing and fiction finding expression in the heterosexualizing of lesbian desire. It is only in the fiction, however, that Nin conceives of cross-gendered lesbian desire other than in terms of penis envy, and more in terms of female fetishism. Reading the diaries as a 'supplement' to the fiction has resulted in problems for critics, not least because the creative process for Nin begins in the diaries. In response to Nin's assertion that the diaries 'supply the key' to the fantasy of the fiction, Maxine Molyneux and Julia Casterton have raised important questions on the subject of the precise status and function of the diary: 'are the Journals, then, the truth behind the fictions, the clue which facilitates one's escape from the fictional labyrinth? Or do the fictions represent realities lying behind the "truthful" observances of the Journals, realities which the veils of control and discretion have shrouded?'[5] Susan Kavaler-Adler has read the creative process as Nin's means of repairing 'defects within the self and its inner world of object relations'; this kind of reading presents the fiction as the locus of unproblematic self-reparation.[6] The aim in this study is to analyse the shift from introspection in the diary to fiction-writing in terms of Nin's representation of female cross-gendering, rather than to read the fiction in terms of Nin's personal 'integration' and 'developmental growth'.

Initially Nin remained resistant to psychoanalysis because of an aversion to theories of contemporary sexuality ('the most powerful

---

[4] I borrow the term 'convert' from Deirdre Bair to resonate with Kenneth Burke's 'per-version, in-version, con-version' nexus. *Anaïs Nin: A Biography* (London: Bloomsbury, 1995), 139. Nin herself used the term: 'Books convert me and de-convert me'. *The Early Diary of Anaïs Nin* (1994; London: Penguin, 1995), 256. She also used it to convey her struggle to define herself as a woman writer, 'to convert what I was learning from men into a knowledge that would be adapted, made of possible use to me', and to conceptualise psychoanalysis, which 'converts' negatives into positives. *Conversations*, ed. DuBow, 112, 185.

[5] Maxine Molyneux and Julia Casterton, 'Looking Again at Anaïs Nin', *Minnesota Review*, NS 18 (Spring 1982), 86–101: 94.

[6] Susan Kavaler-Adler, *The Compulsion to Create: A Psychoanalytic Study of Women Artists* (New York: Routledge, 1993), 1.

charm in the world has been left to the devils by a few prudish old men[7]), but analysis was recommended to her by her cousin Eduardo Sànchez who had undergone a classic Freudian analysis in 1928; he thought analysis would enable her to free herself of whatever blocked her from writing fiction. Nin, however, was 'proud of never having to turn to another for any explanations of myself', and refused analysis at first because her diary writing was a form of self-analysis: 'I owe to it what some people owe to psychology: knowledge of myself, extreme consciousness of what in others is vague and unconscious, a knowledge of my desires, of my weaknesses, of my dreams, of my talents.'[8] She soon, however, embraced psychoanalysis, believing that it could activate her creativity, and she considered becoming an analyst herself. From the beginning of 1931, she began to transcribe her dreams, and to read 'murky Freud'.[9] She was particularly stimulated by Freud's attempts to access the unconscious; her reading for 1931 consisted mostly of psychology and psychoanalysis.[10] For the first time Nin 'filtered' her interpretations of Freud, Jung, and Adler through her own consciousness, reading, or as Deirdre Bair has phrased it, 'misreading', the psychoanalytic writings, 'doggedly insisting on applying the theories to her own life'.[11] She was especially interested in the implications of the theories for artists and writers; she believed that Freud did not attend to how the artist used the 'transposition, sublimation, transfiguration of our physical and mental elements'.[12] For theories of art she inevitably turned to Jung's theory of the collective unconscious.[13] She was also concerned with the notion of a divided self.

In 1932 Nin consulted René Allendy, one of the most prominent of the first generation psychoanalysts in France, who founded the Société Française de Psychoanalyse with Marie Bonaparte and René Laforgue, and introduced psychoanalysis into criminal court cases. Allendy was classically Freudian in his early years of practice, but

---

[7] Nin, *Early Diary*, 24.   [8] Ibid. 96, 95.   [9] Ibid. 372.
[10] According to Bair she read Freud's *Beyond the Pleasure Principle, The Future of an Illusion, The Collected Papers of Volume 7*, and *Leonardo da Vinci*; Alfred Adler's *The Science of Living* and *Le Tempérament nerveux*; W. B. Pillsbury's *The History of Psychology*; Elizabeth E. Goldsmith's *Life Symbols* and Ramón Fernández's *De la personalité. Anaïs Nin*, 545 n. 6.
[11] Bair, *Anaïs Nin*, 110. For an example of Nin's self-analysis see *Early Diary*, 437–39.
[12] Nin, *Early Diary*, 372.
[13] See C. G. Jung, 'Psychology and Poetry', *transition*, 19–20 (June 1930), 23–45.

was later influenced by alchemy, numerology, and astrology. While he was sympathetic to the plight of the artist (he believed that neurosis was an illness of which the artist must be cured in order to function and create), Nin continued to suffer from problems with writing. She had written two pages of a 'new novel', but could not write her way out of an impasse which she was now convinced analysis had imposed upon her:

There is a baffling thing about analysis which is a challenge to a writer. It is almost impossible to detect the links by which one arrives at a certain statement. There is a fumbling, a shadowy area. One does not arrive suddenly at the clear-cut phrases I put down. There were hesitancies, innuendos, detours.[14]

It is precisely this 'shadowy area' which marks (or rather obscures) the shift from the diary to the fiction. Nin remained committed to producing a work of fiction, and, significantly, the piece she was working on in the early 1930s was approximately forty typed pages about June Mansfield, Henry Miller's wife, including descriptions of her body, clothes, and gestures, and analytic readings of her behaviour. Nin both conceived of June and her reactions to June's beauty as masculine (Henry Miller compared his wife to Proust's Albertine).[15] Nin hoped that these fragments would coalesce into a more sustained piece of work. She began her own self-analysis, which became frenzied and all-encompassing, but eventually in November 1933 became Otto Rank's patient. While, in Nin's view, Allendy had been a mechanist of the psyche, Rank was more of a philosopher or metaphysician, and most importantly for Nin was interested in extending the applications of psychoanalysis to aesthetics. He had been one of Freud's devotees and intimates, but fell out of favour when he published *The Trauma of Birth* (1924), and had been practising in Paris since 1926. Rank thought it was a contradiction to invoke fetishism as evidence of the importance of the Oedipal phase in relation to the regressive wish for the phallic mother, and argued that castration anxiety masks the prior origin of all anxiety: the traumatic experience of birth. Castration anxiety was a substitute formation in which the phallus acted as a displaced

---

[14] Anaïs Nin, *The Diary of Anaïs Nin*, i. *1931–1934*, ed. Gunther Stuhlmann (New York: The Swallow Press and Harcourt, Brace and World, 1966), 76.
[15] Miller compared Nin to Balzac's Séraphita. See Noël Riley Fitch, *Anaïs: The Erotic Life of Anaïs Nin* (Boston, New York, Toronto, and London: Little, Brown and Company, 1993), 217.

'symbol' for the umbilical cord. Nin had been reading Rank for over a year, including most importantly *Art and Artist* (1932), and she responded to the tenets laid down in this work, most notably that the artist exists on a different plane from other people, and as a consequence was destined to a life of loneliness and misapprehension; most significantly for an understanding of Nin, Rank believed that 'art is born of fear of loss'.[16] As Philip K. Jason has noted, Rank's special interest in the double, his cleavage of the doubling motif with narcissism and incest, was perceived by Nin as an 'authoritative confirmation' of her own poetic motivation, particularly realized in her first published work of fiction *House of Incest*, which Rank read and commented upon.[17]

Nin first met Rank in Paris in 1933, the same year H.D. began analysis with Freud to help her with her writer's block and her sexual ambivalence. (Freud suggested H.D. should read Rank's *Myth of the Birth of the Hero*.) In Nin's analysis Rank tried to break her diary-writing compulsion and initiate a period of creativity by encouraging her to write an 'intermittent notebook, not the need of describing everything'; she did attempt a few pages of what became *House of Incest* but 'wanted [the] diary as one wants opium'.[18] During this period Nin, encouraged by Rank, received patients of her own in New York; she did not perform psychoanalysis as such, but a form of self-help, in which she would counsel and offer support. One of her patients was a masculine woman, or rather 'a girl pretending to be boyish, or a girl who did not dare to be a woman'.[19] After a breakdown in 1942 she consulted Jungian analyst Martha Jaeger, believing that working with a woman would circumvent the problems she had encountered with Allendy and Rank. Jaeger set about exploring issues of the creative self, suggesting that Nin felt guilty about the writing process because, like H.D., she felt she was trying to compete with men.[20] While being treated by Jaeger, Nin

[16] Bair, *Anaïs Nin*, 188.

[17] Philip K. Jason, 'Doubles/Don Juans: Anaïs Nin and Otto Rank', *Mosaic: A Journal for the Comparative Study of Literature and Ideas*, 11.2 (Winter 1978), 81–94: 82.

[18] Nin, *Diary*, i. 301, 307. Rank could not prohibit Nin from continuing to write feverishly in her diary, and indeed admired her diary to the extent that he actually joined her in a 'twin diary'. See Anaïs Nin, *Fire, From a Journal of Love: The Unexpurgated Diary of Anaïs Nin 1934–1937* (London: Peter Owen, 1996), 51.

[19] Nin, *Diary*, ii. 18.

[20] See Anaïs Nin, *The Diary of Anaïs Nin*, iii. *1939–1944*, ed. Gunther Stuhlmann (New York: Harcourt, Brace and World, 1969), 256–60.

began to write more about the lives of women in her diary, such as Frances Brown, Luise Rainer, and later Renate Druks, and to use these portraits in her fiction.

Even by 1946 when *Ladders to Fire* was published it was uncertain whether Nin had broken the reliance on her diary and the analysis that she undertook in it. Certainly Diana Trilling in *The Nation* (16 January 1946) thought that Nin's 'method' was that of 'clinical history', and her stories 'more like case histories'. Nin turned to Inge Bogner in 1947, and finally reconciled the creative problems she experienced throughout her life, and was able to sustain the diary and fiction simultaneously. When *Solar Barque* was published, 'work with Bogner bore fruit at this moment'.[21] Towards the end of her life she turned the diaries, that work which had prohibited her from embarking on fiction, into publishable form: this process became, ironically but inevitably, very much like fiction-writing itself, in that she was able to bring her experience as a novelist to bear upon the editing of the diaries. Nin considered the diaries to be her best work: the novel writing was too formal, while the diary went 'deeper'.[22] Critics most recently have seen the distinction between the diary and the fiction to be 'imaginary': as Anna Balakian suggests they 'are like two communicating vessels . . . they feed each other constantly'.[23]

Nin's diaries are both a form of analysis and a catalogue of the 'conversion' from solipsistic and narcissistic notation into fiction. From the beginning the diaries were always the place where Nin would work through problems with her analysis; they also functioned as a depository for fantasies and ideas for stories.[24] The distinction between the diary and the fiction is not clearly defined; from the outset, Nin treated her diary as both self-analysis and as a form of 'fiction': for her it remained 'the eternal problem—turn the

---

[21] Nin, quoted in Bair, *Anaïs Nin*, 419.

[22] Nin, quoted in Molyneux and Casterton, 'Looking Again at Anaïs Nin', 87.

[23] Anna Balakian, 'The Poetic Reality of Anaïs Nin'. Quoted in Barbara J. Griffin, 'Two Experimental Writers: Djuna Barnes and Anaïs Nin', in Maurice Duke, Jackson R. Bryher, and M. Thomas Inge (eds.), *American Women Writers: Bibliographical Essays* (London and Westport, Conn.: Greenwood Press, 1983), 135–66: 159.

[24] The diaries began as 'a journey, to record everything for my father', who left the family when Nin was a child. *Diary*, i. 202. Later the diary, which her father jealously read, told the story of her incestuous affair with her father. See *Incest: From 'A Journal of Love', The Unexpurgated Diary of Anaïs Nin, 1934–1935* (San Diego: Harcourt Brace Jovanovich, 1992).

Journal into a novel?'[25] The published diary was in a constant process of being rewritten over a number of years, and reads like a public document, self-censored and rigidly controlled. The unexpurgated material, eventually published as *Fire, Incest, Journal of a Wife* and *Henry and June* after Nin's death, fill in some of the gaps created by the 'official' publication: incest, adultery, sexual fantasy, but also her marriage. In the published *Early Diary*, the narration oscillates between the 'conventional' narrative, and fantasy: these changes in the narration are clearly demarcated in the text as 'Imagy's Journal', which transcribed her transformations into a sexual being. Importantly, for Nin the diary can go two ways, between the real and the imagined, between 'I' and 'they', and between subjective and objective. This is an indication of the creative split Nin encountered in her attempt to wrest fiction from her Imagy-nation; it is the negotiation of this split, and the obsession with the masculine girl, which render Nin's fiction fetishistic.

It was uncovered in analysis that the split Nin experienced was located along the lines of gender: 'I must continue the diary because it is a feminine activity, it is a personal and personified creation, the opposite of the masculine alchemy. I want to remain on the untransmuted, untransformed, untransposed plane.'[26] This suggests that Nin conceived of diary writing as a pre-Symbolic activity—as demonstrated in the name 'Imagy'—in which she remained whole unto herself, in which she protected herself against loss ('personal and personified'). There is no 'death' in the diary, because 'there is no distance. The living moment is caught.'[27] In contrast fiction was the place where division occurs through the process of trans-mutation, trans-formation, and trans-position.[28] For Nin 'magic words are all in the dictionary under the prefix *trans*'; they are identified by her as instrumental to the creative process, leading her 'out of the

---

[25] Nin, *Early Diary*, 14.

[26] Nin, *Diary*, ii. 172. Rank reinforces Nin's rigid gender categorization: 'When the neurotic woman gets cured, she becomes a woman. When the neurotic man gets cured, he becomes an artist. Let us see whether the woman or the artist will win out. For the moment, you need to become a woman'. *Diary*, i. 291. He too ascribes a feminine gender to the diary, as does Lawrence Durrell who encouraged Nin to 'make the leap outside of the womb'. *Diary*, ii. 24, 232. In *Fire* Nin says that she puts her diary away secretly with 'perfumed dresses' (384), accentuating its status as a specifically feminine genre.

[27] *Conversations*, ed. DuBow, 22.

[28] Sharon Spencer has similarly defined the distinction imposed by Nin: the diary is 'maternal', while fiction possesses a 'hard, polished quality'. *Collage of Dreams: The Writings of Anaïs Nin* (Chicago: Swallow Press, 1977), 103.

present, away from the painful, paralyzed spot in our lives', converting 'dross into gold'.[29] Words with the prefix 'trans-' remain a
stumbling-block for Nin, however: they signify the problems she
encounters in crossing from the diary into fiction. The product of
this *trans*ition is the cross(*trans*)-gendered woman. In *Collages*,
Varda the collage-artist tells Renate that he wanted to teach her all
the 'trans-' words, 'transfigure, transport, transcend, translucent,
transgression, transform, transmit, transmute, transpire, all the
trans-Siberian voyages', but Renate significantly replies that he 'forgot the word transvestite' (88).[30]

Nin publicly presented her diary writing as an unproblematic
activity in which she expressed her 'real' self, as opposed to her
'ideal' self which she presented to other people: the diary 'first helps
you to create the real self'.[31] Later she said in lecture performances
that she would hold a metal mask before her face and say that she
was 'unmasking and showing her true face'. She then removed the
mask and read from the diaries.[32] The diaries, however, reveal that
Nin was in the process of constructing an ideal self, or a transfigured
persona, for public consumption. She recognized with hindsight that
she was producing a public record of her life after the diaries were
published: she intimated that she censored herself as she wrote the
diary, and was not up to 'facing certain truths' because of the 'fear of
someone reading over our shoulders, of someone passing judgment
on our secret selves'.[33] The first-person plural used here is suggestive:
not only did Nin precisely allow others to read her diary long before
it was published, but she conceived of herself as multiple, someone
who was trying on different masks in the diary. From the very early
entries when she was 11 years old, and said she 'wished to turn
myself into lots of words, lots of sentences',[34] and later when she

[29] Anaïs Nin, *A Woman Speaks: The Lectures, Seminars and Interviews of Anaïs Nin*,
ed. Evelyn J. Hinz (Chicago: Swallow Press, 1975), 182, 25.

[30] This speech is also echoed in *Children of the Albatross*; Jay tells Djuna that he
found her in 'one page of the dictionary under trans: transmutations, transformation,
transmitting etc'. *Children of the Albatross* (New York: E. P. Dutton, 1947), 152.

[31] Nin, *A Woman Speaks*, 167. See also Anaïs Nin, *The Novel of the Future* (1968;
London: Peter Owen, 1969), 144.

[32] Anaïs Nin, *The Diary of Anaïs Nin*, vii. 1966–1974, ed. Gunther Stuhlmann (New
York: Harcourt Brace Jovanovich, 1980), 243.

[33] Nin, *A Woman Speaks*, 151.

[34] Anaïs Nin, *Linotte: The Early Diary of Anaïs Nin 1914–1920* (New York: Harcourt
Brace Jovanovich, 1978), 145.

claimed that 'becoming a work of art interests me more than creating one', she self-consciously presented her self as text.[35]

In the published diary Nin presented a self that revelled in her femininity: there are sensuous descriptions of her beauty and her clothing throughout the journals. The *Early Diary* is punctuated by testimonies from both men and women to her physical attraction, which led contemporary critics to judge her diaries as a 'narcissus pool'.[36] In the unexpurgated diaries, particularly *Henry and June*, the portrayal of a feminine and pliant woman is complicated by other modes of presentation, most notably female masculinity. Nin adhered to Freud's early theory of the bisexual nature of all human beings, that men and women were each composed of a combination of feminine and masculine characteristics that would compete for dominance:

I have had masculine elements in me always, knowing exactly what I want . . . I acted delicately and yet as a man. It would have been more feminine to have been satisfied with the passion of other admirers, but I insisted on my own selection, on a fineness of nature which I found in a man weaker than I was . . . Now Hugo is strong, but I am afraid it is too late. The masculine in me has made too much progress . . . I have discovered the joy of a masculine direction of my life by my courting of June.[37]

The presence of masculinity also manifests itself in her self-presentation: 'my breasts are small perhaps because I have masculine elements in me and half of my body may therefore be adolescent.'[38] Nin is a self-confessed invert in her feelings for June: 'I was like a man, terribly in love with her face and body, which promised so much.'[39] (Otto Rank confirmed that in loving June Nin was becoming her unfaithful father 'courting women'.)[40]

But it is not as simple as this. Her presentation of June Mansfield in *Henry and June* oscillates wildly in its avowal and disavowal of Freudian theorizing, and, as in the passage above, the 'masculine elements' in her signify her sexual freedom and autonomy. When Nin is faced with the reality of lesbian desire she feels anger and jealousy,

[35] Anaïs Nin, *The Diary of Anaïs Nin*, iv. 1944–1947 (New York: Harcourt Brace Jovanovich, 1971), 177.

[36] Nin is dismissive of Leon Edel's appropriation of her term to describe her diary in a review. *Novel of the Future*, 145.

[37] Anaïs Nin, *Henry and June, From the Unexpurgated Diary* (1986; London: W. H. Allen, 1988), 50–1.

[38] Ibid. 144.   [39] Ibid. 17.   [40] Nin, *Diary*, i. 281.

particularly because June extols another woman's instrument of penetration (the hand): 'Jean's hands were so very lovely, so very supple because she handled clay a lot. The fingers tapered.'[41] While she says that she has wanted to possess June 'as if I were a man', she has also 'wanted her to love me with the eyes, the hands, the senses that only women have. It is a soft and subtle penetration.'[42] This speaks quite specifically and distinctly about lesbian sexuality. In the first published diary, desire for June is also expressed through erotic hand imagery: 'she pressed my hand to her breast, and I kept her hand and I was not ashamed of my adoration.'[43] June is conceived in the 'official' diary according to an encoded lesbian iconography: while she has 'manlike strength', a voice which is 'dark, heavy, husky', and large hands, she is also, as in H.D. and Bryher's encoding, a white Artemisian burning with phosphorescence:

I saw for the first time the most beautiful woman on earth. A startlingly white face, burning dark eyes, a face so alive I felt it would consume itself before my eyes. Years ago I tried to imagine a true beauty; I created in my mind an image of just such a woman. I had never seen her until last night. Yet I knew long ago the phosphorescent color of her skin, her huntress profile, the evenness of her teeth.[44]

June enters Nin's life from her (lesbian) imagination: she has known her all her life, as Her had known Fayne, as Bryher had known H.D. The use of the word 'consume' points to the myriad desires that June inspires, but also the oral (homophobically understood as vampiric) component of lesbian sex. While watching women perform 'lesbian poses' at a nightclub with her husband, which include penetration of one woman by another wearing a dido, and clitoral manipulation, Nin feels that she is 'no longer woman; I am man. I am touching the core of June's being.'[45] Nin conceptualizes her belief that she is ultimately incapable of satisfying a woman in terms of lack: attracted to her masseuse, she is 'stirred madly' but is frustrated in her desire because 'what I could do did not seem satisfying

[41] Nin, *Henry and June*, 17. [42] Ibid. 18.
[43] Nin, *Diary*, i. 28. Interestingly the eroticism is slightly neutralized in *Henry and June*: 'she had pressed my hand. I was not ashamed of my adoration' (20).
[44] Nin, *Diary*, i. 20.
[45] Nin, *Henry and June*, 72. In *Diary*, vol. i, Nin visits the club with Henry Miller; the phrase 'no longer woman [etc]' has been excised (20). This substitution of her lover Henry for Hugo Guiler, her husband, is symptomatic of the elimination, at Hugo's request, of any reference to her married life in the expurgated journals.

enough'. She dreams that she performs oral sex on June but does not satisfy her; in the dream Nin endows her lover with a penis who triumphantly remarks 'Yes, I have a little one; aren't you glad?'[46]

June conceives of their desire for each other in a different way, most importantly in terms of identification, similarity, and fetishism. She desires a pair of shoes like Nin's: 'Everything I wore she would wear, although she had never wanted to imitate anyone else before', and Nin too begins to respond to June using the same kind of language of mutuality: 'I have a feeling that I want to be you. I have never wanted to be anyone but myself before. Now I want to melt into you, to be so terribly close to you that my own self disappears.'[47] The desire for fusion with a female lover is a recurring motif in Nin's fiction, as is the mimicry and identification experienced by both Nin and June: 'the love between women is a refuge and an escape into harmony and narcissism in place of conflict . . . Two women do not judge each other. They form an alliance. It is, in a way, self-love. I love June because she is the woman I would like to be.'[48]

In the diaries, however, which are the testing ground for her understanding of psychoanalysis, the polarization of gender is transferred from her desire for June to her difficulties with writing. Problems with Nin's analysis had implications for ways in which she conceived of psychic dramas in her fiction. For Allendy, as for Freud, women's sexuality was an enigma; psychoanalysis had an 'imperfect' understanding of women, based as it was on 'men's knowledge'.[49] Despite this imperfect knowledge, Allendy convinced Nin that she was in a competitive relation with men, especially her father, who resented her creativity but doubted her talents, and that most of her adult relations with male writers, such as Henry Miller,

[46] Nin, *Henry and June*, 80, 91. Compare this with the short story 'Artists and Models'. Elena, the artists' model of the title, indulges in an affair with the masculine, cross-dressed Leila; Leila's finger was 'firm, commanding, like a penis', her tongue 'stabbing, agile and sharp'. *Delta of Venus* (1969; London: Penguin, 1990), 137. Lynette Felber suggests compellingly that Nin 'rewrites the Freudian scenario of the daughter's supposed horror at finding that her mother has no penis' by suggesting that in her dream Nin discovers 'not lack but the potentiality of her own genitalia, asserting the "triumphant" presence of the clitoris'. Similarly she reads the scene in the nightclub, in which the 'gazer gazes upon herself (the "little woman") in a union with the preoedipal mother' as reversing 'the usual psychoanalytical conception of the daughter's discovery of her mother's "castration" '. 'The Three Faces of June: Anaïs Nin's Appropriation of Feminine Writing', *Tulsa Studies in Women's Literature*, 14.2 (Fall 1995), 309–24: 319–20.
[47] Nin, *Henry and June*, 25, 52.   [48] Nin, *Diary*, i. 41.   [49] Ibid. i. 77.

were structured according to her penis envy, which was a facet of her 'Diana Complex': 'there is a desire to punish and castrate men.'[50] Allendy noted that there was a strong masculine element in her writing, which he interpreted negatively since it illustrated her 'lack of confidence in her womanly power' (see extract below). These concepts are integrated into her fiction. In the following passage, Nin demonstrates how creativity, cross-gendering (as inversion), and desire for women were interconnected:

> Do I love Henry because I identify myself with him and his love and possession of June? No, this is false. I think of the night Henry taught me to lie over him and how I disliked it. I was happier when I lay under him, passively. I think of my uncertainty with women, not being sure of the role I want to play. In a dream it is June who has a penis. At the same time, I admit to Allendy, I have imagined that a freer life would be possible to me as a lesbian because I would choose a woman, protect her, work for her, love her for her beauty while she could love me as one loves a man, for his talent, his achievements, his character. (I was remembering Stephen in *The Well of Loneliness*, who was not beautiful, who was even scarred in the war, and who was loved by Mary.) This would be a relief from the torment of lack of confidence in my womanly powers. It would eliminate all concern with my beauty, health, or sexual potency.[51]

The invocation of Stephen Gordon, another troubled writer, indicates that Nin connects the need to be loved by a woman with creative proficiency and narcissistic feelings of self-worth. Only if we also note that Allendy's diagnosis of Nin as 'neurotic' acted upon her as if 'he touched an open wound' (reminiscent of Stephen's scars), and also that Nin provoked Allendy into lyrical invocations of her beauty, charm, grace, and wit, can we then begin to understand Nin's self-conceptualization in the diaries other than in terms of penis envy. While Nin still clings to this interpretation, the diary also speaks of the specific anxieties of the female artist who is unable to accede to fiction-writing, not because of penis envy, but due to a failure of narcissism.

CONVERSION, FRAGMENTATION, AND NARRATIVE
INSTABILITY: NIN'S FICTION 1936–1946

The *Early Diary* charts the splitting of the ego under the pressure to produce fiction. This is evident in the demarcation between 'Anaïs'

---

[50] Quoted in Bair, *Anaïs Nin*, 143.   [51] Nin, *Henry and June*, 132–3.

and 'Imagy', between self-censorship and fantasy, and in the numerous allusions to this split: 'I was tempted today to keep a double journal, one for things which do happen, and one for imaginary incidents . . . I live *doubly*. I'll write *doubly*.'[52] Imagy is born of the imagination, of fantasy and desire, and represents the split side of herself struggling into fictive discourse.[53] The aim is to 'fuse both' selves, to 'surrender the real me and Imagy to the world as One'.[54] This other book is paradigmatic of all her future novels: 'Yesterday I began the second Book drawn from my Journal; it will be full of inventions, exaggerations, Imagy's life, unreality. I am beginning to feel the need of fiction, of a disguise.'[55]

While Otto Rank had tried to instil in Nin an idea of the integrated self, she experimented with the multiplying selves that her diary and the *trans*formation of it impelled. The number of personas she used in the diary proliferated, suggesting to her that there was no fixed self, and this idea was transferred into her fiction with the use of open-ended narratives, the image of the multiplying woman in Marcel Duchamp's *Nude Descending a Staircase*, and the replication of characters in a continuous state of 'development' from one narrative to the next. The publishing history of Nin's works also contributed to this as shorter pieces were transplanted from one text into another, and recontextualized. But if fragmentation is embraced and extolled in the later fiction (note the title *Collages*) and diaries, anticipating post-modern multiplicity, there was an acute anxiety about fragmentation in the early fiction. As in *Nightwood*, the novel Nin admired and wanted to emulate, fetishism is used to allay anxiety about proliferating gendered selves.

The need to write fiction emanated from the recognition that diary writing 'left unsaid what can only be said with creative work'; the diary resulted in partial portraits, like statues 'without arm or head', awaiting the Pygmalion-like touch of the artist.[56] Nin realized that the same 'fear of loss' motivated both the diarist and the artist. The transition to fiction-writing, however, was a slow and painful

---

[52] Nin, *Early Diary*, 56.

[53] Nin also describes to Allendy the feeling of being a 'shattered mirror': 'each piece has gone off and developed a life of its own'. *Diary*, i. 103. Her books are also conceived in terms of a split: 'the dream on one side, the human reality on the other' (264). The mirror is a persistent motif in the diaries and in the fiction. See for example *Diary*, ii. 180–2.

[54] Nin, *Early Diary*, 118.   [55] Ibid. 128.   [56] Nin, *Diary*, ii. 112.

process: 'and yet my novel is terrible. Thirty-five pages of rot.'[57] Nin brought to it material from the diary ('the depository of the living moments'), and a self-styled form of psychoanalysis that resulted in an experimental, 'abstract' novel that 'left out so much of the realistic trappings', and concentrated on the psychological drama.[58] The weight of psychoanalytic influence in her early forays into fiction was great: in writing a sequel to her short story 'The Woman No Man can Hold', she said that 'from the point of view of the woman, the logic of analysis brought it to an equation which was never formulated in my own mind'.[59] Nin based much of her fictive ethos upon the Jungian concept of 'proceeding from the dream outwards' to a 'psychological reality', and was encouraged by Freud's belief that the poet possessed an innate understanding of psychoanalytic truths.[60] Nin is concerned only with the transcription of fantasy and desire as they emanate from dreams, in her fiction: 'what may seem unreal or invented in my writing is the natural outcome of dramatizing the conflict between the conscious and unconscious self.'[61] Most importantly, fiction, in its symbolization and creation of myth, enables a way out of the self-censoring limits imposed upon the diary: 'When you are faithful to a portrait, you cannot go beyond the portrait, and faithfulness is part of the diary. But in the novel you can push this discovery to many more dimensions. It doesn't matter, you're free.'[62]

House of Incest (1936) was the first sustained attempt to convert the diary into fiction. It was begun under Rank's analysis and is a narrative of the 'fear of loss' that he had identified as a component of art, proceeding from within the dream itself.[63] Given these particular conditions, Nin's fiction-writing might be conceived as in the throes of a fetishistic split. In *House of Incest* issues of self-hood, identity, and similarity are probed in fiction that descends into the 'real womb'.[64] Cross-gendered desire as an expression of identification and fetishistic desire for the self-same is explored more fully in the *Cities of the Interior* series, but it is significant that while she was

[57] Nin, *Early Diary*, 137.   [58] Nin, *Novel of the Future*, 117, 2.
[59] Nin, *Early Diary*, 374.
[60] Nin, *Novel of the Future*, 5. Nin demonstrated this instinct: 'Once, when he [her husband Hugo] asked me a question, I did not remember Freud's answer to it. I invented one that I thought to be logical. When I looked up, I found it was Freud's. That's what you call real knowledge'. *Early Diary*, 451.
[61] Nin, *Novel of the Future*, 44.   [62] Nin, *A Woman Speaks*, 175.
[63] Nin, *Novel of the Future*, 120.   [64] Nin, *Diary*, ii. 235.

in analysis Nin was attempting to fictionalize a confrontation with the Other as an incestuous object of desire. In Nin's sexual framework, incest is an expression of narcissism, what Balakian calls a 'metastasized affliction', this love of self in the other.[65]

The frontispiece to *House of Incest* speaks of the act of writing as a bodily function, precisely as the disgorging of the writer's heart, which painfully illustrates the effort involved in the creative process: 'the morning I got up to begin this book I coughed. Something was coming out of my throat: it was strangling me. I broke the thread which held it and yanked it out. I went back to bed and said: I have just spat out my heart.'[66] It begins with a vision of a womb-bound subject who is wrenched from the bodily interior too soon: 'I looked with chameleon eyes upon the changing face of the world, looked with anonymous vision upon my uncompleted self' (15). The subject compares the pain of this experience where 'food seeped through invisible pores' to being 'thrown up on a rock' (17). This is one of the few representations of maternity in Nin's fiction, but the primal separation from the mother sends repercussions across her later work.[67]

The narrator of *House of Incest* mythologizes love between women as fusion of the self-same: 'There is no mockery between women. One lies down at peace as on one's own breast' (24). This sense of completeness, similarity, and intermingling seems to emanate from the evocation of intrauterine existence. Between women there is no immediately identifiable difference:

Your beauty drowns me, drowns the core of me. When your beauty burns me I dissolve as I never dissolved before man. From all men I was different, and myself, but I see in you that part of me which is you. I feel you in me; I feel my own voice becoming heavier, as if I were drinking you in, every thread of resemblance being soldered by fire and one no longer detects the fissure. (25)

The same terms as this desire for Sabina are employed by Lillian in *Ladders to Fire*: the dissolution of the self is here pleasurable as it is connected to sexual desire; the need to introject and consume the

[65] Anna Balakian, 'Anaïs Nin, the Poet', in Suzanne Nalbantian (ed.), *Anaïs Nin: Literary Perspectives* (Basingstoke: Macmillan, 1997), 63–78: 73.

[66] Anaïs Nin, *House of Incest* (1936?; Denver: Alan Swallow, 1961), frontispiece. Further page references will be cited in the text.

[67] In *Collages*, for instance, Renate takes the place of the mother 'and voiced accusations her mother had never uttered' (9).

loved one is overwhelming. In *House of Incest* desire for Sabina, whom critics have recognized as a thinly disguised portrait of June Mansfield, is also desire for the self in the lover: the name Sabina is almost anagrammatic of Anaïs: Banais, that is, 'be Anaïs'.[68] This lyrical rendering of lesbian desire is largely repressed in the diaries; but here in its fetishistic mode it is enacted as an impossible, fantasmatic co-mingling of protagonists. But the soldering of their bodies suggests the possible instability of this union: there is a fissure whether it can be seen or not. Importantly the female lover in *House of Incest* is a twin sister whom the narrator feels is missing; the narrator is a 'protector' of the missing half:

Cease trembling and shaking and gasping and cursing and find again the core which I am. Rest from twistedness, distortion, deformations. For an hour you will be me; that is, the other half of yourself. The half you lost. What you burnt, broke, and tore is still in my hands: I am the keeper of fragile things and I have kept of you what is indissoluble. (27)

It is in being 'inextricably woven', gathering together all the fragments of the lover in order to restore her to herself, that the narrator of the *House of Incest* finally confronts its other. This is the discourse of fetishism, explored throughout this study as the loss of the female lover/self, the 'other' half. Fetishism works as a displacement of meaning through synecdoche, through the displacement of the object of desire on to something else: in this schema, the lover is fetishized as a 'part' of the self. If the object of desire is the lost female self, this is registered through a fetish which is incorporated as part of the self. In the *House of Incest* the narrator chooses to become the object she desires: 'I choose a body then a face, a voice. I become you' (27). Only later in the *Cities of the Interior* series is this mode of desire rewritten in terms of female cross-gendering.

Sabina is not merely the Other in *House of Incest*; she is also the fantasized image of the speaking subject, the fetishized object of

[68] In Nin's own early print of *House of Incest*, the Sabina figure is called Alraune (Gemor Press, n.d.). 'Alraune' was also an early title for *House of Incest*. I have chosen to use the Swallow edition because, in the naming of Sabina, it registers its continuity with the later series of novels. Nin was ambivalent about her identification with her characters: in *Diary*, vol. iii, she said that Djuna, Lillian, and Sabina were herself, leading some critics to suggest that Sabina is her id, Lillian her ego, and Djuna her superego. In *The Novel of the Future*, however, she discounted such claims. Anaïs's name was used in anagrammatic form in the 'Siana' press she established with Henry Miller, Alfred Perlès, and Michael Fraenkel in 1935.

desire.[69] In *Ladders to Fire* and *A Spy in the House of Love*, Nin fully reveals Sabina's duplicity and deceitfulness, her 'twistedness, distortion, deformations' (27). In *House of Incest*, however, Sabina's lover is lulled into a false sense of security, attracting her into a misrecognition of her self: 'I AM THE OTHER FACE OF YOU' (Nin's upper casing, 28). The insistent question 'DOES ANYONE KNOW WHO I AM?' is answered by 'YOU ARE THE WOMAN I AM'. That this answer co-opts the subject, and that the word 'soldered' recurs throughout *House of Incest*, speaks of the provisional nature of the bond between the two women, the fusing of two broken pieces: 'Our faces soldered together by soft hair, soldered together, showing two profiles of the same soul' (28).

The fantasy of fusion continues to be rendered as unstable. In a scene before the mirror, the narrator experiences her body as a collection of fragmented and disembodied parts: 'Here are a pair of eyes, two long braids, two feet. I look at them like dice in a box, wondering if I should shake them, would they still come out and be ME. I cannot tell how all these separate pieces can be ME. I do not exist. I am not a body' (47–8). The nightmare of the forest of decapitated trees and women with 'faces cut in two by the sculptor's knife, showing two sides forever separate, eternally two-faced' (55) seems to emanate from this redramatized 'mirror-phase'.[70] The narrator is also a 'marionette pulled by unskilled fingers, pulled apart, inharmoniously dislocated' (29); the integrated Other vies for individuation: there are 'two women in me freakishly bound together, like circus twins. I see them tearing away from each other' (30). The pain of separation is horrifying: 'the insanity of things pulling, pulling within oneself' (30). *House of Incest* is a narrative of desire which attempts to reinstate what has been experienced as absence or loss; it is not phallic lack, but the loss of an incestuous lover, a twin sister: 'I am constantly reconstructing a pattern of something forever lost and which I cannot forget' (39).

House of Incest mimicked and intensified the fragmented style of the diary. This first creative production outside the diary, but which

---

[69] In talking later about her desire for June Mansfield, Nin provides a gloss for what is ultimately the negation of lesbian desire in *House of Incest*: 'It seemed to me that my love of June was really not *for* June; she was the woman *I* wanted to be. There was this attraction to a projected part of myself'. *A Woman Speaks*, 64.

[70] This passage is transcribed almost directly from Nin's description in *Diary*, vol. i, of the sculpture of Zadkine (178).

transplants many extracts from it into its text, is generically neither one thing nor the other: a prose poem. This illustrates the instability of Nin's entire oeuvre: parts of previous texts are excluded in later editions; revisions of novels become new novels in their own right; and the diary is constantly threatening the very status of the fiction itself, and vice versa.

Two short stories, written after *House of Incest*, illustrate Nin's creative model, how she conceptualized the function and status of the diary, and her employment of the terms of fetishism. 'The Labyrinth' (published in *Under a Glass Bell* in 1944), uses a favourite metaphor of Nin's to suggest the way the diary structures experience. The narrator of the story 'was eleven years old when I walked into the labyrinth of the diary', and retracing that journey now, she finds herself in a nightmare of fragmented images and dismembered body parts ('white bleached bones, sand, ashes, decomposed smiles, eyes full of holes like cooled lava').[71] She wonders whether she should have counted the number of moves she made, 'the mediated displacements, the obsessional repetitions' (66), but the obsessions became infinite, and she is lost. The purpose of the diary is to chart the development of the self, but its linguistic obsessions—'I was walking on the word obsession with naked feet' (67)—perform so many displacements between the authorial self and the self in the diary that she can only feel 'an anguish over something lost' (66). She wonders why she had not numbered the pages, but the linearity that this would have imposed on the diary was not what she wanted: 'so much was left out that I had intended to insert, and numbering was impossible, for numbering would mean I had said everything' (67). She finds herself walking up a 'stairway of words', but then she is not walking and 'the word died' (67). She searches desperately for a sign she can recognize, but she is sucked violently into darkness into a cave of dismembered body parts ('legs and arms and ears of wax', 68). This space is the realm of (male) fetishism: 'The flesh and fur walls breathed and drops of white blood fell'; the narrator's feet are 'covered with fur, my hand with leather, my legs wrapped in accordion-pleated cotton' (68). The narrator sinks into silence, only able to move her lips like a sea anemone. She is awakened by 'a sound of paper unrolling' (as paper unfurled out of Tinguely's

---

[71] Anaïs Nin, 'The Labyrinth', in *Under a Glass Bell* (1947; London: Penguin, 1978), 66–7. Further references will be cited in the text.

machine), her feet 'treading paper', and realizes that the way out is, perversely, to write (170). She confronts her 11-year self as she emerges.

'Ragtime' (also published in *Under a Glass Bell*), a fragment that uses the motif of the fragment, offers an explanation of the creative process and fetishism. The ragpicker collects discarded objects, which become in their turn desired in his imagination; this is the imagination of the artist, in which the detached object becomes whole:

> The ragpicker worked in silence and never looked at anything that was whole. His eyes sought the broken, the worn, the faded, the fragmented. A complete object made him sad. What could one do with a complete object? Put it in a museum. Not touch it. But a torn paper, a shoelace without its double, a cup without saucer, that was stirring. They could be transformed, melted into something else. A twisted piece of pipe. . . . Wonderful, half a dress, the ribbon off a hat, a fan with a feather missing. . . . Fragments, incompleted worlds, rags, detritus, the end of objects, and the beginning of transmutations.[72]

The broken objects are precisely like fetishes, because they become detached from their wholes, but can be conceived to make new wholes, *trans*muted and *trans*formed. This says something about Nin's relationship to the creative process, particularly her anxiety about public perception of her work (a constant worry) and her methodology: transformation proceeds through fragmentation and dismemberment, but also more importantly via transformative objects that enable the envisioning of new wholes. The narrator suggests, however, that transformations are highly provisional and subjective (the old shoe that children play with is not a boat), and the story ends in nightmare, as the narrator doubts her own physical integrity: she finds amongst the lost objects her own torn blue dress which reminds her of the intensity of adolescent desire. This acts as the catalyst to a re-membrance of her past as the ragpicker also restores to her a wisdom tooth and her long hair that she had cut off. In the final scene the ragpicker collects her into his bag as he would do any other broken item, but the very last line suggests that she too will be transformed, 'made new' according to the modernist mantra. Transformation is something that the *House of Incest* completely denied: there can only be such 'crossing' in the Symbolic.

---

[72] Anaïs Nin, 'Ragtime', in *Under a Glass Bell* (1947; London: Penguin, 1978), 60–1. 'Ragtime' was originally 'Rag Time': the cleavage of the two words perhaps suggests the making of a new whole.

What 'Ragtime' and 'Labyrinth' both illustrate are the anxieties concerning the convergence of textual and physical integrity. The narrator's fear of losing parts of herself, is a fear of projecting the self into the public domain to be read, and, as Nin anticipated, misread. (Up until her last successful years she obsessively transcribed negative criticism into her diary.) Nin remained troubled by a nightmare that she had before the publication of the first diary: she opened her front door and was blasted by a fatal wave of radiation: 'This was the fear of the world, the fear of judgement, the fear of not being loved, the fear of having everyone say, this is a monster. I have accumulated all these fears because the diary is the real self.'[73] The pull is always to fragmentation because that is for Nin the ideal mode to transform lived experience into fiction; but fragmentation, as the fiction so painfully shows, is acutely damaging to the concepts of ego integrity. Nin stresses that the diary helped her to construct an identity: 'What everyone forgot is that you can not be a valuable member of the universal life unless you first become a complete, unified and balanced entity.'[74] The crux for Nin is to reconcile the need for structure, form, and generic/gendered boundaries with the desire to be liberated from (masculine) literary form. These are crucial ideas for theorizing 'women's writing', within which category critics have recuperated Nin as an exponent of *l'écriture feminine*. Nin first underwent analysis not only to understand how to transfer from the diary to fiction, but also to find a way to reconcile and unify her 'different' and fragmented selves in her work—to become 'recomposed'. For Nin, as for Barnes and H.D., articulating the unconscious as the essence of achievement of establishing an ego and 'genuine consciousness', is a constant, unresolved struggle. The criticism of Nin speaks over and over again of the lack of unity and coherence in her work, but Nin avowed and disavowed 'unity' as the governing principle of her narratives, and she questioned the very nature of the incompatibility of disunity and unity precisely because it was through dispersal that her ego related to her empirical experiences. This was a process that had no *telos* for Nin: she was not moving inexorably towards integration but putting the disunity/unity opposition under constant erasure. Nowhere is this more palpably and physically evident than in the publication of the *Cities of the Interior* series.

[73] *Conversations*, ed. DuBow, 81.   [74] Ibid. 20.

PLAYING THE DON JUAN: PSYCHOANALYSIS AND
CROSS-GENDERING IN *LADDERS TO FIRE*

Cities of the Interior, which has a complicated publishing history, comprises *Ladders to Fire* (1946), *Children of the Albatross* (1947), *The Four-Chambered Heart* (1950), *A Spy in the House of Love* (1954), and *Solar Barque* (1958), which was expanded, renamed, and published separately as *Seduction of the Minotaur* (1961). The latter was the first to be written without the aid of the diary. *Ladders to Fire* was first published as 'This Hunger', comprising 'Hejda', 'Stella', and 'Lillian and Djuna'. When Dutton published it in 1946 Nin took out 'Hejda' (it subsequently appeared in the 1948 version of *Under a Glass Bell*), and it was retitled. This edition was made up of two parts, 'This Hunger' (a reduced version) and the additional 'Bread and the Wafer'; 'This Hunger' was further fragmented in this edition into two pieces, 'Stella' and 'Lillian and Djuna'. In the Swallow edition 'Stella' was removed (and transplanted into *Winter of Artifice*), and 'Lillian and Djuna' renamed 'This Hunger'; 'Bread and the Wafer' remained unaltered. *Cities* was issued in a final authorial one-volume version in 1974.[75]

If *House of Incest* is a pre-Oedipal narrative of the womb, then the *Cities of the Interior* series is wholly Symbolic, in which the reconstruction of patterns of loss are played out in terms of fetishistic cross-gendering, and through the metaphor of costuming as identity. *Ladders to Fire* was, according to Nin, the 'story of woman's development'. Most women, Nin argued, 'followed man's pattern and could not integrate within them the feminine part of themselves'. In this assumption of masculinity, the woman 'lost contact with her nature', and became a split subject, a 'woman at war with herself'.[76] And yet because of the rigidity of her generic gendering of diary writing as specifically feminine, to accede to masculine fiction-writing was to result inevitably in conflict. *House of Incest* in its descent into the womb presented the female artist as 'the mermaid with her fish-tail dipped in the unconscious'.[77] In the

[75] See Philip K. Jason for a full itemization of the publishing history of *Cities of the Interior. Anaïs Nin and her Critics* (Columbia, SC: Camden House, 1993), 55–7.
[76] Nin quoted by Gunther Stuhlmann, Introduction, *Ladders to Fire* (London: Peter Owen, 1991), 5.
[77] Nin, *Diary,* ii. 235.

Cities of the Interior series Nin moves away from the solipsism of the *trans*itional text *House of Incest* to a more 'individuated' style. The original edition of *Ladders to Fire* begins with 'Stella', which was first published in *Winter of Artifice* (1945), a collection of three 'novelettes'. The inclusion of 'Stella' in *Ladders* provides an appropriate bridge between *House of Incest* and *Cities*.[78] It dramatizes the 'dedoublement' diagnosed by Allendy and rendered in *House of Incest*: 'Stella sat in the small, dark room and watched her own figure acting on the screen. Stella watched her "double" moving in the light, and she did not recognize her.'[79] She sees herself as a child-woman in her own 'interior mirror', solipsistically inverted. Self-reflection is associated with humiliation and failure of narcissism; Stella is wearing a dress that belonged to a cousin and does not fit her: 'The girl looks at the blue dress with shame' (39). Self-contemplation is the site of pain and of splitting of the ego, and anxiety is displaced on to the body and on to clothes. Stella experiences herself as the girl who looks meagre, poor, and shrunken in her borrowed clothes.

Ladders to Fire traces Lillian's development incorporating the same fetishistic motifs of splitting, failure of narcissism, and a sense of gender dysphoria. It was published the same year as Otto Fenichel's *The Psychoanalytic Theory of Neurosis*, which emphasizes the close relation between (male) transvestism and fetishism, and homosexuality. Fenichel admits the possibility of the existence of female transvestites but argued that women cross-dress according to male motives; since it is only a failed copy, it cannot offer any 'serious' psychic assuagement. The female fetishist is a woman who simply covets the penis. *Ladders* offers a serious challenge to this belief that 'female transvestism has a "pretending" character'.[80]

When 'Stella' was first published it appeared alongside 'The Voice' in *Winter of Artifice*, which dramatizes the importance of the psychoanalytic experience and of the psychoanalyst:

---

[78] Marie-Claire Van der Elst has documented that in the manuscript of 'This Hunger' the pronoun 'she' referring to Stella is changed to 'Lillian', thus becoming the second section of the Dutton edition of *Ladders to Fire*. 'The Manuscripts of Anaïs Nin at Northwestern', *Mosaic*, 11.2 (Winter 1978), 59–63: 60.

[79] Anaïs Nin, *Ladders to Fire* (New York: E. P. Dutton, 1946), 15. Further references will be cited in the text.

[80] Otto Fenichel, *The Psychoanalytic Theory of Neurosis* (London: Routledge & Kegan Paul, 1946), 345.

Djuna, lying down, remembers all this that she lived, and that so many others are living after her. This dark in the dark with one who becomes part of herself, who answers all the doubts in her. This man without identity, the Voice of all she did not know but which was in her to bring to light. The Voice of the man who was helping her to be born again.[81]

The Voice, a thinly disguised portrait of Otto Rank, also treats Lilith and Lillian, who are split-off parts of Lillian in *Ladders to Fire*. He uncovers Lilith's 'wars against herself', which form one of the main narratives of *Ladders to Fire*; she sees herself either as too weak or too strong, 'bursting with a power which makes me believe I can rule the whole world' (142). In *Ladders* Lillian's 'development' is circumscribed; in 'The Voice' Lilith speaks of her errant father, and her wounded mother, 'left maimed, like someone who had lost an arm' (143). Reading 'The Voice' as a psychoanalytic 'commentary' on *Ladders* partially accounts for why Lillian should express her 'wars against herself' in terms of cross-gendering; she fears 'a second loss, a second abandon, a second wound', and responds to the weakness in other people (144). This 'second wound' is genital. Lilith is classically 'frigid', and her husband persuades her to have her hymen cut surgically: 'I tried to feel as a woman afterwards. It was a terrible thing, it was as if the knife had made me close forever rather than open, as if it had made me cold forever' (146). She fantasizes that she is phallicized, decorated, and emblazoned ('I see myself standing very rigid, and I am covered with jewelry and luxuriant robes'), but it is a hyper-performance of femininity to which she can only hopelessly aspire ('Do you think I will ever turn into a woman?', 147). She desires to be 'shattered into bits', which ultimately finds expression in the concluding sequence of *Ladders to Fire*. The wearing of 'strange clothes' is, in 'The Voice', a defence mechanism to repulse other people; in *Ladders* male clothes become an armour of strength, also the fetishes via which desire for lost or denigrated femininity is expressed. The Lillian of 'The Voice' seeks out treatment for her gender ambiguity, but The Voice recognizes immediately that she is not masculine, because of her feminine hands and feet: 'She was deluding herself and others about it' (126). She too has been surgically mutilated: an operation supposedly for appendicitis leaves her without her 'woman's parts' (128). She

---

[81] Anaïs Nin, 'The Voice', *Winter of Artifice* (1945; Chicago: Swallow Press, 1948), 122. Further references will be cited in the text.

announces her 'perversion' to The Voice—that she is a lesbian who does not want sex with a man. But she dreams of injecting mercury into her hands—poisoning her lesbian sexual tool—and fantasizes of passing a violin bow between her legs, playing herself. Ever since her encounter with June Mansfield, Nin had been obsessed by female cross-gendering. In April 1944 she recorded her ideal of a new image of women, Valentina Orlikova, the first female captain of the Soviet merchant navy:

A photograph of her had appeared, which all of us fell in love with. Short dark hair, regular features but fleshly and sensuous, beautiful dark eyes, clear-cut and stylised in her captain's uniform. She conveyed firmness and capability, without hardness or coldness. She became a symbol of woman's most secret wishes: to be able to be free and in command of her own destiny, responsible without loss of her womanliness.[82]

Inspired by Orlikova, Nin cross-dressed in her husband's tuxedo, and her portrait haunts *Ladders to Fire*, which inscribes both the beauty of the masculine woman, and yet the instability of her representation. In the novel Lillian's infantile cross-dressing, her adult assumption of a 'masculine' position, and her subsequent attachment to Djuna is a performance of fetishism that, as in *The Well of Loneliness*, stages desire for the lost female sexual body. As in *HER* and *Nightwood*, this fetishistic desire is compounded by textual splitting and dismemberment. Reading *Ladders* through 'The Voice' and *House of Incest*, Nin employs patterns of reference in her representation of the relationship between two women; this later text provides a model for female fetishism which bears comparison with that dramatized in *The Well*. Lilith's genital wound in 'The Voice' is internalized by Lillian in *Ladders*; it is the mark of her castration signifying not phallic lack but a wounded sense of female sexual integrity.

The residue of Nin's psychoanalytic experience is found in both 'The Voice' and *Ladders to Fire*. In the short story Lilith wants a man who satisfies her the way Djuna does, but she believes that Djuna nullifies the desire between them: there is no love between the two women because they are precisely the same.[83] But the eroticism

[82] Nin, *Diary*, iv. 10.
[83] This is reiterated in *Seduction of the Minotaur*: love for women is identity, not desire for the Other, 'closeness but not desire': 'It was hope for an exchange of selves'. *Seduction of the Minotaur* (1961; Chicago: The Swallow Press, 1969), 126.

of the pairing cannot ultimately be negated in 'The Voice': 'What softness between women. The marvelous silences of twinship. To turn and watch the rivulets of shadows between the breasts, to lie on the down of the bed sleeping over one's body' (161). *Ladders to Fire* is similarly schizoid in its representation of desire, oscillating between valorization of the erotics of sameness, and conversely the compulsion to 'heterosexualize' lesbian encounters. Lillian's adult masculine strivings are figured in terms of the annihilation she enacts upon her lover Gerard, and are understood as an assumption of power that phallicizes her but leaves her ultimately defeated and empty. Their relationship is 'delusive' because Lillian is 'too strong' and Gerard is 'not strong enough', and both elements would, in Nin's apocalyptic emotional language, 'destroy them' (74). Moreover, Lillian cannot enjoy her strength: 'At the same time as this urge to triumph continuously, she felt no appeasement or pleasure from her victories. What she won was not what she really wanted. Deep down, what her nature wanted was to be made to yield' (75). Both Gerard and Lillian are figured in terms of an unsuccessful cross-gendering which leaves them sexually unfulfilled and narcissistically devalued. It is the cross-gendering of Freudian theory which casts the masculine woman as a deficient man, and the feminine man as a weak and duplicitous woman: 'Gerard (like a woman) wore false pretexts' (74). While Lillian desires power, she imagines that it makes her unlovely and unwomanly: 'I did not arouse his love. I was not beautiful enough' (74). Lillian's masculinity in relation to men is figured exclusively and negatively in terms of her own devaluation. After Gerard's disappearance, Lillian 'became the warrior', in not an offensive, but a defensive attitude towards men (74). The sources of female pleasure in this model are not mutuality and reciprocity of desire, but 'being invaded . . . being conquered' (75). Her assumption of masculinity, of the costume and accoutrements of psychic strength, is transvestic: it comprises the armour and chain-mail of the male warrior.

Lillian and Djuna's relationship is similarly structured according to polarized attributes, and Lillian's masculinity acquires a different value and valence: Lillian has 'the physical strength, the physical dynamism, the physical appearance of strength. She carried tailored clothes well, her gestures were direct and violent. Masculinity seemed more possible to her, outwardly. Yet inwardly she was in a state of chaos and confusion. Inwardly she was like nature, chaotic and irrational' (82). Djuna is conversely the 'essence of femininity' (82). But such a diamorphic figuration does not necessarily spell out a neat distribution of gendered attributes. In contrast to Lillian's relationship with Gerard, Lillian and Djuna's union is presented as an 'encounter of equal forces', a 'meeting of equal speed, equal fervour, equal strength' (77). Lillian comes to this encounter initially in her guise of strength, but must hastily withdraw: 'Why Djuna, when I heard your voice over the telephone I thought you were delicate and fragile. And you look fragile but somehow not weak. I came to . . . well, to protect you. I don't know what from' (78, Nin's ellipsis). Their relationship is most effectively symbolized by a see-saw in which the women take turns to be the protector (93); both recognize the pain in the other and wish to assuage it. Nin explores the full range of gendered position in the *Cities* series producing what Diane Richard-Allerdyce has usefully termed a linguistic over-determination of gender: she cites the episode when Djuna, who upsets Lillian when she says that Lillian has a 'real maternal capacity' (she has a husband and two children), offers to write a personalized dictionary for Lillian 'which would stabilize the meaning of language by listing all non-injurious connotations of phrases that others use'.[84] Lillian's impossible desire to fix language speaks of the needs of the fetishist: she is fixated with her flawed outward appearance—missing buttons, runs in her stocking which suggest that her identity too is an imperfect costume. As Richard-Allerdyce glosses, she 'cannot hold her self together'.[85]

While Lillian gives Djuna something 'wonderful'—her presence, her 'eyes and ears, and hands and warmth and interest and alertness' (80)—Djuna also has something to give Lillian: it is her beautiful feminine body. Like Stephen Gordon, Lillian is presented as wearing her figurative masculine costume of armour as a sign of her 'castration', and of her desire for the female body, which she craves anaclitically as the object of desire, and narcissistically for herself, as a sign of her ideal self. In this model, the literal masculine costume of her childhood and the figurative transvestiture of her womanhood are fetishes that ward off narcissistic anxiety and

[84] Diane Richard-Allerdyce, *Anaïs Nin and the Remaking of Self: Gender, Modernism, and Narrative Identity* (Dekalb, Ill.: Northern Illinois University Press, 1998), 102.
[85] Ibid. 102.

signify her desire for what has been lost. This is the second model of cross-gendering employed by Nin in *Ladders to Fire*, and the one that transgresses the boundaries of psychoanalytic theory because it allows the intrusion of female fetishism as a mode of desire.

Lillian believes that if a woman seduces a man in a masculine manner, if she 'plays the Don Juan', then she is 'mutilated in some way' (81). This realization emanates from the failure of narcissism that she experiences with Gerard; the costume of strength which she appropriates covers over her own weakness, but it also occludes both her beauty and her femininity, which Nin problematically formulates as the desire to 'yield' and to be 'invaded'. Djuna, in response to Lillian's comment, observes that the feeling of mutilation emerges from guilt: 'For a man it is natural to be the aggressor and he takes defeat well. For woman it is a transgression, and she assumes the defeat is caused by the aggression' (81). Djuna wonders when woman will cease to be 'ashamed of her strength', when she will desist from experiencing power as a mark of castration (81).

COSTUMES OF STRENGTH AND COSTUMES OF UTTER FEMININITY: HOMEOVESTISM AS AN EXPLANATION FOR FEMALE CROSS-GENDERING

But Djuna's own gender identity is also shown to be unstable, her femininity an appropriation or a performance. This is more fully expressed in *Children of the Albatross*: 'she felt herself re-entering a smaller house of innocence and faith, and that what she shed was merely a role: she had played a role of woman, and this had been the torment, she had been pretending to be a woman, and now she knew she had not been at ease in this role.' With one of her male lovers 'she felt she was being transformed into a stature and substance nearer to her true state'.[86] In *Ladders* she is 'ashamed' of her female strength and wears the accoutrements of excessive femininity as if to mask masculine cravings. This performance is in some senses presented as a reparation of guilt:

While wearing the costume of utter femity [*sic*], the veils and the combs, the gloves and the perfumes, the muffs and the heels of femininity, she nevertheless disguised in herself an active lover of the world, the one who was actively

---

[86] Nin, *Children of the Albatross*, 81.

roused by the object of his love, the one who was made strong as man is made strong in the center of his being. (98)

Beneath the 'starched undulating petticoat or a ruffled ballet skirt', her 'nature was clarified, ordered, understood, dominated' (82). In her case history 'Womanliness as Masquerade' (1929), Joan Riviere attempted to show 'that women who wish for masculinity may put on a mark of womanliness to avert anxiety and the retribution feared from men'.[87] She presents the history of an intellectual woman (who many thought was herself), successful in business and a devoted wife and mother, who nevertheless flirted with older men after an 'intellectual performance'. In the 1970s George Zavitzianos coined the term 'homeovestism' after reading Riviere to mean behaviour that uses same-sex clothes as fetishes. His subject, aptly named Lillian, is a psychopathic female kleptomaniac. While Zavitzianos insists that the fetish is an illusory penis, his case studies identify a range of female fetishes which include clothing and jewellery to 'enhance' Lillian's 'appearance as a woman', and significantly books. He insists that the fetish for women is not necessary for coitus as it is for the male fetishist, but satisfies a more generalized need.[88] Might Lillian's behaviour in *Ladders to Fire*, read through Riviere and Zavitzianos, constitute a form of homeovestism, which rather than performing the desire for the father's penis stages the desire for the lost female body?

Riviere's radical discovery or female masquerade influenced modern feminist theory with such statements as: 'the reader may now ask how I define womanliness or where I draw the line between genuine womanliness and the "masquerade". My suggestion is not, however, that there is such a difference; whether radical or superficial, they are the same thing.'[89] But because Riviere analyses her subject according to a phallic economy she creates a problematic impasse: the female subject is revealed either as phallically castrated (incapable of pleasure) or wishing to castrate (unable to welcome the penis by gratification).[90] Nin reaches a similar formal impasse in

---

[87] Joan Riviere, 'Womanliness as Masquerade', *The International Journal of Psycho-Analysis*, 10 (1929), 303–13: 303.

[88] George Zavitazianos, 'Homeovestism: Perverse Form of Behaviour Involving Wearing Clothes of the Same Sex', *The International Journal of Psycho-Analysis*, 53 (1972), 471–7, and 'Fetishism and Exhibitionism in the Female and Their Relationship to Psychopathology and Kleptomania', *The International Journal of Psycho-Analysis*, 52 (1971), 297–305.

[89] Riviere, 'Womanliness as Masquerade', 306.   [90] Ibid. 307.

both her fiction and her diaries. Moreover in *Ladders to Fire*, Djuna's disguise of femininity is a mere 'inversion': where Djuna is outwardly feminine, she possesses a masculine mind. Furthermore, in what is the dominant Freudian text of *Ladders*, Nin still conceives of lesbian desire according to a heterosexual frame. While watching women perform the can-can, Djuna 'forgot that she was a woman and looked at the women dancing with the eyes of an artist and the eyes of a man' (102). In her relationship with Lillian each one wishes the other were a man (82).

But Nin does write herself out of this difficulty; it is not wholly the case that in Djuna the masquerade of femininity conceals either the castrating or castrated woman. Having lived a life of abject poverty, Djuna has conceived the ability to fantasize and create rich psychic dramas for herself which stimulate and nourish her: 'I saw in my dreams houses, forests, entire cities, and such a variety of personages that even today I wonder how a child, who had not even seen pictures, could invent such designs in textures' (94). Djuna incorporates what is lacking in her life: 'Whatever was missing she became: she became mother, father, cousin, brother, friend, confidant, guide, companion to all' (98). Need is converted through vision into nourishment, and hunger becomes love. While wearing the costume of femininity, she disguises not merely her masculinity, but her ability to love, not human strength, but weakness, not plenitude but need:

They needed each other. Djuna experienced deep in herself a pleasure each time Lillian exploded, for she herself kept her gestures, her feeling within an outer form, like an Oriental. When Lillian exploded it seemed to Djuna as if some of her violent feeling, so long contained within the forms were released . . . Djuna contained in herself a Lillian too, to whom she had never given a moment's freedom, and it made her strangely free when Lillian gave vent to her anger or rebellions. But after the havoc, when Lillian had bruised herself, or more seriously mutilated herself (war and explosion had their consequences) then Lillian needed Djuna. For the bitterness, the despair, the chaos submerged Lillian, drowned her. The hurt Lillian wanted to strike back and did so blindly, hurting herself all the more. And then Djuna was there, to remove the arrows implanted in Lillian, to cleanse them of their poison, to open the prison door, to open the trap door, to protect, to give transfusion of blood, and peace to the wounded. (99)

The image of the see-saw is now forsaken; Djuna assumes the dominant role in terms of protection and nurture and this stimulates

Lillian's desire for her: 'Lillian knew only one thing: that she must possess Djuna' (99). She does not consciously desire Djuna's 'masculine' core-self, but rather her ability to restore Lillian's female body to herself which is played out through Djuna's *trans*fusion of blood, and her performance as the Mother (she continues this role with male lovers in *Children of the Albatross*). Lillian's seduction of Djuna is initiated through the conferring of gifts, significantly feminine accoutrements, such as perfume and jewellery, upon her lover.[91]

In the 'covert' anti-Freudian text of *Ladders*, Nin suggests an alternative psycho-sexual framework for the representation of cross-gendering. The key to understanding the figuration of Lillian's masculine identification and her cross-dressing is through a reading of her clothes fetish, not only for her own masculine clothing, but also for Djuna's feminine costumes. The relationship for both women is like a fetish in its anthropological sense, a 'primitive figure to which both enjoyed presenting proofs of worship and devotion. It was an active continuous ceremony in which there entered no moments of indifference, fatigue, or misunderstandings or separations, no eclipses, no doubts' (81). This cleaving together, or *trans*fusion, this ceremony of indifference is ritualized through the fetishes of difference.

Lillian's desire for Djuna is most specifically indexed in terms of sartorial display; she secretly investigates Djuna's wardrobe, obsessed by the 'sheer femininity' of her clothing, and is struck by the 'world of artifice' unveiled by the wardrobe (85). Jay conducts a similar survey of Djuna's wardrobe and bathroom in *Children of the Albatross*, opening jars and bottles to see what they contain and pulling at her eyelashes: 'even though he always had the feeling that women resorted to tricks and contrived spells which man must watch out for, he still felt that she was more than a woman, and that given the right moment, she was willing to shed the veils, the elusiveness, and to be completely honest.'[92] In *Ladders*, Lillian stimulates her craving by showering gifts of slippers and shoes upon Djuna, an act which seems to serve a complex psychological need:

---

[91] In *Children of the Albatross* Lawrence similarly pays tribute to Djuna's femininity bringing her 'gifts of chokers, headdresses, earrings made of painted clay'. But the gifts are 'like the trappings for a costume play' indicating the self-conscious constructedness of Djuna's gendered identity (74).

[92] Ibid. 142–3.

'Lillian became the mother who wanted to dress her child out of her own substance, Lillian became the lover who wanted to slip the shoes and slippers on the beloved's feet so he could contain these feet. The dresses were not chosen as Djuna's dresses, but as Lillian's choice and taste to cover Djuna' (100). The word 'cover' with it connotation of 'veiling' carries some anxiety about Djuna's own feminine status: is it phallicism (as mother), her castration, or something else that is being veiled?[93] The key element of this extract is that Lillian's engagement in some form of displacement activity that fetishizes Djuna is crucial to her own psychic health. Lillian's fetishization of masculine clothing on herself, and feminine clothing on Djuna, serve the same purpose: to cover over the narcissistic wound and access to the female body that can provide sexual satisfaction and (self-)love. Lillian exists in a position of lack to Djuna's feminine abundance; what Lillian could not attain 'she at least reached by way of Djuna' (107). She is not Djuna, but desires to be her and imagines that she could be her; through the power of this conviction she speaks the discourse of fetishistic disavowal: 'I know that I am not her, but I choose to believe that I am.' With this statement, Lillian can construct a fetish (masculinity) on to which are displaced all her feelings of anxiety and desire which emanate from her own female body and the sight of Djuna's ultra-femininity.

The cross-gendering of Lillian must be understood in terms of this displaced investment in feminine display, which spills over into her own self-presentation. She buys a black lace gown like Djuna's, and desires to own all the objects 'which carried Djuna's personality or spirit' (101). Djuna perceives that Lillian wants to become her 'so that she communicate with man', but there is clearly more at stake, which Nin dramatizes in Lillian watching Djuna walk: 'In front of Lillian walked Lillian's lost femininity, imprisoned in the male Lillian. Lillian's femininity imprisoned in the deepest wells of her being, loving Djuna, and knowing it must reach her own femininity at the bottom of the well by way of Djuna. By wearing Djuna's feminine exterior, swaying her hips, becoming Djuna' (107). Richard-Allerdyce suggests that Lillian's desire to 'be' Djuna 'leads her not to a "true" sense of self or of femininity but to a memory

---

[93] The word 'cover' is also a term used in animal reproduction (the bull 'covers' the cow). This adds a phallic connotation to Lillian's desire for Djuna. I am grateful to Ros Ballaster for suggesting this.

that points to the fictional status of engendered identity'.[94] The memory is of childhood trauma: the first time she is hurt by a boy, she cross-dresses in her brother's suit wanting to 'feel as the boy felt' (108). She conducts future relationships while dressed in men's clothes. The clothing becomes a 'costume of strength', which not only makes her feel confident, but restores a sense of self-worth (108). The story of Lillian's childhood cross-gendering is retold in *Seduction of the Minotaur* with a few significant embellishments: 'Lillian had no confidence in herself as a woman. She thought that it was because her father had wanted her to be a boy. She did not see herself as beautiful, and as a girl loved to put on her brother's clothes at first to please her father, and later because it gave her a feeling of strength.'[95] In an adolescent relationship she is not passive enough, cycling too fast to meet a lover and losing him as a result; she is a Romeo 'who had to leap across space' to join her Juliet (110). The two gendered components of her schizoid identity, the 'prone figure of the woman, apparently passive, apparently receptive', and the 'taut and anxious shadow' of the woman cycling too fast who 'plunges forward' and is defeated (as Lillian is defeated by Gerard) remain unreconciled and create a split in Lillian's figuration (111). What emerges is the 'shadow of anxiety', the fetish of masculine clothing, enabling Lillian to assume 'man's active role to quieten its anguish' (111).

Djuna, however, penetrates to the depths of Lillian's disguise, beneath the aggression and the strength, to the 'hidden, secret, frightened Lillian who had created such a hard armor and disguise around her weakness', taking up the 'man's lance' in a gesture of overt phallicism (108–9). Lillian's cross-gendered identification is presented as a fetish against which value in oneself is secured. Djuna sees through the armour to the wounded body beneath; Lillian comes to her with the armour destroyed, and the fragments inflicting wounds upon her, 'like cruel pieces of mail which had wounded her more than they had protected her from the enemy' (109). What is uncovered when the armour has 'melted' is 'bruised feminine

---

[94] Richard-Allerdyce, *Remaking of Self*, 103. Richard-Allerdyce finds Nin's concept of gender 'difficult to define when Lillian tries to "be" Djuna' to find the 'lost femininity . . . imprisoned in the deepest wells of her being'. This is partly due to Nin's ambivalence in her presentation of Lillian and Djuna, but also because Richard-Allerdyce does not take into account the discourse of fetishism.

[95] Nin, *Seduction of the Minotaur*, 124–5.

flesh' (109). Like Stephen Gordon, Lillian's self-concept is entirely projected on to her body; in de Lauretis's terms the mark of her 'castration' is what makes her unsuitable as the object of desire.[96]

In the subsequent volumes of the *Cities of the Interior* series, it is Sabina's cape that becomes the armour of strength. In *Children of the Albatross* she lends it to Lillian:

Her first instinctive, blind gesture of escape was to don the black cape copied from Sabina's at the time of their relationship.

She wrapped Sabina's cape around her, and put two heavy bracelets around her wrist (one for each wrist, not wanting any more to be in bondage to her, never to one; she would split the desire in two, to rescue one half of herself from destruction).[97]

This is a conscious recognition of the fetishist in Lillian in her desire to save and protect one aspect of herself by displacing anxiety and fear on to a piece of clothing (which is significantly a 'copy'). In *A Spy in the House of Love* Sabina, who wears the cape as a memorial to masculinity ('the cape held within its fold something of what she imagined was a quality possessed exclusively by man') experiences a similar splitting: 'she was startled by the appearance of a woman at her left, who walked in step with her. Sabina glanced at her profile and was comforted by her tallness, the assurance of her walk.'[98] But for Lillian the excitement of the performance, of being Sabina, pales: 'The clothes had not fitted very well.'[99]

CLOSING DOWN POSSIBILITIES FOR FEMALE CROSS-GENDERED FETISHISM

But, as Djuna's explanation of Lillian's fetishization of her augurs, Lillian's cross-gendering is ultimately fed back into the authoritative Freudian text. Into Djuna's mouth is put Nin's master-narrative:

---

[96] The nature of this wound is to be contrasted with that referred to in the short story 'Artists and Models'. Despite the masculine Leila's performance of strength, Elena recognizes in her a 'secret wound'. Nin, *Delta of Venus*, 128.

[97] Nin, *Children of the Albatross*, 138. This is a passage from the diary: the bracelets serve a multiple purpose: to bind the lover, to signify twinship, and to protect against the possibility of loss. *Diary*, ii. 40. June Mansfield also gives Nin a bracelet, 'a part of her': the 'joy of wearing her bracelet filled me'. *Diary*, i. 85. It pinches her wrists like fingers.

[98] Anaïs Nin, *A Spy in the House of Love* (Paris: British Book Centre, 1954), 12, 14.

[99] Nin, *Children of the Albatross*, 141.

'[Lillian] wants something of me that only a man can give her. But first of all she wants to become me, so that she communicate with man. She has lost her ways of communicating with man. She is doing it through me!' (107). The tenderness, pleasure, and desire that had been part of this lesbian relationship are lost. Nin's writing can not maintain the bond between Djuna and Lillian, and collapses notions of female cross-gendering into psychoanalytic common-places: that the 'masculine' woman desires refeminization in order to assume a correct and rightful position in relation to man. She is renourished at the mother's breast so that she can in turn offer sus-tenance to her male mate.

Thus renewed, Lillian becomes a fetishized phallic mother for her lover, Jay: 'she felt immense, and strong, and illimitable, the bound-less mother opening her arms and her wings flying to carry him somewhere; she his shelter and refuge, his secret hiding place, his tent, his sky, his blanket' (116). Jay is a classic Freudian male fetishist; Lillian is sexually enjoyed as a fur object, 'the pocket, the warmth that sheltered him' (116): she envelops and sustains him and he sleeps in her 'warmth and furriness' (116). The maternal warmth displaced on to an image of fur allows Jay to enjoy sexual fulfilment: 'He caressed the fur, he feared no claws, he abandoned himself'; this is mutually erotic (116).[100] He desires to be taken into the lover's/mother's body and Lillian answers this need by completely introjecting him: 'She never felt him outside of herself' (121). Jay comes to Lillian as a 'man who limps'; he suffers with an intense cas-tration anxiety, dreaming that his mother is a cripple, and that he deprived her of the 'lower half of her body' (166–7). In their rela-tionship, as a result of Jay's psychic damage, Lillian enjoys a vicari-ous maternal masculinity in which she replenishes him so that he can perform in the world; by smothering him with love and support she, in effect, phallicizes him, and phallicizes herself: 'he treated her as if she were a man (or the mother)' (122). This confusion between the man and the mother indicates that Nin constructs all-powerful maternity in terms of phallicism, and male fetishism; it also explains why Djuna's inner core of masculinity provides sustenance to Lillian.

[100] Jay's fur fetish is traced back to his mother's deprivations, specifically her refusal to allow his cold hands inside her fur muff. The pornographic possibilities are manifest. Psychoanalytic explanation is ventriloquized by Lillian: 'What she overtly extended to him was one who seemed done with her child self and who would replace the harsh mother, extend the muff and the warm naked hands' (152).

But Lillian's union with Jay does not ultimately replenish her: 'Jay had not made her woman, but the husband and mother of his weakness' (136). She is unable to carry the child fathered by Jay because he does not want it; she voices a desire to her unborn child that is central to *House of Incest*: 'All of us forever seeking this warmth and this darkness, this being alive without pain, this being alive without anxiety, fear or loneliness' (137). She resorts to assuming 'the man's costume' in order to protect herself, and to attempt again to access the 'core' of her femininity. Acting like a lover to Helen, she seduces her as if she were a man, putting herself in Jay's position and experiencing Helen vicariously. It is ambiguous whether Lillian does so in order to help Helen, to restore 'warmth and fervour', or to take the place of Jay, to enact the seduction of which she feels she has deprived Helen. There is some suggestion that Lillian recognizes herself in Helen, who is also physically large and imposing and wears masculine clothing such as severely tailored suits. Like Lillian, she is also conceived as a split personality, as both passively feminine and rigidly masculine; this is registered somatically: 'she had two voices, one which fell deep like the voice of a man, and another light and innocent. Two women disputing inside of her' (131). More significantly, as Djuna experienced with Lillian, so Lillian recognizes in Helen: 'All around her there were signs, signs of danger and loss' (133). Helen responds to Lillian's performances of femininity, but Lillian ultimately rejects her.

Lillian's relationship with Sabina breaks the pattern imposed by Lillian's inability to occupy a stable gendered position. While Lillian had wanted to possess Djuna for her own narcissistic sustenance, in Sabina she recognizes an erotic ideal: 'Lillian saw for the first time the woman she had always wanted to know. She saw Sabina's eyes burning, heard her voice so rusty and immediately felt drowned in her beauty. She wanted to say: I recognize you. I have often imagined a woman like you' (169). Djuna had provided a template of fetishized femininity; Sabina provides an image of an ideal self: while Lillian wanted to mimic Djuna, to appropriate her magical gifts, in an echo of *House of Incest* she wants to be Sabina: 'I never wanted to be anyone but myself before . . . If I were to unmask you Sabina, I would only be revealing myself' (174–5).[101] Their sexual encounters are couched in the language of erotica, veiling the vagina

---

[101] Nin later explicated wanting to 'be' the female lover—it was not to be confused with 'genuine lesbianism' or with love, but was narcissistic. *Conversations*, ed. DuBow, 124.

and uterus in lyricism: 'They entered a softly lighted place, mauve and diffuse, which enveloped them in velvet closeness' (177). In this enclosed womb-like space the two women experience a reciprocal mystic fusion of selves and bodies: 'Their individuality washed down and effaced the world: they stood at the beginning of everything, naked and innocent of the past . . . No bodies touching would answer this mysterious craving in them to become each other. Not to possesses each other but to become each other' (182, 185). What Sabina desires in Lillian is her 'newness', and what Lillian desires in Sabina is her corruption:

'You're so extraordinarily white.' With a strange sadness, like a weight, she spoke, as if it were not the white substance of Lillian but the whiteness of her newness to life which Sabina seemed to sigh for. 'You're so white, so white and smooth.' And there were deep shadows in her eyes, shadows of one old with living: shadows in the neck, in her arms, on her knees, violet shadows. (184)

Lillian's sense of wholeness, of being desired not as man, and not as a mother, is restored through Sabina's desire. The white unmarked body connotes innocence and wholeness for Sabina before she was stained by the vicissitudes of desire; Sabina sees herself as a child in the mirror of Lillian, and she wants to return to this pristine self. But whiteness, as discussed in the work of H.D. and Hall, also denotes lesbian decadence and eroticism. Lillian's contrasting desire for Sabina is indexed according to Sabina's marks of castration, the violet shadows that are indicative of the 'loss of herself'.

But this union is ruptured at the break of day; Lillian concludes that she wants to be Sabina because Jay desired her. Sabina attempts to restore the 'magic' of their alliance: 'He is not as aware of us as we are of each other. We have loved in each other all he has failed to love and see' (186). This is an important admission: it is an awareness of the specificity of women's bodies and desires. But, as we have already witnessed in Nin, lesbian desire is rarely represented outside a heterosexual frame: this time a man creeps between the two women, 'now lying at their side, between their caresses, slipping in between them like an enemy' (186).[102] Lillian had entrusted Jay with

[102] Similarly in the short story 'Mallorca', a Mallorcan girl is seduced into the sea by a boyish American girl. But once in the water a displacement occurs: when Maria is embraced by who she thinks is the girl, she is surprised not to feel her breasts against her own but a penis between her legs. The American girl has been replaced by her younger brother. In 'The Basque and Bijou' this displacement is repeated. Observing a man and a woman watching 'lesbian poses' in which Bijou had performed with a dildo the Basque intercedes: 'You wanted a man and here I am, *Delta of Venus* (1969; London: Penguin, 1990), 167.

the moulding of her image as a woman, 'someone of value', but Djuna points to the vanity of this hope: 'Lillian, no one should be entrusted with one's image to fashion, with one's self-creation. Women are moving from one circle to another, rising towards independence and self-creation' (193). In the final pages of *Ladders to Fire* Lillian casts off the guise of her constructed self, tearing off her dress, jewels, her facial expression; Djuna's image of her restored self also lies in tatters: 'Nothing to salvage. A mere pile of flaws' (209).[103]

The proliferation of multiple and fragmented selves is emblematized on the front cover of an edition of *Ladders to Fire* in which Nin appears photographed in different guises as characters from the novel. The photograph of her as Lillian with short hair and a tailored man's suit causes a 'negative' reaction and 'gave rise to the legend that I was a Lesbian'.[104] Nin was indignant that the photograph of herself as 'the author' had not been used; instead the 'real' self was supplanted by a fantasized and idealized cross-gendered image. The crossing of the boundary that marks off confession and autobiography from fiction was traversed by Nin allowing her to indulge in the discourse of fetishism. Djuna Barnes's spelling out of the limits of the representation of gendered subjects through such a discourse is finally played out by Nin, but within the bounds of that failure an understanding of female fetishism had been transformed.

[103] In *A Spy in the House of Love*, Sabina, in training as an actress, feels that 'parts of me tear off like a fragment, fly here and there. I lose vital parts of myself.' She is a 'composite', not whole (22).
[104] Nin, *Diary*, iv. 175.

Afterword

Even though Anaïs Nin figured female cross-gendering as a performance of fetishism in her *Cities of the Interior* series in the 1940s, Djuna Barnes had already mapped out the limits of that figuration in *Nightwood*, the novel Nin longed to emulate. The disavowal of the discourses of psychoanalysis and sexology in that text is eventually relinquished in favour of 'impossibility': this makes *Nightwood*, in a sense, the repressed in the unconscious of the texts under discussion in this study. In *The Well of Loneliness*, Radclyffe Hall oscillated fetishistically between modes of presenting the invert/pervert: while the subtext of female fetishism was available to be read, it was the dominant text of inversion that influenced the readership of *The Well* for the next sixty years. Nin incorporated similarly opposing means of presentation in *Ladders to Fire* and her diaries, oscillating between Freudian and anti-Freudian discourses, while H.D. explored the possibilities of fetishizing the object of desire in order to stabilize the self, only to narrativize its failure in *HER*. The pervasive nature of fetishism in *Nightwood* as a sexual/textual practice signals the breakdown of fetishistic textuality explored in Nin, Hall, and H.D., as well as exhausting and frightening its author. Fetishistic cross-gendering would not be refigured as a textual practice until the second wave of feminism had re-evaluated its importance, most significantly in the work of Jeanette Winterson. Barnes would prove to have left the most compelling legacy to a second generation of modernist women writers.[1]

Throughout this study, the texts have been read as engaging with (psychoanalytic and sexological) theory, and while *Nightwood* is a 'theoretical' text, it is also perversely anti-theoretical. Following the explosion of (feminist) theory during and after the 1970s, which reformulated psychoanalytic models and concepts through poststructuralism, Jeanette Winterson produced self-conscious 'fictions of theory', in which the cross-gendered woman re-emerged as a

---

[1] For an analysis of Barnes's influence on Winterson see Carolyn Allen, *Following Djuna: Women Lovers and the Erotics of Loss* (Bloomington, Ind.: University of Indiana Press, 1996).

problematic figure of representation. During the 1950s and 1960s, the representation of female cross-gendering was largely the preserve of pulp fiction, and was typically assimilated into the literature which flourished around the butch-femme lesbian subculture (notably the 'Beebo Brinker' series by Ann Bannon).[2] Cross-gendering only re-entered 'high art' after post-structuralist feminist theory had been thoroughly digested. Post-structuralism allowed precisely the reading of what is 'disavowed' in a text, or what is not overtly articulated.

Jeanette Winterson's particular fascination with modernism and sexual representation makes her a direct descendant of Djuna Barnes. Her novel *Written on the Body* (1992) withholds the gender of the protagonist in an effort to focus attention upon what Carolyn Allen has termed the 'erotics of loss'. The ungendered 'I' of the novel reflects on losing the beloved Louise as loss of the (female) body, through extended tropes of dismemberment culled from Monique Wittig's *The Lesbian Body*. In *The Passion* (1987), Winterson poses female cross-gendering in precisely the same terms as discussed in this study; as both the threatened loss of female subjectivity, and as an enhancement of the body/self. Villanelle's cross-dressing is presented as a performance of fetishism which overtly and joyously glorifies and takes pleasure in the sexual female body, while it refigures her love for another woman in terms of the erotics of loss: 'She thought I was a young man. I was not. Should I go to see her myself and joke about the mistake and leave gracefully? My heart shrivelled at this thought. To lose her again so soon.'[3] When Villanelle finally removes her man's shirt to reveal her breast to her beloved, this uncovering is presented as the erotic corollary of their relationship.

In *The Passion* Winterson engages in a discussion about the coterminous nature of sex and gender and the notion of a unitary self ('And what was myself?' asks Villanelle).[4] Given the proliferation of recent theories about the performativity of gender and sex, the cross-gendered woman remains compelling to both feminist critics

[2] For an overview of butch-femme fiction see Ann Herrmann, 'Imitations of Marriage: Cross-Dressed Couples in Contemporary Lesbian Fiction', *Feminist Studies*, 18.3 (Fall 1992), 612–25, and Michèle Aina Barale, 'When Jack Blinks: Si(gh)ting Gay Desire in Ann Bannon's Beebo Brinker', in Henry Abelove, Michèle Aina Barale, and David Halperin (eds.), *The Lesbian and Gay Studies Reader* (New York: Routledge, 1993), 604–15.
[3] Jeanette Winterson, *The Passion* (1987; London: Penguin, 1988), 65–6.
[4] Ibid. 66.

and women writers alike because of her position as a figure of unde-cidability. Cross-gendering has re-entered the gender/sex debate in terms of both a figure for cultural anxiety (Marjorie Garber, *Vested Interests*), and as the focus for a reformulation of masquerade or 'drag' (Judith Butler, *Gender Trouble*). Winterson's novels return to Barnes having been sifted through feminist and post-structuralist theory. However, while Barnes had radically alienated desire from passion, Winterson in her curiously sermonizing theoretical fictions re-fuses them. Her newly *trans*figured version of modernism is, however, at odds with its style, which leaves the cross-gendered woman as the fetish of theory itself. It is an oddly sanitized view of female cross-gendering, and one comparatively free from anxiety. For the 'dark unconscious' of fetishistic desire, one that defines the very limits of engendering, we must return to the novels of Radclyffe Hall, Anaïs Nin, H.D., and Djuna Barnes.

Bibliography

PRIMARY MATERIAL

Literary works

BARNES, DJUNA, 'Dusie', in Carl Van Doren, (ed.), *Americana Esoterica* (New York: Macy-Masius, 1927).

—— *Ladies Almanack* (1928; Elmwood Park, Ill.: Dalkey Archive Press, 1992).

—— 'A Night Among the Horses', in *Spillway* (London: Faber & Faber, 1962).

—— *Nightwood: The Original Version and Related Drafts*, ed. Cheryl J. Plumb (1936; Normal, Ill.: Dalkey Archive Press, 1995).

—— *The Antiphon*, in *Selected Works of Djuna Barnes* (London: Faber & Faber, 1962).

—— 'James Joyce', in *I Could Never Be Lonely Without a Husband: Interviews*, by Djuna Barnes, ed. Alyce Barry (1985; London: Virago, 1987).

—— 'Madame Collects Herself', in *At the Roots of the Stars: The Short Plays*, ed. Douglas Messerli (Los Angeles: Sun and Moon Press, 1995).

BRYHER, *Development* (London: Constable, 1920).

—— *Two Selves* (Paris: Contact, [1923?]).

—— *The Heart to Artemis* (London: Collins, 1963).

GRAND, SARAH, *The Heavenly Twins* (1893; Ann Arbor: University of Michigan Press, 1992).

—— 'The New Aspect of the Woman Question', *The North American Review* (Mar. 1894).

GREGG, FRANCES, 'Male and Female', in Bronte Adams and Trudi Tate (eds.), *That Kind of Woman: Stories from the Left Bank and Beyond* (London: Virago, 1991).

—— *The Mystic Leeway*, ed. Ben Jones (Ottawa: Carleton University Press, 1994).

GUIRL-STEARLEY, G. C. (ed.), 'The Letters of Djuna Barnes and Emily Holmes Coleman (1935–1936)', *The Missouri Review*, 22.3 (1999): 105–46

HALL, RADCLYFFE, *A Sheaf of Verses* (1908; Windsor: Gaby Goldscheider, 1985).

—— *The Unlit Lamp* (1924; London: Virago, 1981).

—— 'Miss Ogilvy Finds Herself', in *Miss Ogilvy Finds Herself* (London: William Heinemann, 1934).

—— *The Well of Loneliness* (1928; London: Virago, 1991).

—— *Your John: The Love Letters of Radclyffe Hall*, ed. Joanne Glasgow (New York and London: New York University Press, 1997).

HAMILTON, CICELY, *Life Errant* (London: J. M. Dent and Sons, 1935).

H.D., 'Narthex', in Alfred Kreymborg, Lewis Mumford, and Paul Rosenfeld (eds.), *The [Second] American Caravan: A Yearbook of American Literature* (New York: Macaulay, 1928).

—— *Kora and Ka (Mira-Mare)* (Dijon: Imprimerie Darantière, 1934).

—— *Nights* (1936; New York: New Directions, 1986).

—— *Tribute to Freud* (1956; Boston: David R. Godine, 1974).

—— *The Gift* (1969; New York: New Directions, 1982).

—— *End to Torment: A Memoir of Ezra Pound With the Poems from 'Hilda's Book' By Ezra Pound*, ed. Norman Holmes Pearson and Michael King (Manchester: New Directions, 1979).

—— *Her* (1981; London: Virago, 1984).

—— *Notes on Thought and Vision and the Wise Sappho* (San Francisco: City Lights Books, 1982).

—— 'Hymen', in *Collected Poems 1912–1944*, ed. Louis L. Martz (Manchester: Carcanet Press, 1984).

—— 'The Master', in *Collected Poems 1912–1944*, ed. Louis L. Martz (Manchester: Carcanet Press, 1984).

—— 'Pygmalion', in *Collected Poems 1912–1944*, ed. Louis L. Martz (Manchester: Carcanet Press, 1984).

—— *Asphodel*, ed. Robert Spoo (Durham and London: Duke University Press, 1992).

—— *Paint It Today*, ed. Cassandra Laity (New York and London: New York University Press, 1992).

JACOB, NAOMI, *Me—and the Swans* (London: William Kimber, 1963).

LOWRY, MALCOLM, *Selected Letters*, ed. Harvey Breit and Margerie Bonner Lowry (1965; London: Penguin, 1985).

MOORE, GEORGE, 'Albert Nobbs', in *Celibate Lives* (London: Heinemann, 1927).

NIN, ANAÏS, *House of Incest* (1936?; Denver: Alan Swallow, 1961).

—— 'The Voice', *Winter of Artifice* (1945; Chicago: Swallow Press, 1948).

—— *Ladders to Fire* (New York: E. P. Dutton, 1946).

—— *Under a Glass Bell* (1947; London: Penguin, 1978).

—— 'The Labyrinth', in *Under a Glass Bell* (1947; London: Penguin, 1978).

—— 'Ragtime', in *Under a Glass Bell* (1947; London: Penguin, 1978).

—— *Children of the Albatross* (New York: E. P. Dutton, 1947).

—— *A Spy in the House of Love* (Paris: British Book Centre, 1954).

—— *Seduction of the Minotaur* (1961; Chicago: The Swallow Press, 1969).

—— *Collages* (1964; London; Virago, 1993).

—— *The Diary of Anaïs Nin*, i. *1931–1934*, ed. Gunther Stuhlmann (New York: The Swallow Press and Harcourt, Brace and World, 1966).

—— *The Diary of Anaïs Nin*, ii. *1934–1939*, ed. Gunther Stuhlmann (New York: The Swallow Press and Harcourt, Brace and World, 1967).

—— *The Novel of the Future* (1968; London: Peter Owen, 1969).

—— 'Artists and Models', in *Delta of Venus* (1969; London: Penguin, 1990).

—— 'The Basque and Bijou', in *Delta of Venus* (1969; London: Penguin, 1990).

—— *The Diary of Anaïs Nin*, iii. *1939–1944*, ed. Gunther Stuhlmann (New York: Harcourt, Brace and World, 1969).

—— *The Diary of Anaïs Nin*, iv. *1944–1947* (New York: Harcourt Brace Jovanovich, 1971).

—— *A Woman Speaks: The Lectures, Seminars and Interviews of Anaïs Nin*, ed. Evelyn J. Hinz (Chicago: Swallow Press, 1975).

—— *Linotte: The Early Diary of Anaïs Nin 1914–1920* (New York: Harcourt Brace Jovanovich, 1978).

—— *The Diary of Anaïs Nin*, vii. *1966–1974*, ed. Gunther Stuhlmann (New York: Harcourt Brace Jovanovich, 1980).

—— *Henry and June, From the Unexpurgated Diary* (1986; London: W. H. Allen, 1988).

—— *Incest: From 'A Journal of Love', The Unexpurgated Diary of Anaïs Nin, 1934–1935* (San Diego: Harcourt Brace Jovanovich, 1992).

—— *The Early Diary of Anaïs Nin* (1994; London: Penguin, 1995).

—— *Conversations With Anaïs Nin*, ed. Wendy DuBow (Jackson, Miss.: University Press of Mississippi, 1994).

—— *Fire, From a Journal of Love: The Unexpurgated Diary of Anaïs Nin 1934–1937* (London: Peter Owen, 1996).

POUND, EZRA, 'Sancta Patrona Domina Caelae', in *End to Torment: A Memoir of Ezra Pound With the Poems from 'Hilda's Book' By Ezra Pound*, by H.D., ed. Norman Holmes Pearson and Michael King (Manchester: New Directions, 1980).

POWYS, JOHN COWPER, *Autobiography* (1934; London: Macdonald, 1967).

[ST JOHN, CHRISTOPHER], *Hungerheart: The Story of a Soul* (London: Methuen, 1915).

—— 'Close-Up' (1949), in Eleanor Adlard (ed.), *Edy: Recollections of Edith Craig* (London: Frederick Muller, 1949).

STEIN, GERTRUDE, 'A Sontina Followed By Another', in *The Yale Gertrude Stein*, ed. Richard Kostelanetz (New Haven: Yale University Press, 1980).

WINTERSON, JEANETTE, *The Passion* (1987; London: Penguin, 1988).

WOOLF, VIRGINIA, *Orlando: A Biography* (London: The Hogarth Press, 1928).

—— *A Change of Perspective: The Letters of Virginia Woolf*, iii. *1923–1928*, ed. Nigel Nicolson and Joanne Trautmann (London: The Hogarth Press, 1977).

WOOLSON, CONSTANCE FENIMORE, 'Felipa', in Joan Myers Weimer (ed.), *Women Artists, Women Exiles: 'Miss Grief' and Other Stories* (New Brunswick, NJ, and London: Rutgers University Press, 1988).

Sexology and Psychoanalysis

ABRAHAM, KARL, 'Manifestations of the Female Castration Complex' (1920), in *Selected Papers of Karl Abraham*, trans. Douglas Bryan and Alix Strachey (London: The Hogarth Press and the Institute of Psycho-Analysis, 1927), 338–69.

BARAHAL, HYMAN S., 'Female Transvestism and Homosexuality', *Psychiatric Quarterly*, 27 (1953), 390–438.

BINET, ALFRED, 'Le Fétichisme dans l'amour', *Revue Philosophique*, 24 (1887), 142–67, 252–74.

BLAND, LUCY, and DOAN, LAURA (eds.), *Sexology Uncensored: The Documents of Sexual Science* (Oxford: Polity Press, 1998).

BREUER, JOSEPH, 'Case 1. Fräulein Anna O', in *The Standard Edition of the Complete Works of Sigmund Freud*, trans. James Strachey *et al.*, 24 vols (London: The Hogarth Press and the Institute of Psycho-Analysis, 1953–74), 2. 21–47.

CAPRIO, FRANK S., *Variations in Sexual Behaviour: A Psychodynamic Study of Deviations in Various Expressions of Sexual Behaviour* (1957; London: John Calder, 1966).

CARPENTER, EDWARD, 'On the Connection Between Homosexuality and Divination and the Importance of the Intermediate Sexes Generally in Early Civilizations', in *American Journal of Religious Psychology and Education*, 4 (1911), 219–43.

CHARCOT, JEAN-MARTIN, and MAGNAN, VALENTIN, 'Inversion du sens génital et autres perversions sexuelles', *Archives de Neurologie*, 3 (Jan.–Feb. 1882), 53–60, and 4 (July 1882), 296–322.

CHIDECKEL, MAURICE, *Female Sex Perversion: The Sexually Aberrated Woman As She Is* (1935; New York: Brown Book Company, 1968).

DICKES, ROBERT, 'Fetishistic Behaviour: A Contribution to Its Complex Development and Significance', *Journal of the American Psychoanalytic Association*, 11 (1963), 303–30.

—— 'Parents, Transitional Objects and Childhood Fetishes', in S. A. Grolnick and L. Barkin (eds.), *Between Reality and Fantasy* (New York: Jason Aronson, 1978), 307–19.

DOCTER, RICHARD F., *Transvestites and Transsexuals: Toward a Theory of Cross-Gender Behaviour* (New York: Plenum Press, 1988).

ELLIS, HAVELOCK, *Man and Woman: A Study of Human Secondary and Sexual Characters* (London: Walter Scott, 1894).

—— *Studies in the Psychology of Sex*, i. *Sexual Inversion* (London: The University Press, 1897).

—— *Studies in the Psychology of Sex*, vii. *Eonism and Other Supplementary Studies* (Philadelphia: F. A. Davis, 1928).

—— *Psychology of Sex* (1933; London: Heinemann, 1948).

—— *Studies in the Psychology of Sex*, ii. *Sexual Inversion* (New York: Random House, 1936).

FELDMAN, SANDOR S., 'On Homosexuality', in Sandor Lorand and Michael Balint (eds.), *Perversions, Psychodynamics and Therapy* (1956; London: The Ortolan Press, 1965), 71–96.

FENICHEL, OTTO, *The Psychoanalytic Theory of Neurosis* (London: Routledge & Kegan Paul, 1946).

FREUD, ANNA, *Normality and Pathology in Childhood: Assessments of Development* (London: The Hogarth Press and the Institute of Psycho-Analysis, 1966).

FREUD, SIGMUND, *The Standard Edition of the Complete Works of Sigmund Freud*, trans. James Strachey *et al.*, 24 vols. (London: The Hogarth Press and the Institute of Psycho-Analysis, 1953–74). Individual volumes cited below as *SE*.

—— 'Three Essays on the Theory of Sexuality' (1905), *SE* 7. 135–243.

—— 'Fragment of an Analysis of a Case of Hysteria ('Dora')' (1905 [1901]), *SE* 7. 1–122.

—— 'On the Sexual Theories of Children' (1908), *SE* 9. 205–26.

—— 'On Narcissism: An Introduction' (1914), *SE* 14. 69–102.

—— 'The Taboo of Virginity' (1918 [1917]), *SE* 11. 191–208.

—— 'The Uncanny' (1919), *SE* 17. 217–56.

—— 'The Psychogenesis of a Case of Homosexuality in a Woman' (1920), *SE* 18. 145–72.

—— 'Some Consequences of the Anatomical Distinction Between the Sexes' (1925), *SE* 19. 241–58.

—— 'Fetishism' (1927), *SE* 21. 147–57.

—— 'Civilization and its Discontents' (1930 [1929]), *SE* 21. 57–145.

—— 'Female Sexuality' (1931), *SE* 21. 221–43.

—— 'New Introductory Lectures on Psycho-Analysis, Lecture 33: Femininity' (1933 [1932]), *SE* 22. 112–35.

—— 'Splitting of the Ego in the Process of Defence' (1940 [1938]), *SE* 23. 275–78.

GUTHEIL, EMIL, 'Analysis of a Case of Transvestism', in *Sexual Aberrations: The Phenomena of Fetishism in Relation to Sex*, ed. Wilhelm Stekel, trans. S. Parker (London: John Lane, The Bodley Head, 1930), ii. 281–318.

HIRSCHFELD, MAGNUS, *Transvestites: The Erotic Drive to Cross-Dress*, trans. Michael Lombardi-Nash (1910; Buffalo, NY: Prometheus, 1991).

—— *Sexual Anomalies and Perversions: Physical and Psychological Development and Treatment (A Summary of the Works of the Late Professor Dr. Magnus Hirschfeld Compiled as a Humble Memorial by his Pupils)* (London: Francis Aldor [1937]).

JUNG, C. G., 'Psychology and Poetry', *transition*, 19–20 (June 1930), 23–45.

KRAFFT-EBING, RICHARD VON, *Psychopathia Sexualis, with Especial Reference to Contrary Sexual Instinct: A Medico-Legal Study*, trans. Charles Gilbert Chaddock (Philadelphia: F. A. Davis, 1892).

LACAN, JACQUES, and GRANOFF, WLADIMIR, 'Fetishism: The Symbolic, the Imaginary and the Real', in Sandor Lorand and Michael Balint (eds.), *Perversions: Psychodynamics and Therapy* (1956; London: The Ortolan Press, 1965), 265–76.

MOLL, ALBERT, *Untersuchungen über die Libido Sexualis* (Berlin, 1897).

RANK, OTTO, *Beyond Psychology* (New York: Dover, 1958).

RIVIERE, JOAN, 'Womanliness as Masquerade', *The International Journal of Psycho-Analysis*, 10 (1929), 303–13.

STOLLER, ROBERT J., *Observing the Erotic Imagination* (New Haven: Yale University Press, 1985).

WESTPHAL, CARL, 'Die Konträre Sexualempfindung', *Archiv für Psychiatrie und Nervenkrankheiten*, 2 (1869), 73–108.

WOLFF, CHARLOTTE, *Love Between Women* (London: Duckworth, 1971).

WULFF, M., 'Fetishism and Object Choice in Early Childhood', *Psychoanalytic Quarterly*, 15 (1946), 465–8.

ZAVITAZIANOS, GEORGE, 'Fetishism and Exhibitionism in the Female and Their Relationship to Psychopathology and Kleptomania', *The International Journal of Psycho-Analysis*, 52 (1971), 297–305.

—— 'Homeovestism: Perverse Form of Behaviour Involving Wearing Clothes of the Same Sex', *The International Journal of Psycho-Analysis*, 53 (1972), 471–7.

SECONDARY MATERIAL

ACKROYD, PETER, *Dressing Up, Transvestism and Drag: The History of an Obsession* (London: Thames and Hudson, 1979).

ALLEN, CAROLYN, 'The Erotics of Nora's Narrative in Djuna Barnes's *Nightwood*', *SIGNS*, 19.1 (Autumn 1993), 177–200.

—— *Following Djuna: Women Lovers and the Erotics of Loss* (Bloomington, Ind.: Indiana University Press, 1996).

APTER, EMILY, *Feminizing the Fetish: Psychoanalysis and Narrative Obsession in Turn-of-the-Century France* (Ithaca, NY: Cornell University Press, 1991).

—— and Pietz, William (eds.), *Fetishism as Cultural Discourse* (Ithaca, NY: Cornell University Press, 1993).

ARDIS, ANN L., *New Women, New Novels: Feminism and Early Modernism* (New Brunswick, NJ: Rutgers University Press, 1990).

BAIR, DEIRDRE, *Anaïs Nin: A Biography* (London: Bloomsbury, 1995).

BAIRD, JAMES, 'Djuna Barnes and Surrealism: "Backward Grief" ', in Kenneth H. Baldwin and David K. Kirby (eds.), *Individual and Community: Variations on a Theme in American Fiction* (Durham, NC: Duke University Press, 1975), 160–81.

BAKER, MICHAEL, *Our Three Selves: The Life of Radclyffe Hall* (London: Hamish Hamilton, 1985).

BALAKIAN, ANNA, 'Anaïs Nin, the Poet', in Suzanne Nalbantian (ed.), *Anaïs Nin: Literary Perspectives* (Basingstoke: Macmillan, 1997), 63–78.

BARALE, MICHÈLE AINA, 'Below the Belt: (Un)Covering *The Well of Loneliness*', in Diana Fuss (ed.), *Inside/Out: Lesbian Theories, Gay Theories* (New York: Routledge, 1991), 235–57.

—— 'When Jack Blinks: Si(gh)ting Gay Desire in Ann Bannon's Beebo Brinker', in Henry Abelove, Michèle Aina Barale, and David Halperin (eds.), *The Lesbian and Gay Studies Reader* (New York: Routledge, 1993), 604–15.

BARTHES, ROLAND, *The Pleasure of the Text*, trans. Richard Miller (1975; Oxford: Basil Blackwell, 1990).

BAXTER, CHARLES, 'A Self-Consuming Light: *Nightwood* and the Crisis of Modernism', *Journal of Modern Literature*, 3.5 (July 1974), 1175–87.

BENSTOCK, SHARI, *Women of the Left Bank: Paris 1900–1940* (1986; London: Virago, 1994).

BJØRHOVDE, GERD, *Rebellious Structures: Women Writers and the Crisis of the Novel 1880–1990* (Oslo: Norwegian University Press, 1987).

BOCK, MARTIN, *Crossing the Shadow-Line: The Literature of Estrangement* (Columbus, Oh.: Ohio State University Press, 1989).

BRANDON, RUTH, *The New Women and the Old Men: Love, Sex and the Woman Question* (London: Secker and Warburg, 1990).

BREDBECK, GREGORY W., 'Narcissus in the Wilde: Textual Cathexis and the Historical Origins of Queer Camp', in Moe Meyer (ed.), *The Politics and Poetics of Camp* (New York and London: Routledge, 1994), 51–74.

BRITTAIN, VERA, *Radclyffe Hall, A Case of Obscenity?* (London: Femina, 1968).

BROE, MARY LYNN, 'My Art Belongs to Daddy: Incest as Exile, The Textual Economics of Hayford Hall', in Mary Lynn Broe and Angela Ingrams (eds.), *Women's Writing in Exile* (Chapel Hill, NC: University of North Carolina Press, 1989), 41–86.

—— (ed.), *Silence and Power: A Reevaluation of Djuna Barnes* (Carbondale, Ill.: Southern Illinois University Press, 1991).

BRONFEN, ELISABETH, 'Wandering in Mind and Body: Death, Narration and Gender in Djuna Barnes' Novel *Nightwood*', *Amerikastudien*, 33.2 (1988), 167–77.

BUCK, CLAIRE, 'Freud and H.D.: Bisexuality and a Feminine Discourse', *m/f*, 8 (1983), 53–66.

—— *H.D. and Freud: Bisexuality and a Feminine Discourse* (Hemel Hempstead: Harvester Wheatsheaf, 1991).

BURKE, CAROLYN, ' "Accidental Aloofness": Barnes, Loy, and Modernism', in Mary Lynn Broe (ed.), *Silence and Power: A Reevaluation of Djuna Barnes* (Carbondale, Ill: Southern Illinois University Press, 1991), 67–79.

240 *Bibliography*

BURKE, KENNETH, 'Version, Con-, Per-, and In-: Thoughts on Djuna Barnes's Novel *Nightwood*', in *Language as Symbolic Action: Essays on Life, Literature and Method* (Berkeley: University of California Press, 1968), 240–53.

BUSST, A. J. L., 'The Image of the Androgyne in the Nineteenth Century', in Ian Fletcher (ed.), *Romantic Mythologies* (London: Routledge & Kegan Paul, 1967), 1–95.

BUTLER, JUDITH, *Gender Trouble: Feminism and the Subversion of Identity* (London: Routledge, 1990).

—— *Bodies that Matter: On the Discursive Limits of Sex* (New York: Routledge, 1993).

—— *The Psychic Life of Power: Theories in Subjection* (Stanford, Calif.: Stanford University Press, 1997).

CAPLAN, JANE, 'Sexuality and Homosexuality', in Cambridge Women's Studies Group (ed.), *Women in Society: Interdisciplinary Essays* (London: Virago, 1981), 149–67.

CARLSTON, ERIN G., *Thinking Fascism: Sapphic Modernism and Fascist Modernity* (Stanford, Calif.: Stanford University Press, 1998).

CASTLE, TERRY, *The Apparitional Lesbian: Female Homosexuality and Modern Culture* (New York: Columbia University Press, 1993).

—— *Noel Coward and Radclyffe Hall: Kindred Spirits* (New York: Columbia University Press, 1996).

CHISHOLM, DIANNE, *H.D.'s Freudian Poetics: Psychoanalysis in Translation* (Ithaca, NY: Cornell University Press, 1992).

—— 'Obscene Modernism: *Eros Noir* and the Profane Illumination of Djuna Barnes', *American Literature*, 69.1 (Mar. 1997), 167–206.

CIXOUS, HÉLÈNE, and CLÉMENT, CATHERINE, *La Jeune Née* (Paris: Union Générale d'Editions, 1975).

CLINE, SALLY, *Radclyffe Hall: A Woman Called John* (London: John Murray, 1997).

COCKIN, KATHARINE, *Edith Craig (1869–1947): Dramatic Lives* (London and Washington: Cassell, 1998).

COLLECOTT, DIANA, *H.D. and Sapphic Modernism 1910–1950* (Cambridge: Cambridge University Press, 1999).

COLLIS, ROSE, *Colonel Barker's Monstrous Regiment: A Tale of Female Husbandry* (London: Virago, 2001).

DEKOVEN, MARIANNE, 'Gendered Doubleness and the "Origins" of Modernist Form', *Tulsa Studies in Women's Literature*, 8.1 (Spring 1989), 19–42.

DE LAURETIS, TERESA, 'Perverse Desire: The Lure of the Mannish Lesbian', *Australian Feminist Studies*, 13 (Autumn 1991), 15–26.

—— 'Habit Changes', *differences: A Journal of Feminist Cultural Studies*, 6.2 and 3 (Summer/Fall 1994), 296–313.

—— *The Practice of Love: Lesbian Sexuality and Perverse Desire* (Bloomington, Ind.: Indiana University Press, 1994).

DeVore, Lynn, 'The Backgrounds of *Nightwood*: Robin, Felix, and Nora', *Journal of Modern Literature*, 10.1 (Mar. 1983), 71–90.

Doan, Laura, *Fashioning Sapphism: The Origins of a Modern English Lesbian Culture* (New York: Columbia University Press, 2001).

DuPlessis, Rachel Blau, 'Romantic Thralldom in H.D', *Contemporary Literature*, 20.2 (Spring 1979), 178–203.

Eliot, T. S., Introduction, *Nightwood* by Djuna Barnes (1936; London: Faber & Faber, 1985), 1–7.

Faderman, Lillian, *Surpassing the Love of Men: Romantic Friendship and Love Between Women from the Renaissance to the Present* (1981; London: The Women's Press, 1985).

Farrer, Peter, '120 Years of Male Cross-Dressing and Sex–Changing in English and American Literature', in Richard Ekins and Dave King (eds.), *Blending Genders: Social Aspects of Cross-Dressing and Sex–Changing* (London and New York: Routledge, 1996), 123–32.

Felber, Lynette, 'The Three Faces of June: Anaïs Nin's Appropriation of Feminine Writing', *Tulsa Studies in Women's Literature*, 14.2 (Autumn 1995), 309–24.

Ferguson, Suzanne C., 'Djuna Barnes's Short Stories: An Estrangement of the Heart', *The Southern Review*, 5.1 (Jan. 1969), 26–41.

Field, Andrew, *The Formidable Miss Barnes: A Biography of Djuna Barnes* (London: Secker and Warburg, 1983).

Fields, Kenneth, Introduction, *Tribute to Freud*, by H.D. (1956; Boston: David R. Godine, 1974).

Fitch, Noël Riley, *Anaïs: The Erotic Life of Anaïs Nin* (Boston, New York, Toronto, and London: Little, Brown and Company, 1993).

Fleischer, Georgette, 'Djuna Barnes and T. S. Eliot: The Politics and Poetics of *Nightwood*', *Studies in the Novel*, 30.3 (Fall 1998), 405–35.

Foster, Jeanette H., *Sex Variant Women in Literature: A Historical and Quantitative Study* (London: Frederick Muller, 1958).

Frank, Joseph, *The Widening Gyre: Crisis and Mastery in Modern Literature* (1963; Bloomington, Ind.: Indiana University Press, 1968).

Friedman, Susan Stanford, *Psyche Reborn: The Emergence of H.D.* (Bloomington, Ind.: Indiana University Press, 1981).

—— *Penelope's Web: Gender, Modernity, H.D.'s Fiction* (Cambridge: Cambridge University Press, 1990).

—— and DuPlessis, Rachel Blau, ' "I Had Two Loves Separate": The Sexualities of H.D.'s *HER*', in Susan Stanford Friedman and Rachel Blau DuPlessis (eds.), *Signets: Reading H.D.* (Madison: University of Wisconsin Press, 1990), 205–32.

Fuchs, Miriam, 'Djuna Barnes: "Spillway" into Nightmare', *The Hollins Critic*, 18.3 (June 1981), 2–9.

—— 'Dr. Matthew O'Connor: The Unhealthy Healer of Djuna Barnes's *Nightwood*', in Anne Hudson Jones (ed.), *Literature and Medicine*, ii.

Images of Healers (Baltimore and London: Johns Hopkins University Press, 1985), 125–34.

FUCHS, MIRIAM., 'The Triadic Association of Emily Holmes Coleman, T. S. Eliot, and Djuna Barnes', *ANQ: A Quarterly Journal of Short Articles, Notes, and Reviews*, 12.4 (Fall 1999), 28–39.

GALVIN, MARY E., *Queer Poetics: Five Modernist Women Writers* (Westport, Conn., and London: Praeger, 1999).

GAMMAN, LORRAINE, and MAKINEN, MERJA, *Female Fetishism: A New Look* (London: Lawrence and Wishart, 1994).

GARBER, MARJORIE, *Vested Interests: Cross-Dressing and Cultural Anxiety* (1992; London: Penguin, 1993).

GERSTENBERGER, DONNA, 'The Radical Narrative of Djuna Barnes's *Nightwood*', in Ellen G. Friedman and Miriam Fuchs (eds.), *Breaking the Sequence: Women's Experimental Fiction* (Princeton: Princeton University Press, 1989).

GILBERT, SANDRA M., 'Costumes of the Mind: Transvestism as Metaphor in Modern Literature', in Elizabeth Abel (ed.), *Writing and Sexual Difference* (1980; Brighton: Harvester, 1982), 193–219.

—— and GUBAR, SUSAN 'Ceremonies of the Alphabet: Female Grandmatologies and the Female Autograph', in Domna C. Stanton (ed.), *The Female Autograph: Theory and Practice of Autobiography from the Tenth to the Twentieth Century* (1984; Chicago and London: University of Chicago Press, 1987), 21–48.

—— *No-Man's Land: The Place of the Woman Writer in the Twentieth Century*, i. *The War of Words* (New Haven and London: Yale University Press, 1988).

—— *No-Man's Land: The Place of the Woman Writer in the Twentieth Century*, ii., *Sexchanges* (New Haven and London: Yale University Press, 1989).

GILMAN, SANDER L., *Difference and Pathology: Stereotypes of Sexuality, Race and Madness* (Ithaca, NY: Cornell University Press, 1985).

GILMOUR, LEIGH, 'Obscenity, Modernity, Identity: Legalizing *The Well of Loneliness* and *Nightwood*', *Journal of the History of Sexuality*, 4 (Apr. 1994), 603–24.

GLASGOW, JOANNE, Introduction, *Your John: The Love Letters of Radclyffe Hall* (New York and London: New York University Press, 1997), 1–17.

GLENDINNING, VICTORIA, *Vita: The Life of Vita Sackville-West* (London: Weidenfeld and Nicolson, 1983).

GORDON, RICHARD A., *Anorexia and Bulimia: Anatomy of a Social Epidemic* (1990; Oxford: Basil Blackwell, 1991).

GRIFFIN, BARBARA J., 'Two Experimental Writers: Djuna Barnes and Anaïs Nin', in Maurice Duke, Jackson R. Bryher, and M. Thomas Inge (eds.), *American Women Writers: Bibliographical Essays* (London and Westport, Conn.: Greenwood Press, 1983), 135–66.

GROSSKURTH, PHYLLIS, *Havelock Ellis: A Biography* (1980; New York: New York University Press, 1985).

GROSZ, ELIZABETH, 'Lesbian Fetishism?', in Emily Apter and William Pietz (eds.), *Fetishism as Cultural Discourse* (Ithaca, NY, and London: Cornell University Press, 1993), 101–15.

—— *Space, Time, and Perversion: Essays on the Politics of Bodies* (New York and London: Routledge, 1995).

GUBAR, SUSAN, 'Blessings in Disguise: Cross-Dressing as Re-Dressing for Female Modernists', *The Massachusetts Review*, 22.3 (Autumn 1981), 477–508.

GUEST, BARBARA, *Herself Defined: The Poet H.D. and Her World* (London: Collins, 1985).

HALBERSTAM, JUDITH, *Female Masculinity* (Durham, NC, and London: Duke University Press, 1998).

HAMER, EMILY, *Britannia's Glory: A History of Twentieth-Century Lesbians* (London and New York: Cassell, 1996).

HARMS, VALERIE, 'Anaïs and Her Analysts, Rank and Allendy: The Creative and Destructive Aspects', in Suzanne Nalbantian (ed.), *Anaïs Nin: Literary Perspectives* (Basingstoke: Macmillan, 1997), 112–19.

HARRIS, ANDREA L., *Other Sexes: Rewriting Difference from Woolf to Winterson* (Albany, NY: State University of New York Press, 2000).

HEKMA, GERT, 'A History of Sexology: Social and Historical Aspects of Sexuality', in Jan Bremmer (ed.), *From Sappho to de Sade: Moments in the History of Sexuality* (1989; London: Routledge, 1991), 173–93.

HENKE, SUZETTE A., '(En)Gendering Modernism: Virginia Woolf and Djuna Barnes', in Kevin J. H. Dettmar (ed.), *Rereading the New: A Backward Glance at Modernism* (Ann Arbor: University of Michigan Press, 1992), 325–41.

HENNEGAN, ALISON, Introduction, *The Well of Loneliness*, by Radclyffe Hall (London: Virago, 1991), pp. vii–xvii.

HENSON, LESLIE J., ' "Articulate Silence[s]": Femme Subjectivity and Class Relations in *The Well of Loneliness*', in Laura Harris and Elizabeth Crocker (eds.), *Femme: Feminists, Lesbians, and Bad Girls* (New York and London: Routledge, 1997), 61–7.

HERRING, PHILLIP, 'Djuna Barnes and Thelma Wood: The Vengeance of *Nightwood*', *Journal of Modern Literature*, 18.1 (Winter 1992), 5–18.

—— *Djuna: The Life and Work of Djuna Barnes* (1995; London: Penguin, 1996).

HERRMANN, ANN, 'Imitations of Marriage: Cross-Dressed Couples in Contemporary Lesbian Fiction', *Feminist Studies*, 18.3 (Autumn 1992), 612–25

HERZIG, CARL, 'Roots of Night: Emerging Style and Vision in the Early Journalism of Djuna Barnes', *The Centennial Review*, 31.3 (Summer 1987), 255–69.

HOPE, TREVOR, 'Mother, Don't You See I'm Burning? Between Female Homosexuality and Homosociality in Radclyffe Hall's *The Unlit Lamp*', in Elizabeth Wright, Mandy Merck, and Naomi Segal (eds.), *Coming Out of Feminism?* (Oxford: Blackwell, 1998), 123–53.

HOWLETT, CAROLINE, 'Femininity Slashed: Suffragette Militancy, Modernism and Gender', in Hugh Stevens and Caroline Howlett (eds.), *Modernist Sexualities* (Manchester and New York: Manchester University Press, 2000), 72–91.

IAN, MARCIA, *Remembering the Phallic Mother: Psychoanalysis, Modernism and the Fetish* (Ithaca, NYand London: Cornell University Press, 1993).

INNESS, SHERRIE, 'Who's Afraid of Stephen Gordon?: The Lesbian in the United States Popular Imagination of the 1920s', *NWSA Journal*, 4.3 (Autumn 1992), 303–20.

JACKSON, MARGARET, 'Sexology and the Social Construction of Male Sexuality (Havelock Ellis)', in L. Coveney, M. Jackson, S. Jeffreys, L. Kaye, and P. Mahoney (eds.), *The Sexuality Papers: Male Sexuality and the Social Control of Women* (London: Hutchinson in association with the Exploration in Feminism Collective, 1984), 45–68.

JASON, PHILIP K., 'Doubles/Don Juans: Anaïs Nin and Otto Rank', *Mosaic: A Journal for the Comparative Study of Literature and Ideas*, 11.2 (Winter 1978), 81–94.

—— *Anaïs Nin and Her Critics* (Columbia, SC: Camden House, 1993).

JEFFREYS, SHEILA, ' "Free from all Uninvited Touch of Man": Women's Campaigns Around Sexuality 1880–1914', in L. Coveney, M. Jackson, S. Jeffreys, L. Kaye, and P. Mahoney (eds.), *The Sexuality Papers: Male Sexuality and the Social Control of Women* (London: Hutchinson in association with the Exploration in Feminism Collective, 1984), 22–44.

JONES, BEN, 'Surprised by Frances: Travel and Recognition in *The Mystic Leeway*', *The Powys Journal*, 5 (1995), 35–53.

KAIVOLA, KAREN, *All Contraries Confounded: The Lyrical Fiction of Virginia Woolf, Djuna Barnes, and Marguerite Duras* (Iowa City, Ia.: University of Iowa Press, 1991).

KANNENSTINE, LOUIS F., *The Art of Djuna Barnes: Duality and Damnation* (New York: New York University Press, 1977).

KAPLAN, JOEL, and STOWELL, SHEILA, *Theatre and Fashion: Oscar Wilde to the Suffragettes* (Cambridge: Cambridge University Press, 1994).

KAPLAN, LOUISE J., *Female Perversions: The Temptations of Madame Bovary* (1991; London: Penguin, 1993).

KAUTZ, ELIZABETH DOLAN, 'Gynaecologists, Power and Sexuality in Modernist Texts', *Journal of Popular Culture*, 28.4 (Spring 1995), 81–91.

KAVALER-ADLER, SUSAN, *The Compulsion to Create: A Psychoanalytic Study of Women Artists* (New York: Routledge, 1993).

KERSLEY, GILLIAN, *Darling Madame: Sarah Grand and Devoted Friend* (London: Virago, 1983).

KING, DAVE, 'Gender Blending: Medical Perspectives and Technology', in Richard Ekins and Dave King (eds.), *Blending Genders: Social Aspects of Cross-Dressing and Sex–Changing* (London and New York: Routledge, 1996), 79–98.

KNUTSON, LIN, 'Arrested Moments: Communitas and Liminality in H.D.'s *HER*', *Sagetrieb*, 15.1/22 (Spring and Fall 1996), 35–50.

KOFMAN, SARAH, 'Ça cloche', in Philippe Lacoue-Labarthe and Jean-Luc Nancy (eds.), *Les Fins de l'homme: à partir du travail de Jacques Derrida* (Paris: Galilee, 1981).

—— *The Enigma of Woman in Freud's Writings*, trans. Catherine Porter (1986; Ithaca, NY: Cornell University Press, 1985).

KUCICH, JOHN, 'Curious Dualities: *The Heavenly Twins* (1893) and Sarah Grand's Belated Modernist Aesthetics', in Barbara Leah Harman and Susan Meyer (eds.), *The New Nineteenth Century: Feminist Readings of Underread Victorian Fiction* (New York and London: Garland Publishing, 1996), 195–204.

LAITY, CASSANDRA, *H.D. and the Victorian Fin de Siècle: Gender, Modernism, Decadence* (Cambridge: Cambridge University Press, 1996).

LANSER, SUSAN SNIADER, 'Speaking in Tongues: *Ladies Almanack* and the Discourse of Desire', in Mary Lynn Broe (ed.), *Silence and Power: A Reevaluation of Djuna Barnes* (Carbondale, Ill.: Southern Illinois University Press, 1991), 156–68.

LEE, JUDITH, '*Nightwood*: "The Sweetest Lie" ', in Mary Lynn Broe (ed.), *Silence and Power: A Reevaluation of Djuna Barnes* (Carbondale, Ill.: Southern Illinois University Press, 1991), 207–18.

MCCABE, SUSAN, ' "A Queer Lot" and the Lesbians of 1914: Amy Lowell, H.D., and Gertrude Stein', in Joyce W. Warren and Margaret Dickie (eds.), *Challenging Boundaries: Gender and Periodization* (Athens, Ga., and London: University of Georgia Press, 2000), 62–90.

MCNEIL, HELEN, Introduction, *Her* by H.D. (London: Virago, 1984), pp. v–xi.

MACPIKE, LORALEE, 'Is Mary Llewellyn an Invert? The Modernist Supertext of *The Well of Loneliness*', in Elizabeth Jane Harrison and Shirley Peterson (eds.), *Unmanning Modernism: Gendered Re-Readings* (Knoxville, Tenn.: University of Tennessee Press, 1997), 73–89.

MANGUM, TERESA, *Married, Middlebrow, and Militant: Sarah Grand and the New Woman Novel* (Ann Arbor: University of Michigan Press, 1998).

MARCUS, JANE, 'Laughing at Leviticus: *Nightwood* as Woman's Circus Epic', in *Silence and Power: A Reevaluation of Djuna Barnes* (Carbondale, Ill.: Southern Illinois University Press, 1991), 221–50.

MARCUS, LAURA, *Auto/biographical Discourses: Theory, Criticism, Practice* (Manchester: Manchester University Press, 1994).

MARTIN, BIDDY, *Femininity Played Straight: The Significance of Being Lesbian* (New York: Routledge, 1996).

MATLOCK, JANN, 'Masquerading Women, Pathologized Men: Cross-Dressing, Fetishism, and the Theory of Perversion, 1882–1935', in Emily Apter and William Pietz (eds.), *Fetishism as Cultural Discourse* (Ithaca, NY: Cornell University Press, 1993), 31–61.

MAZLISH, BRUCE, 'Autobiography and Psychoanalysis: Between Truth and Self-Deception', *Encounter*, 35 (Oct. 1970), 28–37.

MICHEL, FRANN, 'All Women Are Not Women All: *Ladies Almanack* and Feminine Writing', in Mary Lynn Broe (ed.), *Silence and Power: A Reevaluation of Djuna Barnes* (Carbondale, Ill.: Southern Illinois University Press, 1991), 170–82.

MITCHELL, JULIET, *Psychoanalysis and Feminism* (London: Allen Lane, 1975).

MOLYNEUX, MAXINE, and CASTERTON, JULIA, 'Looking Again at Anaïs Nin', *Minnesota Review*, NS 18 (Spring 1982), 86–101.

MOORJANI, ANGELA, *The Aesthetics of Loss and Lessness* (London: Macmillan, 1992).

—— 'Fetishism, Gender Masquerade, and the Mother-Father Fantasy', in Joseph H. Smith and Afaf M. Mahfouz (eds.), *Psychoanalysis, Feminism and the Future of Gender* vol. xiv of *Psychiatry and the Humanities* (Baltimore and London: Johns Hopkins University Press, 1994), 22–41.

NEWTON, ESTHER, 'The Mythic Mannish Lesbian: Radclyffe Hall and the New Woman', in Estelle B. Freedman, Barbara C. Gelpi, Susan L. Johnson, and Kathleen M. Weston (eds.), *The Lesbian Issue: Essays from SIGNS* (Chicago: University of Chicago Press, 1985), 7–25.

NICOLSON, NIGEL, *Portrait of a Marriage* (1973; London: Weidenfeld and Nicolson, 1990).

NYE, ROBERT A., 'The Medical Origins of Sexual Fetishism', in Emily Apter and William Pietz (eds.), *Fetishism as Cultural Discourse* (Ithaca, NY: Cornell University Press, 1993), 13–30.

O'NEAL, HANK, '*Life is Painful, Nasty and Short . . . In My Case It has Only Been Painful and Nasty': Djuna Barnes 1978–1981, An Informal Memoir* (New York: Paragon House, 1990).

O'ROURKE, REBECCA, *Reflecting on 'The Well of Loneliness'* (London: Routledge, 1989).

PARKER, ALAN MICHAEL and WILLHARDT, MARK, *The Routledge Anthology of Cross-Gendered Verse* (London: Routledge, 1996).

PLUMB, CHERYL J., *Fancy's Craft: Art and Identity in the Early Works of Djuna Barnes* (London: Associated University Presses, 1986).

PROSSER, JAY, 'Transsexuals and the Transsexologists: Inversion and the Emergence of Transsexual Subjectivity', in Lucy Bland and Laura Doan (eds.), *Sexology in Culture: Labelling Bodies and Desires* (Oxford and Cambridge: Polity Press, 1998), 116–23.

—— *Second Skins: The Body Narratives of Transsexuality* (New York: Columbia University Press, 1998).

PYKETT, LYN, *The 'Improper' Feminine: The Women's Sensation Novel and the New Women Writing* (London: Routledge, 1992).

RADFORD, JEAN, 'An Inverted Romance: *The Well of Loneliness* and Sexual Ideology', in Jean Radford (ed.), *The Progress of Romance: The Politics of Popular Fiction* (London: Routledge & Kegan Paul, 1986), 96–111.

RICHARD-ALLERDYCE, DIANE, *Anaïs Nin and the Remaking of Self: Gender, Modernism, and Narrative Identity* (Dekalb, Ill.: Northern Illinois University Press, 1998).

ROBINSON, JANICE S., *H.D.: The Life and Work of an American Poet* (Boston: Houghton Mifflin, 1982).

ROBINSON, PAUL, *The Modernization of Sex: Havelock Ellis, Alfred Kinsey, William Masters and Virginia Johnson* (London: Paul Elek, 1976).

ROOF, JUDITH, *A Lure of Knowledge: Lesbian Sexuality and Theory* (New York: Columbia University Press, 1991).

ROSE, LOUIS (ed.), 'Freud and Fetishism: Previously Unpublished Minutes of the Vienna Psychoanalytic Society', trans. Louis Rose, *Psychoanalytic Quarterly*, 57 (1988).

ROWLETTE, ROBERT, 'Mark Twain, Sarah Grand, and *The Heavenly Twins*', *Mark Twain Journal*, 16.2 (Summer 1972), 17–18.

RUEHL, SONJA, 'Inverts and Experts: Radclyffe Hall and the Lesbian Identity', in Rosalind Brunt and Caroline Rowan (eds.), *Feminism, Culture and Politics* (London: Lawrence and Wishart, 1982), 15–36.

RULE, JANE, *Lesbian Images* (1975; London: Peter Davies, 1976).

SAHLI, NANCY, 'Smashing: Women's Relationships Before the Fall', *Chrysalis*, 8 (Summer 1979), 8–27.

SCHOR, NAOMI, 'Female Fetishism: The Case of George Sand', *Poetics Today*, 6.1–2 (1985), 301–10.

—— 'Fetishism and Its Ironies', *Nineteenth-Century French Studies*, 17 (Autumn 1988), 89–97.

SCOTT, BONNIE KIME, *Refiguring Modernism*, ii. *Postmodern Feminist Readings of Woolf, West, and Barnes* (Bloomington, Ind.: Indian University Press, 1995).

SENF, CAROL A., Introduction, *The Heavenly Twins*, by Sarah Grand (1893; Ann Arbor: University of Michigan Press, 1992), pp. vii–xxxvii.

SEVERO, SARDUY, 'Writing/Transvestism', *Review*, 9 (Autumn 1973), 31–3.

SHOWALTER, ELAINE, *The Female Malady: Women, Madness and English Culture 1830–1980* (1985; London: Virago, 1993).

—— *Sexual Anarchy: Gender and Culture at the Fin de Siècle* (1990; London: Bloomsbury, 1991).

SINGER, ALAN, 'The Horse Who Knew Too Much: Metaphor and the Narrative of Discontinuity in *Nightwood*', *Contemporary Literature*, 25.1 (Spring 1984), 66–87.

SMITH, SIDONIE, *A Poetics of Women's Autobiography: Marginality and the Fictions of Self-Representation* (Bloomington, Ind.: Indiana University Press, 1987).

SMITH, VICTORIA L., 'A Story Beside(s) Itself: The Language of Loss in Djuna Barnes's *Nightwood*', *PMLA (Publications of the Modern Language Association of America)*, 114.2 (Mar. 1999), 194–206.

Smith-Rosenberg, Carroll, *Disorderly Conduct: Visions of Gender in Victorian America* (1985; New York: Oxford University Press, 1986).

Souhami, Diana, *Gluck 1895–1978: Her Biography* (1988; London: Weidenfeld and Nicolson, 2000).

—— *The Trials of Radclyffe Hall* (London: Weidenfeld and Nicolson, 1998).

Spencer, Sharon, *Collage of Dreams: The Writings of Anaïs Nin* (Chicago: Swallow Press, 1977).

Spoo, Robert, Introduction, *Asphodel*, by H. D. (Durham, NC: Duke University Press, 1992), pp. ix–xxi.

Sprengnether, Madelon, *The Spectral Mother: Freud, Feminism, and Psychoanalysis* (Ithaca, NY: Cornell University Press, 1990).

Studlar, Gaylyn, *In the Realm of Pleasure: Von Sternberg, Dietrich, and the Masochistic Aesthetic* (New York: Columbia University Press, 1988).

Stuhlmann, Gunther, Introduction, *Ladders to Fire*, by Anaïs Nin (London: Peter Owen, 1991), 5–6.

Taylor, Melanie A., ' "The Masculine Soul Heaving in the Female Bosom": Theories of Inversion and *The Well of Loneliness*', *Journal of Gender Studies*, 7.3 (Nov. 1998), 287–96.

Trotter, David, 'Lesbians Before Lesbianism: Sexual Identity in Early Twentieth-Century British Fiction', in Billie Melman (ed.), *Borderlines: Gender and Identities in War and Peace, 1870–1930* (New York and London: Routledge, 1998), 193–211.

Troubridge, Una, *The Life and Death of Radclyffe Hall* (London: Hammond, 1961).

Tyler, Carole-Anne, 'The Feminine Look', in Martin Kreiswirth and Mark A. Cheetham (eds.), *Theory Between the Disciplines: Authority/Vision/Politics* (Ann Arbor: University of Michigan Press, 1990), 191–212.

—— 'Passing: Narcissism, Identity, and Difference', *differences: A Journal of Feminist Cultural Studies*, 6.2 and 3 (Summer/Autumn 1994), 212–48.

Vandenburg, Margaret, 'Aryan *Mundus* and Sexual Inversion: Eliot's Edition of *Nightwood*', *Prospects: An Annual of American Cultural Studies*, ed. Jack Salzman, 23 (Cambridge: Cambridge University Press, 1998), 329–55.

Van der Elst, Marie-Claire, 'The Manuscripts of Anaïs Nin at Northwestern', *Mosaic*, 11.2 (Winter 1978), 59–63.

Vicinus, Martha, ' "They Wonder to Which Sex I Belong": The Historical Roots of the Modern Lesbian', in Henry Abelove, Michèle Aina Barale, and David Halperin (eds.), *The Lesbian and Gay Studies Reader* (New York: Routledge, 1993), 432–52.

—— 'Turn-of-the-Century Male Impersonation: Rewriting the Romance Plot', in Andrew H. Miller and James Eli Adams (eds.), *Sexualities in Victorian Britain* (Bloomington and Indianapolis, Ind.: Indiana University Press, 1996), 187–213.

Winkiel, Laura, 'Circuses and Spectacles: Public Culture in *Nightwood*', *Journal of Modern Literature*, 21.1 (Summer 1997), 7–28.

Index

Aldrich, Thomas Bailey 41
Allen, Carolyn 149–50, 156, 158, 173–4, 230
Allen, Mary 61
Allendy, René 194–5, 196, 202–3, 213
anorexia 39 n. 26
Apter, Emily 10–11, 89 n. 66
Arkell-Smith, Valerie [Colonel Barker] 104

Bair, Deirdre 194
Baird, James 168
Baker, Michael 76
Balakian, Anna 197, 206
Balzac, Honoré de 39, 124–5 n. 57
Bannon, Anne 230
Barahal, Hyman S. 5
Barnes, Djuna 228, 230
  The Antiphon 188
  and Natalie Clifford Barney 156
  The Book of Repulsive Women 165
  'Cassation' 167
  and Emily Coleman 152 n. 5, 153, 155, 158–9, 160, 188, 189
  and cross-gendering 160, 191
  'Dusie' 88 n. 65, 160, 163
  and James Joyce 153 n. 11, 189
  Ladies Almanack 156–7, 165, 185, 189
  'Madame Collects Herself' 182
  'A Night Among the Horses' 166
  Nightwood 79, 128, 149–90, 191, 215, 229
  and Anaïs Nin 191–2, 229
  and psychoanalysis and sexology 155–9, 190
  'The Rabbit' 166
  Ryder 165 n. 57
  and Thelma Wood 161–2
Barney, Natalie Clifford 156
Barry, James 43
Barthes, Roland 14–15
Bennett, Arnold 59
Benstock, Shari 176
bisexuality 106, 108–9, 110, 113, 142, 200
Bock, Martin 170, 179

body, the 9, 10, 49, 78–9, 82–3, 95, 99–102, 163, 182–5, 200, 206, 217
Bogner, Inge 197
Bonaparte, Marie 194
Breuer, Joseph 168–9 n. 70
Brittain, Vera. 68 n. 28, 79 n. 53
Broe, Mary Lynn 179–80
Bryher [Winifred Ellerman] 75, 94, 201
  and cross-dressing 62, 105
  and cross-gendering 62–4
  Development 62–3
  and Havelock Ellis 105
  and H.D. 114, 129, 145
  The Heart to Artemis 125
  and psychoanalysis 106, 145
  Two Selves 62–4, 125, 131
Buck, Claire 107, 142
Burke, Carolyn 189
Burke, Kenneth 162
Butler, Judith 18, 186

Caplan, Jane 49
Caprio, Frank 6
Carlston, Erin G. 179
Carpenter, Edward 45, 59 n., 77
Castle, Terry 14, 79
castration 4, 7, 8, 9, 11, 13, 86, 89, 92, 108, 111, 112, 136, 142, 144, 147–8, 167, 183, 195, 215, 217, 219
Chadwick, Mary 106
Charcot, Jean-Martin 53
Chisholm, Dianne 107, 116, 135, 136, 138, 181
Cixous, Hélène 115
  and Catherine Clément 38
Clérambault, Gatian de Gaeton de 53
Cline, Sally 68 n. 28, 75, 76–7
clothing 60–1, 72, 77, 86–88, 90–3, 96–7 n. 76, 97, 123, 155, 163, 214
Coleman, Emily 152 n. 5, 153, 155, 158–9, 160, 188, 189
Collis, Rose 104
Craig, Edy 57–8, 97 n. 78

cross-dressing 3, 66, 17, 18, 19, 46, 48,
    54–5, 60–1, 62, 77, 90–3, 104, 214
  and Bryher 62, 105
  and Radclyffe Hall 77, 104
  and H.D. 122, 144
  in *The Heavenly Twins* 24–5, 27,
    28–9, 30–2, 35–7, 43, 56
  in *HER* 126, 128
  in *Ladders to Fire* 215, 221, 223
  in literature 39, 41–2, 75
  in *Nightwood* 158, 159, 171, 180
  and Anaïs Nin 215
  in *The Passion* 230
  in *The Well of Loneliness* 82, 85–8,
    99
  see also transvestism
cross-gendering 2–3, 43–4, 52–3, 54, 57,
    60–1
  and Djuna Barnes 160, 191
  and Bryher 62–4
  female 1–2, 9, 11, 18, 19, 20–3, 46,
    50, 74, 78, 81, 90, 92, 93, 107–8,
    229–31
  and Sarah Grand 25, 43
  and Radclyffe Hall 74, 103–4
  in *The Heavenly Twins* 27–33, 35–7
  and H.D. 125, 133, 141
  in *HER* 118, 122, 146–7, 149
  in *Hungerheart* 58
  in *Ladders to Fire* 212–28
  in literature 39–43, 230
  male 41–2
  in *Nightwood* 149, 150–1, 155, 163,
    179
  and Anaïs Nin 193, 203, 205
  in psychoanalysis 107–8
  in sexology 43–56
  in *The Unlit Lamp* 77
  in *The Well of Loneliness* 14, 76, 78,
    82, 94, 102–3, 158

Dane, Clemence 59
DeKoven, Marianne 14
de Lauretis, Teresa 9–10, 12, 89–90,
    147–8, 150–1
desire, *see under* lesbianism
Dickes, Robert 8 n. 20, 86 n. 64
Dietrich, Marlene 163 n. 53
disavowal, 4–5, 8–11, 14, 81, 142, 147,
    168, 186, 189, 200, 229, 230
dismemberment, 182–3, 208, 215
Dixie, Florence 42
Doan, Laura 43, 60–1, 77

double, the 102, 171, 196, 213; *see also*
    twin the,
Doyle, Arthur Conan 41
drag 18, 186 n. 107, 231
Duc, Aimée 51 n. 62
DuPlessis, Rachel Blau, *see under*
    Friedman, Susan Stanford

Eliot, T. S. 151 n. 4, 153, 155, 158, 165,
    176, 189
Ellis, Edith 47
Ellis, Havelock 47–9, 51, 55, 62, 76,
    77–9, 105–6, 108
eonism 55; *see also* inversion

Faderman, Lillian 50
Farrer, Peter 41–2
father figure, the 112, 137–8, 143,
    197 n. 24
Fenichel, Otto 213
Féré, Charles 68
Ferguson, Suzanne C. 152–3, 166
fetishism 120, 131, 142, 150, 157, 167,
    169, 175, 178, 189, 195, 202, 207,
    209, 222–3, 229
  female 5–12, 13, 16, 53–5, 80–5, 94,
    126, 150–1, 193, 213, 215, 224
  in *HER* 117–23
  in *Ladders to Fire* 224–8 *passim*
  and literature 13–14
  male 4–5, 9, 109, 209, 213, 225
  in *Nightwood* 151–2, 177–82 *passim*
  in *The Well of Loneliness* 80–90,
    93–103
Field, Andrew 188
First World War 60, 74, 114
Fitzroy, A. T. 59
Fleischer, Georgette 163
Ford, Charles Henri 153–4
Forel, August 61
Foster, Jeanette 40, 74
Fowler, Ellen Thorneycroft 59
Frank, Joseph 152, 158, 159
French literature 39–41, 74–5
  Honoré de Balzac 39, 124–5 n. 57
  Philip Cuisin 39, 43
  Jacques Lacretelle 74
  Henri de Latouche 39, 124–5 n. 57
  Victor Margueritte 74
  Sâr Josephin Péladan 41, 42
  Rachilde [Marguérite Aymery
    Vallette] 41, 42
  Romain Rolland 74

Émile Zola 89 n. 66
see also Gautier, Théophile
Freud, Anna 5
Freud, Sigmund 105–13, 190, 193, 196,
    200, 202
    and Bryher 62
    and H.D. 105–7, 129, 135–40, 142–8
    'Female Sexuality' 112
    'Femininity' 112–13
    'Fetishism' 80–1
    'On the Genesis of Fetishism' 81
    'The Infantile Genital Organization'
      111
    'Mourning and Melancholia' 4, 186
    'On Narcissism' 111, 146–7, 150
    'Some Psychical Consequences of
      theAnatomical Distinction
      Between the Sexes' 111
    'The Psychogenesis of a Case of
      Homosexuality in a Woman' 52,
      110–11
    'Three Essays on the Theory of
      Sexuality' 4, 80, 108–9
Friedman, Susan Stanford 63, 106–7,
    114–15, 123–4, 125, 142, 145
    and Rachel Blau DuPlessis 120, 121,
      129
Fuchs, Miriam 163, 190

Gamman, Lorraine and Merja Makinen
    8, 80
Garber, Marjorie 18, 169, 231
Gautier, Théophile 39, 40, 124–5 n. 57
Gilbert, Sandra M, *see under* Gubar,
    Susan
Gilman, Sander L. 46
Gluck [Hannah Gluckstein] 60
Grand, Sarah [Frances McFall], 64
    'The Baby's Tragedy' 25
    The Beth Book, 26, 37, 39
    and cross-gendering 25, 43
    A Domestic Experiment 26
    The Heavenly Twins 24–39, 42–3, 44,
      56, 60, 104
    Ideala 26
    and the New Woman 43–4
    sexology 28
    and Gladys Singers-Bigger 34
    Singularly Deluded 26
    'Two Dear Little Feet' 25
Gregg, Frances 105, 114, 123 n. 53, 124–5
    n. 57, 127, 129, 141, 144, 145
Grosskurth, Phyllis 47

Grosz, Elizabeth 7–8, 11, 20
Gubar, Susan and Sandra M. Gilbert
    17, 22, 26
Guest, Barbara 127
Gunter, Archibald and Fergus Redmond
    42
Gutheil, Emil 90–3
Gynecocracy 42

Halberstam, Judith 11, 89 n. 69
Hall, Radclyffe 61
    'The Career of Mark Anthony Brakes'
      68 n. 28
    and cross-dressing 77, 104
    and cross-gendering 74, 103–4
    The Master of the House 68 n. 28
    'Michael West' 68 n. 28
    'Miss Ogilvy Finds Herself' 73–4
    'The Scar' 101–2 n.
    and sexology 73–80
    and Evguenia Souline 96–7 n. 76
    and Una Troubridge 68 n. 28, 73,
      76–7
    The Unlit Lamp 64–73, 74, 97, 99,
      100, 101
    The Well of Loneliness 75–90,
      93–104, 105, 150, 156, 158, 163,
      185, 203, 215, 217, 224, 229
    'The Woman in the Crêpe Bonnet'
      68 n. 28
hand symbolism:
    and H.D. 127, 133, 134
    and Radclyffe Hall 68 n. 28
    in *Nightwood* 183–5
    and Anaïs Nin 201
    in *The Unlit Lamp* 67–8
    in *The Well of Loneliness* 97–101
Harris, Andrea L. 157
Hatch, Mary 42
H.D. [Hilda Doolittle] 201
    Asphodel 114, 132–5
    Bid Me to Live (A Madrigal) 114,
      132–3
    and bisexuality 106, 113, 142
    and Bryher 62–4, 105–6, 114, 129
    and cross-dressing 122, 144
    and cross-gendering 125, 133, 141
    and Havelock Ellis 105–6, 137 n.
    and Sigmund Freud 105–7, 129,
      135–40, 142–8
    The Gift 129, 148
    and Frances Gregg 105, 114,
      123 n. 53, 127, 129, 141, 144, 145

H.D. [Hilda Doolittle] (*cont.*):
  HER 107, 114, 117–32, 133, 136,
    146–8, 149, 162, 163, 185, 215
  'Hymen' 125
  Kora and Ka (Mira-Mare) 124
  'The Master' 144 n. 100
  and the mother figure, 136–40, 144,
    146, 147–8
  Nights 124
  Notes on Thought and Vision 142–3
  Paint It Today 106, 114, 123, 125,
    132–5
  Palimpsest 123
  and Ezra Pound 114, 115 n. 35, 123,
    127
  Sea Garden 127
  Tribute to Freud 106, 122–3, 129,
    130, 135–48
Hekma, Gert 47
Henke, Suzette 157–8
Hennegan, Alison 79
Herring, Phillip 188
Herzig, Carl 154
Hirschfeld, Magnus 45, 54, 55, 77
homeovestism 7, 218–19
homosexuality, male 32–3, 213
Hope, Trevor 70
Howlett, Caroline 60
Huneker, James Gibbon 40
hysteria 38–9, 110

Ian, Marcia 12
Inness, Sherrie 40–1
inversion 43–56, 62–3, 103, 157, 163,
    200
  and *The Well of Loneliness* 73–80

Jackson, Margaret 50
Jacob, Naomi 88 n. 65
Jaeger, Martha 196–7
Jason, Philip K. 196
Joyce, James 153 n. 11, 189
Jung, Carl 194, 205

Kaivola, Karen 153, 166
Kannenstine, Louis F. 154
Kaplan, Joel and Sheila Stowell 44
Kaplan, Louise 6–7
Kavaler-Adler, Susan 193
Kersley, Gillian 25–6
King, Dave 54
Kipling, Rudyard 41
Kofman, Sarah 8–9, 109–13

Krafft-Ebing, Richard von 33, 46–7, 51,
    52, 53, 54, 76, 77, 78
Kucich, John 26–7

Lacan, Jacques and Wladimir Granoff
    4, 14
Laforgue, René 194
Laity, Cassandra 124, 127, 130–1
Lanchester, Elsa 76 n. 37
Lawrence, D. H. 59, 137 n., 140, 141
Lee, Judith 177, 187–8
Lee, Vernon [Violet Paget] 75
Lehmann, Rosamund 75
lesbianism:
  and desire 10, 11, 14, 34, 39, 70–3,
    99–102, 110–11, 114, 124, 127,
    132, 133, 147, 149, 150, 173, 184,
    193, 200–1, 206–7, 220, 227
  in literature 59
  in psychoanalysis 113, 145–6
  and sexuality 163, 183, 201–2
  and subjectivity 9, 132
Linton, Elizabeth Lynn 42
Loringhoven, Elsa von Freytag 161 n. 43

Mangum, Teresa 26, 37
Mansfield, June 195, 200–3, 207, 215
Marcus, Jane 158
Marcus, Laura 16
masculinity complex 107
masquerade, female 219, 220, 231
Matlock, Jann 53
Mazlish, Bruce 16
melancholia 4, 186
Miller, Henry 195, 202
modernism 11, 12, 14–15, 17–18, 114,
    115–16, 229–31
  and *The Heavenly Twins* 24–8, 56
  and *Nightwood* 153, 190
  and *The Well of Loneliness*, 95
Moll, Albert 54–5
Molyneux, Maxine and Julia Casterton
    193
Moore, George 75 n. 36
Moorjani, Angela 13
mother, the, and mothering 112–13, 221
  in *HER* 128–9
  in *Nightwood* 178–9
  in *Tribute to Freud* 136–40, 144, 146,
    147–8
  in *The Unlit Lamp* 65–9, 73
  in *The Well of Loneliness* 82–5, 87
  see also phallic mother

narcissism 10, 11, 87, 111, 146–8, 150,
    158, 169, 170, 196, 203, 206; *see
    also* Freud, Sigmund, 'On
    Narcissism'
New Woman 33, 43, 50, 77, 78
Newton, Esther 77, 78
Nin, Anaïs 142, 153
    and René Allendy 194–5, 196, 202–3,
        213
    and Djuna Barnes 191–2, 229
    'The Basque and the Bijou' 227 n.
    and Inge Bogner 197
    'Bread and the Wafer' 212
    Children of the Albatross 199 n. 30,
        212, 218, 221, 224
    Cities of the Interior 205, 211,
        212–13, 224, 229
    Collages 191–2, 199
    and cross-dressing 215
    and cross-gendering 193, 203, 205
    diaries 192–204
    Fire 198
    The Four-Chambered Heart 212
    'Hejda' 212
    Henry and June 198, 200–3
    House of Incest 196, 205–9, 212, 213,
        226
    Incest 198
    and Martha Jaeger 196–7
    Journal of a Wife 198
    and Carl Jung 194, 205
    'The Labyrinth' 209–10, 211
    Ladders to Fire 197, 206–7, 208,
        212–28, 229
    'Lillian and Djuna' 212
    'Mallorca' 227 n.
    and June Mansfield 195, 200–3, 207,
        208 n. 69, 215
    and Henry Miller 195
    and Valentina Orlikova 215
    and psychoanalysis 193–8, 200, 202,
        205, 215
    'Ragtime'210–11
    and Otto Rank 195–6, 200, 204,
        214
    Solar Barque 197, 212
    A Spy in the House of Love 191, 208,
        212, 224
    'Stella' 212, 213
    'This Hunger' 212
    'Under a Glass Bell' 143
    Under a Glass Bell 209
    'The Voice' 213–15

Winter of Artifice 212, 213
'The Woman No Man Can Hold' 205
Nye, Robert 53

Oedipus complex 111
O'Neal, Hank 161
Orlikova, Valentina 215
O'Rourke, Rebecca 78

penis envy 107, 109, 112, 193, 203
perversion 6–9, 64–73, 103–4 *see also*
    fetishism
phallic mother 12–13, 40, 110, 112, 129,
    169, 179, 195, 222, 225
phallus, the 4, 8, 9, 80, 89, 92, 110, 112,
    195–6
Plath, Sylvia 143 n. 99
Plumb, Cheryl J. 152, 166, 185
post-structuralism 230
Pound, Ezra 114, 115 n. 35, 123, 127
Powys, John Cowper 105 n. 1, 124–5 n.
    57
Prosser, Jay 51–2, 89 n. 69
psychoanalysis 105–13; 117–18, 193–8,
    202, 205, 213 *see also* castration;
    disavowal; fetishism; Freud,
    Sigmund; narcissism; penis envy;
    phallic mother; phallus
    and homosexuality 108
    Lacanian 190
    object-relations theory 8, 10
Pyket, Lyn 39

Radford, Jean 84–5, 102
Rank, Otto 123, 195–6, 200, 204, 214
    Art and Artist 196
    Myth of the Birth of the Hero 196
    The Trauma of Birth 195
Richard-Allerdyce, Diane 217, 222–3
Riviere, Joan 219
Roof, Judith 99
Rule, Jane 45

Sachs, Hanns 106
Sackville-West, Vita 21, 75, 88 n. 65
    and Violet Trefusis 60, 68 n. 28
Sahli, Nancy 50
St John, Christopher [Christabel
    Marshall]
    and Edy Craig 57–8, 97 n. 78
    Hungerheart 57–9
Sand, George 16–17, 37, 43, 57 n. 1, 75,
    190

Schor, Naomi 16–17
Severo, Sarduy 13
sexology 43–56, 73–80, 94, 105–6
Showalter, Elaine 38
Singer, Alan 154, 168, 175
Singers-Bigger, Gladys 34
Smith, Victoria L. 169
Southworth, E. D. E. N. 42
Spoo, Robert 132
Sprengnether, Madelon 10
Stein, Gertrude 17–18, 22, 59
Stoker, Bram 43 n. 34
Stoller, Robert 6
Symonds, John Addington 47

Taylor, Melanie A. 89–90 n. 69
transsexualism 52, 61, 63
transvestism 22–3, 5, 13, 18, 20, 22, 48,
   77, 89, 199
   female 5, 6, 49–56, 61, 85–93, 105,
      199, 213
   in *The Heavenly Twins* 35, 36–9
   and literature 17, 26
   male 5, 6, 9, 34, 40, 213
   in *Nightwood* 158, 179
   in *The Well of Loneliness* 86–90, 93–4
   see also cross-dressing
Trefusis, Violet 60, 68 n. 28
Trilling, Diana 197
Troubridge, Una 68 n. 28, 73, 76–7

Twain, Mark 41
twin, the 102, 171, *see also* Grand,
   Sarah, *The Heavenly Twins*
   in *HER* 123–35
   in *Tribute to Freud* 140–5
Tyler, Carole-Anne 4–5, 6

Ulrichs, Karl Heinrich 44–5, 52, 94
Urania magazine 43 n. 34
uranism 43–4

vampirism 65, 69
Vicinus, Martha 32–4

Webster, Henry Kitchell 59
Westphal, Carl 45, 52, 54
Winterson, Jeanette 229–31
   The Passion 230
   Written on the Body 230
Winthrop, Theodore 42
Wittig, Monique 230
Wolff, Charlotte 82
Women Police Service 61; *see also*
   Allen, Mary
Wood, Thelma 161–2
Woolf, Virginia 21–22, 67 n., 75
Woolson, Constance Fenimore 98 n.
Wulff, M. 8 n. 20

Zavitzianos, George 219